Hellenic Studies 45

KLEOS IN A MINOR KEY

D'où vous vient, jeune étranger, cette témérité d'aborder en mon île? (P. 34.)

Telemachos meets Kalypso. *Les aventures de Télémache par Fénelon*, nouvelle edition, Madrid, 1883.

KLEOS IN A MINOR KEY: THE HOMERIC EDUCATION OF A LITTLE PRINCE

J. C. B. PETROPOULOS

CENTER FOR HELLENIC STUDIES
Trustees for Harvard University
Washington, DC
Distributed by Harvard University Press
Cambridge, Massachusetts, and London, England
2011

Kleos *in a Minor Key: The Homeric Education of a Little Prince*
  by J. C. B. Petropoulos
Copyright © 2011 Center for Hellenic Studies, Trustees for Harvard University
All Rights Reserved.
Published by Center for Hellenic Studies, Trustees for Harvard University,
  Washington, DC
Distributed by Harvard University Press, Cambridge, Massachusetts, and
  London, England
Production: Nancy Wolfe Kotary
Cover Design: Joni Godlove

EDITORIAL TEAM:
Senior Advisors: W. Robert Connor, Gloria Ferrari Pinney, Albert Henrichs,
  James O'Donnell, Bernd Seidensticker
Editorial Board: Gregory Nagy (Editor-in-Chief), Christopher Blackwell,
  Casey Dué (Executive Editor), Mary Ebbott (Executive Editor),
  Scott Johnson, Olga Levaniouk, Anne Mahoney, Leonard Muellner
Production Manager for Publications: Jill Curry Robbins
Web Producer: Mark Tomasko

LIBRARY OF CONGRESS CATALOGING-IN-PUBLICATION DATA

Petropoulos, J. C. B.
 Kleos in a minor key : the Homeric education of a little prince / by J. C. B.
  Petropoulos.
    p. cm. -- (Hellenic studies ; 45)
 Includes bibliographical references and index.
 ISBN 978-0-674-05592-6 (alk. paper)
 1. Homer. Odyssey. 2. Homer--Characters--Telemachus. 3. Epic poetry,
  Greek--History and criticism. 4. Telemachus (Greek mythology) in
  literature. 5. Princes in literature. 6. Glory in literature. 7. Maturation
  (Psychology) in literature. 8. Education of princes in literature. 9. Fathers
  and sons in literature. I. Title.
PA4167.P49 2010
883'.01--dc22
                        2010045796

Contents

Foreword

THIS BOOK BY PROFESSOR PETROPOULOS is a veritable tour de force in Homeric scholarship. It combines the best traditions of classical *Strengphilologie* with the most highly refined methods of social anthropology and linguistics. More broadly, it is literary criticism at its best. Taking as his point of departure the first four rhapsodies of the *Odyssey*, commonly known as the "*Telemachy*," Petropoulos shows how the mentality of "rites of passage," as firmly grounded in the customs and linguistic usages of Greek-speaking peoples in the last two millennia before our era, pervades the plot- and character-development of not only the *Telemachy* but also the entire *Odyssey*. The book illuminates in refreshingly new ways the highly complex social and poetic notion of *kleos*, demonstrating that the narratives about younger and older generations of heroes interweave from the beginning all the way to the very end of the *Odyssey*.

This demonstration by Professor Petropoulos is a truly major achievement in the world of Classics. It is a most convincing proof of the artistic unity of the Homeric *Odyssey*, viewed in the historical context of 'Homeric poetry in the making', as Milman Parry and Albert Lord would describe it. The late Albert Lord, who was a teacher of Petropoulos at Harvard, would be so proud of this luminous book by one of his most gifted students. We see here a quantum leap in the proud tradition of Homeric scholarship pioneered by Parry and Lord.

Gregory Nagy
Director, Center for Hellenic Studies

Author's Prologue

ʽἤδη γὰρ νοέω καὶ οἶδα ἕκαστα,
ἐσθλά τε καὶ τὰ χέρεια· πάρος δ' ἔτι νήπιος ἦα.'

Odyssey 20.309–310 (cf. *Odyssey* 18.228–229)

*"because now I perceive and know each and every thing,
good and bad alike, whereas before I was still childish."*

ʽαἴ κεν ἐᾷ πρόφρων με Διὸς θυγάτηρ ἀγελείη
αὐτόν τε ζώειν καί μοι φίλον υἱὸν ἀέξῃ.'

Odyssey 13.359–360

*"if Zeus' daughter, she who leads the army shall in her graciousness
grant me to live and my dear son to grow to maturity."*

MOST LIKELY COINED BY the German scholar P. D. C. Hennings in 1858, the term *Telemacheia* refers to the rather minor adventures of Telemachos as recounted in the first four books of Homer's *Odyssey* and parts of Books 15, 16, and 17. Like many scholars today, I balk at the suggestion that the *Odyssey* is the result of the conflation of three disparate poems—the lesser tales of Telemachos, the tales of Odysseus' travels and sea adventures, and the tale of his vengeance at Ithaka.[1] Nonetheless, I admit that two main narrative currents are discernible in the *Odyssey* as a whole. There is, on the one side, the overarching story about Odysseus' marine adventures and *nostos* and, on the other, a reduplication—in the narratological sense—of the first tale, namely, the story of his son's journey, or *hodos*, in search of news (in Homeric Greek, *kleos*) regarding his father. That these two storylines coalesce makes sense if they are appreciated, as I believe they were in antiquity, as parallel and eventually overlapping quests, the *Telemacheia* being necessarily (on account of the protagonist's relative immaturity) a search for masculine identity—ultimately a social concept connoted,

---

[1] See Dawe 1993:8 and Heubeck and Hoekstra 1990:5–6 for the views of Kirchhoff, Wilamowitz, Focke, and Page; see also Μανακίδου 2002:13–68.

as R. Redfield most sensitively has suggested, also by the term *kleos*.[2] The *incipit* Ἄνδρα μοι ἔννεπε 'Of the man tell me' in the *Odyssey*'s proem is doubly apposite; besides Odysseus the emphatic first word alludes to the process (I stress the processual aspect) of Prince Telemachos' ἀνδροποίησις 'becoming a man'.[3]

From my 'developmental' vantage point, what I find most interesting is the fact that, of the father-son duo, Telemachos is the one who traverses a much longer psychological distance. His *hodos* 'journey' is geographically shorter and less exotic than his father's but more momentous in an inner sense. In the course of his micro-Odyssean travels (Books 1–4 and part of 15), but also subsequently through his assistance in the combat at home (Book 22) and extra *muros* (Book 24), the young Prince progressively if unevenly assimilates the masculine identity which his father and grandfather acquired long before him. Telemachos' travels involve considerable physical risk and one narrow, last-minute escape from assassination (see especially *Odyssey* 16.365–370); for all that, they constitute first and foremost an 'educational' drama. This is scarcely a novel finding, as witness the views of the neo-Platonist Porphyry in the fourth century AD and, in the early twentieth century, the classicist J. A. Scott, who was followed by others.[4] What is novel however is the fresh evidence, textual and largely social-anthropological and psychoanalytic, which I adduce in support of this thesis.

In common with other scholars, I assume that qua literary genius Homer frequently strove to portray at least certain of his characters in a psychologically plausible manner.[5] The more I read and reread Telemachos' words, the more 'realistic' or at least credible he sounds in respect of certain crucial psychological details. These details pertain to ancient society synchronically and to non-Greek societies diachronically, reflecting as they do certain universal constants of post-adolescent and male behavior. The hypothesis of synchronic verisimilitude is borne out by the aesthetic principle Odysseus in effect formulates in *Odyssey* 8.487–491:[6]

'λίην γὰρ κατὰ κόσμον Ἀχαιῶν οἶτον ἀείδεις,
ὅσσ' ἔρξαν τ' ἔπαθόν τε καὶ ὅσσ' ἐμόγησαν Ἀχαιοί,
ὥς τέ που ἢ αὐτὸς παρεὼν ἢ ἄλλου ἀκούσας.'

---

[2] See Chapter 1 below.

[3] Calame 1999:278 uses this term.

[4] For Porphyry's view, see Chapter 1 below; also Scott 1917–1918, esp. 427. Dawe, an opponent of the 'developmental' interpretation of the *Telemachy*, admits that the Prince is indeed roused to manhood despite the fact that "the trouble is that the progression from boy to man does not take place in a straight line: e.g. he is weak and unsure at 2.60–61, but so he is again at 16.71ff." (Dawe 1993:878, who also cites Porphyry and Scott.)

[5] Thus Copley 1993, passim and Devereux 1976, esp. xi: "great art is located at the confluence of culturally imposed artistic means and objectives and of a *subjectively psychological realism*" (my italics).

[6] See also Dawe 1993:341 *ad Odyssey* 8.488 and Chapter 2 n64.

"for you sing of the Achaians' fate in exceedingly proper order,
both of the many things the Achaians suffered and their many hardships—
as if somehow you were there yourself or had heard of these things from
someone else."

Though he does not cite it explicitly, the ethno-psychiatrist Georges Devereux
discerns this principle also in Greek tragedy. In his classic work, *Dreams in Greek
Tragedy* (1976), Devereux likens the realistic depiction of dreams in tragedy
to the extreme verisimilitude of Rembrandt's still lifes.[7] Yet why should, say,
Aischylos have adhered to this aesthetic rule, particularly in portraying the
dreams of his characters? Devereux's answer to this question has to do not only
with dreams in tragedy but also with the refined, plausible manner in which
Homer shows Telemachos' coming of age: "he [sc. the poet] tried to write the
best drama (and dream) he could devise."[8] By the same token, the poet Homer
tried to compose the best 'educational drama' he could conceive.

---

[7] Devereux 1976:xviii. Lloyd-Jones accepts that in a number of cases Greek tragedy depicted
madness in a psychologically plausible fashion: Lloyd-Jones 1990, chapter 23.

[8] Devereux 1976:xviii. Psychological 'realism' can also be detected in other contexts in the *Odyssey*.
See, for instance, Russo, Fernández-Galiano, and Heubeck 1992:9–12 on the exchange between
Penelope and the beggar Odysseus in Book 19.

Acknowledgments

THIS BOOK WAS BORN in the classroom. Starting in 2000, I taught the *Telemachy* first in translation in the School of Education and then in the original in the Department of Greek Philology in the Democritean University of Thrace. With few research sources to hand I resorted to the standard commentaries on the *Odyssey*. Commentaries, I found out anew, can be daunting, at times throttling, yet at others times they may deliver piercing perspectives, and when they skirt the Mandarin disease they can be positively beneficial, even if merely as a fillip for disagreement and further thought. This book grew out of my attempts to explain the *Odyssey*, particularly Books 1–4 and 15, to my students with the help of the relevant commentaries, after having first subjected the modern day scholiasts to close interrogation. My debts to S. West, I. de Jong, R. D. Dawe, and P. V. Jones, among others, will be apparent both in the main text and especially the footnotes. Without too much philological dalliance—and sometimes with arrow-like swiftness—they have guided me and my students as we moved through the *Telemachy*, trying to make sense of the ways in which the Little Prince expresses and experiences the process of growing up.

As my lecture notes proliferated the outlines of a book emerged. My subsequent phenomenological progress through the *Telemachy* would literally have been unthinkable had I not had direct access to a number of fine libraries, fine scholars, and academic audiences. Intermittently over the years 2004–2006 I worked in the libraries of the University of London (UCL) and the Center for Hellenic Studies (CHS) in Washington, DC. I am grateful to the staff of these libraries. I would like also to express heartfelt thanks to Lady Marina Marks and her son, Mr. Alex Collins, for friendship and support in difficult days. My stay at the CHS in the summers of 2005 and 2006 was funded by the Center. Earlier versions of Chapters 2, 5, and 6 were presented as lectures and seminar papers at the European Cultural Center of Delphi, the CHS's facility in Nafplion, the Chinese Academy of Social Sciences in Beijing, and, thanks to the generous support of the University Seminars Program of the Alexander S. Onassis Public Benefit Foundation in 2008, at Harvard, Stanford, and Ohio State Universities and Rhodes College. For their salutary comments and criticism I therefore thank Professors E. Bowie, P. Themelis, Ph. Kakridis, D. N. Maronitis, A. Mayor, K. Morrell, Gregory Nagy, and A. Rengakos as well as the members of my American audiences. I am moved to record my appreciation for the priceless translation of the *Odyssey* by the late Robert Fitzgerald, who immersed me as an undergraduate in the world of Telemachos and his parents. The Department of Classical Studies at the University of Pennsylvania kindly appointed me Visiting Scholar in the summer of 2009. This enabled me to work, in considerable comfort, on the English version of this book in the University's Van Pelt-Dietrich Library. Many thanks to Professor Joseph Farrell for his scholarly feedback and to the staff—especially the student staff—of this philoxenous library. I wish to thank the editor-in-chief, Professor Gregory Nagy, the executive editor, Professor Casey Dué, and the entire production team of CHS publications, particularly the production manager Ms. Jill Curry Robbins and Mr. Noel Spencer, for their patience and professionalism. Finally, I wish to thank Ms. Lydia Hadjidakis for her long-suffering technical assistance in preparation of the original version of this text and Fathers Vlasie and Chrysotomos of the St. Gregory Palamas Monastery (Etna, CA) for further technical aid.

This book is dedicated to my sister, Vicki, ἰφθίμη κασιγνήτη τῇ ὁμοῦ ἐτρεφόμην. I hope that she and her family will derive many hours of pleasure from the *Odyssey*. As Eumaios tells Odysseus, 'ἔστι δὲ τερπομένοισιν ἀκούειν' ("There is ample time to enjoy hearing a story").

J. C. B. P.
Alexandroupolis/Athens

Note

The critical texts of the *Iliad* are those of D. B. Monro and T. W. Allen, eds., *Homeri opera* I–II, 3rd ed. (Oxford, 1902, 1920); the texts of the *Odyssey* are those of T. W. Allen, *Homeri opera* III–IV, 2nd ed. (Oxford, 1908, 1917–1919); the text of the *Homeric Hymns* is that of T. W. Allen, *Homeri opera* V (Oxford, 1912). (All the Greek in the main text has been translated; the rather literal and workmanlike renderings have been provided by me.)

1

Kleos and Oral History

"Es Tagträumt in mir."
Ernst Bloch, *Das Prinzip Hoffnung*

'αὐτὰρ ἐγὼν Ἰθάκην ἐσελεύσομαι, ὄφρα οἱ υἱὸν
μᾶλλον ἐποτρύνω, καί οἱ μένος ἐν φρεσὶ θείω,
εἰς ἀγορὴν καλέσαντα κάρη κομόωντας Ἀχαιοὺς
πᾶσι μνηστήρεσσιν ἀπειπέμεν, οἵ τέ οἱ αἰεὶ
μῆλ' ἀδινὰ σφάζουσι καὶ εἰλίποδας ἕλικας βοῦς.
πέμψω δ' ἐς Σπάρτην τε καὶ ἐς Πύλον ἠμαθόεντα,
νόστον πευσόμενον πατρὸς φίλου, ἤν που ἀκούση,
ἠδ' ἵνα μιν κλέος ἐσθλὸν ἐν ἀνθρώποισιν ἔχησιν.'

Odyssey 1.88–95

"But as for myself, I shall go to Ithaka, so that I might rouse for him his son
still more and instill determination in his mind,
after summoning the long-haired Achaians to a public assembly
to serve notice to all the suitors, who are constantly
slaughtering his huddling flocks of sheep and his oxen of shambling feet
        and curved horns.
After that I shall send him off to Sparta and sandy Pylos
to seek information about his dear father's return, if perhaps he may hear
        of it,
and so that a fine reputation (*kleos*) among human beings may accrue to
        him."

T HE *ODYSSEY* BEGINS essentially with the melancholy reverie of a twenty-year-old *kouros*—by modern standards, a male at the "psychic boundary between adolescence and adulthood"—who is supposed to gain *kleos* as the action unfolds.[1]

---

[1] See Copley 1993:107 on this age. On Telemachos' age: *Odyssey* 4.112, 11.67–68, 174, and esp. 447–450, etc. (For the 'initiatory' significance of this age cf. Jason who at 20 embarked on the

This *kleos* will also amount to his social identity and indeed his profounder identity as an adult and a man.[2] Amid the commotion (ὀρυμαγδός) of the suitors deep in their cups (see *Odyssey* 1.106ff., 133),[3]

ἧστο γὰρ ἐν μνηστῆρσι φίλον τετιημένος ἦτορ,
ὀσσόμενος πατέρ' ἐσθλὸν ἐνὶ φρεσίν, εἴ ποθεν ἐλθὼν
μνηστήρων τῶν μὲν σκέδασιν κατὰ δώματα θείη,
τιμὴν δ' αὐτὸς ἔχοι καὶ κτήμασιν[4] οἷσιν ἀνάσσοι.
τὰ φρονέων, μνηστῆρσι μεθήμενος, εἴσιδ'Ἀθήνην.

Odyssey 1.114–118

[Telemachos] was sitting among the suitors aggrieved in his heart,
picturing his noble father in his mind, if he were to come from
     somewhere
and send those suitors scampering in the palace
and were himself to regain honor and to rule over his possessions.
Reflecting on these things as he sat among the suitors, he caught sight
     of Athena.

This passage is cast in the form of a ring-composition.[5] Its centerpiece describes schematically the content of the abstract image that passes through Telemachos' mind (*Odyssey* 1.115: ὀσσόμενος . . . ἐνὶ φρεσίν 'picturing . . . in

---

Argonauts' expedition. See Woronoff 1978:246 and Chapters 5–6 below.) The ancients apparently did not distinguish between dreams, visions, and daydreams: see also nn13–14 below. Martin 1993:239 aptly calls Telemachos "the gateway to the *Odyssey*." According to this scholar Telemachos' focalization is identical to the poet's, just as Achilles' focalization is coextensive with Homer's. At *Odyssey* 1.94–95, incidentally, the motif of 'the *kleos* of Telemachos' is sounded for the first time (by Athena); on the narratological function of this motif, see Rengakos 2002:87–98.

2   Cf. *Odyssey* 1.1: Ἄνδρα μοι ἔννεπε . . . The proem pre-announces as the poem's subject the much-wandering *man* who, though not mentioned by name, is readily identified by the audience yet remains a fuzzy idea for Telemachos (see also n24). The prince will have to prove just how much of an ἀνήρ he is (see verse 1.358 and discussion below). On ἀνήρ as a strongly "gendered term," see further Graziosi and Haubold 2003:71 *ad loc.* and Chapter 3 below.

3   For the pejorative term ὀρυμαγδός (of the incoherent, loud cacophony of cultural inferiors), see Heath 2005:64; on drunkenness, a rare phenomenon that characterizes Kyklops, Elpenor, and the Centaurs, ibid.

4   κτήμασιν: δώμασιν. Both *lectiones* are satisfactory, esp. because, as Jones 1992:86 observes, "For Telemachus, the central issues are what the house used to be like when Odysseus was at home, especially the way in which Odysseus won it for him (Telemachus has a strong sense of his responsibility for his father's possessions) . . ." On the motif of the erstwhile prosperity of Odysseus' household, see *Odyssey* 1.21–218 (where κτεάτεσσιν occurs) and discussion below.

5   See in general van Otterlo 1944. Jones 2002:10 *ad loc.* (but not de Jong 2001:20–21) also notes this structure.

his mind').[6] As others have observed, the *Odyssey* is in large part "psychological drama."[7] The poet evinces a marked penchant for recording or representing internal, psychological states already in *Odyssey* 1.114ff., where he gives the first information about Telemachos.[8] To be sure, as Friedrich Klingner remarks in one of the most penetrating articles ever written on the *Telemachy*, the poem does not commence with the violence of the *Iliad* or the *Aeneid* but instead (as he shows) with inner conflict, represented by the youth's festering mental anguish.[9] This "helpless martyr" daydreams, "plunged into isolation and humiliation" or in Homer's words, "aggrieved in his heart" (*Odyssey* 1.114). The unseen but keenly felt "spiritual presence of Odysseus" overshadows from the outset the entire scene with Mentes; this presence haunts the prince's thoughts, rendering him especially susceptible to Mentes' ensuing psychological intervention. Telemachos is well prepared for a process in which each, prince and guest, will "seek after and find in the other elements of Odysseus."

The mental state of grief (*Odyssey* 1.114)[10] characterizes the young man in varying degrees of intensity, particularly in the first two books. Only in Book 4 is this mood reversed temporarily (though not entirely) thanks to Helen's magical "antidepressant."[11] The very moment we meet him, Telemachos is fixated on his suffering (πένθος, *Odyssey* 1.342),[12] immobilized in a phantasy in which his father occupies center stage in exterminating the suitors.[13] This daydream, which lacks the structure of a typical dream,[14] condenses (to use a Freudian

---

[6] This, in effect, is the *imago* (see *Odyssey* 1.115: ἐνὶ φρεσίν, 1.118: τὰ φρονέων, and discussion below) of his father, which stands in counterpoint to the non-phantastical (i.e. real) appearance of the suitors and Athena. ὀσσόμενος πατέρ' ἐσθλὸν . . . , εἴ . . . (*Odyssey* 1.115) = σκοπῶν or σκοπούμενος + oblique question. (According to Jones 1991:42 ad *Odyssey* 1.116, θείη and ἔχοι are pure optatives; see also nn13–14 below.) The oblique questions in *Odyssey* 1.115–117 are a rare example of *silent* internal monologue.

[7] Rutherford 1992: "psychological drama of suspense and deception" (9–10, esp. 10).

[8] Dawe 1993:54 ad *Odyssey* 1.114: "As Homer gives us the first picture of Telemachos, he avails himself several times of set phrases like 'in his heart' and 'in his mind' to convey to us in full the young man's *mood of introspection*" (my emphasis).

[9] Klingner 1944:26. The passages quoted in this paragraph are taken from Klingner 1944:27, 28, 30, 31; the translation of p30 is by Jones and Wright 1997:206.

[10] See n12 and n15 below.

[11] *Odyssey* 4.220–331, 290–295, and de Jong 2001:100–101, 104 ad loc.

[12] Jones 1991:113 ad *Odyssey* 1.114–117: "a typically significant first sight of Telemachus, almost as depressing as our first sight of Odysseus (5.81–4, cf. 4.556). Telemachus is *incapable of taking action himself: all he can do is think* about the possibility of his father returning" (my emphasis). (Cf. also Martin 1993: "we cannot see Telemachus without instantly hearing of his father." [234])

[13] In British psychoanalytical circles the term *phantasy* (as opposed to 'fantasy') is "more akin to imagination than to whimsy": see Rycroft 1995:55–56, s.v. 'fantasy and phantasy'. De Jong 2001:21 ad *Odyssey* 1.113–118 considers this wish a *prolepsis* of the *Odyssey*'s vengeance; *prolepseis* are often expressed as wishes. See n14.

[14] Cf. n1 above. In *Odyssey* 15.1–47, Athena counsels Telemachos in what is otherwise a typical dream scene, despite the fact that he is awake: see de Jong 2001:363–364 ad loc. (and 120–121 ad *Odyssey* 4.795–841). From a cultural point of view it was assumed that an actual ὄνειρος (*Odyssey*

term) the precarious power vacuum that Odysseus has left behind: one of the leitmotifs of the *Telemachy* is the "absence of Odysseus" and the fluctuating intensity of the emotions of loss, powerlessness, and sorrow this causes to his intimates, or *philoi*.[15] The content of this *Tagtraum* betrays the relative unpreparedness of the youth: it is not he who undertakes the act of vengeance (as will also happen later) but his father. Book 1.117 is most telling, for here Odysseus is said to 'regain honor' (ἔχοι . . . τιμήν), which is equivalent to the social status and recognition enjoyed by a member (male or female) of the hereditary elite. As H. van Wees has shown in his historical study, the heroes' continual efforts to uphold their *timê* is the main cause of the violence endemic in Homeric society.[16] This pathological state arises out of the paradox that a hero can only achieve status through conflict,[17] but rightful authority and the defense of ownership presuppose his use or threat of violence. In Telemachos' phantasy, Odysseus—with whom his son does not identify, however—behaves no differently from a typical Homeric *basileus* 'king' who, being *primus inter pares*, would be required to show in practice that he was *basileuteros* 'more kingly' or, better yet, *basileutatos* 'kingliest' vis-à-vis other 'peers of the realm'.[18] C. Antonaccio, drawing on others, notes that a *basileus* is comparable to the big man of 'primitive' micro-societies studied by social anthropologists, given that political authority in the Iron Age and the Archaic period in the Greek world "was achieved, not heritable," for "such a position is only partly heritable."[19]

From Pain to Strength and Back Again

Book 1.114–118, just examined, merits two further comments. First, to judge from Telemachos' fanciful reverie, which, as noted, is rather exiguous and

---

19.535) or a genuine ὄναρ (19.547) was not only prophetic (a kind of *prolepsis*) but also sometimes a form of wish-fulfillment: at *Odyssey* 19.547 the eagle, the protagonist of Penelope's dream, makes this diagnosis in the course of the dream! Telemachos' reverie in Book 1 is comparable to his mother's ὄναρ-ὕπαρ in Book 19.

[15] See de Jong 2001:25 *ad Odyssey* 1.158–160. For the political vacuum, see Osborne 2004: "The *Odyssey* examines issues of political succession in an extreme situation of political vacuum and uncertainty" (212). The political uncertainty regarding the succession at Ithaka is homologous to the psychological vacuum and the deeper uncertainty caused by Odysseus' absence.

[16] Van Wees 1992, esp. 61ff.

[17] See Graziosi and Haubold 2003, esp. 68, 74–75, Chapter 3 n12, and Chapter 4 n35 below: the plot and epic vocabulary itself concur in showing that self-harming, antisocial ἀγηνορίη/ἀγήνωρ θυμός are tempered in both Homeric poems by a countervailing tendency to social cooperation and solidarity between the heroes.

[18] Cf. Taplin 1992:47–48.

[19] Antonaccio 1993:64, to whom now add Murray 1993:323 and Hall 2007:122–123.

schematic (note the indefinite enclitic ποθεν 'from somewhere', *Odyssey* 1.115), the youth is deprived of a convincing image of his father. Indicative of this particular lack is the contrapuntal image that Mentes later conjures up for his benefit (*Odyssey* 1.253–258, 265–266). Serving as a kind of encouragement, the imaginary scene evoked practically corresponds in every detail to the manner in which the prince articulates his wish-fulfillment (compare *Odyssey* 1.114–117 and 163–164) but is much more detailed and hence convincing, especially because it is supposedly an actual reminiscence (*Odyssey* 1.257ff.).[20] Telemachos thus has now before him a diptych version of Odysseus to which presently, in *Odyssey* 1.298ff., will be added the *imago* of the grand exterminator Orestes.[21] Suddenly, however, even before he moves on to the related *exemplum* of Orestes, Mentes himself corrects his exhortation (compare *Odyssey* 1.166–168 and see below):

'τοῖος ἐὼν μνηστῆρσιν ὁμιλήσειεν Ὀδυσσεύς·
πάντες κ' ὠκύμοροί τε γενοίατο πικρόγαμοί τε.
ἀλλ' ἦ τοι μὲν ταῦτα θεῶν ἐν γούνασι κεῖται,
ἤ κεν νοστήσας ἀποτίσεται, ἦε καὶ οὐκί,
οἷσιν ἐνὶ μεγάροισι· σὲ δὲ φράζεσθαι ἄνωγα
ὅππως κε μνηστῆρας ἀπώσεαι ἐκ μεγάροιο.'

Odyssey 1.265–270

"If only Odysseus, just the way he was then, could mingle with the suitors:
the whole lot of them would be swift to die during their bitter-tasting
       'wedding.'
But of course these matters lie on the knees of the gods:
whether after returning home he will exact revenge—or *not*—
in his palace. Now as for you, I urge you to consider
how you might drive the suitors out of the palace."

The phrase ἦε καὶ οὐκί 'or not' (*Odyssey* 1.268), though common enough, is perhaps one of the most startling and cruel occurrences of a disjunction in ancient Greek literature. Klingner has already remarked the descent from "idealisation" (we might say 'phantasy') to unadorned reality expressed in theological terms (*Odyssey* 1.266–267).[22] According to this scholar, Athena calculatingly raises the alternative of abandoning Odysseus as idealized avenger in

---

[20] Olson 1995:71 also notes: "Athena now imagines the hero's return in concrete terms which echo Telemachos' own fantasies . . ." Cf. Menelaos' even more vivid remembrance of Odysseus in *Odyssey* 4.341–346 (Odysseus as a triumphant wrestler) and Jones 1992:79 *ad loc.*

[21] The Freudian term for 'internal object'; see below.

[22] Klingner 1944:34–35.

order to force Telemachos to realize his *duty to act* (as opposed, one might add, merely to daydreaming): 'σὲ δὲ φράζεσθαι ἄνωγα' ("Now as for you, I urge you to consider," *Odyssey* 1.269). The divine interlocutor, in other words, resumes her encouragement of the youth but coarsens it for outright "paedagogical" reasons, converting Telemachos' pain to strength, as Klingner also notes.[23]

Tucked away at a discreet distance from the carousers (*Odyssey* 1.132), the prince can converse almost without distraction (he actually whispers; see *Odyssey* 1.157) with the mysterious 'Mentes'.[24] The withdrawal of the two in a corner of the palace symbolically connotes Telemachos' marginalization in the constitutional and symposiastic order.[25] As if performing an impromptu lament-speech (γόος), the youth unexpectedly bewails the situation in the palace:[26]

'Ξεῖνε φίλ', ἦ καί μοι νεμεσήσεαι ὅττι κεν εἴπω;
τούτοισιν μὲν ταῦτα μέλει, κίθαρις καὶ ἀοιδή,
ῥεῖ', ἐπεὶ ἀλλότριον βίοτον νήποινον ἔδουσιν,
ἀνέρος οὗ δή που λεύκ' ὀστέα πύθεται ὄμβρῳ
κείμεν' ἐπ' ἠπείρου, ἢ εἰν ἁλὶ κῦμα κυλίνδει.
εἰ κεῖνόν γ' Ἰθάκηνδε ἰδοίατο νοστήσαντα,
πάντες κ' ἀρησαίατ' ἐλαφρότεροι πόδας εἶναι
ἢ ἀφνειότεροι χρυσοῖό τε ἐσθῆτός τε.
νῦν δ' ὁ μὲν ὣς ἀπόλωλε κακὸν μόρον, οὐδέ τις ἡμῖν
θαλπωρή, εἴ πέρ τις ἐπιχθονίων ἀνθρώπων
φῇσιν ἐλεύσεσθαι· τοῦ δ' ὤλετο νόστιμον ἦμαρ.

---

[23] Klingner 1944:34.

[24] From the outset they sit ἔκτοθεν ἄλλων, in the words of the poet (*Odyssey* 1.132), their voices drowned out by the ὀρυμαγδός (*Odyssey* 1.106ff., 133). Afterwards, though, when Phemios performs and everyone grows silent (*Odyssey* 1.155; cf. 1.325–326), they are forced to whisper (*Odyssey* 1.156–157). Klingner 1944:27–28 remarks that initially the cacophony of the ἀγήνορες suitors and subsequently the *aoidos'* song provide the secrecy that makes it possible for both to conjure up in their midst the spiritual presence of Odysseus. According to Klingner, this scene harks forward to the "subsequent concealment of the physically present Odysseus" (1944:27–28). I might add that whispering—in effect, a disguising of normal speech—suits the general climate of concealment and disguise evoked by 'Mentes'.

[25] See also Rutherford 1992:14.

[26] See de Jong 2001:25 ad *Odyssey* 1.158–77. Dawe 1993:58 is both salutary and amusing: " . . . unburdening oneself in this way to the total stranger Mentes is not how we expect a son of Odysseus to behave" (a gentleman, indeed a prince, should not let on about his personal worries!). But Dawe aptly notes: "Here Telemachus' words are of a self-tormenting savagery, right for a man suffering grief and oppression" (1993:58). According to Jones 2002:12 ad *Odyssey* 1.160–168, the youth's extravagant grief is a plausible way to protect himself from worse news. Telemachos' rhetorical resort to *pathos* in his speech is also a desperate *captatio benevolentiae*, framed by his opening apology in verse 158; see also Jones 1991:116 ad *Odyssey* 1.159–168.

ἀλλ' ἄγε μοι τόδε εἰπὲ καὶ ἀτρεκέως κατάλεξον·
τίς πόθεν εἰς ἀνδρῶν; πόθι τοι πόλις ἠδὲ τοκῆες;'

Odyssey 1.158–170[27]

"Dear stranger, will you be indignant at me if I speak?
These men are only interested in this, the *kitharis* and song,
[which is] easy for them, since they're eating up with impunity the liveli-
       hood of someone else,
 indeed, of a man whose white bones rot in the rain
as they lie on land or the surge of the sea turns them over and over.
If they saw *that* man returned to Ithaka,
all of them would pray to be faster on their feet
than richer in gold and clothing.
Yet as it is, this man perished with an evil doom and we haven't any
heart-warming consolation, not even if some earth-dwelling human
said that he will come, for this man's day of homecoming is lost.
But come, tell me this and recount it accurately:
Who are you and from where? Where are your city and your parents?"

The Implied, Anonymous Man

Telemachos does not mention the name of the owner of the palace. The significant missing person is an anonymous male (see ἀνέρος 'of a man', *Odyssey* 1.161;
κεῖνον γ᾽ 'that one', 1.163; ὁ μὲν 'this one', 1.166; τοῦ δ᾽ 'this one's', 1.167), and
the youth defines his relation to him only indirectly (at the end of his opening
speech), camouflaging the referent under the adjective πατρώϊος 'stemming
from my father or forefathers' (*Odyssey* 1.175).[28] To an unsuspecting stranger
the speaker might initially create the impression that he is simply referring to
an unspecified third person. Then, in the short span of three verses (*Odyssey*
1.163–165), Telemachos reverts fleetingly to his earlier silent phantasy, which
this time he expresses out loud, again in the form of a conditional sentence in
the optative, only to deconstruct the wishful supposition with a typical *epanor-*

---

[27] Cf. also *Odyssey* 1.161–162, 166–168, echoing faithfully an Iliadic *goos* (γόος) speech, as does
Odyssey 1.241–251: on the generic *goos*-speech, see Tsagalis 2004. See also the (emotionally meaningful?) assonance 'κείμεν' … κῦμα κυλίνδει' in *Odyssey* 1.162 (not noted in the commentaries *ad
loc.*). Elsewhere, e.g. *Odyssey* 5.296, the selfsame assonance occurs twice.

[28] See also de Jong 2001:18, 25 *ad Odyssey* 1.163. Nor does Penelope utter the name Ὀδυσσεύς,
despite the fact that when she first comes on stage in the poem she recollects him with heart-
rending tenderness and pride (*Odyssey* 1.342–344). On the other hand, as de Jong 2001:18 remarks,
'Mentes' repeatedly cites the absent hero ὀνομαστί (*Odyssey* 1.196, etc.). To be precise, Athena
has already cited his name at *Odyssey* 1.48 in her response to Zeus: 'ἀμφ' Ὀδυσῆϊ δαΐφρονι δαίεται
ἦτορ.'

thosis: 'νῦν δ' . . .' ("Yet, as it is," *Odyssey* 1.166–168). The sole certainty is that the implied, anonymous man has died; only the manner and place of his death (on land? at sea?) remain uncertain. At *Odyssey* 1.234–240 Telemachos reformulates these dark thoughts and adds the affecting observation that the unnamed man lacks even a grave (*Odyssey* 1.239).[29]

Mentes,[30] exactly like his *Doppelgänger* Mentor (in Books 2 and 3) and to a degree like Peisistratos (especially in Books 3 and 4), will prove to be an effective teacher and interlocutor, indeed arguably the most successful.[31] He will be the first adult to elicit certain psychological reactions in the immature, self-doubting youth, which will bring him closer to maturity. Significantly, Mentes will accomplish this even before Telemachos sets out for the Peloponnese.

Heubeck, West, and Hainsworth play down the importance of the voyage, pointing out—correctly—that the prince's "awakening" and "real psychological change" (as they put it) take place in Book 1 (320ff.) and are merely corroborated thereafter in the next book.[32] It might however be more accurate to say that *in cultural and social terms* the voyage per se (in Books 3–4)

---

29   See below.

30   Μέντης (as also most probably the equivalent name Μέντωρ) < *men* 'to think'; its meaning must be 'adviser, counselor': Jones 1991:117 *ad Odyssey* 1.180. Frame 2009:25–28 posits the verb *μένω 'I make eager, incite' and hence argues that the proper names Mentes and Mentor mean 'he who instils μένος', 'he who incites', and also 'he who reminds'. Here and elsewhere the poet brings out mental operations and attributes: e.g. *Odyssey* 1.3: νόον ἔγνω, the name of the Ithakan noble Νοήμων, etc.

31   Mentor's sole appearance and speech *in propria persona* occur at *Odyssey* 2.224ff. 'Mentor'/ Athena appears in *Odyssey* 2.267ff. and accompanies Telemachos to Pylos (*Odyssey* 2.399–406). The only adult on the ship, the goddess is a *"guide initiatique"* comparable to e.g. Herakles and Orpheus on the Argonauts' expedition: Woronoff 1978:246–247, 252–253, and Chapters 5 and 6 below. For Mentes and Mentor, see also de Jong 2001:59–60; for Peisistratos, de Jong 2001:70–71 *ad Odyssey* 3.34–64 and 366 *ad Odyssey* 3.49–55. At *Odyssey* 3.371–373 'Mentor' leaves Pylos and is replaced by Peisistratos, the prince's contemporary who like him is unwed; Peisistratos accompanies him to Sparta (*Odyssey* 4.156ff.), acts as a real 'mentor' at *Odyssey* 15.49–55, and returns to Pylos at *Odyssey* 15.202–216, his mission ended.

32   Heubeck, West, and Hainsworth 1988:54–55, 67, evidently following Allione 1963, esp.15 (Athena metamorphoses the lad instantaneously into a man by causing him to reflect on his father; this overall cognitive process is a single "atto spirituale," sealed by the goddess' miraculous disappearance at 319ff.). Klingner 1944:34 argues along similar lines, assigning the transformation more specifically to the duration of Athena's long pep talk in verses 253–305, as will be noted. For the degrees of Telemachos' psychological change (*Entwicklungsgang*) in Book 1 and beyond, see further Clarke 1963:140–141n16 (bibliography), Wöhrle 1999:129–131 (on *Mannwerdung*), chapter 4 of Olson 1995, and Heath 2005:92n34. Fundamental to my approach throughout this study, and particularly in Chapter 5 below is Jaeger 1939:27–34: The 'antitype' of the recalcitrant former pupil Achilles of *Iliad* 9, Telemachos gradually develops (albeit not in a modern sense) in the course of the *Odyssey*, which has a "deliberately educational outlook *as a whole*" (29; my emphasis). I follow Jaeger in being a gradualist while admitting that Athena's exhortations in *Odyssey* 1 work pretty much as typical inspiration in the form of a divine command (which Jaeger 1939:31 expressly rules out in this book). In my view, Athena gives Telemachos a supernatural fillip—or kick—in the middle of Book 1,

is intrinsic and instrumental to Telemachos' coming of age, which is set in motion in Book 1 and formally culminates after the *Telemacheia* proper when the prince participates in the slaying of the suitors and especially in the war against their relatives (see Chapter 6). As noted, the *Telemacheia* revolves around the psychosocial maturation of the Little Prince; unless he matures he will be unable to help his father to take revenge on the usurpers and regain power.[33] By the third century AD, Porphyry had already defined Telemachos' journey as a *paideusis*.[34] H. W. Clarke and P. V. Jones have in their turn aptly brought out the 'paideutic' dimension in the Tale of Telemachos. As they argue, in the course of Books 1–4 the princeling receives from Athena, Nestor, Menelaos, and Helen successive accounts and versions of himself, among other narratives, all of them characteristic of a performance culture.[35] By means of these accounts the protagonist harmoniously matches—and reconciles—his inner world with his outer appearance.[36] That this process of harmonization is highly important can be inferred from the leitmotif of (in de Jong's formulation) "Telemachus' resemblance to Odysseus, both in his appearance and his manner of speaking,"[37] which Klingner calls the "theme of the father inside the son"—and which we might call the "theme of Odysseus' *nostos* in the mental world of his son."[38]

The Father's *Imago*

If the young man can only realize how much he resembles his father in physiognomy and *potentially* in mental traits, he will be able to resolve the *aporia* regarding his identity: Is he or is he not the *worthy* son of Odysseus? (He does not really doubt that Odysseus is his father.) Is he or is he not an extension

---

and from then until the end of the poem he evolves according to a distinct cultural logic, which I hope to explore.

[33] See esp. Jones 1988:496–506 and discussion below.

[34] Scholia *ad Odyssey* 1.284, noted by Clarke 1963:140n16 and others. For Athena's intervention as instruction, cf. *Odyssey* 1.384 ('θεοὶ διδάσκουσι'), etc.

[35] Clarke 1963, esp. 140–143; Jones 2002:7–8, stressing Telemachos' need for approval by others of his mode of self-presentation, on which also see below. Cf. also Olson 1995, esp. 89: "Telemachus can accordingly expect to be described to anyone who visits Pylos . . . in an awed and respectful manner . . . So too in Sparta . . . By the time Telemachus is ready to leave Sparta in Book XV . . . , he has got himself a good reputation among men . . ."

[36] Clarke 1963: "The burden of the next few books is to harmonize Telemachus' inner and outer selves" (131n6, a superb précis of the *Telemachy*). Wöhrle 1999:118, too, underscores the discrepancy between Telemachos' outer and inner maturity. Martin 1993:232–233 well remarks, along with others, that the entire poem revolves generally around the gap between, on the one hand, *Schein* 'seeming'—hence the importance attached to disguise—and, on the other, *Sein* 'being' or 'reality' and *real competence*.

[37] See de Jong 2001:27–28 *ad Odyssey* 1.206–212 and below.

[38] Klingner 1944:35 (this terminology is especially fitting for Book 1). I have replaced Klingner's "return" with *nostos*.

9

(almost an instantiation) of his father, as his very name, *Telemachos*, would suggest?[39] These are standard questions, which every hero (even Achilles, the son of a goddess) is necessarily bound to put to himself (even if indirectly) or to encounter in epic society. There are at least two reasons for this. The first touches on Homer's interest in the disparity between *Schein* and *Sein*, between seeming and being—in the case of Telemachos between, on the one hand, his promising, godlike appearance (θεοειδής 'of godlike appearance', *Odyssey* 1.113; compare ἰσόθεος 'godlike', 1.324), which Mentes and the poet himself register, and, on the other, the lad's Odyssean capabilities.[40] The other reason reflects a particular psychosocial constant, given the fact that the consolidation of a male's sense of 'masculinity' presupposes in myth as in social reality the individual's *self-definition in relation to his father*.[41] Indeed, the trajectory towards self-definition and hence maturity featured in the *Telemacheia* largely concerns the son's relation to the *imago* of his father, as will be shown. In this sense as well the *Telemacheia* may be said to describe a symbolic 'education'. This particular process is pretty far advanced in Book 1 (even before the assembly and Telemachos' departure in Book 2), since the conversation between the prince and Mentes has induced the youth to cite Odysseus at first by name (*Odyssey* 1.396, 398) and then as "my father" (*Odyssey* 1.413).[42]

In general the recognition of Odysseus' secret presence in the midst of Telemachos and Mentes comes about through the mutual mirroring of outer signs and psychological associations; each mirrors the absent hero in the other's eyes. From a psychological perspective the successive mental images of Odysseus that Mentes will bring to life for the youth's benefit will amount to the *imago* or, as B. Copley would argue,[43] the "unconscious object" of his father. Because Telemachos will, in the course of his interaction with Mentes, concretize and begin to come to terms with this 'object', it may be as well to examine in greater detail the stages of their interaction.

The stranger startles the young man with his initial 'news', a virtual *non sequitur* (*Odyssey* 1.194) that he hastens to correct by offering more 'news',

---

[39] See de Jong 2001:27–28 and Jones 2002:7–8: *Iliad* 4.370–400 (Diomedes is the worthy son of Tydeus), 6.476–481 (Astyanax will hopefully surpass Hektor in bravery), 8.281–285 (Teukros is the worthy son of Telamon). A patronymic used in addressing a hero is honorific particularly because it evokes his ethos: van Wees 1992:69; in general, a patronymic suggests the social status or the achievements of a hero's ancestors: Wöhrle 1999, esp. 18–22, 19 (with n31), and 49.

[40] See Martin 1993:234–235 and n36 above. (According to this scholar, the fact that Telemachos lags behind his father particularly in respect of μῆτις suggests that Homer acknowledges that a living epic tradition has come to an end: see Chapter 6 on the end of the *Odyssey*.)

[41] *Pace* Graziosi and Haubold 2003:68–69: see Chapters 4 and 6 below. For a bibliography of the ethnography of masculinity, see Graziosi and Haubold 2003:75–76.

[42] See de Jong 2001:18 *ad Odyssey* 1.96–324 and further below.

[43] I rely here on chapter 4 of Copley 1993, a psychoanalytical discussion.

schematic but hopeful, which in turn he transforms into an equally hopeful prophecy:

'νῦν δ' ἦλθον· δὴ γάρ μιν ἔφαντ' ἐπιδήμιον εἶναι,
σὸν πατέρ'·ἀλλά νυ τόν γε θεοὶ βλάπτουσι κελεύθου.
οὐ γάρ πω τέθνηκεν ἐπὶ χθονὶ δῖος Ὀδυσσεύς,
ἀλλ' ἔτι που ζωὸς κατερύκεται εὐρέϊ πόντῳ,
νήσῳ ἐν ἀμφιρύτῃ, χαλεποὶ δέ μιν ἄνδρες ἔχουσιν,
ἄγριοι, οἵ που κεῖνον ἐρυκανόωσ' ἀέκοντα.
αὐτὰρ νῦν τοι ἐγὼ μαντεύσομαι, ὡς ἐνὶ θυμῷ
ἀθάνατοι βάλλουσι καὶ ὡς τελέεσθαι ὀΐω,
οὔτε τι μάντις ἐὼν οὔτ' οἰωνῶν σάφα εἰδώς.
οὔ τοι ἔτι δηρόν γε φίλης ἀπὸ πατρίδος αἴης
ἔσσεται, οὐδ' εἴ πέρ τε σιδήρεα δέσματ' ἔχῃσι·
φράσσεται ὥς κε νέηται, ἐπεὶ πολυμήχανός ἐστιν.'

Odyssey 1.194–205

"And now I have come, because indeed they said he was among his people,
your father; but surely the gods are deflecting him from his course.
Divine Odysseus is not yet dead on this earth;
rather, alive still, he is kept back somewhere on the broad sea,
on a sea-washed island, and harsh men are holding him,
savages, they are detaining him, I take it, against his will.
But now I shall prophesy to you, just as in my spirit
the immortals are impelling me and as I believe it is coming to pass
although I am scarcely a seer nor one well-versed in omens:
No doubt he will not be away from his beloved country any longer,
no, not even if chains of iron hold him;
he will devise a way of returning, for he is a man of many devices."

As Klingner (1944:30) says of this passage, "the image of Odysseus appears to his son in an ever new perspective and shape" (though, one might add, this image remains amorphous despite its undeniable emotional charge). Immediately afterwards, in his reminiscence in the same passage about the young Odysseus, Mentes transfers the image of the young commander bound for Troy onto Telemachos (*Odyssey* 1.206–212; see below). Here, as Klingner (1944:30) remarks, the goddess "builds a bridge of thought between the young Odysseus who once went to war and his image who is now standing in front of the guest. Yes, in addressing Telemachos she is close to addressing an Odysseus who has grown up again and (so to speak) returned . . ." A little later Mentes portrays Odysseus in considerable detail, albeit only momentarily, as an idealized avenger (*Odyssey*

1.255–265; see n52 and discussion below). In this same passage Mentes allusively assimilates this image to the heartening example of the equally young avenger Orestes (*Odyssey* 1.296–302). In evoking these paradigmatic figures the goddess exploits deliberately the topic of her host's outer resemblance to the two heroes (*Odyssey* 1.206–209, 301–302). This topic is deployed as a rhetorical argument meant to persuade the prince that he combines the physical and mental attributes that render him a *new Odysseus-Orestes* capable of achieving *kleos*. See *Odyssey* 1.269–270 discussed above and especially 1.301–302, where Telemachos is cast as Orestes:

'καὶ σύ, φίλος, μάλα γάρ σ' ὁρόω καλόν τε μέγαν τε,
ἄλκιμος ἔσσ', ἵνα τίς σε καὶ ὀψιγόνων ἐῢ εἴπῃ.'

Odyssey 1.301–302

"You too, friend—for I see that you are very handsome and
        impressive-looking—
be brave [sc. like Orestes] so that even in future people will speak well of
        you."

Just as Mentes detects "elements of Odysseus within Telemachos," as Klingner notes, so too does the prince begin, by the end of the book, to notice reflections of Odysseus in Mentes.[44] It is no coincidence that moments before the stranger disappears with the speed of (or, less probably, in the form of) a bird Telemachos likens him gratefully to a father:

'ξεῖν', ἦ τοι μὲν ταῦτα φίλα φρονέων ἀγορεύεις,
ὥς τε πατὴρ ᾧ παιδί, καὶ οὔποτε λήσομαι αὐτῶν.'

Odyssey 1.307–308

"Stranger, truly you speak these [sc. words] in the spirit of intimacy,
like a father to his son, and never shall I forget them."

G. Wöhrle would account for this comparison as a nearly automatic politeness typical in a patriarchal society wherein senior men have the status of *Ersatzväter*.[45] But social reflexes aside, Telemachos' reaction suggests something deeper on which Homer's 'objective' comment may cast psychological illumination:

---

[44] Cf. the mutual mirroring of Achilles and Priam in *Iliad* 24.486–492, 540–542.
[45] Cf. Wöhrle 1999:36–37.

> τῷ δ' ἐνὶ θυμῷ
> θῆκε μένος καὶ θάρσος, ὑπέμνησέν τέ ἑ πατρὸς
> μᾶλλον ἔτ' ἢ τὸ πάροιθεν.

Odyssey 1.320–322

> and in his heart
> she instilled determination and courage, and called his father to his mind
> even more than before.

The 'internal object' of the father is starting to become more concrete in the depressed youth's mind. It is suggestive at least that he assimilates Mentes to the 'internal object of the good father', as Melanie Klein might have argued.[46] In general Telemachos' references to his father, by name and otherwise, together with the theme of 'Odysseus' *nostos* in Telemachos' mental world' (see also below) indicate his need for a father. (*Mutatis mutandis* this need is implied by Odysseus' declaration on first meeting his son: 'ἀλλὰ πατὴρ τεός εἰμι, τοῦ εἵνεκα σὺ στεναχίζων / πάσχεις ἄλγεα πολλά, βίας ὑποδέγμενος ἀνδρῶν' ["Rather, I am your father, on whose account you, groaning, / have been suffering much pain, putting up with the abuses of men," *Odyssey* 16.188–189].) What this early post-adolescent most clearly lacks is "a sense of a firmly established relationship with inner objects," particularly an internal father.[47] (Even the *exemplum* of Orestes is a disguise for the image of Odysseus.) According to Copley, an introjective relationship of this kind provides a developing person with a "deeper experience of identity" required for the "formation and maintenance of a mature adult state of mind."[48]

If a crucial step in the youth's 'education' is the establishment, or re-establishment, of a relationship particularly with his internal paternal object, the next step, equally indicative of his progress, can be seen in the episode (*Odyssey* 1.365–425) in which apparently for the first time—indeed, in public rather than in a purely optative private reverie—he lays claim to his rights as heir and head of Odysseus' *oikos* (see especially *Odyssey* 1.397–398: 'αὐτὰρ ἐγὼν οἴκοιο ἄναξ ἔσομ' ἡμετέροιο / καὶ δμώων, οὕς μοι ληΐσσατο δῖος Ὀδυσσεύς' ["but I shall be lord of our house / and of our male servants whom illustrious Odysseus took as plunder for my sake."]). As Klingner notes,[49] the episode, taking place as it does immediately after the "awakening" (which this scholar situates in *Odyssey* 1.253–305), points up how substantive this change is, inasmuch as the prince's forthright words precipitate and "bring to the fore the dynamic of opposition to

---

[46] Klein 1932 and 1948.
[47] Copley 1993:109.
[48] Copley 1993:109–111.
[49] Klingner 1944:34.

Penelope and the suitors." In particular, as will be seen, the youth's opposition to his mother is psychologically and culturally plausible, and because it also raises the matter of the meaning of *kleos* it will be analyzed shortly.

Σὸν πάτερ': Putting a Name to the Indefinite

Celibate Athena is, incidentally, the ideal dedicated teacher; her combination of strategic and intellectual resourcefulness makes her Telemachos' best motivator.[50] Moreover, she is an exotic figure enjoying a liminal status, given that her sexual ambiguity corresponds to the liminal status of a (possibly Phoenician) slave trader who conducts business with the Ithacans without belonging to their society.[51] Socially, being a generic *kakos* 'lowly person' on account of her occupation, she would not have been deemed threatening by the suitors. (In fact, Eurymachos' "seemingly generous remark"—so Dawe 1993:79 *ad Odyssey* 1.411—about the mysterious, evanescent stranger would seem to confirm the very opposite, namely, that Mentes is of κακός social status: 'οὐ μὲν γάρ τι κακῷ εἰς ὦπα ἐῴκει' ["because he definitely did not at all look, eye in eye, like a lowly person."].) She also has the advantage, qua Mentes, of having been a *philos* of Odysseus since the latter's youth; he is, as noted, the emotional and educational link between the liminal adult Telemachos and the liminal adult Odysseus, irrespective of whether the goddess's account about the stranger's junior mission at Ephyre is true (as de Jong believes) or an ad hoc invention (as others hold).[52]

Mentes takes Telemachos aback, though not Homer's audience, when, introducing himself, he announces:

'νῦν δ' ἦλθον· δὴ γάρ μιν ἔφαντ' ἐπιδήμιον εἶναι,
σὸν πατέρ'· ἀλλά νυ τόν γε θεοὶ βλάπτουσι κελεύθου.
οὐ γάρ πω τέθνηκεν ἐπὶ χθονὶ δῖος Ὀδυσσεύς. . .'

Odyssey 1.194–196

---

[50] See also Clarke 1963: "Athena, herself half native and half intruder, also childless and kinless . . ." (142). For Athena as a teacher of εὐβουλία, see Chapter 3 below.

[51] 'Mentes' is by definition a pirate: *Odyssey* 15.427, 16.426. He belongs to the category of Hartog's *hommes frontières*: Hartog 1996:12–14 (who does not cite Mentes, however). Perhaps this character foreshadows the liminal traveler Odysseus himself. (Klingner 1944:27n8 regards specifically the scene with Mentes as a "shadow of the scene with Eumaios" [see *Odyssey* 14.122–172].)

[52] De Jong 2001:32 *ad Odyssey* 1.255–264 notes that this is the first anecdote about the young Odysseus. Cf. Jones 1991: the narrative is a fictitious *prolepsis* of the murder of the suitors (123); Heubeck, West, and Hainsworth 1988:107 *ad loc.* remain undecided on whether the anecdote is an ad hoc invention or not.

"And now I have come, because indeed they said he was among his people,
your father; but surely the gods are deflecting him from his course.
Divine Odysseus is not yet dead on this earth . . ."

σὸν πατέρ' 'your father', emphatic at the beginning of verse 195, is nothing short of breathtaking. By 'μιν . . . ἐπιδήμιον' ("him . . . among his people," *Odyssey* 1.194) the young man would understand his grandfather Laertes, to whom the stranger had just been referring (*Odyssey* 1.189–93). The shock value is redoubled when Mentes utters "Ὀδυσσεύς" ("Odysseus") at the end of verse 196. The audience would have waited with bated breath for the name of the absent hero during this conversation,[53] especially after Mentes' earlier proleptic remark that he and Odysseus were 'ξεῖνοι . . . πατρώϊοι . . . / ἐξ ἀρχῆς' ("guest-friends . . . going back to our fathers . . . / from old times," *Odyssey* 1.187–188). Surely enough, the newcomer pronounces the name, confirming (as if he had to!) the identity of 'σὸν πατέρ' ("your father"). Mentes has in effect adduced the two ingredients, the cognitive coordinates—Ὀδυσσεὺς 'Odysseus' and σὸν πατέρ' 'your father'— that Telemachos will have to explore both intellectually and psychologically in the next books. Yet the prince is taken aback by more than the two nouns just mentioned, for his guest at first speaks as if Odysseus were already in Ithaka ('ἐπιδήμιον εἶναι' ["to be among his people," *Odyssey* 1.194]). These unexpected tidings of great joy are an explanation, tacked on to the stranger's statement 'νῦν δ' ἦλθον' ("And now I have come," *Odyssey* 1.194), which, as noted, is something of an *anacolouthon*. The news would have pained the prince as much as raised his hopes.[54] Before long Telemachos will utter these emotive words,[55] individually or together, in the same book (*Odyssey* 1.354, 396, 398, 413)[56] and subsequently in Book 2 (*Odyssey* 2.46, 59, 71)[57], Book 3 (*Odyssey* 3.83–84, 98ff.) and Book 4 (*Odyssey* 4.328)[58].

Telemachos, in addressing Nestor at *Odyssey* 3.83–84, combines the proper name with the phrase 'πατὴρ ἐμός' ("my father"), as he had already done in his speech before the assembly at *Odyssey* 2.71. He repeats the combination at *Odyssey* 3.98ff., his impassioned plea to the Pylian ruler for information about

---

[53] So also Heubeck, West, and Hainsworth 1988:102 *ad Odyssey* 1.196.

[54] See also Klingner 1944:31.

[55] On hearing the mention of his father's name in *Odyssey* 4.113–116 Telemachos cries, which indicates the emotional charge of this name.

[56] See de Jong 2001:18 *ad Odyssey* 1.96–324. In the verses above, Telemachos in fact believes the opposite, i.e. that Odysseus is alive: de Jong 2001:37, 38, 41 *ad Odyssey* 1.345–359, 353–355, 396, and 413–421, respectively; see also n57 immediately below.

[57] These passages occur in Telemachos' first public address before the Ithakans, in which, aiming as he does to arouse pity for himself, among other emotions, he feigns that he believes his father to be dead: see *Odyssey* 2.131, 218ff., and de Jong 2001, esp. 49 *ad Odyssey* 1.39–81. For other similar passages in Book 2: see *Odyssey* 2.131, 215, 218, 264, 352, and 360.

[58] See n28 above.

his father. He is here claiming the glorious past, in essence the very *kleos* of Odysseus:[59]

ʻλίσσομαι, εἴ ποτέ τοί τι πατὴρ ἐμός, ἐσθλὸς Ὀδυσσεύς,
ἢ ἔπος ἠέ τι ἔργον ὑποστὰς ἐξετέλεσε
δήμῳ ἔνι Τρώων, ὅθι πάσχετε πήματ᾿ Ἀχαιοί·
τῶν νῦν μοι μνῆσαι . . .ʼ

Odyssey 3.98–101

"I beg you, if ever my father, noble Odysseus
promised you and carried out any word or any deed
in the country of Troy where you Achaians were experiencing much
        suffering:
now remember these things for my sake . . ."

In nomine patris

In addressing Nestor in the passage just cited, the young guest hyposta-tizes the generic *kleos* of a Homeric hero from its two defining constituents, namely, *epos* and *ergon* (see Chapter 3). Borrowing as it were the *kleos* of his father,[60] he projects it onto himself in the hope of prompting Nestor to give him 'news' (the secondary meaning of the term *kleos*; see below). As he told the king slightly earlier:

ʻπατρὸς ἐμοῦ κλέος εὐρὺ[61] μετέρχομαι, ἤν που ἀκούσω,
δίου Ὀδυσσῆος ταλασίφρονος, ὅν ποτέ φασι
σὺν σοὶ μαρνάμενον Τρώων πόλιν ἐξαπαλάξαι.ʼ

Odyssey 3.83–85

"I come in quest of news (*kleos*) of my father that has spread from afar,
        on the chance I may hear
about divine Odysseus the steadfast, who once, they say,
after fighting together with you sacked the Trojans' city."

Generally speaking, *kleos* as such, especially when it emanates from a military deed, can be transferred to the *laos* 'people' (see *Iliad* 12.315–328)

---

[59] See Jones 2002:29 *ad Odyssey* 3.98–101 and discussion on *kleos* below. Cf. *Odyssey* 2.70–74 (Telemachos' ironical reference to Odysseus' *kleos*).

[60] Cf. *Odyssey* 1.263–266, where Odysseus appropriates (cf. Segal 1994:96) the *kleos* of Marshal Agamemnon. See also n62 below.

[61] See Heubeck, West, and Hainsworth 1988:165 *ad Odyssey* 3.83 (κλέος εὐρὺ) and Segal 1994:96 (with n27) noting that in Indoeuropean poetry and the *Odyssey* alike the adjective εὐρύ may typify κλέος. See also n119 below.

or less diffusely to the *philoi* 'friends, intimates' of a hero. This associative, or synecdochic, transference is a predictable concomitant of a "shame culture."[62] Jones remarks that the young man is appropriating, by hereditary right, the *consequences* of his father's deeds.[63] Moreover the youth's resort to an *exemplum* in order to validate his request is highly conventional.[64] What is of particular relevance to the educational dimension of the *Telemachy* is the fact that in his plea the prince consciously interweaves the past and present and in so doing substitutes his father (living or dead) for himself.

If, as will be remarked, *kleos* subsumes a person's social identity, a *hypallage*, or 'mutual exchange', of identity may be at play here: by way of 'persuasive association'—which is at once a rhetorical and deeply social argument—the *exemplum* ascribes Odysseus' mighty panoply of accomplishments to Telemachos while Telemachos' role as a son in search of his father devolves upon Odysseus, who travels in quest of his πατρὶς γαῖα 'native country'. This crisscrossing of identities may underlie the parallels in the adventures of Odysseus and his son that many scholars have detected. D. E. Bynum has invoked in this connection the "role transference between father and son," remarking that this theme also occurs in Serbo-Croatian epic poetry.[65] At least as regards Telemachos, the theme may imply an educational process. Throughout his ὁδός 'journey' the Little Prince in fact imitates in a symbolic way the travels of his father, and particularly his temptations, as A. J. Apthorp has shown.[66] Καθ' ὁδόν 'on his way' Telemachos comes of age, absorbing both consciously and unconsciously elements of his father's personality. Imitation of such a duration and nature typifies both the educational practice of apprenticeship per se and the process of growing up as a figurative apprenticeship, which will be discussed in Chapter 5.[67] For the time being it is perhaps sufficient to observe that the ancient scholia registered that as a result of his ἀποδημία 'going abroad' the prince developed— we might say 'grew up'—from a modestly tongue-tied, overprotected youth to a more Odyssean man:

> ἄτοπος δοκεῖ εἶναι Τηλεμάχου ἡ ἀποδημία . . ., ἀλλ' ἔδει τὸν ἐν γυναιξὶ
> τεθραμμένον, λύπαις τεταπεινωμένον, ῥητορειῶν οὐ πεπειραμένον
> οὐδεπώποτε, πολύτροπον γενέσθαι παραπλησίως τῷ πατρὶ, . . . καὶ
> κοινωνεῖν τῷ πατρί τῶν κατορθωμάτων ἐν τῇ μνηστηροκτονίᾳ

---

[62] Cf. again *Odyssey* 9.263–266 and Clarke 2004:77 *ad Iliad* 12.315–328 (Sarpedon's and Glaukos' *kleos* devolves upon the Lykians). For the transferral of *kleos* in general: LfgrE i.1330, 1α abb, s.v. ἄρνυμαι c. dat. pers. For shame culture, see e.g. Petropoulos 2003:161n323.

[63] Jones 1988:501n10. See n60 above.

[64] For the *exemplum* in prayers, supplications, and magic spells, see e.g. Petropoulos 2008:44–45.

[65] Bynum 1968:1296–1303 (also cited by Jones 1988:498n5).

[66] Apthorp 1980:1–22. See also Chapter 5 below.

[67] See also Chapter 6 for the *hypallage* in the simile in *Odyssey* 16.17–21.

Telemachos' going abroad seems absurd . . . yet having been raised among women, having been humiliated by sorrows, never having had any experience in public speaking, he had to become *polutropos* nearly like his father . . . and to take part in the success of the murder of the suitors.[68]

To return to *Odyssey* 3.98–99, the condition 'εἴ ποτέ τοί τι πατὴρ ἐμός, ἐσθλὸς Ὀδυσσεύς . . .' ("if ever my father, noble Odysseus . . .") in Telemachos' petition bears comparison to Odysseus' manifestly unorthodox yet telling oath in *Iliad* 2.260:

'μηδ' ἔτι Τηλεμάχοιο πατὴρ κεκλημένος εἴην'
"nor may I any longer be called father of Telemachos"

Instead of highlighting his relation to his father Laertes, the hero defines himself in relation to his son Telemachos: Odysseus reverses the obvious hallmark of his son's masculine identity ('Telemachos, son of Odysseus') and applies the rearranged terms to himself ('Odysseus, father of Telemachos'). R. B. Rutherford regards this unique reversal as an indirect indication that Homer was aware of tales about Odysseus' *nostos* and, one might add, about the role that his relationship with Telemachos plays in this *nostos*.[69] The *hypallage* in the Iliadic oath may at first seem curious; in Book 16 however the patronymic relationship—and, by extension, the son's relation to (or reception of) the *kleos* of his father—will be fully elucidated when the prince lives up to his father's call to action. Such a *protropê* 'exhortation' concerning the importance of a warrior's ancestry is routine in martial rhetoric:[70]

'εἰ ἐτεόν γ' ἐμός ἐσσι καὶ αἵματος ἡμετέροιο,
μή τις ἔπειτ' Ὀδυσῆος ἀκουσάτω ἔνδον ἐόντος. . .'

Odyssey 16.300–301

"If you really are mine and of our blood,
then let nobody hear about Odysseus being inside . . ."

---

68 EM *ad Odyssey* 1.93 (Dindorf); see Jones 1988:498n5. For πολυμήχανος Telemachos, see Jones 1988, esp. 505–506, (who relies on Austin 1969:45–63). See Martin 1993:239–240 for a metapoetic exegesis of the fact that at a formal level Telemachos is described as πεπνυμένος though never πολύμητις; see Chapter 3 (on Telemachos πεπνυμένος) and Chapter 6 (further on Martin's exegesis).

69 Cf. also *Iliad* 4.354 and Rutherford 1992:18–19 *ad loc.*

70 For this *topos*, see below, esp. Chapter 6. Wöhrle 1999:133–135, notes that the command serves as a kind of "testing" of Telemachos after father and son have recognized one another.

When Nestor asks him outright, "Who are you?" (*Odyssey* 3.71) Telemachos could—in theory—answer just as directly as his father does in Book 9.19–20 (in response to Alkinoos' questions):

'εἴμ' Ὀδυσεὺς Λαερτιάδης, ὃς πᾶσι δόλοισιν
ἀνθρώποισι μέλω, καί μευ κλέος οὐρανὸν ἵκει.'

"I am Odysseus, son of Laertes, who because of my tricks
am on the minds of all human beings, and my reputation (*kleos*) reaches
the sky."

As it happens, Telemachos has not (yet) gained the requisite military and other kinds of experience to warrant even a faintly similar (and typically self-regarding) heroic boast.[71] Even when he avails himself of his father's *kleos* the youth distances himself from it by using the phrase 'ὅν ποτέ φασι' ("who once [upon a time], they say," *Odyssey* 3.84), which imparts a fairy-tale-like coloring to the existence and deeds of his father.[72] On the one side, Telemachos grounds his relation to his father on the collocation of πατὴρ ἐμός 'my father' and Ὀδυσσεύς 'Odysseus' in Book 2 and in his address to Nestor in Book 3. On the other, as remarked, he tempers the certainty even of his father's existence. Admittedly such diminuendo may in large measure be rhetorical; but even so, we may allow for some echo of general uncertainty besetting the prince.[73] This psychological reaction is plausible, despite the fictional plot of the *Telemachy*: the little ἄναξ 'lord' emerges as an "ordinary young person" who is much nearer to everyday life than most of his predecessors, the relentless heroes of the *Iliad*.[74]

The Little Prince's Lineage

The Little Prince's progression towards adult confidence and competence will go through many fluctuations in the *Telemachy*. For example, the poet at first describes him, even before he meets Mentes, as "aggrieved in his heart" (*Odyssey* 1.114); the selfsame phrase will be used to describe his mood at the end of Book 2 (298), right after Athena delivers the longest of her exhortations (this

---

[71] On bragging about one's *kleos*, see Martin 1989:94 with n15 (cross-cultural and Homeric evidence). See e.g. Diomedes' remarks to Glaukos, *Iliad* 6, esp. 150–151, 206–211, Segal 1994:93 *ad loc.* and discussion of *kleos* below. De Jong 2001:72 (*contra* Heubeck, West, and Hainsworth 1988:165 *ad Odyssey* 3.83) rightly points out that Telemachos keeps mum about his own name because of shyness or uncertainty about himself (I prefer the latter).

[72] Cf. *Cypria* fr. 1.1 Davies: ἦν ὅτε μυρία φῦλα κατὰ χθόνα, recalling the *incipit* of a fairy tale; also Plato *Protagoras* 320c: Ἦν γάρ ποτε χρόνος. See de Jong 2001:73 *ad loc.*: κείνου (88), φασι, and the indefinite article ποτέ (84) evoke either genuinely or affectedly (and with rhetorical effect) the pessimistic conviction that the youth is separated from his father by *space* as well as *time*. (In *Odyssey* 1.189, 220 Telemachos also employs the verb φασὶ/φασι.) See below on rumors.

[73] See nn71–72 above.

[74] For Telemachos as an "ordinary youth," see Clarke 2004:86.

time in the guise of 'Mentor'). The spiraling, vacillating course towards self-awareness as the 'adult son of Odysseus' is set in motion, as already noted, by Mentes in his first speech:

'ἀλλ' ἄγε μοι τόδε εἰπὲ καὶ ἀτρεκέως κατάλεξον,
εἰ δὴ ἐξ αὐτοῖο τόσος πάϊς εἰς Ὀδυσῆος.
αἰνῶς μὲν κεφαλήν τε καὶ ὄμματα καλὰ ἔοικας
κείνῳ, ἐπεὶ θαμὰ τοῖον ἐμισγόμεθ' ἀλλήλοισιν,
πρίν γε τὸν ἐς Τροίην ἀναβήμεναι . . .'

Odyssey 1.206–210

"But come now, tell me this and recount it frankly,
   whether being so grown, you really are the son of the very man
      Odysseus.
Uncannily, to be sure, in your head and beautiful eyes you look like
   him, [sc. I say this] because we often associated with one another like
      this,
well before he embarked for Troy . . ."

"Now tell me, being so large and tall, whether you are Odysseus' own son?"— so, in effect, begins Mentes' provocative oblique question. Given that Athena has already identified her interlocutor as the son of Odysseus (see especially *Odyssey* 1.195–196), her query is superfluous. Yet it provides Telemachos with a springboard for further thought and psychological searching. Contradicting her previous statements, Athena feigns ignorance in order to elicit from him an anxious reaction (*Odyssey* 1.214–220); acting as a mirror, she forces him to re-examine his relationship with his absent progenitor.[75] From a strictly logical point of view the syntax of her question is elliptical; this is the ellipsis of collo-quial speech. Mentes immediately corrects this, explaining the reasons for his question. First, as an *adult* (a secondary implication of τόσος, literally, 'so big', *Odyssey* 1.207; compare τηλίκος 'of such an age', *Odyssey* 1.297), the young man bears a surprising (see αἰνῶς 'uncannily', *Odyssey* 1.208) and attractive (see κεφαλήν τε καὶ ὄμματα καλὰ 'in your head and beautiful eyes') resemblance (ἔοικας 'you look like') to his father's physiognomy.[76] Second, inasmuch as τοῖον 'to such an extent' in verse 209 does not modify the adverb θαμά 'often'

---

[75] See also de Jong 2001:27–28 *ad Odyssey* 1.206–212 ("suggestive questions").

[76] Cf. τοσοῦτον, *Iliad* 9.485 in the sense of 'adult'. For Telemachos' height and handsomeness, see *Odyssey* 14.174–177, 18.215–220, 175–176 (his beard). See van Wees 1992: heroes are invari-ably and by definition impressive in appearance and strength, e.g. *Odyssey* 20.194: ἔοικε δέμας βασιλῆϊ ἄνακτι (78ff.). See also Chapter 3. Epic descriptions however of a hero or an important woman (such as Helen) are as a rule schematic and indirect, evoking only the impression made on a third party: Edwards 2001:52–53, 111; Petropoulos 2003:24.

but may be connected instead in sense to the verb ἐμισγόμεθ' 'we associated with, were intimate with',[77] the goddess is citing another element that father and son share: "because we often associated with one another so closely or so well [sc. as you and I are now doing]." Athena's recognition of these points in common reflects a leitmotif of the *Telemacheia* that has already been observed by other scholars.[78] She is the first character to mention this resemblance, and she does so in a manner that cannot but flatter her interlocutor (compare ὄμματα καλὰ 'beautiful eyes').

Here and in verses 224ff. her words must mean a great deal to a young man whose relationship to his father is precarious, particularly given that he has never seen his father and talks with considerable reservation about his ancestry. (De Jong acutely comments that the prince does not really doubt his descent from Odysseus but rather stresses that his conviction is based entirely on hearsay.)[79] The prince answers the goddess's query as follows:

'τοιγὰρ ἐγώ τοι, ξεῖνε, μάλ' ἀτρεκέως ἀγορεύσω.
μήτηρ μέν τ' ἐμέ, φησι τοῦ ἔμμεναι, αὐτὰρ ἐγώ γε
οὐκ οἶδ'· οὐ γάρ πώ τις ἑὸν γόνον αὐτὸς ἀνέγνω.
ὡς δὴ ἐγώ γ' ὄφελον μάκαρός νύ τευ ἔμμεναι υἱὸς
ἀνέρος, ὃν κτεάτεσσιν ἑοῖς ἔπι γῆρας ἔτετμε.
νῦν δ' ὃς ἀποτμότατος γένετο θνητῶν ἀνθρώπων,
τοῦ μ' ἔκ φασι γενέσθαι, ἐπεὶ σύ με τοῦτ' ἐρεείνεις.'

Odyssey 1.214–220

"Very well, then, Stranger, I shall speak to you quite frankly:
My mother, to be sure, keeps saying I am his, but I for my part
do not know, for [generally speaking] no one knows for certain his own
        stock.
If only I were the son of some blessedly fortunate
man whom old age has come upon in the midst of his possessions.
As it is, that man has proved the most unfortunate of mortal humans—
from him they say I was born since you ask me about this."

His words form a ring-structure.[80] The particle τε in verse 215 lends the nuance of repetition: Penelope persistently defends her son's patriline, as Stanford (1958:225) and Jones (1991:50) remark ('keep on saying'). The gnomic cast of

---

77 *Contra* Heubeck, West, and Hainsworth 1988:102, as Stanford 1958:225 *ad loc.* ("τοῖον emphasises θαμά"). Compare *Odyssey* 3.496: τοῖον γὰρ ὑπέκφερον ὠκέες ἵπποι.
78 See nn36–37 above.
79 De Jong 2001:28 *ad Odyssey* 1.214–220. Cf. n72 and n81.
80 This appears to have escaped the notice of scholars. See also n5 on this structure.

the youth's opening words (*Odyssey* 1.216) is clever, as it gives him an excuse for generalizing his 'predicament'.[81] The central component of the ring structure is an unrealistic wish: the μάκαρ ἀνήρ 'blessedly fortunate man' who grows old among his possessions may also be an embellished allusion to his grandfather Laertes, whom Mentes mentions earlier (*Odyssey* 1.188–193) or a *prolepsis* of Nestor in Book 3. What is more, this wish is associated with two admittedly minor themes of the *Odyssey*: first, the self-consciousness of many characters about the stages of life (see *Odyssey* 1.218: 'ὃν . . . γῆρας ἔτετμε ["whom old age has come upon"]),[82] and second, the nostalgic theme of 'the former prosperity of Odysseus' household'.[83] Wishful thinking, in any event, is the only escape for those who yearn for Odysseus and cannot act—or, like Telemachos, hesitate to act.[84]

The Consequences of Lineage

The prince, we noted, does not doubt his mother's fidelity or Odysseus' paternity. Though he uses the adverb ἀτρεκέως 'frankly' (*Odyssey* 1.214) in his asseveration,[85] he is rather tendentiously and imaginarily renouncing his real father (who he assumes is long lost) and replacing him with an idealization—the father who returns home and dies in old age among his loved ones.[86] This phantastical image—old man Odysseus dying in happiness in Ithaka—is at once a wish and a prophecy (and hence a virtual φήμη);[87] compare Teiresias' prophecy in Book 11 (134–137). Shortly afterwards (*Odyssey* 1.236–240) the Little Prince will proceed to refashion this image into a variation, also inspired by desperate *Wünscherfüllung*. In this variant wish, Odysseus, deprived of his homecoming, nevertheless dies gloriously at Troy, bequeathing customary *kleos* to his son, as we will see.

Telemachos' rhetoric of misfortune wavers between two phantastical versions of his father's fate, both of them comforting. The first eventuality is rooted in the post-heroic world of the audience: 'Old man Odysseus dies [without *kleos*] among his intimates and possessions in Ithaka' (motif A). The

---

[81] See esp. Heubeck, West, and Hainsworth 1988:102 *ad Odyssey* 1.215–216 (Telemachos' ironical disposition and modesty); *pace* Rutherford 1992:28 (the youth, suspecting his mother's infidelity, doubts that he is the son of Odysseus); de Jong 2001:28 *ad loc.* (Telemachos, for all these uncertainties, does not doubt Odysseus' paternity).

[82] See Reinhardt 1960: the *Odyssey* stresses the contrast and the differences between the older and the younger generation (41). See also Chapter 6.

[83] See *Odyssey* 1.117 and n4 above.

[84] For nostalgic wishes in the pure optative, see de Jong 2001:32 *ad Odyssey* 1.253–269.

[85] In verse 214 he responds to Mentes' command 'εἰπὲ καὶ ἀτρεκέως κατάλεξον.'

[86] Jones 1991:120 *ad Odyssey* 1.215–220, to which the present paragraph is indebted, rightly notes that this disavowal is striking rhetorically.

[87] For φήμη, see Bakker 2002a:139 and Chapter 2 below.

second eventuality is the very opposite and a throw-back to the remoter, earlier cosmos of Iliadic *kleos*: 'Middle-aged Odysseus dies gloriously [i.e. with *kleos*] in battle but far away from Ithaka' (motif –A).[88] If this son renounces his real father by resorting to alternative wishes, this is because, as S. Olson comments,[89] he does not doubt his mother's faithfulness but rather wants to avoid as conveniently as possible a role he realizes that Mentes thrusts upon him but which he feels he cannot assume. If he accepts Athena's statements and insinuations about his likeness to Odysseus, he must admit also that this ancestry is imperatively relevant, obliging him to take action (see *Odyssey* 1.228–229).[90] Scholars have overlooked that in order to help this post-adolescent resolve his "identity crisis,"[91] as a result of which he shirks all responsibility, the goddess emphasizes Telemachos' biological, and simultaneously social, status, situated 'betwixt and between' adolescence and adulthood (see again τόσος πάϊς 'so grown', *Odyssey* 1.207], with Chapter 3 n4 below). At length Athena will repeat to the prince that he has indeed come of age: 'οὐδέ τί σε χρὴ / νηπιάας ὀχέειν, ἐπεὶ οὐκέτι τηλίκος ἐσσί' ("it is not fitting for you / to carry on your childish ways, because you no longer are of such an age," *Odyssey* 1.296–297).

In verses 222–224 the goddess pointedly reinforces her earlier remark about the youth's appearance (*Odyssey* 1.206ff., see below):

'οὐ μέν τοι γενεήν γε θεοὶ νώνυμνον ὀπίσσω
θῆκαν, ἐπεὶ σέ γε τοῖον ἐγείνατο Πηνελόπεια.
ἀλλ' ἄγε...'

Odyssey 1.222–224

"Surely the gods have not made you a family [that will be] nameless in
          future
since Penelope has given birth to someone of your kind.
But come..."

She very reasonably shifts from the theme of outer resemblance to the related topic of γενεή 'family' (compare the expression 'family resemblance' in English). Γενεή as invoked here, however, is a purely qualitative (internal) criterion by which to evaluate and hearten Telemachos (compare τοῖον ἐγείνατο 'someone of your kind', *Odyssey* 1.223). The mere reminder of a hero's γενεή or γένος 'stock, family' is usually enough to move him to carry out his utmost duty. Thus, to cite the famous example in *Iliad* 6, Glaukos confidently recites his own immediate

---

[88] Jones 1991:120 compares *Odyssey* 1.215–220 to Achilles' heroic disjunction in *Iliad* 9.410–416.
[89] Olson 1995:70–71.
[90] Olson 1995:71 ("the relevance of Odysseus' story for his own," "the relevance of Telemachos' ancestry and the promise it holds out for the future").
[91] Among others, Jones 2002:7 employs the term 'identity crisis'.

pedigree (contrast this with Telemachos' uncertainty at *Odyssey* 1.215ff. and especially 220) and then recalls the standard and, from a sociological point of view, plausible paternal injunction (compare ἐπέτελλεν 'he instructed', verse 207 below):[92]

> Ἱππόλοχος μ' δέ ἔτικτε, καὶ ἐκ τοῦ φημι γενέσθαι·
> πέμπε δέ μ' ἐς Τροίην, καί μοι μάλα πολλ' ἐπέτελλεν,
> αἰὲν ἀριστεύειν καὶ ὑπείροχον ἔμμεναι ἄλλων,
> μηδὲ γένος πατέρων αἰσχυνέμεν, οἳ μέγ' ἄριστοι
> ἔν τ' Ἐφύρῃ ἐγένοντο καὶ ἐν Λυκίῃ εὐρείῃ.
> ταύτης τοι γενεῆς τε καὶ αἵματος εὔχομαι εἶναι.'

Iliad 6.206–211[93]

"But Hippolochos begat me, and I assert that I was engendered by him.
And he sent me to Troy, and sternly instructed me
always to be best and to be superior to others,
and not to shame the family of our forefathers, who by far the best
were in Ephyre and Lykia alike.
Of *this* lineage and bloodline do I avow to be."

Kirk well notes that a father's role in passing on the dictum of ἀεὶν ἀριστεύειν 'always to be best' is not necessarily as decisive as Homer's heroes make it out to be.[94] Even when Hektor says that his father 'taught' him the code of *kleos* as epitomized in the notion of ἀριστεύειν 'to be best', he really implies that his instruction and inspiration stemmed from the wider context of growing up and participating in his particular class of elites:

---

[92] Like others Kirk 1993:187 *ad Iliad* 6.207–208 remarks that Peleus gave the same typically heroic advice verbatim to his son in *Iliad* 11.783ff., namely, 'αἰὲν ἀριστεύειν καὶ ὑπείροχον ἔμμεναι ἄλλων.' (The phrase καὶ ὑπείροχον ἔμμεναι ἄλλων is notionally almost identical to αἰὲν ἀριστεύειν.)

[93] The long syllable τοῦ (*Iliad* 6.206) lends a note of *gravitas*, as possibly does the spondee ταύτης in the recapitulating verse 211. Aineias sounds even more self-assuredly boastful when he advertises his divine descent at *Iliad* 20.200ff., esp. 208–209: 'αὐτὰρ ἐγὼν υἱὸς μεγαλήτορος Ἀγχίσαο/εὔχομαι ἐκγεγάμεν, μήτηρ δέ μοί ἐστ' Ἀφροδίτη,' and 241: 'ταύτης τοι γενεῆς τε καὶ αἵματος εὔχομαι εἶναι.' Cf. *Iliad* 6.211 (= 20.241) and *Odyssey* 1.220.

[94] See Kirk 1993:187, 220 *ad Iliad* 6.209–211 and 444–446, respectively. This scholar echoes the emphasis characteristically given by British social anthropologists to the imperatives of social class. *Per contra* Wöhrle 1999:32–48 stresses the primary, exclusive role of the father in transmitting the tenet ἀεὶν ἀριστεύειν; in his view the rigid patriarchal hierarchy dominant in both epics imposes the father as a behavioral model for his son. This scholar admits however that a son, once mature, enters a system of collective 'fathers' (*Väterkollektiv*) and contemporary 'brothers' (36–37).

'οὐδέ με θυμὸς ἄνωγεν, ἐπεὶ μάθον ἔμμεναι ἐσθλός
αἰεὶ καὶ πρώτοισι μετὰ Τρώεσσι μάχεσθαι,
ἀρνύμενος πατρός τε μέγα κλέος ἠδ' ἐμὸν αὐτοῦ.'

Iliad 6.444–446

"Nor does my heart bid me [sc. to shirk battle], because I have learnt to be
    brave
always and to fight alongside Trojans in the front line,
seeking to gain great glory (*kleos*) for my father and myself."

(Another excellent 'student' of war is the young Trojan Euphorbos. As the poet remarks parenthetically, this hero proves from his very first battle to be the best among young warriors: *Iliad* 16.808–811.)

Glaukos and Hektor (and, for that matter, Aineias) will automatically emulate the ethic of excellence in battle because it is required by their social status as ἄριστοι 'best, preeminent'.[95] By achieving *kleos* they will confer it—by association—not only on their fathers but, more importantly, also on the dynasty to which they belong.[96] Indeed, as Glaukos attests (*Iliad* 6.206–211), an aristocrat's γένος 'family, stock',[97] exactly like his synonymous γενεή, sets exacting precedents and standards of behavior (αἰεὶν ἀριστεύειν 'always to be best'), and any deviation from them will shame the πατέρων γένος (in effect, 'ancestors'). Odysseus expresses this very sentiment when he forewarns his son at the end of the *Odyssey*:

'μή τι καταισχύνειν πατέρων γένος, οἳ τὸ πάρος περ
ἀλκῇ τ' ἠνορέῃ τε κεκάσμεθα πᾶσαν ἐπ' αἶαν.'

Odyssey 24.508–509

"how not in any way to shame the family of our forefathers, us who since
    times past
have excelled in warfare and masculinity throughout the whole world."

---

[95] See also below. In epic ideology the members of the heroic elite are brave warriors and their bravery in battle conversely justifies their elevated status (τιμή): van Wees 1992, esp. 79ff., 100; Clarke 2004:77–78.

[96] Moreover, in support of Kirk's comment (n94 above) we can compare πατρός τε . . . κλέος (*Iliad* 6.446) with e.g. γένος πατέρων (*Iliad* 6.209). In *Odyssey* 24.508–509 (immediately below) the father is elided with the entire γένος, which is traced to the past. See also Chapter 6 on the continuation and end of generations in the *Odyssey*.

[97] On the term γένος as used in modern historiography, see chapters 1–2 of Patterson 1998. This scholar glosses γένος in Homer as 'family, kin' (but not 'clan').

By contrast, then, to Glaukos and other heroes, the Ithakan prince lacks (for the time being) the father who would be expected to give him this customary command.[98] It is Athena who in her vital paideutic role will supplement his peculiar deficit. She will do so not only by citing his celebrated γενεή 'family, pedigree' (*Odyssey* 1.222–223) but also, as has been shown, by instilling in him, through the course of Book 1, an increasingly vivid mental image of his father (see ὑπέμνησέν τε ἑ πατρός ["she called his father to his mind," *Odyssey* 1.321]).

Kleos and the Shame of Not Having a Tomb

Athena's *litotes* in *Odyssey* 1.222–223, an affirmation of the reputation of the prince's family, is part and parcel of the Homeric ideological construct embraced by the concept of *kleos*. Later (see especially *Odyssey* 1.239–240 below) her interlocutor rebuts her enthusiastic prediction, particularly in verses 222–223: the youth's rejection of the eventuality of κλέος ὀπίσσω 'kleos in future' disposes of Athena's anticipation of the continuance ὀπίσσω 'in future' of his family's 'name'. Telemachos' speech, which is bitter throughout but soars intermittently to rhetorical heights, now dwells on the tragic shame of the 'anonymity'[99] inevitably attending a hero when he is deprived even of a σῆμα 'burial marker' or τύμβος 'tomb', the latter being among the concomitants needed for the preservation ὀπίσσω of a hero's *kleos* and, secondarily, that of his family:[100]

'ξεῖν', ἐπεὶ ἄρ δὴ ταῦτά μ' ἀνείρεαι ἠδὲ μεταλλᾷς,
μέλλεν μέν ποτε οἶκος ὅδ' ἀφνειὸς καὶ ἀμύμων
ἔμμεναι, ὄφρ' ἔτι κεῖνος ἀνὴρ ἐπιδήμιος ἦεν·
νῦν δ' ἑτέρως ἐβόλοντο θεοὶ κακὰ μητιόωντες,
οἳ κεῖνον μὲν ἄϊστον ἐποίησαν περὶ πάντων
ἀνθρώπων, ἐπεὶ οὔ κε θανόντι περ ὧδ' ἀκαχοίμην,

---

[98] According to Martin 1989:128–130, Glaukos is fighting a verbal duel (as is Diomedes earlier on in his allusively malicious speech: *Iliad* 6.123–143) wherein each speech is "an act of self-presentation that attempts to wrest authority." What is pertinent is Glaukos' youthful inexperience (if we accept Diomedes' comments at *Iliad* 6.123–126). Yet the Lykian hero, Martin remarks, insinuates unmistakably that he even surpasses his grandfather Bellerophon in courage. He expressly recalls his father's injunction ('αἰὲν ἀριστεύειν . . .,' *Iliad* 6.208), while Diomedes expressly admits that he does not even remember his father Tydeus ('Τυδέα δ' οὐ μέμνημαι, ἐπεί μ' ἔτι τυτθὸν ἐόντα / κάλλιφ,' *Iliad* 6.222–223).

[99] See esp. *Odyssey* 24.93 and Hesiod *Works and Days* 154: those belonging to the third (Bronze) Generation are condemned to being νώνυμνοι after death.

[100] Bakker 2002b:18 observes that in epic a dead hero's *kleos* is disseminated and maintained only through song. Yet surely his tomb also contributes to a hero's post mortem *kleos*: de Jong 2001:228 *ad Odyssey* 9.19–20; further, Nora 1989, esp. 22–24 (generally on *lieux de mémoire*). See also n103 below.

εἰ μετὰ οἷς ἑτάροισι δάμη Τρώων ἐνὶ δήμῳ,
ἠὲ φίλων ἐν χερσίν, ἐπεὶ πόλεμον τολύπευσε.
τῷ κέν οἱ τύμβον μὲν ἐποίησαν Παναχαιοί,
ἠδέ κε καὶ ᾧ παιδὶ μέγα κλέος ἤρατ' ὀπίσσω.
νῦν δέ μιν ἀκλειῶς ἅρπυιαι ἀνηρείψαντο·
οἴχετ' ἄϊστος ἄπυστος, ἐμοὶ δ' ὀδύνας τε γόους τε
κάλλιπεν· οὐδ' ἔτι κεῖνον ὀδυρόμενος στεναχίζω
οἶον, ἐπεί νύ μοι ἄλλα θεοὶ κακὰ κήδε' ἔτευξαν.'

Odyssey 1.231–244

"Stranger, since you're asking me about these things and inquiring,
this household here probably was once bountiful and beautiful
as long as that man was still among his folk.
But as it is, gods plotting evil willed things otherwise—
they made him vanish unseen, him above all other
human beings. For I would not grieve like this if he had simply died,
if he had been slain in the country of Troy in the company of his
          comrades-in-arms
or in the hands of intimates, after he had finished winding the thread of
          war.
In that case Achaians from everywhere would have erected a tomb for
          him,
and he would have won great glory (*kleos*) for his son too for the future.
But as it is, Harpy-storm-winds snatched him away so that there is no
          news of him (literally *without kleos*).
He's gone unseen, unreported, while to me pain and lamentation
he has left as a legacy; nor, what is more, do I moan and mourn over
only that man, because now gods have created other worries for me."

    Heubeck, West, and Hainsworth (1988:104) and R. Dawe (1993:63) unneces-
sarily suggest that *Odyssey* 1.238 be obelized; the formers' view, in particular,
that φίλων 'of friends, intimates' must refer to Odysseus' family is debatable.[101]
In a foreign and, moreover, hostile land such as Troy, all Greeks would have
been φίλοι 'friends, intimates'. I suggest keeping verse 238 but reading ἠδὲ 'and'
instead of the disjunctive conjunction ἠὲ 'or'. (If emended in this way the verse
suits even better the context of *Odyssey* 4.490, where it is repeated.) Telemachos,
in effect, wishes that his father had been killed in action at the conclusion of the

---

[101] *Contra* Heubeck, West, and Hainsworth 1988:105.

war ('ἐπεὶ πόλεμον τολύπευσεν'; compare *Odyssey* 5.308–512) at Troy, where Achaians of widely diverse origins would have buried him:[102]

'ἠδὲ φίλων ἐν χερσίν, ἐπεὶ πόλεμον τολύπευσε.'

"and in the hands of intimates, after he had finished winding the thread of war."

In Archaic society a hero's post-mortem *kleos* vitally depended on, above all else, the existence of an oral tradition concerning him; proper burial rites and the physical evidence of a tomb were not enough.[103] A mute tomb on its own, as Telemachos assumes—robbed of a narrative about, say, Odysseus' death in battle—could scarcely sustain the hero's particular *kleos*.[104] A memorializing oral tradition arising out of ritual lamentation at the funeral would, of course, have been a significant step towards preserving this *kleos* ὀπίσσω 'for posterity' (that is, in a systemic sense; see below). Yet no funeral took place and no one—neither Nestor nor Menelaos nor *a fortiori* Telemachos—knows "the end to Odysseus' story" as S. Murnaghan has remarked (1989). Given this incomplete record, the integrity of Odysseus' *kleos*, which definitionally has a commemorative aspect, is at risk. His presumably posthumous *kleos* indeed exists but only as an unfinished story. It is its incompleteness that Telemachos—with some exaggeration—believes will thwart the transferral of his father's *kleos* to himself.

The youth is enervated, then, not only by the disastrous predicament of having no father (*Odyssey* 1.244–251) but also by the consideration that his father has an open-ended life story and no grave—not even (he must imply) a cenotaph.[105] These particular shortfalls create a major stigma for Odysseus himself; additionally, they have dire 'metaphysical' repercussions for his family. As early as *Odyssey* 1.161–162 Telemachos cites the absence of a grave when he melodramatically speculates that his father's bones 'πύθεται ὄμβρῳ / κεῖμεν' ἐπ' ἠπείρου, ἢ εἰν ἁλὶ κῦμα κυλίνδει' ("rot in the rain / as they lie on land or the surge of the sea turns them over and over"). To be sure, the

---

[102] The prefix παν- brings out the pluralistic variety of the individual groups of Achaians: Hall 2002:132 with n28. When the Παναχαιοί, and not simply Ἀχαιοί set up the tomb, it is understood that the participation in the burial, and hence its magnificence, are maximal.

[103] Cairns 2001:31–32, with n103 *contra* Vernant. See also Sourvinou-Inwood 1995:139ff. (for the reciprocally magnifying relation between the splendor of a τύμβος/σῆμα and the diffusion of κλέος); also n100 above.

[104] See *Odyssey* 1.240: 'ᾧ παιδὶ … κλέος ἤρατ ὀπίσσω' and LfgrE i.1329 s.v. ἄρνυμαι, 1a α: construed with the immaterial objects κῦδος, κλέος, and εὖχος, this verb refers to the 'glory and fame' that arise from individual martial action; also LfgrE i.1330, 1a abb. (For a different reading of Telemachos' sentiments in this passage, see Murnaghan 1989:157, 159.)

[105] On the "mound of earth over the grave with or without a stele," see Sourvinou-Inwood 1995:128ff., n107 and Chapter 6 below.

cruelest fate conceivable in antiquity for a hero at death was to be carrion for birds of prey (on land) or fish (at sea) and to be denied the customary ritual lament and burial.[106] Such a death was regarded as superlatively desolate and, socially speaking, most humiliating; for the unmourned hero—lost at sea, for instance—was unlikely to be joined with his family in Hades (whence the preventive customary practice, which reached back to the Mycenaean period, of placing a stone or cenotaph to stand synecdochically for the deceased).[107] The tomb Telemachos desiderates would thus also have guaranteed the integrity of his family.[108] Under the circumstances, this integrity has been jeopardized not only in the afterlife through the lack of a tomb, but also in the present, on account of Odysseus' disappearance. This deeply tragic sense of double loss underlies his words at *Odyssey* 1.234ff., where, as noted, he effectively wishes at least that his father had been buried at Troy.[109]

This speech, we remarked earlier, has a studiedly rhetorical texture. Compare especially: a) the ambiguity of the adverb ἀκλειῶς 'without report' at *Odyssey* 1.241,[110] which following on the noun κλέος 'fame, glory' at 1.240 is an example of *paronomasia*;[111] and b) the *asyndeton* at *Odyssey* 1.242, which juxtaposes two privative (and in fact, rhyming) adjectives counterpointed by the remainder of the run-on verse.[112] Cumulatively the phraseology in verses 240–244, the punning assonance and especially the unconnected, emotive adjectives in verse 242, recall the style of an actual lament.[113] Odysseus (whom the prince does not mention by name) has vanished without a trace, depriving his family and society at large of reports (κλέος). Synchronically, these oral accounts would feed into the sum total of the narratives about him; diachronically, they would make up his κλέος, rendering it much more intricate than mere 'news' or 'gossip'.[114]

---

[106] See again e.g. *Odyssey* 5.308–312 and Vermeule 1979:12, 184–185, 187.

[107] Vermeule 1979:12, 45, 221n4 (to her bibliography of the σῆμα and cenotaph now add Sourvinou-Inwood 1995 above). The cenotaph is mentioned at *Odyssey* 5.584 (see Heubeck, West, and Hainsworth 1988:228 *ad loc.*).

[108] For the triumph of the cohesion of a *genos*, see Chapter 6.

[109] This has not been remarked by modern-day commentators.

[110] Cf. *Odyssey* 4.728: [sc. ἀνηρείψαντο Τηλέμαχον] ἀκλέα ἐκ μεγάρων, where the adjective ἀκλεής is explained by the adjoining sentence οὐδ' ὁρμηθέντος ἄκουσα (see also Heubeck, West, and Hainsworth 1988:239 *ad loc.*). Cf. also the synonym ἀπευθής, *Odyssey* 3.88.

[111] See also Jones 1991:121 *ad loc.* Puns are more characteristic of the *Odyssey* than the *Iliad*; In *Odyssey* 1.48 and 62 *paronomasia* foreshadows Odysseus' playfully polytropic ethos: Silk 2004:33.

[112] For the evolution of the *asyndeton*, see e.g. Σαρίσχουλη 2000:7–34. The adjective ἄϊστος also occurs in *Odyssey* 1.235 above; see also Jones 1991:242. Instead of *kleos* Odysseus bequeaths grief to his son (*Odyssey* 1.240–243); Penelope makes the same ironical statement about herself at *Odyssey* 19.127–129 (see also below).

[113] For a stylistic analysis of the generic lament, see Alexiou 2002; also n27 above.

[114] Κλέος < *κλύω, 'to hear', cf. Autenrieth, Kaegi, Willi 1920 s.v.v. For the basic, synchronic meaning 'things heard, news, rumor(s)', cf. *Iliad* 2.486, *Odyssey* 3.83, 16.461 ('τί δὴ κλέος ἔστ' ἀνὰ ἄστυ;'), and Olson 1995, esp. 9–16; also *Odyssey* 14.179: πατρὸς ἀκουήν 'news about his father'; but cf.

Homeric Man as a Version of Narrative

Kleos can be predicated also of objects and songs, places and events (e.g. war, a military mission).[115] Thus an object (e.g. Nestor's shield)[116] but especially a deity (e.g. Poseidon at *Iliad* 7.458), a hero, or a heroine (e.g. Penelope; compare κλέα γυναικῶν)[117] possesses his or her own 'objective history' (in the sense of E. Benveniste's *histoire*),[118] to the extent that certain accomplishments or qualities credited to him or her are relayed widely in society as 'things heard' or hearsay.[119] These *énoncés* are preserved, in theory forever, through various

---

Nagy 2003:45, on the limited usefulness of a strictly synchronic reading of *kleos*, and Chapter 2 below. The next two paragraphs have been inspired by Redfield 1994:30–33, a nuanced analysis showing the process of κλύειν and ἀκούειν to be primarily social. See also Segal 1994 and Nagy 2003:45. For a recent bibliography of *kleos*: Sourvinou-Inwood 1995:374 (with n28) and Currie 2005, esp. 71–88.

115 Redfield 1994:32, who however does not cite song per se (cf. *Odyssey* 8.74). De Jong 2001:228 ad *Odyssey* 9.19–20 observes that, while in the *Iliad* *kleos* mainly pertains to military deeds, in the *Odyssey* it is won in many other ways. Hence the relevant range of actions embraces not only excellence in warfare but also the following: 1.) *Adventuresome voyages*: this category as postulated by de Jong is false because her three examples, *Odyssey* 1.19, 3.78, and 13.422, refer to Telemachos' investigative mission, which, as will be seen, is comparable to reconnaissance or espionage missions in the *Iliad,* which also confer *kleos* (see *Iliad* 9.212). 2.) *Conjugal fidelity*: *Odyssey* 6.185 (inter-spousal solidarity), 24.196 (Penelope's faithfulness); see Katz below. 3.) *Dolos*: *Odyssey* 9.19–20 (de Jong's other instance, *Odyssey* 16.241–2, is not relevant; see no. 5 below), possibly *Odyssey* 4.725–726 = 815–816 (neither passage in de Jong). 4.) *Combination of martial skill and intelligence*: *Odyssey* 16.241–242. 5.) *Athletic victory*: *Odyssey* 8.147. This is the first attested instance—*pace* de Jong 2001:203 ad loc.—of the notion that *kleos* won through the quintessentially aristocratic activity of sport is absolutely legitimate: see also Murray 1993:69, 202. 6.) *Song*: see *Odyssey* 8.74, 83. 7.) *Adherence to justice, piety towards the gods, and other moral virtues*: *Odyssey* 19.108ff. (Penelope) [not in de Jong]. On Penelope's particular *kleos*, see Katz 1991, a largely narratological treatment of the queen's ambiguous, problematic, and complex *kleos*. (For a general bibliography of Penelope, see Heath 2005:76n110.) The classification of *kleos* on the basis of beauty is not entirely valid, as will be seen; *contra* de Jong 2001, citing 18.255. 8.) *Seafaring*: 'Φαίακες . . . ναυσίκλυτοι', *Odyssey* 16.227.

116 *Iliad* 8.192–193: 'ἀσπίδα Νεστορέην, τῆς νῦν κλέος οὐρανὸν ἵκει/πᾶσαν χρυσείην ἔμεναι . . .' See also *Iliad* 7.451 (the Achaians' wall, built largely of bricks).

117 Although the term 'the glories of women' is unexampled, the corresponding notion is discernible: see *Iliad* 2.742, κλυτὸς Ἱπποδάμεια and the catalogue of heroines in *Odyssey* 11.234ff. The plural κλέα, as in the phrase κλέα ἀνδρῶν (*Iliad* 9.189), in effect means 'epic poetry' (Heubeck, West, and Hainsworth 1990:88 ad loc.) or "a given tradition of [sc. epic] composition" (Nagy 1990:202).

118 Benveniste 1966, esp. 238ff., 258ff.

119 *Kleos* (= 'news' in its primary sense) is said to be εὐρύ in relation to its starting point and the extent of its diffusion in space-time (*Odyssey* 3.83) and space (*Odyssey* 1.344 = 4.726 = 4.816; cf. 23.333). In *Odyssey* 19.333–334 κλέος εὐρὺ is carried *by word of mouth* on a universal scale 'πάντας ἐπ' ἀνθρώπους' after being crystallized into laudatory fame ('πολλοί τέ μιν ἐσθλὸν ἔειπον', cf. the gnomic aorist, which consolidates the ἐσθλὸς quality of the *laudandus*). Not surprisingly, the sky into (or across) which positive *kleos* is transmitted is said to be εὐρύς: *Odyssey* 8.74ff. (of the *kleos* of Demodokos' song) = 19.108ff. (of the *kleos* of Penelope and the

media, but principally through epic poetry and hero cult.[120] Diachronic, that is, systemic, *kleos*, because it has become detached from (subjective) *discours*, presupposes as a rule a more objective communication process, and it is diffused by third parties in the form of a narrative. Hence in the *Iliad* a hero rarely says ἐμὸν κλέος 'my *kleos*' (and he never refers to it as already accomplished), while in the *Odyssey* only Odysseus speaks of his own *kleos*, when he represents it as a *fait accompli* moments before launching on the subjective speech (or *discours*) of the *Ich-Erzählung* of Books 9–12. But in the court of Alkinoos he occupies the unique, paradoxical position of a supposedly objective *aoidos*.[121]

A worthy hero enjoys certain exceptional qualities or special qualifications (e.g. excellence in fighting or in giving counsel, or both) or moral virtues. More concretely, he may be associated with specific achievements (e.g. the taking of a city, an athletic victory, or, in the case of a married couple, ὁμοφροσύνη 'harmony of mind'). Either way, the hero will attract to himself successive layers of reports or more extensive oral narratives bound up indissolubly with his name.[122] These 'stories' become crystallized over time into virtual objects—permanent organic ingredients, as it were, of the social universe encompassing both the subject of *kleos* and its recipients or audience.[123] From a sociological point of view, as R. Redfield has noted, a hero's *identity or role in epic society* is defined by the narratives concerning him.[124] Ultimately *kleos* is commensurate with the hero's iden-

---

generic good king); cf. *Iliad* 8.112 (of the *kleos* of Nestor's shield), 7.451 (of the wall) and n61 above.

[120] Ἐσαεί: *epos* does not talk directly about (catastrophic) time, far less about eternity; see Bakker 2002b:27–28 and Nagy 2003, esp. 41–43. Because of its inherent self-referentiality this poetic genre represents itself tendentiously as the only vehicle for the perpetuation of *kleos*: e.g. *Iliad* 6.356ff., *Odyssey* 8.580, 24.200ff.; cf. Segal 1994: "The 'message' appears . . . as the creation of its 'medium'" (89), "*kleos* as a self-conscious creation of bardic tradition" (90), et passim; also Nagy 1990, esp. 147–148 and 2003, esp. 41–43. Yet in an oral society non-poetic legends and, particularly from the eighth century BC on, hero cults would have had at least some contributory role in the formulation and diffusion of *kleos*: see e.g. also Griffin 1995 and n100 and n114 above.

[121] Segal 1994:88, citing Reinhardt 1960, notes the anomalous running together of objectivity and subjectivity. On the *Apologoi*, see also the fine analysis in Murnaghan 1989:170–171.

[122] Redfield 1994:32. See also n115 above. Additionally compare e.g. the lengthy narrative, as performed by Agamemnon, of Tydeus' 'personal story' (*Iliad* 4.372–399), which was however related to him by others (*Iliad* 4.374–375: 'οὐ γὰρ ἔγωγε / ἤντησ' οὐδὲ ἴδον· περὶ δ' ἄλλων φασὶ γενέσθαι'). The stories circulating about actions and attributes of a hero—for instance, 'δίου Ὀδυσσῆος ταλασίφρονος, ὅν ποτέ φασι / σὺν σοὶ μαρνάμενον Τρώων πόλιν ἐξαπαλάξαι' (*Odyssey* 3.84–85)—can be condensed in a formulaic adjective such as, in the case of Odysseus, ταλασίφρων (as here) or πτολίπορθος (elsewhere). See also the discussion of Odysseus' 'personal story' and *kleos* below and Chapter 2 on news narratives.

[123] See further Segal 1994:87, following Nagy 1974:241ff., a comparative treatment of Homeric and Sanskrit epic poetry.

[124] Redfield's observation in 1994:34 is seminal and almost revolutionary: "*Kleos* is thus a specific type of *social identity*. A man has a history . . . His story is in a certain sense himself—or one version of himself—and, since his history can survive his personal experience and *survive his enactment of a social role*, his story is . . . the most real version of himself . . . *in Homer a man*

tity in relation not merely to others but also to himself. Hence *kleos* is not, *stricto sensu*, 'glory or fame', as indeed G. Nagy has shown: the latter meaning is only the *consequence* of *kleos*, which by extension may on occasion be rendered even as 'songs that praise gods and men on account of their deeds'.[125]

As a concept *kleos* lends itself to other distinctions than the linguistically inspired juxtaposition of 'objective' *histoire* and 'subjective' *discours*, with the corollary differentiation of *énoncé* from *énonciation*. Thus, according to the degrees in which Homer's characters perceive 'pastness' in relation to particular instances of *kleos*, we may distinguish two broad types, roughly comparable with *oral history* and *oral tradition*, respectively. As Jan Vansina, the historian of Africa has proposed, 'oral history'—which in essence is 'oral testimony'—comprises personal reminiscences, eyewitness accounts, rumors, commentary, and other 'things heard' (compare again *kleos* in its radical denotation) regarding events that took place during the lifetime of an informant (who may have also been an eyewitness of these events). On the other hand, 'oral tradition', in Vansina's formulation, is based on oral narratives and information reaching back to several generations prior to the informant's lifetime.[126] W. Kullmann is right to note that the Homeric epics are not the end-products of (naive) 'oral history' and 'oral tradition' in the ethnographic sense of these terms.[127] As Kullmann argues, Homeric characters demonstrate a much more sophisticated awareness of history and a richer thought world than their counterparts in the African epics, which purport to record events but do so rather ingenuously and within a shallow time frame. The findings of historians and ethnographers such as Vansina and Jack Goody therefore have no heuristic value with regard to Homeric poems. We cannot, Kullmann stresses, extract historical events from the Greek epics inasmuch as they are

---

may be conceived as narrative, may conceive himself as a narrative" (my emphases). See *inter alios* Jones 1988, esp. 499–500 and Wöhrle 1999:130. But cf. Olson 1995:88n54: "κλέος in the *Odyssey* always reflects what others think and say of one, not what one thinks of oneself." *Contra* Olson, it may be urged that in a face-to-face culture such as we find in epic a) 'what others think and say of one' inevitably determines the hero's self-opinion (see *Odyssey* 9.19–20); and b) 'what others think and say of one' constitutes by definition the hero's social identity. Hence *kleos* is connected directly to social identity in the twin social-anthropological sense of 'identity in relation to others and to oneself'. See *Encyclopedia of Social and Cultural Anthropology*, s.v. 'identity' (Barnard and Spencer 1996:292). For the comparative notions of the person and personhood, see Carrithers, Cohen, and Lukes 1985.

[125] Cf. *Odyssey* 1.338: ἔργ' ἀνδρῶν τε θεῶν τε, τά τε κλείουσιν ἀοιδοί, Hesiod *Theogony*, esp. 100–101 (discussed below), and Nagy 1974:246–250 ("κλέος was the singer 's own word for what he sings in praise of gods and men" [250]). But see also *Iliad* 9.524 and discussion below.

[126] Vansina 1985, esp. 12–13. Marwick 2001:136 prefers the term 'oral testimony' as opposed to 'oral history', which he considers an exaggeration. For the difference between oral history and oral tradition, see Thomas 1989:10–12 (following Vansina) and now Thomas 1992:108–113 (with further bibliography of oral tradition, 108n25).

[127] Kullmann 1992, esp. 159, 162, 168–169.

not the result of genuine 'oral history'. Yet, I would like to suggest, because of this very sophistication, a poet living as he did during the transition from orality to literacy, as Kullmann emphasizes, designedly represented societies that in earlier stages interpreted history, both collective and individual, on the basis of purely oral testimony and traditions. Thus the epics may *show how, in synchronic terms, people perceived 'history'*. It is impressive at least that a) epic poets as a rule limit themselves to a maximum of three generations, the upper limit recognized by social historians such as Keith Thomas,[128] and b) the *Odyssey* gives special prominence to the fundamental importance of oral testimony and narrative, as will be shown in the next chapter.

The Personal Narrative

> *"Reminiscences are perhaps the most typical product of human memory . . .*
> *Reminiscences are bits of life history . . . Reminiscences are part of an organized*
> *whole of memories that tend to project a consistent image of the narrator*
> *and, in many instances, a justification of his or her life."*[129]

The *kleos* that Odysseus solipsistically announces in the same breath as his name in Book 9 alludes retrospectively to experiences from his life. That is, it emerges from his 'personal story', in which he has proved harmful to the collectivity of his ἑταῖροι 'comrades':

'εἴμ' Ὀδυσεὺς Λαερτιάδης, ὃς πᾶσι δόλοισιν
ἀνθρώποισι μέλω, καί μευ κλέος οὐρανὸν ἵκει.'

"I am Odysseus, son of Laertes, who am on the minds of all men for my
tricks; my reputation reaches to the sky."[130]

In epos, incidentally, 'history' per se may be conceived as little more than a series of separate 'personal narratives', the equivalent of oral 'life stories' or 'autobiographies' delivered by heroes in the course of the action. Sometimes heroes will resort to reminiscences derived from 'family traditions' or straightforwardly cumulative accounts such as genealogies—both being classes of interpretative testimony with African analogues (see Vansina 1985:17–24.) In the instance of a

---

[128] See Thomas 1983 and Chapter 6 below.

[129] Vansina 1985:8.

[130] Dawe's trans. (1993:354). According to Haubold 2000:128 this hero's fame "feeds on collective disaster," the utter destruction he inflicts on the *laos* (i.e. his comrades and later the suitors). This *kleos* is depicted as spreading *vertically* ("reaches the sky") on account of its unprecedented magnitude; the same can be said of negative *kleos*, e.g. of the suitors (*Odyssey* 15.329: 'τῶν ὕβρις τε βίη τε σιδήρεον οὐρανὸν ἵκει'). See also n119 and n133.

genealogical reminiscence that traces back spectacularly to a god, as Aineias'
at *Iliad* 20, the hero may be rehearsing a chapter in 'cosmic history', which, as
B. Graziosi and J. Haubold argue (2005), is the general subject of the Homeric
and Hesiodic epics. In the *Odyssey*, where the actions of gods and mortals are
emphatically, indeed programmatically, separated (see Graziosi and Haubold
2005, especially 76–77, 80–81, 143, 146), 'history' is by and large based on
stories in which gods only rarely play a visible role. This more 'secular' focus,
for all the primitive, strange supernatural or semi-mortal beings (e.g. the
goddess Kalypso, Poseidon, half-divine Kyklops), is, in my view, an advance
on cosmic history. Returning to the 'personal (experience) story', modern
folklorists and ethnographers recognize the genre,[131] and it is with the help
of such evidence, much of it drawn from fieldwork in the United States, that
we might approach the *Apologoi* and the *Telemacheia*. As defined by S. Stahl,
the 'personal story' is "a prose narrative relating a personal experience; it is
usually told in the first person" and its content is "seemingly idiosyncratic"
(hence 'nontraditional') while at the same time expressing "folklore attitudes,
values, prejudices, and tastes" (Stahl 1989:12–13, 19). In the setting of an interview or discussion, the teller relates his or her 'actual' experiences, much as
Odysseus publicly records his adventures, albeit in verse, in the *Apologoi*. The
three cardinal features of this 'literary folk genre' may recall the *Apologoi* still
further. These are, in Stahl's words (1989:15): "(1) dramatic narrative structure, (2) a consistently implied assertion that the narrative is true, and (3) the
selfsame identity of the teller and the story's main character (the *Ich-Bericht*
form)." But Odysseus' proud promulgation of his *kleos* in Book 9 clearly
touches something more than anecdotal, multi-episode 'personal narration'.
It adumbrates also the domain of impersonal 'history' he has just entered. The
conflation of a 'personal experience story' with collective 'history' in Homer,
particularly in the *Apologoi* and the *Telemachy*, makes sense sociologically: for
the narration of personal experiences (by which, as will be noted shortly, the
reminiscing narrator aims to convey and to fix his well-defined identity) is
shaped in a social environment which subsumes and at the same time tran-
scends exponentially the aggregate of individual memories. As the sociolo-
gist M. Halbwachs argues, autobiographical memory—the stuff of a 'personal
story'—intersects collective memory and is decisively influenced by it.[132]

[131] Stahl 1989, esp. 12–21. Cross-cultural examples of this genre include the 'yarns' told by Nova Scotian fishermen (14).
[132] See again *Odyssey* 9.19–20: 'πᾶσι ... / ἀνθρώποισι μέλω,' an allusion to the collective memory of the self-memorializing πολύμητις Odysseus. For the interdependence of collective and individual memory: Halbwachs 1980, esp. 44–47, 50–51. Halbwachs's analysis is noteworthy, particularly his insightful observation that collective memory, *impersonal* as it is, is the accu-mulation of the *personal* recollections of individuals yet different from particular memories. See also Chapter 2 n14.

Compared to the characters of the Old and New Testaments, Homer's heroes have their eyes trained narcissistically on the *hic et nunc* of their society and ultimately—at least in theory—on the indefinite future, again in society, after their death.[133] The sole meaning and aim of 'history' lie in the acquisition of *kleos* in life, its transferral at death to one's *epigoni*, and its preservation thereafter, mainly through song. Consider *Iliad* 6.146–149, the renowned comparison of the generation of mortals with ephemeral, falling leaves: *sub specie aeternitatis* one generation succeeds another, only to hand on to the next the account about its descent, and so forth. (Compare in this connection Glaukos' *historiola* about his ancestors, *Iliad* 6.150–206, already noted, which features the feats of his grandfather Bellerophon.) The layers upon layers of generations following one another—gathering like an ever mounting heap of mulching leaves—all contribute to these cumulative accounts, which perpetuate the *kleos* of ancestors and in turn corroborate the *kleos* of their proud descendants. *Iliad* 20.203–204 ("For we know each other's ancestry, and we know [each other's] parents, / hearing as we do the accounts heard of old of mortal men"), from Aineias' *historiola* in support of his pedigree, shows with particular lucidity that the *kleos* affiliated with genealogy may be transmitted in the long term by means of non-poetic narrative (see φασὶ 'they say', *Iliad* 20.206). As Glaukos does earlier, Aineias recounts *in extenso*, indeed performs, the tale of his famous forebears. It is legitimate to ask whether his tale necessarily emerges from song (see e.g. Helen's words to Hector, *Iliad* 6.357–358: "so that even in the future / we might be subjects of song for future human beings.")[134] or from 'prose accounts', including hearsay and generally oral media other than song. It seems in any event certain that Aineias' narrative is based on 'πρόκλυτ' . . . ἔπεα θνῆτων ἀνθρώπων' ("the *proklut(a)* accounts of mortal men," *Iliad* 20.204), where the adjective *proklut(a)* means 'that have been heard from the distant past', and therefore alludes to an 'oral tradition' in Vansina's sense.

At the same time, Odysseus' first-person 'life story' (see *Odyssey* 9.19–20 above)—or 'personal story'—forms a part of broader 'oral history' and is recorded synchronically in the epic poem itself, as will be seen, in sung and 'prose' narratives. Using the selfsame formulation, the poet described earlier (*Odyssey* 8.73ff.) the *kleos* attaching to Demodokos' song about the colossal *neikos* between Odysseus and Achilles, a confrontation that may well have juxtaposed the former's characteristic *dolos* 'trickery' to the latter's *biê* 'physical force'.[135]

---

[133] As Penelope suggests at *Odyssey* 19.328–334, *kleos* might also be understood as recompense in the here-and-now for morally correct behavior: given that, as Penelope says, 'ἄνθρωποι δὲ μινυνθάδιοι τελέθουσιν' (328), this reward—essentially a collective *makarismos*—has an immediate and purely sociological, and not a metaphysical, character.

[134] See also Martin 1989:16, following Nagy.

[135] The poet paraphrases (in *oratio obliqua*) the content of this ἀοιδή: see de Jong 2001:195 and Nagy 2003:13–15 *ad loc.* This conflict a) suggests the innate instability and impermanence of power in

The *kleos* of the song—or more precisely, of the cycle of songs (see οἴμης, *Odyssey* 8.74) from which this particular song originates[136]—radiates, metaphorically, outward to the broad sky: οἴμης τῆς τότ' ἄρα κλέος οὐρανὸν εὐρὺν ἵκανε ('from the point in the tale [or cycle of tales] of which the fame/*kleos* at that time [already] reached the broad sky'). But in what sense can a song about an event in a hero's career (actually two heroes' careers) have *kleos* that rises to the sky? Dawe suspects that Homer has conflated almost out of oversight the song (the medium) with the event (message): the exceptional nature of the *neikos* has 'rubbed off' on the song commemorating it.[137] This *catechresis* is, I think, revealing. If we accept Redfield's view (see above, especially n124) that a multi-episode narrative about a hero (living or dead) contributes to, in effect defines, his *kleos*,[138] then the two instances of sky-high *kleos* just cited are homologous. First, the event will possess *kleos* by dint of synecdoche; a hero's overall life story, of which the event is a chapter, is conceptualized as *kleos*. Second, because the song about the conflict is in itself an oral narrative, the poet can readily associate it with *kleos*, ultimately an oral phenomenon. Together, the particular medium (song) and message (the event) have a relatively fixed and quasi-objective character. In the poem's social universe both have the status of (immaterial) cultural goods, as noted,[139] entitling Odysseus to represent his *kleos* as something already 'there' and complete. True enough, at least two ἔργα 'deeds' performed by the hero,[140] namely, the great *neikos* 'quarrel' (some twenty years earlier) and the episode of the Wooden Horse (ten years ago; see *Odyssey* 8.499–520), are—in synchronic terms—well-known themes in Demodokos' fixed repertory. And Helen previously recounts (*Odyssey* 4.240–260) a selected episode, the sack of Troy; she pre-announces

---

Homeric society (see below), and b) shows the poet to be indirectly comparing the respective advantages of δόλος and βίη as means for handling crises; the poet decides in favor of δόλος: Osborne 2004:213, cf. Clarke 2004:82. Cunning is one of the main themes of the *Odyssey*: de Jong 2001:196 *ad loc.*

[136] De Jong 2001:197 *ad Odyssey* 8.73–5 on οἴμη; cf. Nagy 2003:13n70 (οἴμη = 'story-thread').

[137] Dawe 1993:308 *ad Odyssey* 8.74: "One can see a kind of blurring in the poet's own mind between ballad and event." Yet the confusion that Dawe condemns may have arisen from associational transference (on which see n60 above), which supports my arguments below on the 'objectification' of *kleos*.

[138] Herewith a comparison—which, I hope, is not far-fetched—based on conventional Byzantine iconography: a thirteenth-century icon of St. George from Mt. Sinai features in the center the saint in military uniform surrounded by twenty scenes, practically vignettes, illustrating his life, e.g. the slaying of the dragon and his martyrdom. Each scene is a figurative narrative and as an aggregate these make up his 'personal story', or, better, they reflect his 'oral biography', serving thus to establish his saintliness. In similar fashion the various episodes of Odysseus' life underpin and define his 'notoriety' or *kleos*.

[139] See n123.

[140] Cf. *Odyssey* 1.338: 'ἔργ' ἀνδρῶν τε θεῶν τε, τά τε κλείουσιν ἀοιδοί' and see Chapter 3 on the conjunction of deeds and words in heroic conduct.

it, significantly, as one of the innumerable ἄεθλοι 'feats' (*Odyssey* 4.241) that in the aggregate would have constituted the 'personal tradition' about Odysseus.[141]

According to Vansina (1985:18–19), a 'personal tradition' will often revolve around the adventures of a leader or someone otherwise prominent in his community. If sufficiently memorable, such a tradition ordinarily will survive only one or two generations after his death. So far, Odysseus' story conforms to this scheme. Transmitted in song and 'prose' alike, his 'personal tradition' already belongs, synchronically, to collective 'oral history'.[142] Odysseus is thereby bound to society in much the same manner as an extraordinary material object such as Nestor's shield (noted earlier):

'ἀσπίδα Νεστορέην, τῆς νῦν κλέος οὐρανὸν ἵκει
πᾶσαν χρυσείην ἔμεναι . . .'

Iliad 8.192–193

"Nestor's shield, the reputation (*kleos*) of which now reaches the sky
that it is all of gold . . ."

The *kleos* of this material object is widespread not only on account of its uncommon qualities (which are analogous to Odysseus' δόλοι 'tricks') but also because of the 'oral history' regarding its use by Nestor in battle:[143] in like fashion the 'personal tradition' about Odysseus, having found its way into collective

---

[141] Helen narrates the episode involving Odysseus' reconnaissance mission prior to the sack of Troy, an episode treated in the *Little Iliad*: see e.g. de Jong 2001, esp. 102–103 *ad Odyssey* 4.234–289, 240–243; Heubeck, West, and Hainsworth 1988:208–209 *ad Odyssey* 4.242ff.; and Dowden 2004:199 (on the *Little Iliad*). The choice of this particular scene is not, *pace* de Jong 2001:102–103, simply a rhetorical *recusatio*, but an indication that Helen is also acting consciously as an *aoidos* who, well aware of the immense superstructure of oral narratives—in theory, innumerable as Helen also admits—singles out a particular episode, substituting the 'part' for the 'whole' (*Odyssey* 4.240–242: 'πάντα μὲν οὐκ ἂν ἐγὼ μυθήσομαι οὐδ' ὀνομήνω, / ὅσσοι 'Οδυσσῆος ταλασίφρονός εἰσιν ἄεθλοι· / ἀλλ' οἷον τόδ' ἔρεξε. . .'); cf. *Odyssey* 1.10, 8.500. For a singer's metonymic selections, see Fowler's acute observations (2004): "the larger superstructure . . . is always immanent but almost never performed as a sequenced whole . . . Were we to conduct a thorough survey of the world's epic traditions, we would find that this 'immanent' approach to epic performance—letting the part stand for the implied whole—is in fact a very common strategy that reflects the traditional, non-textual nature of composition and reception" (176–177).

[142] See de Jong 2001:195–196 *ad Odyssey* 8.73–82: hearing the song about the νεῖκος (and also the song about the Wooden Horse), Odysseus confronts his own *kleos* after his seven years of total isolation on Kalypso's isle.

[143] In an actual (extra-poetic) society this shield might give rise to the elaboration of aetiological legends—that is, to an *iconatrophy*—about it. According to Vansina 1985:7–8 and esp. 10–11, iconatrophy is one of the interpretative oral genres that feed into the historical consciousness of a people: iconatrophy comprises imaginary explanations *ex post facto* regarding objects, monuments, landscapes, etc. that have extraordinary qualities. Cf. the aetiological 'legend' about Niobe (*Iliad* 24.599–620).

memory, is broadcast to every corner of Hellas and the whole world.[144] Indeed, the two passages just examined, *Odyssey* 9.19–20 and *Iliad* 8.192–193,[145] offer a homology that makes good sense according to Redfield's and Vansina's criteria.

As a subject of *kleos*, Odysseus emerges in his eponymous poem an established, almost objectified figure. In the excursive 'personal experience story' of his *Apologoi* he seeks not only to triumphantly celebrate his identity but also to delineate for his audience its stability. Stahl (1989:21), confirming Vansina (see the epitaph to this section), shows that identity is bound up with the 'personal narrative', the "overall function" of which is "to allow for the discovery of the teller's identity (especially in terms of values and character traits) and to *maintain the stability of that identity for both the teller and listener*" [my emphasis]. Odysseus' *kleos*, hence also his identity, is celebrated self-reflexively in *Odyssey* 9.19–20, but it is also corroborated as a self-existent, as it were, entity in Demodokos' songs and the accounts of others.[146] By contrast, Telemachos' *kleos*, needless to say, is still in a state of becoming. The young ἄναξ 'lord' has not yet produced a 'personal story' (Stahl) or 'personal account' (Vansina) that, duly highlighting conventional competence in ἔργα 'deeds' and ἔπεα 'words' alike, could go down in collective 'oral history' (see Chapter 3).

---

[144] See esp. n132 above.

[145] An 'equivalence' of this kind would be inconceivable in Homer as well as the logocentric Pindar and Simonides. In Homer, what in the ultimate analysis survives—indeed in perpetuity—is neither Agamemnon's and the Achaians' wall (*Iliad* 7.451ff.) nor the walls of Troy (which Poseidon and Apollo built, *Iliad* 7.452–3) nor the rival *kleos* of each of these military constructions. These material objects and their concomitant *kleos* are destined to be overshadowed by the *kleos* of Achaian heroes in their 'incarnation' as ἡμίθεοι, a *kleos* that hero cult and epic poetry will perpetuate. See Hainsworth 1993:230 *ad Iliad* 12.23: ἡμίθεοι and Nagy 1999:160–161. Both Pindar and Simonides scoff at the notion that a material memorial such as a statue (Pindar *Nemean* 1.1–5) or an inscription (Simonides fr. 581 PMG) will gain for someone eternal *kleos*: in their view, as Thomas 1992:114–115 notes, poetry is an eminently flexible medium that, depending on its quality, circulates more widely and potentially forever.

[146] Demodokos and the Phaiakians already know of Odysseus' fame (and at least certain of the concomitant narrative details), though they do not yet know that their shipwrecked guest is the hero himself. This hero's reputation for μῆτις must be widespread throughout Phaiakia since, as Halbwachs 1980, esp. 24ff. argues, collective memory and hence 'oral history' presuppose belonging to a social group (while oblivion is born from the state of not belonging). Thus only the Kyklopes appear to lack collective memory: Polyphemos is therefore not moved by Odysseus' mention of Agamemnon at *Odyssey* 9.263–266. See also Chapter 2 n14.

2

Kleos and Oral News

'ἐγὼ μὲν ἐξ ἐμοῦ τε κοὐκ ἄλλης σαφῆ
σημεῖ' ἰδοῦσα τῷδε πιστεύω λόγῳ.'

Sophokles *Elektra* 885–886

B OTH ORAL HISTORY and oral tradition spring from orally transmitted
messages,[1] or, to use a Homeric term, ἔπεα (literally, 'words').[2] As J.
Vansina's now famous analysis shows, both categories of oral message embrace
"reminiscences, hearsay or eyewitness accounts about events and situations."
Reminiscences, in turn, belong to a broad "class of original messages" referring to "the interpretation of experience," whether it be an "existing situation" or other "existing messages."[3] Vansina also describes another broad class
of communications, usually simpler, that concern the present: 'news' or, in
Homeric Greek, *kleos*, in its primary, synchronic meaning. Thus, for example,
Telemachos' divinely ordained mission, as we know, consists in the gathering of
news regarding his father's homecoming—or not (*Odyssey* 1.93–94). The young
man himself, when he announces the purpose of his mission to Menelaos ("I
come in quest of news (*kleos*) of my father that has spread from afar . . . ," *Odyssey*
3.83), refers expressly to news according to Vansina's definition of "information about something that happened not long ago and is not known to one's
audience."[4] News derives, moreover, from "eyewitnesses, hearsay or internal
experience such as visions, dreams or hallucinations."[5] One of the main components of news, and at later stages of collective historical consciousness, is

---

[1] Vansina 1985:3.
[2] Ἔπος in the sense of 'message': Martin 1989:12.
[3] Vansina 1985:3, 7–8, 9, 12. For differing interpretations of interrelated experiences and events,
cf. Helen's account of the Wooden Horse (*Odyssey* 4.242–264) and Menelaos' corrective version
(*Odyssey* 4.271–289).
[4] Vansina 1985:3. See also below.
[5] Vansina 1985:4–7.

hearsay or rumor, which "deals with . . . sensational news,"[6] a sub-category of oral messages that besets Telemachos as well as Penelope.

According to Chantraine, s.v. φημί ('I speak, say'),[7] the name *Phêmios* is derived from the noun *phêmis*. From a historical-linguistic perspective, *Phêmios* is therefore 'he who has some relation to the action of the verb φημί'. He is, by extension, 'he who is connected to φῆμις' or 'the *phêmis-man*' in E. Bakker's formulation.[8] But what is *phêmis*? Bakker proposes that the term denotes 'unwanted publicity', 'rumor', 'speech of the *dêmos*', in effect 'talk of the town', a patently pejorative connotation when this noun refers to someone; [9] 'talk', which amounts to 'gossip', is usually expressed in the *agorê* 'assembly place'.[10] Even so, it is obvious that *phêmis*, just as the Homeric *phêmê*, which Bakker also examines,[11] is only potentially but not necessarily pejorative.[12] Because ancient Greek societies were almost always, it seems, highly competitive, the public reports about someone were likelier to be uncomplimentary than the contrary. On the other side, the view that "the noun *phêmis* consistently carries the negative sense of . . . undesired publicity" should be reconsidered, as I will argue.[13]

When it is the sum total of the hearsay and rumor circulating among the *dêmos*, *phêmis* exerts considerable, indeed even irresistible social pressure on an individual.[14] Thus, for instance, "harsh *phêmis of the dêmos* pressed upon" the pseudo-Cretan Odysseus (*Odyssey* 14.239), supposedly putting moral pressure on him to fight in the Trojan War.[15] Penelope admits to her disguised husband

---

6   Vansina 1985: "Hearsay is the fountainhead of most tradition or written documents" (6). Hearsay is deified as Ὄσσα . . . ἄγγελος, see esp. *Odyssey* 24.413. Cf. also *Odyssey* 1.282–283: 'ὄσσαν . . . / ἐκ Διός, ἥ τε μάλιστα φέρει κλέος ('news') ἀνθρώποισι,' and Heubeck, West, and Hainsworth 1988:111 *ad loc.*: ὄσσα is hearsay of indeterminate origin.

7   Chantraine 1968–1980:1195, s.v. φημί.

8   Bakker 2002b:142 and passim, who assigns an active sense to the name Φήμιος. Cf. also Heubeck, West, and Hainsworth 1988:117 *ad Odyssey* 1.154 ("the man who speaks report, the rich in tales") and Dawe in n41 below.

9   Bakker, for instance, describes the adjective χαλεπή, one of the Homeric adjectives used of φῆμις, as 'typifying': 2002b:140.

10   Bakker 2002b, esp. 40, also Dawe 1993:142. Nausikaa's comments (*Odyssey* 6.266–269) suggest that the ἀγορή may also be contiguous to or within an 'industrial' zone; this accounts for verse 275 (see below). Similarly, in the classical period the Athenian ἀγορά, with its adjoining small factories, ἐργαστήρια, and especially the barber- and various other shops, was the locus *par excellence* for social commentary and gossip: Lewis 1996:15–18.

11   Bakker 2002b:137–139 ("an utterance with prophetic properties of which the speaker is unaware," 139).

12   By analogy Homeric *phêmê* may be an oral wish (e.g. *Odyssey* 2.33–34) or an oral curse (e.g. *Odyssey* 20.112–119), something that seems to have gone unnoticed by scholars.

13   Cf. Bakker 2002b:140.

14   To be precise, the sum of the individual rumors is a collective entity. Compare Halbwachs 1980:51 for the difference between individual and collective memory.

15   Heubeck and Hoekstra 1990:210 *ad loc.*

that in a sense it is the *phêmis* of the *dêmos* that prevents her from remarrying (*Odyssey* 19.524–527).[16] Here and at *Odyssey* 6.276–285 *phêmis* means in essence 'what others *would say*', which arises out of the basic sense of 'what others say' and by extension 'what everyone is thinking', hence 'public opinion'.[17]

In what sense—active or passive—is Phemios a '*phêmis-man*'?[18] Perhaps the strongest argument in favor of the active sense (= 'he who utters/spreads the rumors and news of the community') is to be found in *Odyssey* 24.192–202, Agamemnon's 'polar' statement that singers (*aoidoi*) do two opposite but related things: on the one hand, they perpetuate with their *khariessa aoidê* 'delightful song' the *kleos* of a man or woman; on the other hand, with their *stugerê aoidê* 'song full of hate' they spread *khalepên phêmin* 'harsh talk' about him/her (this *phêmis* may either be finite but have a long duration or be understood as eternal on the analogy of *kleos*).[19]

Another *phêmis*-man in the *Odyssey* is the messenger (*kêrux*) Medon. The general details concerning this complex profession are somewhat confusing. Medon does not seem to be an exception in this regard. The former *therapôn* 'attendant' to Telemachos while Telemachos was a child (*Odyssey* 22.357–358), he appears in the plot as a manservant—a kind of *aide-de-camp*—of the suitors.[20] At the same time he is by definition a *dêmioergos* 'public worker' (see *Odyssey* 19.134–135),[21] that is, he belongs to the class or category of workers who travel to various localities in order to practice their profession.[22] If he is at all like the other *kêrukes* whom Penelope rejects at *Odyssey* 19.134–135, Medon is also a

---

[16] *Odyssey* 19.527 = 16.75.

[17] In *Odyssey* 6.276–285 the princess quotes the content of the specific φῆμις. See also Russo, Fernández-Galiano, and Heubeck 1992:101 *ad Odyssey* 19.527: φῆμις here = 'the pressure of community opinion'.

[18] This question concerns philologists, not historical linguists who treat the name Φήμιος as diathetically neutral.

[19] For instance, the φῆμις that worries Nausikaa (*Odyssey* 6.273–274, where ὀπίσσω = 'behind my back' according to Stanford [*contra* Garvie 1994:149 *ad loc.*]) is limited in space and time to the contemporaneous microcosm of her island. Contrariwise, the χαλεπή that Agamemnon foresees *sub specie aeternitatis* from Hades (*Odyssey* 24.200–203) is correlative to κλέος, which characteristically, in this hero's words, 'οὔ ποτ' ὀλεῖται' (*Odyssey* 24.196). Ostensibly the diffusion in space (microsocial or Panhellenic?) and duration (limited or perpetual?) of rumor or news is in direct proportion to the magnitude of its impact. Synonymous φάτις, when it is small-scale, 'ἀνθρώπους ἀναβαίνει' (*Odyssey* 6.29): here oral transmission is imagined as horizontal movement; εὐρύ κλέος—the most elevated grade of κλέος—likewise rises upwards and sideways, but it reaches (ἵκει/ἱκάνει) the sky; see Chapter 1.

[20] For Medon: de Jong 2001:117 *ad Odyssey* 4.675–715.

[21] Compare Penelope's generalization here: "Therefore I pay no heed to strangers (ξεῖνοι) or suppliants (ἱκέται) / or at all to *kêrukes*, whose trade is a public one (δημιοεργοί)."

[22] Other public workers (δημιοεργοί) are the seer (μάντις), the healer (ἰητήρ), the builder (τέκτων) and the singer (ἀοιδός): *Odyssey* 17.383–385. For the δημιοεργοί, see Murray 1993:55, 82. Cf. the modern Greek ντελάλης 'town crier, messenger' in Γκίκας 1983:22 (the town criers' preference for village or town squares and crossroads), 24 (they often also work as church cantors).

'courier', as it were, who conveys from one city to another *angelias*, i.e. 'news' in the form of narratives.[23] Eumaios (compare especially *Odyssey* 14.122–132, 166, 372–379) corroborates the obvious point that an *angeliê* is in principle 'news' and that news is to be understood as a narrative (*epos, muthos*).[24] A *kêrux* such as Medon is thus recognized to be a narrator of hearsay and news with all that this implies (see below). Finally, a *kêrux* also has a special professional link to the *agorê* 'assembly place' inasmuch as he might summon the people to the assembly (see *Iliad* 2.51 = *Odyssey* 2.7), he might moderate the discussion in the assembly (*Iliad* 2.97, *Odyssey* 2.38, etc.), or he might preside over certain public ceremonies in the *agorê*.[25] For Medon's affinity with the *agorê*, see below.

In the *Odyssey*, as we will note, Medon retains certain traditional elements of a messenger's involvement with a network of oral news. First, after overhearing at *Odyssey* 4.677ff. the suitors' discussion, he informs Penelope about their conspiracy to kill her son. Second, and more significant, at *Odyssey* 22.373–374 Odysseus, having just decimated the suitors, immediately resorts to Medon as a 'news broadcaster' and in effect instructs him "so that you may know in your heart and then *tell also to another*, / how far better is the doing of good than the doing of evil."[26] The messenger duly appears, at *Odyssey* 24.443–449, in the assembly and gives an eyewitness account of the mass murder. Scholars have noticed that his version of events differs from that of the poet (*Odyssey* 22.297ff.). The divergences between the two versions are small, however,[27] and, according to A. Heubeck,[28] should be put down to the desire of the *kêrux* to play up the role of divine intervention. This divergent account, it should be noted, may betray an 'oral reporter' at work, typically coloring his *angeliê* 'report' with sensationalizing detail and, from an outsider's point of view, distorting it. This distortion suggests that this character is consciously

---

[23] Because at *Iliad* 1.334, 8.274, 384 *kêrukes* carry out their missions by shuttling between military camps, I think it reasonable to suppose that the *kêrukes* mentioned by Penelope move between cities.

[24] See Lewis 1996: "There is no Greek word for news as such, or a newsworthy event; instead, words focus on *process* (my italics) . . . the primary word is *aggellô*, I report, and its cognates . . . clearly the act of reporting is what creates news" (4).

[25] See LfgrE ii.1410–1412, s.v. κῆρυξ. For similar functions of the κῆρυξ, chiefly in the Classical period, see Lewis 1996:51–56, 63–68.

[26] Verse 374 recalls a proverb. Russo, Fernández-Galiano, and Heubeck 1992:284 *ad loc.* calls it a "rather banal apophthegm."

[27] *Sic* Russo, Fernández-Galiano, and Heubeck 1992:408 *ad Odyssey* 24.443–449. Dawe 1993:863 *ad loc.* notes many divergences.

[28] Russo, Fernández-Galiano, and Heubeck 1992:408.

giving a performance meant in large measure to be a diversion (or *terpsis*, to use the Homeric term).[29]

In the passage just cited Medon attends the assembly together with Phemios, who is now, however, a silent character. Generally speaking, as de Jong remarks (but without explanation),[30] Medon "is often mentioned in one breath with Phemius." What these particular characters have in common is, obviously, the fact that they are both attached to the suitors' court and serve them *hyp' anangêi* 'under duress'. But what other (more general) common traits may account for their joint association? First and foremost, messengers and singers are the only mortals in Homer who are endowed with a divine *audê* 'articulate voice',[31] as J. Heath also notes.[32] This extraordinary gift and privilege reflects, in my view, the origins of the *kêrux* as a singer: compare the Vedic *Kāru* 'singer of praises'.[33] Furthermore, as Linear B tablets from Pylos show, *ka-ru-ke* was a religious official.[34] It is likely therefore that he was principally an *aoidos humnôn* 'singer of hymns' much like his mythic prototype, the Panhellenic *Hermahas*.[35] At least it is highly suggestive that Hermes (the avatar of the *Urherold Hermahas*) features as a *kêrux* 'messenger' and an *aoidos* 'singer' alike in the late sixth century BC in the *Homeric Hymn to Hermes*.[36]

Second, just like an *aoidos* a generic *kêrux* is a *dêmioergos* 'public worker',[37] whose mobility inevitably brings him into contact with news in the form of oral narratives.[38] Eumaios' comments (in Book 14) are helpful here. In referring collectively to wandering visitors (compare *Odyssey* 14.122, 124), he highlights

---

29 For such τέρψις: *Odyssey* 1.346–347; cf. θελκτήρια, 1.337 and Τερπιάδης, Phemios' patronymic, 22.330. Cf. *Odyssey* 15.399–400, 486–487. See also Lewis 1996: "The hearer [of news] gains knowledge of public affairs, . . . *diversion* . . . The teller gains prestige . . ., the chance to capture attention, and the opportunity to tell the news *in the way that best suits his or her own purposes*' (2, my emphases).

30 De Jong 2001:117 *ad Odyssey* 4.675–715. Cf. n42 below.

31 Cf. Γκίκας 1983:57.

32 Heath 2005:55.

33 LfgrE ii.1409, s.v. κῆρυξ.

34 LfgrE ii.1410 B. Cf. Γκίκας 1983 (n22 above).

35 LfgrE ii.1410 B. Maslov 2009:1–38 derives the simplex ἀοιδός 'solo performer of hexameter poetry' from the hypothetical compound *θεσπιαοιδός, 'singer of things divine'. Despite this reconstruction, Maslov questions the alignment of poetry and prophecy in Archaic Greece; for a bibliography of this connection, see Maslov 2009:24n52.

36 Verses 54–59 (ἄειδειν/ἐξ αὐτοσχεδίης, etc.), 331. Generally the syncretism of the singer's attributes with those of the 'messenger' reaches back to the Mycenaean period, as noted; at present it is not possible, on the basis of the surviving tablets, to determine whether Mycenaean *Hermahas* already combined both functions. It is nonetheless clear that in the Homeric epics Hermes is a πομπός and ἄγγελος, who holds a (magic) wand, or ῥάβδος (*Odyssey* 5.43–54, 24.153, etc.; see in general LIMC V.i.286–288 but in conjunction with LfgrE *loc. cit.*); cf. the scepter of singers in Hesiod *Theogony* 30 and, in the epics, the scepter of kings, priests, and *kêrukes* (West 1966:163 *ad Theogony* 30).

37 See n22.

38 See n23.

and at the same time stigmatizes the typical professional conduct of a *dêmio-ergos kêrux* (*Odyssey* 14.122–132, 372–381): in return for a material reward he improvises, as noted, a news narrative on the spot. Penelope alludes to just this sort of improvising *logopoios* 'fashioner or fabricator of narratives' when she states, as we have seen, her deep distrust of the news delivered to her by *kêrukes* and other *xeinoi* 'strangers' (*Odyssey* 19.134–135).[39] So a *kêrux*, precisely like an *aoidos*, earns his keep thanks to his godlike voice and by his solo 'oral performances'. The performances are judged by his audience according to the criteria that apply to a (narrative) song of an *aoidos* (compare, for example, *Odyssey* 17.518–521 and de Jong 2001:433 *ad loc.*). The same aesthetic criteria are invoked in both cases because *kêrukes* and *aoidoi* are narrators and hence *logopoioi* 'makers of narratives'; both *katalegousi muthous* 'recount stories [from beginning to end]'.[40]

If the messenger is among other things a narrator of news, what might we say about his relative, the singer? As suggested, the very name of the representative singer *Phêmios* means literally 'he who utters (*phêsi*) talk of the town (*phêmis*)'; this fact, supported considerably by *Odyssey* 24.192–202 (see above), is a strong indication that he too is generally a narrator of news, rumors, and general hearsay.[41] *Odyssey* 22.376 is revealing on this score: having smiled (*epimeidêsas*), Odysseus has, as noted, ordered Medon to announce outside of the palace the triumph of good over evil (*Odyssey* 22.371–374), whereupon he commands him, "sit down outside / in the court, away from the slaughter, you and the *poluphêmos* singer" (*Odyssey* 22.375–376). Frightened, they—*in the dual number* (*Odyssey* 22.378)—head for the altar of *Herkeios* Zeus (see *Odyssey* 22.334–335).[42]

Odysseus' words are a pun. The context (compare especially *epimeidêsas*, *Odyssey* 22.371) implies that he is being ironical. According to Bakker, the adjective *poluphêmos* at verse 376 carries the pejorative sense 'market poet' since the hero is scoffing at the special relationship with (negative) *phêmis* that this singer presumably develops during the suitors' 'tyranny'. It is perhaps implied, Bakker and others argue, that this singer spreads rumors that are pessimistic and/or slanderously unheroic and hence 'untraditional' about Odysseus' fate; naturally, then, such news would prompt Penelope to

---

[39] We will note shortly that *logopoiia* is typical of 'messengers'.

[40] Cf. Alkinoos at *Odyssey* 11.363–369: the unspecified ἐπίκλοπος (because unreliable) bearer of pseudo-news, on the one hand, and the generic singer, on the other, narrate *muthoi* (cf. *Odyssey* 11.368: 'μῦθον . . . κατέλεξας'). Later, as Lewis 1996:4–5 also remarks, the term λογοποιός came to mean 'poet' as well as 'he who spreads (false) news'.

[41] See also Dawe 1993:306 *ad Odyssey* 8.44: the etymology of Φήμιος is connected with "speech, reputation or rumour."

[42] Cf. the address, also in the dual, of Eumaios and Philoitios, both of whom are fellow laborers and in fact slaves, at *Odyssey* 21.85–90 and 209–220.

try to 'shut up' Phemios at *Odyssey* 1.337–342.[43] It is not necessary, however, in my view, to suppose that these reports—many of which correspond extratextually to the *Nostoi* of the epic cycle—are pessimistic or untraditionally slanderous.[44] The only information about these accounts arises out of the *Odyssey* itself:

1. The reports and rumors concern "the woeful return of the Achaians from Troy" (*Odyssey* 1.326–327), an account of the tragic *nostos* of (among others?) Ajax the Lesser.[45]

2. It emerges subsequently from Nestor's and Menelaos' comments (*Odyssey* 3.130ff., 4.499ff.) that this particular account is accurate at least as regards its initial episodes, after which both men loose traces of Odysseus. By contrast, Penelope does not even know whether the first episodes ever transpired inasmuch as she is not in communication with Nestor or Menelaos.

3. The *aoidos*' song afflicts the queen with *penthos* 'grief' (*Odyssey* 1.341). But from *Odyssey* 14.126–130 we also know that she is moved to tears even by the hopeful narratives/*angeliai* she hears from various wanderers.[46] She has tired of receiving heartening, if, as she believes, false, reports.

Despite Odysseus' snide insinuations at *Odyssey* 22.375–376 about the *poluphêmos aoidos*, the hearsay and generally the news Phemios recounts at the palace feasts are not necessarily negative. *They may, on the contrary, be hopeful.* In any event the news becomes cliché for Penelope, who is obliged to submit to the painful routine of listening to it.[47] For Telemachos however these accounts

---

[43] Bakker 2002b:142.

[44] Telemachos' statement 'οὐ γὰρ Ὀδυσσεὺς οἶος ἀπώλεσε νόστιμον ἦμαρ / ἐν Τροίῃ, πολλοὶ δὲ καὶ ἄλλοι φῶτες ὄλοντο' (*Odyssey* 1.354–355) is nothing but pure bluff; he has realized that the encouraging 'Mentes' is in reality a divinity. If, in the light of the prince's pretence, we disregard the conjunction καί, verse 355 adumbrates his only certainty: 'πολλοὶ δὲ καὶ ἄλλοι φῶτες ὄλοντο' (see immediately below). *Pace* Bakker and others, it would moreover be premature to speak in terms of a proper 'tradition' about Odysseus, because only 20 years have elapsed since his departure.

[45] The *nostos* in question was familiar to the poet and his actual audience; for us the account of Ajax's *nostos* is elliptical: see further Heubeck, West, and Hainsworth 1988:116–117 ad *Odyssey* 1.325–327 and esp. Danek 1998:59. Heubeck, West, and Hainsworth 1988:118–119 ad *Odyssey* 343–344 ('τοίην γὰρ κεφαλὴν ποθέω μεμνημένη αἰεὶ / ἀνδρός . . . ') draw our attention to the clear funerary nuances of the noun κεφαλή in Homer. Penelope thus laments over her husband, moved almost inductively by the song about the tragic homecomings of Ajax and others. The pronoun τοίην, too, bears out Penelope's lugubrious associations inasmuch as τοίην = 'such a person [sc. as Ajax and the other Achaians]'. In the suitors' presence Telemachos deliberately confirms his mother's worst fears in verses 354–355, noted above.

[46] 'ἐπὴν πόσις ἄλλοθ' ὄληται' (*Odyssey* 14.130) is Eumaios' supposition, not Penelope's.

[47] See again esp. *Odyssey* 14.126–130, 372–376, and also 1.340–342 ('ταύτης δ' ἀποπαύε' ἀοιδῆς / λυγρῆς, ἥ τέ μοι αἰεὶ ἐνὶ στήθεσσι φίλον κῆρ / τείρει'). In common with Heubeck, West, and Hainsworth 1988:119, Jones 1991:129 ad *Odyssey* 1.352 interprets verses 340–342 poetologically.

are actual news. It seems likely in light of the analysis above that Phemios is *poluphêmos* also in the sense that he presumably broadcasts, with relative freedom, the *dêmoio phêmis* 'talk of the town', whatever it may be.[48] It is not hard to understand, then, why Phemios and Medon depart together, as observed earlier (compare again the dual number at *Odyssey* 22.378–380), and afterwards go to the *agorê* 'place of assembly' to meet the victims' relations. Both of these *logopoioi* of exquisite voice return to the space associated with the function of a *traditional narrator of (oral) news* such as was their common role in Ithakan society.

"Literature is News that Stays News"[49]

I should like now to turn to Telemachos' forthright response to the reaction that Penelope has to Phemios' song. It is worth noting that the singer remains silent and it is the prince who takes up his defense:

'μῆτερ ἐμή, τί τ'ἄρα φθονέεις ἐρίηρον ἀοιδὸν
τέρπειν ὅππῃ οἱ νόος ὄρνυται; οὔ νύ τ' ἀοιδοί
αἴτιοι ...
τὴν γὰρ ἀοιδὴν μᾶλλον ἐπικλείουσ' ἄνθρωποι,
ἥ τις ἀκουόντεσσι νεωτάτη ἀμφιπέληται.'

Odyssey 1.346–348, 351–352

(For other comparable interpretations *ad loc.*, see Nagy in n52 and van Wees in n61 below.) According to Jones, Penelope refers to the (painfully familiar) *content* of Phemios' song.

48 Does the fact that Phemios sings ὑπ' ἀνάγκη (*Odyssey* 1.154) rule out the possibility that he conveys (reliable) news about Odysseus, especially if it is hopeful or at least not dismal? Should we rather assume, along with others, that he censors his songs in order to please the suitors? In Archaic Greek society a singer would have enjoyed a large degree of freedom, and even immunity. For this 'artistic freedom' see *Odyssey* 8.44–45: 'τῷ γάρ ῥα θεὸς πέρι δῶκεν ἀοιδὴν / τέρπειν, ὅππῃ θυμὸς ἐποτρύνῃσιν ἀείδειν' (Demodokos is here presented as an archetypical *aoidos*, not as a poet in a paradise). Moreover, the murder of a singer would be *hubris* against the Muses and Apollo, since by definition he was θεῖος/θέσπις, not to mention περικλυτός (see de Jong 2001:191). This privileged status is strongly implied when Phemios supplicates Odysseus at *Odyssey* 22.344ff.; in the space of four verses the singer understandably but also revealingly employs the word θεός/θεοί three times (*Odyssey* 22.346–347, 349). The treatment accorded to Haliserthes the Ithakan soothsayer may be a comparable case: in *Odyssey* 2.178ff. the suitors simply threaten him verbally. But in *Odyssey* 3.267ff. Klytemnestra's 'mentor-singer', having proven bothersome to the illicit couple, is left to die on a desert island. See also n53 below.

49 Pound 1934:29.

"Mother mine, why do you begrudge the trusty singer (*aoidos*)
the giving of pleasure in whichever direction his mind moves for him?
    Singers certainly
are not to blame . . .
for men would rather praise that song most
that comes the newest round hearers."

In his cross-cultural study of oral genres J. Vansina remarks that "news must interest to some degree its hearers and is often sensational," and, more importantly, that these 'messages' relate to the present and "imply some future."[50] The news that Telemachos seeks, though in reality traceable to the more distant past, is nonetheless never felt by him and his milieu as anything other than 'information about something that did not occur in the too distant past'. Moreover, the consequences of this information undoubtedly concern the present and the immediate future as envisaged explicitly in the *Telemachy*.[51] If we allow that the search for *kleos* (in the sense of 'news') is to prove Telemachos' first step, as it were, in acquiring *kleos* (in the wider sense), then it becomes easy to understand the self-righteous fervor with which he defends Phemios' song, whose subject is the *nostos* of the Achaians:

"men would rather praise that *song* (*aoidê*) most
that comes the *newest* (*neôtatê*) round hearers."

Odyssey 1.351–352[52]

The young prince does not so much uphold, in the name of *terpsis* (*Odyssey* 1.346–347), the singer's 'freedom of expression' or, rather, invention (self-evident to him anyway). Instead, he brings out the alternative social function of song to afford news. Handling without hindrance his *more or less stable content* (compare ἥ τέ μοι αἰεὶ 'which (song) repeatedly', *Odyssey* 1.341), Phemios is entitled to add—as regards *form*—new nuances and emphases, but chiefly—as regards *content*—fresh details, significant and less so, and generally *new information*, much of it derived from eyewitness accounts, even if these are only partly reliable.[53] In such cases song crystallizes news and gossip in the selfsame manner as the (deceptive) narratives of the wandering flatterers who from time to time

---

[50] Vansina 1985:4–5.

[51] See *Odyssey* 1.279–296, 2.214–223.

[52] The literal translation in Nagy 1990:69 is helpful: "Men would most rather give glory [*kleos*] to that song / which is *the newest to make the rounds among listeners*" (my italics). Nagy 1990:67–70 notes that the adjective νεωτάτη [sc. ἀοιδή] alludes to the "overall narrative in progress."

[53] See Vansina 1985:5 on such news. According to Scodel 2002, esp. 84–85, Phemios' song is impartial and hence reliable, and it does not deal with Odysseus' homecoming.

call upon Penelope (*Odyssey* 14.122–130). We might compare the effectively encomiastic 'news from the front' offered by the so-called bards (*bardoi*) who accompanied Celtic aristocrat warriors (Posidonius FGrHist 87 F = Diodorus Siculus 5.31.2).[54] The *neôtatê aoidê* (see *Odyssey* 1.351–352) is potentially as significant a source of information as the most recent *viva voce* testimony of, say, Menelaos, who "was the last of the brazen-shirted Achaians to reach home" (*Odyssey* 1.286). Despite claims to the contrary—he is actually bluffing to the suitors, as the poet notes (*Odyssey* 1.420)—Telemachos has every reason to pursue news (*angeliê*) from various sources: "No longer do I place credence in *tidings* (*angeliê*), from wherever they should come" (*Odyssey* 1.414). The exemplary silence of the suitors, who are otherwise ill-mannered (*Odyssey* 1.325–326, 339–340) and usually omit to offer libations at their meals,[55] may imply that they too treat Phemios' song in particular as potentially news-worthy; compare Eurymachos' anxious query about Mentes, "Does he bring some *news* (*angeliê*) of your father's coming, / or does he come this way [i.e. here] pursuing some business of his own?" (*Odyssey* 1.408–409) and especially *Odyssey* 2.255–256, 14.375–377.

From Homer's much-discussed apostrophe to the Muses at *Iliad* 2.485–492 it is possible to extrapolate the principle according to which these divinities are beyond a doubt unerring eyewitnesses not only of all that happened in the remote past (namely, the oral tradition which the Catalogue of Ships purports to be), but also of the more recent past (namely, oral history; see on both scores *Iliad* 2.485–486: "for you are goddesses and are both present at, and know, all things, / whereas we hear only a *hearsay* (*kleos*) and know nothing," and compare Hesiod *Theogony* 38). Plato *Republic* 424b and scholars such as W. B. Stanford, A. Heubeck, S. West, and J. B. Hainsworth, and I. de Jong *ad loc.* do not cite song as a source of news as established by ethnography.[56] Yet such a function is probable especially in many preliterate societies wherein song is the repository of every manner of information and knowledge.[57] If the repertory which includes Phemios' song about the "woeful *nostos* of the Achaians" (*Odyssey* 1.326–327) refers to events dating from seven years since the fall of

---

[54] εἰσὶ δὲ παρ' αὐτοῖς καὶ ποιηταὶ μελῶν, οὓς Βάρδους ὀνομάζουσιν. οὗτοι δὲ μετ'ὀργάνων ταῖς λύραις ὁμοίων ᾄδοντες οὓς μὲν ὑμνοῦσιν, οὓς δὲ βλασφημοῦσι . . . ἀλλὰ καὶ κατὰ τοὺς πολέμους τούτοις μάλιστα πείθονται καὶ τοῖς μελῳδοῦσι ποιηταῖς . . . ("Among them there are also singers [literally poets] of songs whom they call 'Bards.' These, singing to the accompaniment of instruments similar to lyres, praise some or speak ill of others . . . But also in war they especially obey these [sc. priests] and the chanting singers . . . ")

[55] Lateiner 1993:183.

[56] De Jong 2001:83 acknowledges however (*ad Odyssey* 3.276–302) that Nestor's narrative may already be based on songs. See also van Wees below.

[57] As Ph. Kakrides informs me, in the Ionian Islands oral poets broadcasted local news in rhyme until recently.

Troy to two years ago (see Menelaos' *nostos*, *Odyssey* 1.286 above and 3.318, "for he has only *lately* (νέον) come from abroad"),[58] it stands to reason that a singer could concern himself with news. After all, one of his legitimate objects (and the touchstone by which his performance would be judged) would be to offer *terpsis* 'pleasure, delight' to his audience, irrespective of the relative chronology of his repertory.[59] Moreover, as P. Jones has shown, the *Odyssey's main characters understand the past as more proximate* than is the case in the *Iliad* and as a rule resort to contemporary mortals—rather than gods or distant heroes—as behavioral models or *exempla*.[60]

The implications of the ethnography of news and gossip and their oral practitioners have led me to the conclusion that the *Odyssey*'s characters naturally expect to hear news via song, among other oral media. H. van Wees has recently come to a similar conclusion and urges that Telemachos' spirited defense of Phemios reflects an earlier phase of epic poetry "when legends were still in the making and one could compose new epics on *new epic deeds*" (my italics).[61] Indeed, these 'new epic deeds' were at first simply news. A singer thus behaved much like a messenger, with whom he shared a heritage of song performance and *logopoiia* 'fashioning of narrative'. At the same time, it may be salutary to end this section by superimposing a diachronic perspective on the synchronic interpretation of song I have proposed. As G. Nagy has argued,[62] in the course of continual reperformances by *aoidoi* over time, whatever 'news or hearsay' (*kleos*) was conveyed in song becomes something infinitely more complex: 'news from the war front' (as I call it) confers 'glory' (*kleos*) on its protagonists and ultimately becomes coterminous with it.

The *Telemachy*'s Proliferating News

The bedrock of news, as we noticed, is rumor or hearsay. Our poet scrupulously ranks its trustworthiness while always differentiating it from eyewitness accounts. In the *Odyssey* rumors may be accurate, but their inaccuracy is just as likely or still likelier than not, especially when they are not necessarily based on autopsy.[63] In the *Telemachy*, where they play a major role, rumors may be classified as follows:

---

[58] See Dawe 1993:146, Heubeck, West, and Hainsworth 1988:181 *ad loc.*, and Danek 1998, esp. 168–170, on the chronology of the *nostoi* relative to one another.

[59] See again n29.

[60] Jones 1992:88, 89n26; on time in the *Iliad*, see Edwards 2001:48.

[61] Van Wees 1992:15.

[62] Nagy 2003, esp. 41–43. By this token, as D. N. Maronitis reminds me, a singer may be a 'messenger' synchronically, but poetologically (and diachronically/systemically as G. Nagy would say) the lowly δημιοεργός is transmuted into something more complex: the very poet Homer.

[63] De Jong 2001:28 *ad Odyssey* 1.214–220 and 77 *ad Odyssey* 3.184–187. See Appendix I. See further Marincola 2007, esp. 5–6: The *Odyssey* distinguishes clearly between "second-level type of

1. Unconfirmed reports or hearsay,[64] the truthfulness of which is an open matter: These usually arise from incomplete data, and in turn are supplemented by similar data. At times a character may treat a rumor falling under this neutral category as inherently inaccurate or utterly false. Compare *Iliad* 2.486: ἡμεῖς δὲ κλέος οἶον ἀκούομεν οὐδέ τι ἴδμεν ('whereas we hear mere hearsay and know nothing') and *Odyssey* 1.215–220, especially 220 (Telemachos ostensibly distances himself from rumors that Odysseus is his father; see Chapter 1). Many rumors seem to originate *ex nihilo*. Because of this vacuum of information reports of this kind may become overblown. See *Odyssey* 1.161–162, 3.88: 'κείνου δ' αὖ καὶ ὄλεθρον ἀπευθέα θῆκε Κρονίων' ("even his death [let alone his other troubles] Zeus has made obscure"), 3.89–91, 4.109–110: 'οὐδέ τι ἴδμεν, / ζώει ὅ γ' ἦ τέθνηκεν' ("and we do not at all know, / whether he is alive or dead"), etc. Also compare *Odyssey* 1.282–283: ὄσσαν . . . ἐκ Διός ('the voice of hearsay . . . from Zeus'), which (according to Heubeck, West, and Hainsworth 1988:111 *ad loc.*) is "a rumour of which the origin cannot be traced."[65]

2. Reliable (*prima facie*) rumors: In *Odyssey* 1.189–193, Mentes, in paraphrasing news (circulating in the form of rumors), transmits in his turn the accurate information that Laertes no longer goes to town. See especially *Odyssey* 1.189–191: 'τὸν οὐκέτι φασὶ πόλινδε / ἔρχεσθ' ("who they say no longer comes to this city"); compare 3.186–198. Nestor, too, paraphrases hearsay—see especially *Odyssey* 1.186–187: 'ὄσσα . . . / πεύθομαί' ("as many things as . . . / I am informed about") and 1.188: 'Μυρμιδόνας φάσ' ἐλθέμεν' ("they say the Myrmidons came back")—concerning the return of the Myrmidons and other heroes.[66] Consider also *Odyssey* 3.212–213: Nestor is already *au courant* with reports about the suitors. Compare *Odyssey* 3.212: φασὶ 'they say' and 4.94–95, in which Menelaos hints at reports about the seizure of a portion of his property along with Helen: 'καὶ πατέρων τάδε μέλλετ' ἀκουέμεν' ("and you are likely to have heard these things from your fathers" [94]). Fi-

---

inquiry" and "testimony of an eyewitness" such as Nestor and Menelaos; this "hierarchy of knowledge" sets the standard as it were for "all of the ancient historians' claims to veracity." (Marincola does not document these gradations of certitude in the *Odyssey*, since he is concerned mainly with Odysseus the inquirer and narrator as a role model for ancient historians.)

[64] See de Jong 2001:214 *ad Odyssey* 8.487–491, whose comment I am expanding on.

[65] See n6 above on deified rumor and hearsay. (The translation of *Odyssey* 3.88 is by Heubeck, West, and Hainsworth 1988:166 *ad loc.*)

[66] Cf. *Odyssey* 3.184–185 (on the contrary, Nestor lacks news about the *nostos* of Odysseus and others: 'ὡς ἦλθον . . . ἀπευθής, οὐδέ τι οἶδα, / κείνων . . .' ἀπευθής [184] has an active sense, as Heubeck, West, and Hainsworth 1988:171 *ad loc.* note).

nally, see *Odyssey* 4.199–202: Peisistratos tells Menelaos that his brother Antilochos was 'οὔ τι κάκιστος / Ἀργείων· μέλλεις δὲ σὺ ἴδμεναι· οὐ γὰρ ἐγώ γε/ἤντησ' οὐδὲ ἴδον· περὶ δ' ἄλλων φασὶ γενέσθαι / Ἀντίλοχον . . .' ("[sc. my brother was] hardly the worst of the Argives; / you are likely to know [this]. For certainly I did not meet and know him nor even saw him; but they say he was superior to [all] others, / [was] Antilochos . . . "). The accounts about the *kleos* of his lost brother (who died even before Peisistratos was born), apparently are based in large part on first-hand information such as Nestor's, and can be verified by comparison with the reports of other eyewitnesses such as, in this case, Menelaos.

3. Unreliable (and most probably false) rumors: If we return to Mentes at *Odyssey* 1.194–195 we will notice that he indirectly quotes a second, successive report: 'δὴ γάρ μιν ἔφαντ' ἐπιδήμιον εἶναι,/ σὸν πατέρ. . .' ("because indeed they said he was among his people, / *your father* . . . "), which he later roundly contradicts: 'ἀλλά νυ τόν γε θεοὶ βλάπτουσι κελεύθου' ("but surely the gods are deflecting him from his course" [195]); compare *Odyssey* 1.363–368 and de Jong 2001:103 *ad loc.* Consider also the term ψευδάγγελος 'one who misreports a message' at *Iliad* 15.159.

Generally speaking, the *Odyssey*'s characters have a keen ear (and a vocabulary) for the qualitative gradations of messages and their interpretation.[67] Rumors, which, as Vansina notes, are necessarily "sensational news," may in certain instances "have a basis in fact," yet they may be untruthful, as remarked, especially when they "serve practical purposes such as to dishearten opponents, or to galvanize supporters."[68] Once proven inaccurate, rumors will disappear, only to be replaced by *fresh* ones, as Vansina remarks.[69] Telemachos has grown up amidst just such a vicious cycle of conflicting rumors—presumably expanding at times as they feed on each other, at others shrinking or eventually giving rise to further rumors. At least sometimes, such hearsay will have been dictated by hidden agendas, such as Mentes' untrue but briefly bracing news about Odysseus' return to Ithaka.

---

[67] Their orality is designated by, among other things, the alternative names for this genre: κλέος, ἀκουή, κληηδών, ἀγγελία. See Vansina 1985: "Hearsay or rumor is transmitted from ear to mouth" (6).
[68] Vansina 1985: "Many rumors have a basis in fact . . . Especially when rumors serve practical purposes such as to dishearten opponents, or to galvanize supporters, they are untrustworthy" (6).
[69] Vansina 1985:6.

Seeing is Believing

Telemachos at *Odyssey* 3.93–95 (= 4.323–325) consciously projects the definitive disjunction between first-hand information (autopsy) and second-hand
information (μῦθος) from a party who witnessed some event (in the recent or
more remote past) with his or her own eyes:[70]

> ‘εἴ που ὄπωπας
> ὀφθαλμοῖσι τεοῖσιν ἢ ἄλλου μῦθον ἄκουσας
> πλαζομένου. . .’

> "if you have anywhere seen
> with your eyes or heard from someone else the account
> of that man [sc. Odysseus] wandering . . . "

The testimonies the prince elicits are removed, in fact, from the recent past,[71]
which is the sphere of 'news', as will be seen. In a strict sense these eyewitness accounts are, to use Vansina's term, 'life histories', that is, autobiographical reminiscences—truly "the main input of oral history"[72]—through which
a teller interprets certain experiences, paying special attention to imposing
cohesion on his or her retelling.[73] Indeed, in the *Odyssey* first-hand information is privileged above all other types of communication.[74] The personal
reminiscences of Nestor, Menelaos, and Helen and Odysseus' catalogue-like
Apologoi are in essence eyewitness accounts. The manner in which these
personages articulate their oral—by definition—matter is instructive. In what
follows I will concentrate my analysis on Nestor and Menelaos, the protagonists in Books 3 and 4, respectively.

It is hardly accidental that the poet employs the phrase cited (*Odyssey*
3.93) in indicating the content and the often complex form of Nestor's and
Menelaos' oral recollections. Both veterans recount to Telemachos and
Peisistratos their personal experiences, either basing themselves on their
autopsy or supplementing it, at times expansively, with hearsay or other
secondary communications.[75] The latter, though of indeterminate prove-

---

[70] De Jong 2001:73 cites *ad loc. Odyssey* 8.491; but see also n63 above.

[71] Telemachos is prompting his interlocutor's memory in this passage, as Nestor admits in the
beginning of his answer (*Odyssey* 3.103ff.): ‘ὦ φίλ᾽, ἐπεί μ᾽ ἔμνησας ὀϊζύος . . .’ Cf. also the series
of four questions that the youth puts to him in *Odyssey* 3.248–252. For the oral mechanism of
provoking another's memory, see Vansina 1985:8. (De Jong 2001:82, who does not take this
traditional mechanism into account, ascribes Telemachos' queries to ignorance.)

[72] Vansina 1985:8–9.

[73] Vansina 1985:9. On coherence see n63 above.

[74] See also de Jong 2001:214 *ad Odyssey* 8.487–491.

[75] Cf. again de Jong 2001:83 *ad Odyssey* 3.276–302: Nestor's account of the homecoming of
Menelaos sprang from rumors or possibly songs such as Phemios'. For the differences between

nance, are nonetheless treated as trustworthy both by these tellers and their auditors. Thus, as will be seen, the 'legend' of Agamemnon's murder—to cite a conspicuous example—is 'received' by everyone as ἀληθέα 'the truth'. Both narrators generally revert to secondary material whenever they recollect *nostoi* that they cannot possibly have witnessed themselves: those of the Myrmidons, Agamemnon, Ajax, and even Odysseus.

As remarked, Vansina, in common with many others, has detailed the multifarious messages that alongside eyewitness accounts ultimately generate 'oral history'.[76] We might by analogy suppose that the alternative source of μῦθος 'account, story' that Telemachos entertains in his plea to Nestor (see again *Odyssey* 3.94) implies a considerable range of oral messages.[77] Whether we concur with Heubeck, West, and Hainsworth or not (see n77), the phrase ἄλλου μῦθον ἄκουσας 'you heard from someone else the account' (*Odyssey* 3.94) raises one of two possibilities: either a) the testimony furnished by ἄλλος 'someone else' is based on autopsy or some other form of immediate experience; or b) the account stems from unspecified, indirect sources. No less than Telemachos, Nestor explicitly acknowledges the paramountcy of eyewitness experience. At *Odyssey* 3.184–187 the Pylian king, practically apologizing for his lack of first-hand information, announces with remarkable self-consciousness that he will he will instead quote the accounts he has heard from others in his palace (compare *Odyssey* 3.94):

'ὣς ἦλθον, φίλε τέκνον, ἀπευθής,[78] οὐδέ τι οἶδα
κείνων, οἵ τ' ἐσάωθεν Ἀχαιῶν οἵ τ' ἀπόλοντο.
ὅσσα δ' ἐνὶ μεγάροισι καθήμενος ἡμετέροισι
πεύθομαι, ἦ θέμις ἐστί, δαήσεαι, οὐδέ σε κεύσω.'

Odyssey 3.184–187

"So I came, dear child, without information, that is, I don't know anything
  about which Achaians returned safe and which perished.
On the other hand, as many things as sitting in our
palace I am informed about, as is customary, you will get to know, and I
    will not hide from you."

---

the two versions of Agamemnon's tragic *nostos*, see de Jong 2001:81–83 *ad Odyssey* 3.254–316 and 110–111 *ad Odyssey* 4.512–549.

[76] Vansina 1985:4–7.

[77] Heubeck, West, and Hainsworth 1988:166, as Stanford 1958:253, detach the particle πλαζομένου from the pronoun ἄλλου (*Odyssey* 3.95). In their view the causal sentence following verse 95 suggests that this participle refers, albeit rather gauchely, to Odysseus. Dawe 1993:131, on the other hand, attaches the pronoun to the participle but detaches the latter from Odysseus. All suspect that verse 95 is an interpolation.

[78] For the adjective ἀπευθής, see n66 above.

'οὐδέ τι οἶδα/κείνων' οἵ τ'ἐσάωθεν Ἀχαιῶν...' ("I don't know anything / about which Achaians returned safe...," *Odyssey* 3.184–185) may be comparable with the poet's admission of fallibility in *Iliad* 2.486: ἡμεῖς δὲ κλέος οἶον ἀκούομεν οὐδέ τι ἴδμεν ('whereas we hear mere hearsay and know nothing'); Nestor's confession of ignorance, like Homer's, reduces him to complete reliance on *kleos*. The old man then cites in ascending order of importance the *nostoi* of the Myrmidons (*Odyssey* 3.188–189), Philoktetes (3.190), Idomeneus (3.191–192), climaxing with an allusion to Agamemnon's bloody return (3.193–195). (Later, at verse 254, he will describe as ἀληθέα 'the truth' the substance of the latter 'legend'; see below.) From the parataxis of verses 188–194 we may reasonably infer that the speaker attaches equal weight to these four events not in terms of emotional resonance, to be sure, but in terms of 'historicity'. When in his third account of Menelaos' *nostos* Nestor relates the final, Egyptian phase of this adventure (*Odyssey* 3.286–302), he clearly draws his information from the indirect sources that underlie this 'legend'. De Jong 2001:83 *ad Odyssey* 3.276–302 (see also n75 above) correctly observes that Nestor presumably relies on hearsay and even possibly *songs like Phemios'*.

The details of Agamemnon's pitiable return, for all their indirect 'documentation', are reckoned by all the characters to be true. Although neither Nestor nor Menelaos witnessed the assassination, far less the action preceding it or the ensuing revenge, their interlocutors do not for a moment doubt the veracity of the account each time they hear it.[79] Nestor, we have seen, expressly notes that his information about this particular *nostos* as well as of other *nostoi* is second-hand and oral (see again *Odyssey* 3.184–187); yet, tellingly, before beginning his narrative about Agamemnon's death he avows its truthfulness:

'ἀληθέα πάντ' ἀγορεύσω.'

Odyssey 3.254

"I will tell you the whole truth."

'Mentor' confirmed its accuracy earlier (*Odyssey* 3.234–235), and νημερτὴς 'unerring in his deep knowledge' Proteus (as quoted by Menelaos) will also corroborate the account in the next book (*Odyssey* 4.512–537).

---

[79] The extremely wide diffusion of this legend can be inferred especially from: a) Nestor's comment, 'Ἀτρεΐδην δὲ καὶ αὐτοὶ ἀκούετε, νόσφιν ἐόντες...' (*Odyssey* 3.193ff.) and b) the positive reactions of Telemachos (*Odyssey* 3.201ff.) and 'Mentor' (*Odyssey* 3.234–235). For the differing details, emphases, and ambiguities in Nestor's and Menelaos' respective accounts see: a) de Jong 2001:77–78 *ad Odyssey* 3.193–200; 81–83 *ad Odyssey* 3.254–316, and b) de Jong 2001:95 *ad Odyssey* 4.91–92; 110–111 *ad Odyssey* 4.512–549.

The tale of Agamemnon's murder is thus recounted in no less than four versions in the *Telemachy*—twice by Nestor and twice by Menelaos; none of the versions is contradictory. Cumulatively, through *paraleipsis* (ἔνια παραλείπειν καὶ ὕστερον φράζειν 'the omission of some things and the telling of them after-wards'), often called the technique of 'piecemeal narration' (see de Jong 2001:82), these reminiscences serve to expand and enrich with their different details the image emerging on the canvas, as it were: they throw complementary, mottled shades of light on the recurring 'legend' of the *Oresteia*. The 'truth' of the story of Agamemnon's murder becomes clearer with each accretionary retelling. The differing details, emphases, and omissions also serve to anticipate, from a compositional standpoint, the license with which post-Homeric poets created adaptations, often with innovations, of the *Oresteia* and other epic material.[80] If we treat Nestor's and Menelaos' accounts of Agamemnon's return as individual *récits* of 'oral history', then we should perhaps resist splicing these complementary narratives together and reading them as a unified whole. It may be more useful to read them in much the same manner as a historian reviewing the inter-locking reminiscences of two real-life informants: in the words of Halbwachs (1980:41–42) we should be "considering the two groups simultaneously, but each from the viewpoint of the other." In sum, Nestor and Menelaos accommodate their accounts of the legendary *nostos* to their didactic agenda and other consid-erations.[81] And the freedom with which they do this harks forward, as noted, to later literary treatments of epic sagas. Still more striking, the two heroes (and Helen) may roughly recall informants at work, the men and women who recount to interviewers their experience of a momentous event in collective contempo-rary history—in the case of modern Greece, say, the 'Asia Minor disaster'. Some informants will have participated in the event—and hence in history in the making—themselves. In every case, the participants' account will be shaped by exogenous and/or purely subjective factors, indeed even by the subconscious structures of folk tradition.[82] Could Homer be representing, in effect, the vagaries of recollection that inescapably bedevil oral testimony? His subtle awareness of the calibrations of 'news' and other types of information may suggest so.

In the *Telemachy*, in particular, Homer seems almost playfully to explore the scale of truth in the oral sources his characters cite. The scale reaches its climax in Book 4. Here Menelaos quotes word for word Proteus' testimony regarding

---

[80] See March 1987:xi, 81–89 for permutations of the *Oresteia* saga in Homer, the epic cycle, Hesiod, Stesichoros, etc. On 'truth' in Archaic poetry, see e.g. Nagy 1990, esp. 60–66.

[81] See n75 above.

[82] See Σώκου 2004, esp. 280–281, 282–283, 292, 304–305 for largely postmodern reservations about recollection as an objective, language-based, and social process; cf. Appendix I (on an oral infor-mant's reliance on 'popular paradigms of recollection') and n75 (on selectivity and differing emphases).

the return voyages of Ajax (*Odyssey* 4.499–511), Agamemnon (4.512–537), and Odysseus (4.555–560). In his rather schematic prologue—which operates like a "table of contents speech" in miniature[83]—the "unerring old man of the sea" (*Odyssey* 4.384, compare verse 385) omits the names of all heroes; and when he mentions the third hero's 'happy end' he strikes a demiquaver of vagueness:

'εἷς δ' ἔτι που ζωὸς κατερύκεται εὐρέϊ πόντῳ.'

Odyssey 4.498

"And one man, still alive, somewhere, is being held back on the broad sea."

The enclitic adverb που 'somewhere' is meant to create suspense by casting a pall over the information furnished by the otherwise νημερτής 'infallible one'.[84] However, when he later reveals that the εἷς—the 'one man'—he was just talking about is none other than Odysseus, the Old Man of the Sea dispels outright the vagueness of his previous report. He now assures Menelaos that the information is based, significantly, on autopsy:

'τὸν ἴδον ἐν νήσῳ θαλερὸν κατὰ δάκρυ χέοντα . . .'

Odyssey 4.556ff.

"Him I saw on an island, shedding thick tears . . . "

Proteus may in fact have been an eyewitness of the other *nostoi* besides: this may not be too far-fetched a possibility, especially if we assume that, in addition to being supernatural and a sea deity, he was present at other 'historical' happenings, particularly the quintessentially maritime *nostoi*. If so, he enjoys the same privileged access to 'history' as the Muses do according to *Iliad* 2.485–486. Be that as it may, it is perfectly obvious that Proteus' information about Odysseus, though it scarcely has been diffused to the same extent as the story of Agamemnon's return, is unchallengeable. It is, after all, hard to beat the eyewitness account of a god.

---

[83] See de Jong 2001:15–16 *ad Odyssey* 1.81–95 ("table of contents speeches").

[84] If που is taken to mean 'I suppose', the suspense created is still greater. Dawe 1993:191 *ad loc.* does not consider the verse essential.

3

Kleos and Social Identity

'ὦ πάτερ, ἦ τοι σεῖο μέγα κλέος αἰὲν ἄκουον,
χεῖράς τ' αἰχμητὴν ἔμεναι καὶ ἐπίφρονα βουλήν.'

Odyssey 16.241–242

"Father, truly I used to hear of your great reputation (*kleos*),
that you were warlike with your hands and wise in counsel."

Ἐνὶ οἴκῳ 'At Home'

IN *ODYSSEY* 1.345–359, after Mentes' departure the Little Prince makes the first public demonstration of his maturity or, as others would say, of his psychological change. (This is also the first time the prince pronounces the name Ὀδυσσεύς 'Odysseus', at verse 354.) Here he dumbfounds his mother with his intervention in favor of Phemios Terpiades, which we examined in the previous chapter. As others have also noticed, the youth's antagonistic tone can be explained by reference to his post-adolescent psychology and needs no further comment.[1] What may merit brief attention is the dramatic setting of the brusque outburst in Book 1.

First, Telemachos speaks more generally on behalf of the members of the screened-off sphere of the δαίς 'meal'. In epic, mortal women never participate in the δαίς proper, but may only appear at its conclusion: they neither dine nor drink with the men, but are allowed to take part in post-prandial conversation with them as Helen (*Odyssey* 4.121ff., 216ff.) and Arete (*Odyssey* 8.136ff.) do.[2] In Book 1 the stylized scene of Queen Penelope's diva-like arrival (*Odyssey* 1.328–336) gives us some notion of the degree to which her son will perceive her as

---

[1]   See also Heath 2005: "his first rough stab at growing up" (101). See below on *Odyssey* 21.350–353, a remodeling of this passage.

[2]   See e.g. Heath 2005:71–72 with his n100.

an intruder in the men's quarters even at this advanced stage of after-dinner entertainment. Her face covered with λιπαρὰ κρήδεμνα 'a veil shiny with oil' (*Odyssey* 1.334), she has just come down the stairs from the upper floor escorted by two protective maidservants at either side. Details of dress and living space suggest that she is trespassing in the symbolic world of men (also compare Helen's intrusion at *Odyssey* 4.121–124). The Queen's ensuing instructions to Phemios are about as conventional as Andromache's 'command' to Hektor to station troops at a vulnerable location in the city walls. Heath (2005, especially 69–71) points out that Andromache's proposal, concerning as it does a matter of public, indeed military, strategy, is altogether unorthodox; it is this particular intervention, Heath notes, that draws Hektor's uncharacteristically sharp reaction, which is nearly identical to Telemachos' rude declaration of independence. First, the Trojan hero's words:

'ἀλλ' εἰς οἶκον ἰοῦσα τὰ σ' αὐτῆς ἔργα κόμιζε,
ἱστόν τ' ἠλακάτην τε, καὶ ἀμφιπόλοισι κέλευε
ἔργον ἐποίχεσθαι· πόλεμος δ' ἄνδρεσσι μελήσει
πᾶσι, μάλιστα δ' ἐμοί, τοὶ Ἰλίῳ ἐγγεγάασιν.'

Iliad 6.490–493

"Return to your quarters and attend to your own tasks
with the loom and the shuttle and instruct the maidservants
to go about their work [sc. at the shuttle]; as for war, it will concern
        men,
all [sc. men] who live in Ilios, and especially me."

Telemachos' response as a whole (*Odyssey* 1.345–359)—which the poet himself extols as μῦθον πεπνυμένον 'prudent words, speech' (*Odyssey* 1.361)—is remarkable for at least two reasons.[3] First, the youth, as was argued in the last chapter, alludes (at *Odyssey* 1.346–352) to a particular social function of the epic ἀοιδός 'singer' that has been little explored. Second, in the remainder of his answer the post-adolescent prince deploys μῦθος in order to define himself as a man, except that this move is *still premature according to Homer*.[4] We may consider Telemachos' oft-quoted closing words to his mother:

'ἀλλ' εἰς οἶκον ἰοῦσα τὰ σ' αὐτῆς ἔργα κόμιζε,
ἱστόν τ' ἠλακάτην τε, καὶ ἀμφιπόλοισι κέλευε

---

3 παιδὸς γὰρ μῦθον πεπνυμένον ἔνθετο θυμῷ: the poet-bard takes the side of Telemachos, who has just sided with Phemios. For the adjective πεπνυμένος, see below.

4 Consider the poet's telling comment (*Odyssey* 1.361) that Telemachos spoke very wisely (albeit) as a παῖς, a term which, as Graziosi and Haubold 2003:72 note, *always* refers to "(male and female) children as opposed to adults."

ἔργον ἐποίχεσθαι· μῦθος δ' ἄνδρεσσι μελήσει
πᾶσι, μάλιστα δ' ἐμοί· τοῦ γὰρ κράτος ἔστ' ἐνὶ οἴκῳ.'

Odyssey 1.356–359[5]

"Return to your quarters and attend to your own tasks
with the loom and the shuttle and instruct the maidservants
to go about their work [sc. at the shuttle]; as for speech [represented by
song in the men's quarters], it will concern men,
all [sc. men], and especially me, since *mine* is the authority in this house."

In keeping with social convention, the young prince erects a partition between the respective spheres of the sexes: yet, *pace* Heath and others,[6] women too deliver μῦθοι in the specialized sense of 'speech acts' (which Heath also takes into account in his discussion); thus female μῦθος possesses authority so long as it is spoken in the appropriate sphere, which however falls ultimately ὑπ' ἀνδράσιν 'under the jurisdiction of men' (compare *Odyssey* 7.68, 335ff., 8.433ff.).[7] Through his own speech act (see especially *Odyssey* 1.358) Telemachos loudly and publicly ordains his right more generally to perform speech acts ἐνὶ οἴκῳ 'at home, in his household'. That is, verses 356–359 are themselves a μῦθος 'speech act' that engenders (and validates) future μῦθοι 'speech acts'. At the same time, though, this μῦθος—his very first in this scene—reveals him to be defining (or at least proclaiming) his gender.[8] His statement sums up the multiple ways whereby the notional labels 'male' and 'female' are produced and perpetuated in a society. According to the philosopher Judith Butler,[9] the act of 'girling' or 'boying' that establishes the gender of a child begins the moment when society (for instance, the neonatal specialist or the parents) exclaim, "It's a boy/girl." Defined at first through such constatives, gender is in turn stabilized by speech. Telemachos repeats a constative of the kind that identified him in the past as male when, in effect, he asserts in verses 358–359, "I am a man" (compare the striking 'μῦθος δ' ἄνδρεσσι μελήσει / πᾶσι, μάλιστα δ' ἐμοί' ["as for speech, it will concern men, / all men, and especially *me*"]). Simultaneously he delivers in this passage a speech act that, as noted, is a μῦθος characteristic of a man who performs speech acts ἐνὶ οἴκῳ 'in his house'.[10]

---

[5] Athetized by Aristarchos, whom Dawe 1993:73–74 *ad loc.* faithfully follows. Possibly μῦθος here means 'poetry', a category of authoritative speech presupposing performance. See below.

[6] E.g. Heath 2005:747. Graziosi and Haubold 2003:72 rightly remark: "no matter what Telemachos might claim, μῦθος is not exclusively or unproblematically the prerogative of adult men."

[7] For 'speech acts' see also below. Helen's prophetic speech (*Odyssey* 15.125–129) is an authoritative *muthos*. In general, see Easterling 1991:145–151 on the lament.

[8] For exaggeration in verse 358, see below.

[9] Butler 1997.

[10] Why 'man'? See n4 above.

Καὶ ἐν δήμῳ 'In Public'

'Τηλέμαχ', ἦ μάλα δή σε διδάσκουσιν θεοὶ αὐτοὶ
ὑψαγόρην τ' ἔμεναι καὶ θαρσαλέως ἀγορεύειν.'

Odyssey 1.384–385

"Telemachos, really and truly only the gods are teaching you
to be a lofty speaker and [therefore] to hold forth boldly."

If we accept the salient narrative aspect of *kleos* as analyzed in the previous chapters, we may assume that Iliadic *kleos* refers to something more substantive and complex than dazzling derring-do. As M. Schofield also remarks, the *Iliad* is more than a story of "rash young men"[11] locked in rabid battle.[12] Struck by the military action, we readily foreground the element of ἔργα '[wondrous] deeds'[13] and overlook the fact that the career of a hero in the *Iliad*, if conceived as integral narrative—as his βίος 'way of life', that is, as opposed to his ζωή 'life, existence'[14]—must also illustrate his equally important aptitude for εὐβουλία, namely, "rational discussion" in formulating public policy.[15] Schofield's analysis of εὐβουλία has a signal corollary: military *kleos* in this poem conceptually divides into ἔργα 'deeds' and ἔπεα 'words', as shown, for easy example, by Phoinix's reminder to his former ward Achilles of his (Phoinix's) double educational mission:

---

[11] Schofield 1986, esp. 15 with n20 ("rash young men").

[12] See e.g. Clarke 2004:80–81 on μένος and ἀγηνορίη (= in effect, 'excessive and antisocial manhood'), both of which impel heroes to violent acts. For the definitionally pejorative implications of ἀγηνορίη, see Graziosi and Haubold 2003:60–76.

[13] Cf. *Odyssey* 1.338: 'ἔργ' ἀνδρῶν τε θεῶν, τά τε κλείουσιν ἀοιδοί.' ἔργ' ἀνδρῶν (without an adjective and construed with a genitive of agent) is the object of ἀείδειν and by extension μιμνήσκεσθαι and is the formal equivalent of the κλέα ἀνδρῶν, which Achilles sings (*Iliad* 1.189; see Chapter 1 n125); cf. *Odyssey* 10.199: 'μνησαμένοις ἔργων Λαιστρυγόνος Ἀντιφάταο.' However, in the *Odyssey* a song—and concomitantly *kleos*—have a wider range of reference than πολεμήϊα ἔργα (*Iliad* 2.338, etc.), as we saw in Chapter 1; hence ἔργα in *Odyssey* 1.338 probably means 'wondrous deeds, events, or matters', as in *Odyssey* 11.374: 'σὺ δέ μοι λέγε θέσκελα ἔργα' [sc. Odysseus' encounters with the shades of his companions in Hades]. Ἔργον, incidentally, and in particular the plural ἔργα may generally refer to non-martial contexts in Archaic poetry, e.g. *Odyssey* 2.63, 117, 252 (ἔργα = 'farm plot'), etc. (see further LfgrE ii.676–679, esp. 1e, 3–4, s.v. ἔργον), but also subsequently, see e.g. the funerary inscription, Clairmont, no. 73 (p148, Athens, c. 350 BC): the deceased, aged 22, is praised for his ἔργματα (ἔργ[μασιν], verse 3), which include σωφροσύνη and φιλία (verse 4) as well as his athletic accomplishments (verse 5).

[14] An Aristotelian distinction: e.g. *Nikomachean Ethics* 1905b15 on βίος.

[15] Schofield 1986, esp. 24 ("rational discussion"). To Schofield's testimonia, add *Iliad* 7.288–289 (Ajax combines 'μέγεθός τε βίην τε/καὶ πινυτήν'); see also n47 below.

'τοὔνεκά με προέηκε διδασκέμεναι τάδε πάντα,
μύθων τε ῥητῆρ' ἔμεναι πρηκτῆρά τε ἔργων.'

Iliad 9.442–443[16]

"For this reason he [sc. Peleus] sent me to teach you all these things,
namely, to be to be a speaker of words and a doer of deeds."

The *Odyssey*, as well, attests the same mentality, which evaluates a hero holisti-
cally by the degree to which he successfully combines ἔργα 'deeds' and μῦθοι
'words, speech acts'. In his ironical reaction to Telemachos' abortive 'patriotic'
call to action,[17] the suitor Antinoos patently insinuates that he reckons the
youth—who has just broken into tears—to be incompetent not only in the use of
words, but also in the execution of deeds:

'Τηλέμαχ' ὑψαγόρη, μένος ἄσχετε, ποῖον ἔειπες'[18]

Odyssey 2.85

"Telemachos, lofty speaker, unrestrainable in your vehemence, what a
word is this that you have said!"

Later the same suitor repeats the phraseology above and then effectively glosses
it, thereby confirming this two-fold deficiency:

'Τηλέμαχ' ὑψαγόρη, μένος ἄσχετε, μή τί τοι ἄλλο
ἐν στήθεσσι κακὸν μελέτω ἔργον τε ἔπος τε'

Odyssey 2.303–304

"Telemachos, lofty speaker, unrestrainable in your vehemence, let no other
evil deed or word be of concern to you in your heart"

---

[16] On this passage, see Hainsworth 1993:121 and Griffin 1995:127–128. For ἔργα, see n13 above.
For ἔπεα/ἔπη in the specialized sense of style and tone of speech, see Martin 1989, esp. 7, 21,
34–35. In the Mycenaean formula ϝέργον τε ϝέπος τε the polar dyad of 'deed' and 'word' is a
discernible primeval concept. This composite touchstone for heroic conduct carries over into
epic poetry even as a disjunction, e.g. *Odyssey* 3.99 (of Odysseus), 4.163 (see below), Hesiod *Works
and Days* 710; for straightforward formulations, see e.g. *Odyssey* 2.272 (with Heubeck, West, and
Hainsworth 1988:148 *ad loc.*), 15.375 (with Heubeck and Hoekstra 1993:256 *ad loc.*), etc., Hesiod
Works and Days 710 (with West 1978:331 *ad loc.*); further Chapter 4 n6. Additional testimonia
from Archaic poetry: LfgrE ii.674–675, 1a, s.v. ἔργον. (In Thucydides it is rather the incongruity
between word and action that is stressed; hence the contrast λόγῳ/ἔργῳ = 'pretending'/'in
reality': Hornblower 1991:213, 296, 306, etc.)

[17] In practical terms the address achieves nothing inasmuch as the *dêmos*' only reaction is silent
pity (*Odyssey* 2.81–83) and equally silent inertia, as (the real) Mentor asserts (*Odyssey* 2.239–241).
The youth however scores a moral victory, as de Jong 2001:46 remarks. See further below.

[18] Cf. also the ironical force of the otherwise positive term ἀγορητής in the *Iliad* and *Odyssey*: Heath
2005:89n27.

Ἔπος here, connoting 'authoritative speech' (compare μῦθος at *Odyssey* 1.359),[19] belongs, socially speaking, in the realm of men. We noted in the preceding section that the prince has already claimed the right to speak with authority and, by corollary, to perform deeds. When he reproaches Penelope for daring to dictate Phemios' repertory, Telemachos vouchsafes that a woman's ideological and physical space is her οἶκος, i.e. 'her room(s)' (*Odyssey* 1.356), and that her ἔργον 'work' *par excellence* is weaving.[20] Only men—a rubric under which he most emphatically and contrastively places himself as lord of the manor (*Odyssey* 1.359: 'μάλιστα δ' ἐμοί' ["and especially *me*"])—may translate speech into action at both home and, by clear implication, ἐν δήμῳ 'in public'.

In verses 358–359 Telemachos is guilty of overstatement, for women too, as remarked, are capable of exercising authority via speech acts, albeit ἐνὶ οἴκῳ 'at home, in their quarters', and necessarily ὑπ' ἀνδράσιν 'under the jurisdiction of men'.[21] From a historical and cross-cultural point of view, the strictly hierarchical segregation of the sexes has been substantially based on a tendentious distinction between public and private space. Given that the latter has always been systematically denigrated, it is perhaps no surprise that physical separation has conduced to the "social repression" of women.[22] At the same time spatial discrimination has determined most influentially (and arguably continues to determine even today) the social construction of gender.[23] The *Odyssey* may be a case in point. Here the symbolic taxonomy that relegates women to the private realm promotes, though only indirectly,[24] an ideology of 'male superiority', and this hegemony is reflected in the way in which certain characters construe gender. Thus (to revert once more to the famous passage in Book 1), Telemachos, in audibly counterpoising his gender to his mother's, predictably invokes symbolic topography. As we noted, the junior ἄναξ 'lord' here repeats almost verbatim Hektor's words to his wife in *Iliad* 6.490–493. But this is no mere cross-allusion to the *Iliad*; in my view, it is rather a pointed employment of a common stock of ideological clichés: see also Jones 1991:130 *ad Odyssey* 1.358–359. Coming from the lips of a growing

---

[19] See Martin 1989, esp. 29–30: ἔπος is "the unmarked member," μῦθος "the marked member of the pair." See n5 above.

[20] γυναικήϊα ἔργα (e.g. Herodotos 4.114), as used of aristocratic women, never refers to house-cleaning but to the fabrication of cloth, on which see e.g. chapters 1–2 of Ferrari 2002.

[21] Telemachos 'flexes his muscles before his mother': this explains his absolute and exagger-ated tone. Heath 2005:76n109 describes verses 358–359 as "emotionally driven overstatement, ironic but . . . true." (I do not detect irony here.) See also n25 below: the prince's speech act is in fact a performance that demonstrates his (presumed) ethos.

[22] Rosaldo 1974, esp. 17–30, a Marxist view now widely accepted.

[23] Chodorow 1974, esp. 51 (a sociological-psychoanalytical approach).

[24] See Blundell 1995:56–57.

son, the command to his mother sounds quite different from Hektor's order to his wife. Telemachos is protesting his maleness with nearly the same fervor as his father when he rattles his (phalloid) saber at Kirke in Book 10 (10.321ff., 333–335, especially 340–341). Despite the differing contexts, Telemachos and Hektor are entitled to their common reactions by virtue, ultimately, of the 'circular argument', which upholds the segregation of the sexes and in turn reinforces *ad infinitum* the manifold discrimination against women through segregation.

Speech as the Highest Form of Action

In a culture of oral performance such as Homer's,[25] the words of a hero constitute an ἠθοποιία 'favorable characterization' that individuates his heroic character and especially his status through words.[26] Hence, through his style of speech, a hero will consciously seek to inspire respect (compare τιμή 'honor') and fear in his interlocutors.[27] Consider Eurymachos' refusal to be intimidated by Telemachos' mode of speech: 'ἐπεὶ οὔ τινα δείδιμεν ἔμπης, / οὔτ' οὖν Τηλέμαχον, μάλα περ πολύμυθον ἐόντα' ("since we are afraid of no one, all the same, / not even Telemachos, though he speaks many words," *Odyssey* 2.199–200). The interconnectedness between speech and praxis may moreover be so pronounced that the ἔπεα 'words' of a hero may in themselves make up his *aristeia* (or at the very least contribute to it),[28] as we will see in a moment. Perhaps this explains why Menelaos, extolling Peisistratos' words in Book 4, declares that his speech easily presages his character:

> 'τόσα εἶπες, ὅσ' ἂν πεπνυμένος ἀνὴρ
> εἴποι καὶ ῥέξειε . . .'

Odyssey 4.204–205

"you spoke as many things [i.e. words] as a prudent man might say and do . . . "

---

[25] Straightforward literary works may be classified also as oral-performative, as has been shown by e.g. Finnegan 1977:16–24, esp. 17 and Thomas 1992:3–4, 91–93, 102–104, 107–108, and esp. 117–127 and as Silk 2005:5 notes. In keeping with Aristotle's well-known position in the *Poetics*, Silk argues *contra* Worman 2005 that ancient Greek culture, profoundly logocentric as it was, privileged the speaker's or actor's λέξις as opposed to his ὄψις. Thus ἠθοποιία (on which see immediately below) was reified almost entirely through the λέξις of performance. For the anthropology of performance, see Turner 1974 and 1986; for performance as a hermeneutic principle in Homeric studies, see Nagy 1996, Martin 1989, and Hammer 2002, esp. 26–29 (political processes in the *Iliad* as dramatic performances).

[26] Martin 1989, esp. 91, 95–97.

[27] Van Wees 1992:88ff.

[28] See Schofield 1986:14 and discussion below.

Heubeck, West, and Hainsworth 1988:206 *ad loc.* comment that the phrase καὶ ῥέξειε 'and might do' is redundant, having arisen from attraction, as it were, to the heroic ideal of well-roundedness.[29] Indeed, Menelaos' *catachresis* may suggest that a warrior, ideally, *says what he is capable of accomplishing*: that is, words and actions are perfectly coextensive in Homeric mentality, and a speech may therefore even be equated with a hero's finest hour, or *aristeia*.[30] Epic poetry, I might add, acknowledges that ἔργον 'action' has an intellectual/mental origin and continuum, a fact which makes an ἔργον a reflection and representation of thought and of the μῦθος 'speech, speech act' affiliated with it: consider *Odyssey* 2.236, Mentor's comment about the suitors: 'ἔρδειν ἔργα βίαια κακορραφίῃσι νόοιο' ("to commit violent deeds through the evil scheming of their minds"). Understandably, then, as Schofield concludes (1986:15), "much of what is glorious about them [sc. the heroes] is crystallised in the guile or arrogance or nobility of their talk." Diomedes' impassioned reply to Agamemnon's defeatist proposal (*Iliad* 9.31–49) is, by analogy, "as much a feat of prowess as one of his exploits on the battlefield," since "it wins him an immediate award of honour or glory in the applause of the host."[31] Moreover, Odysseus' "masterly oratorical performance" in *Iliad* 2, at a most critical turning point in the plot, may be accounted "the culmination of . . . his *aristeia*."[32] To be sure, the heroic code of πολεμίζειν 'fighting' is not as simple as we may think. The lengthy deliberative speeches reveal the code to be rich in ambiguity and multilayered: in the exercise of εὐβουλία 'rational discussion' heroes may consciously problematize issues, and especially the code's very values, developing rational analysis alongside the exploitation of emotions.[33] The ideal hero, in Schofield's convincing Aristotelian reading of the *Iliad*, is εὔβουλος 'good at deliberation' above all—the philosopher's φρόνιμος 'prudent' man incarnate.[34] Here Schofield's analysis intersects J. Heath's comprehensive discussion of Telemachos' incremental relationship

---

[29] Heubeck, West, and Hainsworth 1988 do not note that the conjunction καὶ (205) = ἤ. Dawe 1993:72 *ad loc.* comments on another *catachresis*: Menelaos praises the quantity ('τόσα εἶπες'), not the quality of Peisitratos' words. As it is, Menelaos refers to the quality: see *Odyssey* 2.199–200 (πολύμυθον) above. For both speaking and accomplishing a word, see also *Iliad* 1.108 (not noted by commentators).

[30] This correspondence is presupposed by the unspoken premise that a continuum exists between mind and body. Having implied in *Odyssey* 4.204–205 the equivalence of speaking and doing, as noted, Menelaos refers in the next verse (206) to speech in a narrower sense ('τοίου γὰρ καὶ πατρός, ὃ καὶ πεπνυμένα βάζεις').

[31] See n28 above.

[32] See n28 above.

[33] Schofield 1986, esp. 28.

[34] Schofield 1986:18n26.

with the adjective πεπνυμένος 'prudent'.[35] As this scholar demonstrates, the lofty epithet, which is associated especially intimately with Telemachos (a total of 46 times in the *Odyssey*), generally refers to someone who uses the effective, authoritative speech of an experienced man. As he comes of age, the Ithakan princeling comes to "earn" or "grow into" his epithet, as Heath puts it, in a gradual process that can be gauged by the change in his manner of speech (whether sincere or dissembling or silent), and its repercussions for others.[36] As I see it, πεπνυμένος 'prudent', as applied to the prince from the beginning of the poem onwards, signals—proleptically and teleologically—the manly continuum of word and deed or of silence and deferred action for which his ὁδός 'journey' will equip him to an enormous degree. The youth's role model in this journey, Athena assures him, will or should be his father, whose image has been given a new lease of life in his mind (*Odyssey* 1.320–322; see Chapter 1) and who, in the goddess's words, was "so successful a man . . . *both in action and in speech*" (*Odyssey* 2.272; Dawe's translation, italics mine).

Πεπνυμένα βάζειν 'to speak prudent things, talk sensibly' (compare *Iliad* 9.58, *Odyssey* 4.206, etc.) and εὐβουλία thus represent equivalent or nearly identical types of mature male behavior. We have seen that in particular, εὐβουλία, "excellence in counsel or sound judgement" (Schofield 1986:6), can be the supreme form of action, or ἔργον. If the most highly prized quality for a commander such as Agamemnon is εὐβουλία,[37] then we may be justified in taking the cue from Schofield's cogent philosophizing interpretation and considering one of the main positions argued in Book 10 of the *Nikomachea*: given that under Aristotle's scheme the highest activity is ἐνέργεια 'moral action' and that the highest form of *energeia* is θεωρία 'thought, contemplation', then education and the organization of the state should be geared towards teaching citizens to cultivate thought 'καλοῦ ἕνεκα', that is, "for the sake of moral beauty."[38] By direct analogy, under the heroic (i.e. honor-driven) code—let us call it the 'epic

---

[35] Cf. the formula πεπνυμένος ἀντίον ηὔδα, which introduces Telemachos' speech (43 times) and Heath 2005, esp. 92–118.

[36] Heath 2005, esp. 92–93, 96, 100, 117. For the similar adultocentric ideal of circumspect thinking and speech, cf. the western Apache Indians: Martin 1989:11. Also cf. Diomedes' 'training' in the negotiation of public speech: Martin 1989:23–24, 105, 108, 124–130. Further on the assembly as a 'school' for heroes, see Chapter 4 n45 below.

[37] See Schofield 1986: "in a supreme military commander it is *euboulia*, understood as ability in tactics, strategy, and the power to persuade, *not warrior prowess*, that counts most . . . Odysseus' main complaints against Agamemnon in 14 is that his plan is a bad plan, not informed by *euboulia*' (25, my italics). For Odysseus' εὐβουλία as king, see Rutherford 1986:146–147, 156 with n62. The hero mentions in his Ἀπόλογοι the adventures in which he proves less than εὔβουλος, with disastrous consequences for his companions: Rutherford 1986:150–151; see *Kyklopeia*, 151; Aiolos' bag of winds, Kirke, 151–152; Skylla, 153 (the hero occupies a 'gray zone' in terms of responsibility and, I should add, εὐβουλία).

[38] *Nikomachean Ethics*, esp. 1177b27–1178a8, 1179b30–1180b28.

system'—education (which is clearly understood e.g. in *Iliad* 9.442–443[39] and, as will be seen, in *Odyssey* 2.314) and generally the structure of Homeric society (or societies) should encourage ultimately the cultivation of εὐβουλία/πεπνυμένα βάζειν ('excellence in deliberation'/'sensible speaking') mainly for the sake of honor. To a secondary yet still meaningful degree, that is, insofar as it may seek to explore the conflict of heroic and non-heroic values, Homeric 'education' would ideally cultivate εὐβουλία in the direction of *cooperation* and *solidarity* among male φίλοι 'friends' on the war front.[40] This educational ideal (which I believe had a basis in reality) is in fact borne out by an important aspect of εὐβουλία/πεπνυμένα βάζειν often overlooked by scholars: μῦθος 'authoritative speech', through which εὐβουλία is actualized, is as a rule meant to be converted to collective action.[41]

Historically speaking, Homeric society and, in general, other societies across time set store by eloquence particularly of the deliberative kind, which they elide with what is later termed εὐβουλία 'excellence in deliberation'. To paraphrase Schofield: good speaking and good judgment are often not sharply distinguished across cultures and poetic traditions.[42] Naturally, then, a large part of Telemachos' overall education—for Athena has already started teaching him from Book 1 (compare Antinoos' unwitting comment at *Odyssey* 1.384–385)—revolves around the exercise in μῦθοι 'words, speech acts' and more particularly, εὐβουλία. Book 2 gives considerable space to the prince's exposure to both activities; the book is nearly a case study in a prince's faltering attempts at deliberative oratory. In general, Athena functions in the first two books as a patient instructor in 'good speaking and good judgment' (see again *Odyssey* 1.384–385, 2.314–315), coaching her charge privately through her protreptic, itself a well-tempered, often eloquent mix of rational thinking and resort to emotion. Such a combination, as Schofield brings out, is the quintessence of εὐβουλία,[43] which by definition will have a 'bottom line'[44]—τὸ πρακτέον 'things to be done'.[45] Debuting in the *Odyssey* as

---

[39] See n16 above.

[40] See Schofield 1986, esp. 17–18 and Graziosi and Haubold 2003, esp. 68, 75. In the view of the latter two scholars the *Iliad*'s militarist attitude toward masculinity, detectable also in the *Odyssey*, prevents Telemachos from maturing fully as an adult male; but cf. Chapters 5–6.

[41] For example, Πολυδάμας πεπνυμένος 'careful Polydamas' (*Iliad* 18.249), Hektor's contemporary, exercises *euboulia* intellectually and verbally for the common good (though in the end Hektor at 18.295 does not heed him, thereby canceling the former's ability to transmute μῦθος into collective ἔργον). Ideally a hero's ability to convert μῦθος into ἔργον depends ultimately on his ability to induce others to *collective action*. See also Heath 2005:97.

[42] Schofield 1986:7–8, 9 with nn10–11. See also Martin 1989:89–92.

[43] Schofield 1986, esp. 258: "the Homeric hero is heroic in mind as well as in action."

[44] In other words, she guides him with her words just as she literally guides him, leading the way to the shore of Ithaka (*Odyssey* 2.405–406) and Pylos (*Odyssey* 2.12), etc.

[45] Schofield 1986:237.

a deliberative speaker (*Odyssey* 1.45–62, etc.), the goddess subsequently exemplifies the relevant skills and methods of an epic εὔβουλος 'proficient deliberator, counselor' in her covert exchanges with Telemachos, and he takes note.

Odysseus, needless to say, is a seasoned εὔβουλος (see, for example, *Odyssey* 3.125–129), and in *Odyssey* 8.169–177 he gives a programmatic statement in effect about εὐβουλία with which it is fitting to conclude this section.[46] The passage confirms that, in the hierarchy of the poem's values, rhetorical and generally intellectual prowess outranks physical beauty and strength (compare 8.177: 'νόον δ᾽ ἀποφώλιός ἐσσι' ["but you are worthless/uneducated in your mind"]). The rhetorical skill meant here is manifestly tied to the deliberative genre (see especially verse 172 below):

> 'ἄλλος μὲν γὰρ εἶδος ἀκιδνότερος πέλει ἀνήρ,
> ἀλλὰ θεὸς μορφὴν ἔπεσι στέφει, οἱ δέ τ᾽ ἐς αὐτὸν
> τερπόμενοι λεύσσουσιν· ὁ δ᾽ ἀσφαλέως ἀγορεύει
> αἰδοῖ μειλιχίῃ, μετὰ δὲ πρέπει ἀγρομένοισιν,
> ἐρχόμενον δ᾽ ἀνὰ ἄστυ θεὸν ὣς εἰσορόωσιν.
> ἄλλος δ᾽ αὖ εἶδος μὲν ἀλίγκιος ἀθανάτοισιν,
> ἀλλ᾽ οὔ οἱ χάρις ἀμφιπεριστέφεται ἐπέεσσιν,
> ὣς καὶ σοὶ εἶδος μὲν ἀριπρεπές, οὐδέ κεν ἄλλως
> οὐδὲ θεὸς τεύξειε, νόον δ᾽ ἀποφώλιός ἐσσι.'

Odyssey 8. 169–177

"One man is weaker in looks,
but a god puts a crown of beauty on his words, and people
gaze at him in pleasure; and he speaks articulately
with conciliatory sensitivity, and he stands out among those who have
assembled,
and they look up to him, as if he were a god, when he goes through the
city.
Then again another man is similar to the immortals in looks
but charm is not put as a crown round his words:
so also you have outstanding looks, and not any differently [i.e. better]
not even a god could fashion your looks—but you are worthless [or uneducated?] in your mind."

Odysseus is talking to the Phaiakian Euryalos, a handsome but callow champion wrestler; the mature king articulates an ideal that is tailored to the needs

---

[46] Rutherford 1986:145–160 does not cite this testimonium. (Schofield analyzes mainly Iliadic εὐβουλία but notes [1986:10n13] the examination of this attribute outside the *Iliad* in Thalman 1984:182.)

of adult, logocentric society.⁴⁷ It is instructive that his own son Telemachos, for all the godlike glamour he at first exudes in the assembly in Ithaka, falls miserably short of this very ideal.

This is a good point to return to the *Telemachy*. We have seen that—in Homeric ('emic') terms—Telemachos' psychology presents a distinctive 'deficit'. As a child he was deprived of the customary paternal injunction of αἰὲν ἀριστεύειν 'always to be the best', though the elite to which he belonged would have more generally conduced to his immersion in this ethos.⁴⁸ Perhaps more crucial, the ἀκλεής 'unaccounted for' disappearance of his father (dead or alive?) deprived him of the second-hand *kleos* that would have devolved upon him almost instantaneously through the social mechanism, well under-stood by the poet and his audience, of 'synecdochic transferral'. Instead of *kleos* of this kind (compare *Odyssey* 1.240) Odysseus has bequeathed to him in perpetuity the traditional lugubrious double bill, ὀδύνας τε γόους τε 'pain and lamentation' (*Odyssey* 1.242–243).⁴⁹ Telemachos himself admits that he has no narrative version of his father, or at least not a convincing one. It is this lack that impels him under Athena's motivation to embark on a quest for *kleos* in the sense of narratives of—or, rather, about—Odysseus: Is he alive? And regardless of whether he is alive or not, what is the content of his *kleos*? If he knew this Telemachos might be able to live up to the ideal of preserving his father's glory like a proper hero (compare the ideal Iliadic son, Hektor, at *Iliad* 6.444ff.).⁵⁰

If Book 1 brought into close focus the psychological consequences of Odysseus' absence, and indeed represented these in terms of Telemachos' rela-tion to his father's *kleos*, then Book 2, in which the prince officially denounces the suitors, shows up his palpable shortcomings with regard to πεπνυμένα βάζειν 'speaking prudent things' and carrying out ἔργα 'deeds, actions'. As we will note in some detail, this book exposes the distance separating him from κλέος ἔχειν 'the acquisition of *kleos*'. In Book 1 the youth was fortified more than ever before in his conviction that he was the son Odysseus. Now, in the assembly in Book 2, he voices this conviction repeatedly and publicly, citing now his πατήρ 'father' (2.46, 131, 215, 218, 264, 360), now Ὀδυσσεύς 'Odysseus'

---

⁴⁷ See n15 above. See also Hesiod *Theogony* 83ff., a famous parallel. Schofield 1986:25 quotes Kirk: "with few exceptions he [sc. Odysseus in the *Iliad*] is represented as behaving extremely rationally, indeed as initiating complex processes of analysis and decision-making that would do credit to Bertrand Russell himself."

⁴⁸ Cf. also Diomedes (*Iliad* 6.222–223); Chapter 1 n94 and Chapter 4.

⁴⁹ 'ἐμοὶ δ' ὀδύνας τε γόους / κάλλιπεν', *Odyssey* 1.242–243. Cf. the funerary epigram about two brothers, no. 22 (Clairmont, p89, Vari, Attica, end of the fifth century BC), verse 3: πατρὶ φίλωι καὶ μητρὶ λιπόντε ἀμφοῖμ μέγα πένθος. The formulation of *Odyssey* 1.240–243, as a whole, recalls that of a conventional funerary inscription.

⁵⁰ For Hektor as an ideal son, see chapter 4 of Wöhrle 1999.

(2.59, 352), and, once, πατήρ and 'Οδυσσεύς together (2.71).[51] Perhaps these references are signs of the first stage in the process of κλέος ἔχειν 'winning *kleos*'. Now he must move beyond self-confident affirmation to proving that he is a *worthy* son, and filial worthiness will be proved only to the degree that he evinces prestigious well-roundedness at home and abroad.

Telemachos' First Public Performance

In *Odyssey* 1.272–274, Athena instructs the prince to denounce the suitors the next day in the assembly and thereby frighten them to leave the palace for good. At *Odyssey* 1.368–380, especially 373–374, he informs them of his plan, minutes after proclaiming his exclusive right to utter μῦθοι 'words' at home (1.358–359). Μῦθος, we noted, generally means 'a speech act' endowed with authority, and no μῦθος can be more authoritative than a command. Telemachos then quotes the agenda of the next day's assembly: 'ἵν' ὑμῖν μῦθον ἀπηλεγέως ἀποείπω,/ἐξιέναι μεγάρων' ("so that I may forthrightly declare my command [literally, word], / namely get out of the palace," *Odyssey* 1.373–374).[52] The unusual session of the people's assembly breaks up unusually fast and with no results (*Odyssey* 2.256ff.), despite its highly promising start.[53] This, as de Jong comments, is the prince's first public performance.[54] We have seen that in Book 1 Telemachos, far from being a symposiarch, as it were, is forced into a corner. Yet now, thanks to his initiative, Ithaka stumbles out of the constitutional anomaly that has brought it close to the savage *anomie* of Kyklops' isle: this may be the implication of the *analepsis*—at the beginning of the assembly scene—referring to Aigyptios' son Antiphos, the last of Odysseus' crew to be devoured by ἄγριος Κύκλωψ 'savage Kyklops' (*Odyssey* 2.19–20).[55] The phrase ἀγορὴν πολύφημον 'the assembly-place

---

[51] Six out of a total of nine references to his father occur in Telemachos' public speeches. For the celebratory emphasis on the relationship between father (Odysseus) and son (Telemachos) in Book 16, see de Jong 2001:385, Heath 2005:105, and Chapter 5 below.

[52] According to Martin 1993:235, the poet, in deliberately echoing Achilles' phrase at *Iliad* 9.309 ('χρὴ μὲν δὴ τὸν μῦθον ἀπηλεγέως ἀποειπεῖν'), implies that Telemachos is deploying the speaking style of this premier adult hero. Telemachos' advance notice recalls a "table of contents speech" (de Jong 2001:15 *ad Odyssey* 1.81–95), except that the speaker is serving notice to his auditors, not the poem's audience.

[53] See also n17 above. The irregular nature of the assembly can also be inferred from the fact that: a) the convener of the assembly—Telemachos—is not also the first to speak (*Odyssey* 2.15) nor, as would be customary, is he the last; b) Aigyptios, the first speaker, remarks that this is the first assembly in almost 20 years (*Odyssey* 2.26–27): see de Jong 2001:47 *ad Odyssey* 2.15–37. Cf. Jones 1991:136 *ad Odyssey* 2.24: not without precedent (*Iliad* 20.4–18), Aigyptios' age and experience virtually entitle him to be the first to address the assembly. (I do not agree with Heubeck, West, and Hainsworth 1988:131 *ad Odyssey* 2.26–27: "the poet regarded the institution [sc. assembly] as peripheral to the political organization of Ithaca.")

[54] De Jong 2001:47 *ad Odyssey* 2.6–14.

[55] For the Kyklopes' lawlessness, see esp. *Odyssey* 9.112: 'τοῖσιν δ' οὔτ' ἀγοραὶ βουληφόροι οὔτε θέμιστες.' In his first speech Telemachos invokes Themis as the goddess of the ἀγορή (*Odyssey*

where much is talked about', moreover, which the poet later uses in a description in the same scene (*Odyssey* 2.150), may be an ironical allusion to Kyklops' complete ignorance of public matters and public speech.[56]

Under these exceedingly eccentric circumstances Telemachos convokes the ἀγορή 'assembly' with godlike aplomb (*Odyssey* 2.5–7). With Athena's help he arrives radiant in the glow of θεσπεσίην . . . χάριν 'divine . . . charm' (*Odyssey* 2.12), drawing admiration from the crowd and exuding regal *dignitas* and τιμή 'honor' (*Odyssey* 2.10–14, compare 2.33).[57] His aura moves the elders (γέροντες) to cede to him the προεδρία 'place in the front', hence, literally, 'precedence':

βῆ ῥ’ ἴμεν εἰς ἀγορήν, παλάμῃ δ’ ἔχε χάλκεον ἔγχος,
οὐκ οἶος, ἅμα τῷ γε δύω κύνες ἀργοὶ ἕποντο.
θεσπεσίην δ’ ἄρα τῷ γε χάριν κατέχευεν Ἀθήνη.
τὸν δ’ ἄρα πάντες λαοὶ ἐπερχόμενον θηεῦντο·
ἕζετο δ’ ἐν πατρὸς θώκῳ, εἶξαν δὲ γέροντες.

Odyssey 2.10–14

He set out for the assembly-place, and in his hand he grasped a bronze
    spear,
[he was] not alone, two shining dogs followed along with him.
And Athena poured divine charm upon him.
All the people gazed in wonder at him as he approached;
he sat in his father's seat, and the elders made room [sc. for him].

This stylized snapshot depicts Odysseus' heir-apparent striding forth with self-confidence (compare again verse 5) as warlord and king, accompanied almost heraldically with two hunting hounds, obvious status symbols.[58] The image as a whole correlates with the Archaic ideology surrounding the

---

2.68). For the external *analepsis* about the tragic death of Antiphos, see de Jong 2001:47 *ad Odyssey* 2.15–37 who, as the other commentators, does not however detect any political allusions here. (Dawe 1993:93 *ad Odyssey* 2.20 notes that Antiphos is not even mentioned in the *Kyklopeia*. Heubeck, West, and Hainsworth 1988:130 *ad loc.* regard the reference to him in Book 2 as "a slight distraction.")

56 Bakker 2002a:137 remarks this deliberate allusion, connecting it moreover with the φήμη that Aigyptios utters in *Odyssey* 2.33–34. Polyphemos as an inept speaker: Heath 2005:81–83.

57 *Odyssey* 2.33: ‘ἐσθλός μοι δοκεῖ εἶναι, ὀνήμενος . . .’ Τιμή, on which see van Wees 1992, esp. 98–99 and Chapter 1 above, may sometimes be equivalent to Weberian charisma, on which see Gerth and Mills 1958.

58 Heubeck, West, and Hainsworth 1988:129 *ad Odyssey* 2.11–13: "wealthy men may keep them as pets. (xvii 309–10, Il. xxii 69, xxiii 173)." Dogs at a hero's side are however also a signpost of initiation: see Chapter 5 below.

charismatic king.[59] Yet his speech, which will suddenly be interrupted at verse 79, will prove a disappointing performance both dramatically and stylistically.

Aigyptios—bent in his old age and long experience—visually counterpoises Telemachos, tall and upright and inexperienced (see verse 16).[60] Soon the elder will jubilantly hail the prince as ἐσθλόν 'noble' and ὀνημένον 'lucky' (*Odyssey* 2.33). The first epithet, prompted by the youth's charismatic, exalted appearance, surely must reinforce his confidence, while the makaristic overtones of ὀνημένος and the wish that follows (*Odyssey* 2.33–34) must gladden Telemachos; for, as the poet remarks, he considers the exclamation to be good luck (*Odyssey* 2.35: χαῖρε δὲ φήμη 'he was cheered at the saying').[61] In this favorable climate Telemachos is impatient to address the audience (*Odyssey* 2.36). But first he must replace the military emblem of his ἔγχος 'spear' with a σκῆπτρον 'scepter',[62] the symbol of empowerment by his peers.[63]

Rhetorically speaking, the prince's speech is a heterogeneous mixture of personal and public communication that is relatively incoherent (ἀνοικονόμητος 'disorganized'—because of inexperience?—according to Herakleides Pontikos' comment),[64] psychologically maladroit at critical points, and ineffective. The speaker scores a moral victory (as de Jong also remarks),[65] but—crucially—without even proposing any specific action. (In his second speech, however, he will put forward a specific but impracticable proposal in the form of an ultimatum in verses *Odyssey* 2.138ff.[66] In the course of his impassioned oration, Telemachos slowly ascends a scale of emotions, especially from verses 2.66ff. on, climaxing in a "burst of hysteria."[67] Like a

---

[59] This constitutes narrative misdirection, which the ancient scholia also recognized: see de Jong 2001:xv, s.v. 'misdirection'.

[60] ὃς δὴ γήραϊ κυφὸς ἔην καὶ μυρία ᾔδη. Old man Haliserthes and Mentor are the prince's other two Ithakan allies who will speak; all three begin their address in the same manner (Heubeck, West, and Hainsworth:1988:130 *ad Odyssey* 2.25).

[61] Dawe 1993:93 *ad Odyssey* 2.20: "The concluding benediction is ridiculous." This beatitude/ felicitation is however legitimate because: a) Telemachos has an almost supernaturally imposing and handsome appearance, as we have seen; and b) Aigyptios suspects that the speaker bears news about the return of the army. For the requirements for a *makarismos*, see chapter 2 of Petropoulos 2003. For φήμη as a type of *makarismos*, see Chapter 2 n12.

[62] This gesture, dictated by Homeric *savoir faire*, is understood here. See also Heubeck, West, and Hainsworth 1988:88 *ad Odyssey* 1.104.

[63] See e.g. Heubeck, West, and Hainsworth 1988:131–132 *ad Odyssey* 2.37 and Jones 1991:137 *ad loc.*

[64] Heubeck, West, and Hainsworth 1988:132 *ad Odyssey* 2.40ff. also connect the incoherence to Telemachos' inexperience. Cf. *Odyssey* 2.200 (not noted by Herakleides or Heubeck, West, and Hainsworth), where Eurymachos characterizes the prince as πολύμυθος. At present the callow youth is πολύμυθος; later on, having matured and grown self-confident, Telemachos will prove ὀλιγόμυθος, we might say, as Jones 1988:192 *ad Odyssey* 20.338–344 also remarks.

[65] De Jong 2001:46.

[66] Heubeck, West, and Hainsworth 1988:132 *ad Odyssey* 2.40ff.

[67] Dawe 1993:97 *ad Odyssey* 2.70–79.

tapestry his speech unravels hopelessly when he strips himself of the aura of the Weberian charisma with which Athena has invested him.[68]

His speech begins as a private answer to Aigyptios (*Odyssey* 2.40–41):

'ὦ γέρον, οὐχ ἑκὰς οὗτος ἀνήρ, τάχα δ' εἴσεαι αὐτός,
ὃς λαὸν ἤγειρα· μάλιστα δέ μ' ἄλγος ἱκάνει.'

"Old man, this man [about whom you ask] is not far away, and soon you
      will yourself know
who gathered together—I did—the people, because distress has come
      upon me in particular."

The unspecified ἀνήρ who is at hand (compare *Odyssey* 2.40: οὗτος 'this man') is announced from the start, but before Telemachos identifies him he inserts parenthetical information (*Odyssey* 2.40: 'τάχα δ' εἴσεαι αὐτός' ["soon you will yourself know"]) that whets the old man's curiosity still more. Suddenly, to Aigyptios' surprise, the verb (which has no personal pronoun) at the end of the relative clause in the next verse reveals the person who convened the assembly: 'ὃς λαὸν ἤγειρα' ("who gathered together—I did—the people"). Telemachos thus answers the elder's question, 'τὶς ὧδ' ἤγειρε;' ("Who has brought about this assembly like this?" *Odyssey* 2.28). Like an embryonic Odysseus the youth defers the revelation of his identity; but the comparison to his father ends here.

Who, incidentally, are the λαός 'people' and what exactly is implied by Telemachos' move to λαὸν ἀγείρειν 'convene the people'?[69] He creates the λαός 'people', who in principle also include the suitors, in Book 2; yet the suitors resist this grouping and strive for dispersal and individuation, which particularly suits the formulaic-sounding emphasis on ἕκαστος 'each' in Leiokritos' last speech (*Odyssey* 2.252). In Book 2 (to oversimplify Haubold's nuanced discussion), as well as in *Iliad* 2, there is a tug of war between two questions: will the λαός 'people' remain in the background, a passive, malleable mass, or will they emerge an ambivalent power that the protagonists will have to reckon with?

Telemachos' Χρεῖος

The Little Prince's speech subsequently develops into a public oration (*Odyssey* 2.43–79) even as it is still being directed to Aigyptios. This transformation takes place *between* verses 42–43, as is evident from the transition to the plural personal pronoun ὑμῖν 'to you' (*Odyssey* 2.43). This heteroclite fusion of private address and public oration is arguably dictated by a

---

[68] For charisma, see n57 above.
[69] For *laos* in the *Odyssey*: Haubold 2000, esp. 110–115.

clever rhetorical strategy—one that is also highly convenient—on the part of Telemachos. Wishing to forestall any public (political) consequences that may arise from the denunciation he plans to deliver, he *pretends* a priori (*Odyssey* 2.42–45) that the death of his father—the king and quasi-father of the people, as he will put it (*Odyssey* 2.46–47),[70] is, paradoxically, a purely family matter (*Odyssey* 2.44–45: 'οὔτε τι δήμιον . . . / ἀλλ᾽ ἐμὸν αὐτοῦ χρεῖος' ["not something of public interest . . ./ but my own business"]).[71] Under Ithaka's patriarchal system the common denominator of 'father' encourages this intertwining of private and public in Telemachos' speech. As he explains, the news of the fleet's arrival (*Odyssey* 2.42: 'οὔτε τιν᾽ ἀγγελίην στρατοῦ ἔκλυον ἐρχομένοιο' ["I have not heard any message about the army coming"]) would be an altogether different matter: it would be of public interest. Heubeck, West, and Hainsworth 1988:132 *ad Odyssey* 2.44 cite the *Odyssey*'s general tendency to minimize the political consequences stemming from the fate of Odysseus' family. To pursue this comment further: Telemachos' avowedly apolitical stance here may be part of his larger rhetorical strategy, which I wish to illustrate. (A related strategy, aiming at the arousal of pity, likewise impels him to represent his father's death as a foregone conclusion and to treat this as a deeply personal loss; see *Odyssey* 2.46–47.)[72] Another factor that encourages him to 'privatize' the consequences of his father's disappearance is plausibly psychological: his own plight (verging, we might say, on trauma), along with his relative immaturity, leads him to foreground his loss not only in his private conversations but just as persistently in public. It is all too tempting for him psychologically, as well as politically expedient, to play down the objective, communal fallout from his father's absence and to overvalue, somewhat solipsistically, its subjective consequences. As he tells Nestor in *Odyssey* 3.82–83, 'πρῆξις δ᾽ ἥδ᾽ ἰδίη, οὐ δήμιος, ἣν ἀγορεύω. / πατρὸς ἐμοῦ κλέος εὐρὺ μετέρχομαι . . .' ("the business at hand is private, not public, which I am speaking of: / I come in quest of news [*kleos*] of my father . . . ").[73]

The noun χρεῖος (*Odyssey* 2.45) is the overarching theme of the speeches Telemachos makes in Book 2. As Heubeck, West, and Hainsworth 1988:124 *ad Odyssey* 1.409 remark, this term, commonly denoting a 'debt', is used in this verse (as also in *Odyssey* 1.409) in the special sense of 'personal matter'. Yet even in these passages 'personal matter' shades into 'personal business', for,

---

[70] For the motif/comparison of the 'gentle father of his people', see Appendix II.

[71] The boundaries between private life and public interest were indistinct not only for πολιτευόμενοι in Classical Athens (see e.g. Ober 1989:109–111 and Gomme 1970:318 on the motives of the tyrannicides in Thucydides 6.54ff.), but also in Homeric society/societies.

[72] For pity as an instrument in later oratory, see Dover 1994:195–201. De Jong 2001:49 *ad Odyssey* 2.46 notes Telemachos' pretence in this passage but does not link it to his broader apolitical stance.

[73] On *kleos* as 'news', see Chapter 2 above.

as Telemachos will soon admit (*Odyssey* 2.48–58), his paramount concern is the parlous state of his family's possessions. He thus reinstates the primary economic meaning of χρεῖος, as will also be apparent when he ironically envisages receiving compensation from the Ithakans. Τίσις 'requital, revenge' too is a fundamentally economic notion, based on the practice of debt collection. So the prince's personal 'debt' also conceals the dark metaphor of 'settling a score'. Telemachos dreamt of τίσις 'requital' in Book 1, and at the end of his second speech in Book 2 he will announce outright his plan for revenge on the suitors: "but I shall call to the everlasting gods / in case Zeus may perhaps grant that deeds of requital take place. / Then, unavenged you would perish inside this house" (*Odyssey* 2.143–145).[74]

Odysseus' Χρεῖος

It may be instructive to compare the χρεῖος 'debt' pursued by Telemachos with the one Odysseus sought to retrieve as a youth according to Book 21. The passage in question occurs in the lengthy excursus on the hero's bow (*Odyssey* 21.11–41).[75] The parallel phraseology in the excursus and in the prince's first speech suggests, deliberately in my opinion, not only the parallel lives of father and son, but also the *telling contrast in respect of their 'education'*.[76] Here is the *historiola* about Odysseus:

> ἦ τοι Ὀδυσσεὺς
> ἦλθε μετὰ χρεῖος, τό ῥά οἱ πᾶς δῆμος ὄφελλε·
> μῆλα γὰρ ἐξ Ἰθάκης Μεσσήνιοι ἄνδρες ἄειραν
> νηυσὶ πολυκλήϊσι τριηκόσι᾽ ἠδὲ νομῆας.
> τῶν ἕνεκ᾽ ἐξεσίην πολλὴν ὁδὸν ἦλθεν Ὀδυσσεὺς
> παιδνὸς ἐών· πρὸ γὰρ ἧκε πατὴρ ἄλλοι τε γέροντες.

> *Odyssey* 21.16–21

> Odysseus
> had come after [i.e. to recover] a debt which the entire community
>   owed to him.
> For Messenian men had lifted from Ithaka sheep
> and three hundred herdsmen in ships with many benches for oarsmen.
> On this account Odysseus had gone a long way on a mission,
> a 'boy'; for his father and other elders besides had sent him forth.

---

[74] Compare his threat at *Odyssey* 2.316–317, cited in n79 below.
[75] De Jong 2001:506 notes that this excursus is an external *analepsis*. See also Chapter 5 below.
[76] Or to put it differently, 'parallel but dissimilar lives'.

The poet describes objectively the ostensibly conventional social function of the young Odysseus' mission (see *Odyssey* 21.21: παιδνὸς ἐών 'being a boy').[77] The youth's father and other prominent Ithakans assign him a dangerous expedition. Acting *in the name of the dêmos* (see 21.18), Odysseus sets off to recover a straightforwardly economic χρεῖος *from another dêmos* (21.16–17). His mission abroad (21.20: ἐξεσίην 'mission' <ἐξίημι 'I send forth') is conceived as an expressly political and hence public action. In contrast, Telemachos' ἐξεσίη 'mission' is presented in a different light from Book 1 onwards. Because Ithaka lacks a legitimate government, Athena must stand in for the rulers and delegate to the youth the *secret* plan of the ἐξεσίη. Telemachos in his turn is forced to undertake the mission *in secret from the suitors* (and his mother), despite the fact that he formally informs them of his plan earlier in the assembly. It is obvious that the prince—very conveniently—conceives his ὁδός 'journey' as strictly private. Under more normal circumstances he would have been able to be more candid about the public issues raised by the crisis in his οἶκος 'house'.

Homer aptly encapsulates the difference between Telemachos and Odysseus as he is featured in the *historiola* by a paradoxical convergence in phraseology: young Odysseus ἦλθε μετὰ χρεῖος, τό ῥά οἱ πᾶς δῆμος ὄφελλε ('had come [literally, came] after a debt which the entire community owed him', *Odyssey* 21.17); Telemachos, on the other side, as Athena herself foresees, will travel 'νόστον πευσόμενον πατρὸς φίλου, ἤν που ἀκούσῃ' "to seek information about his dear father's return, if perhaps he may hear of it" (*Odyssey* 1.94), and as the prince himself declares, 'πατρὸς ἐμοῦ κλέος εὐρὺ μετέρχομαι, ἤν που ἀκούσω . . .' ("I come in quest of news of my father that has spread from afar, on the chance I may hear . . . ," *Odyssey* 3.83).[78] The χρεῖος 'debt' pursued by the former pertains to a public and economic matter that is entrusted to him mainly by his father; the latter's χρεῖος concerns the quest for news about his absent father. Both expeditions, even so, are similar in that a) they entail military action or at least considerable danger,[79] and b) their underlying rationale is intended ultimately to mark the participants' coming of age. We have seen that Athena signals this educational aspect in her 'table of contents speech' in the beginning of Book 1:[80]

---

[77] See Chapter 5.

[78] See n73 above.

[79] See *Odyssey* 2.316–317: 'πειρήσω ὥς κ' ὕμμι κακὰς ἐπὶ κῆρας ἰήλω,/ἠὲ Πύλονδ' ἐλθών, ἢ αὐτοῦ τῷδ' ἐνὶ δήμῳ.' This homicidal threat includes two disjunctive possibilities that imply, *pace* Dawe, a train of events more complex than a coup that will be planned in Pylos or Ithaka. Following Aristarchos, Dawe 1993:115 *ad loc.* considers these verses inconsequent and therefore spurious, on the grounds that "it is never directly suggested in our *Odyssey* that in his travels Telemachos will be doing anything beyond making inquiries after his lost father." See further Chapter 5.

[80] De Jong 2001:15–16 *ad Odyssey* 1.81–95.

'πέμψω δ' ἐς Σπάρτην τε καὶ ἐς Πύλον ἠμαθόεντα,
νόστον πευσόμενον πατρὸς φίλου, ἤν που ἀκούσῃ,
ἠδ' ἵνα μιν κλέος ἐσθλὸν ἐν ἀνθρώποισιν ἔχῃσιν.'[81]

Odyssey 1.93–95

"After that I shall send him off to Sparta and sandy Pylos
to seek information about his dear father's return, if perhaps he may
> hear of it,
and so that a fine reputation (*kleos*) among human beings may accrue to
> him."

Telemachos' Οἶκος

To return to *Odyssey* 2.46ff., in Telemachos' δημηγορία 'public speech' he dates
his father's certain death to the past twenty years (2.46). He next moves on
to the calamitous here and now, decrying in overly emotional language the
even more serious (compare μεῖζον: literally, 'greater') aspect of his personal
tragedy (2.48–49), namely, the utter waste of his father's estate by the suitors.[82]
The ancient scholia, in common with some modern scholars who apparently
focus on the word βίοτον 'property, livelihood' (2.49), suppose—with embar-
rassment—that the young man is thoughtlessly, "crassly materialistic."[83] Yet
Telemachos is hardly insensitive; for all his hype, he is simply registering a
social truth that he also bewails in Book 1.[84] Archaic and Classical sources
indicate that the οἶκος (see *Odyssey* 2.48: οἶκον ἅπαντα 'the entire *oikos*')
is conceived here as a descent group headed by a κύριος 'head of a family'
and comprising his land assets among other things.[85] Unsurprisingly, then,
Telemachos resorts to the only relevant social and economic concept available to Archaic ideology (*per contra* the concept of, say, a 'wedded couple'
did not exist).[86] Given that the union of a κύριος 'head of a family' and his
assets constituted his οἶκος (*oikos*), Telemachos forthrightly invokes the two
respects in which his or more precisely his father's οἶκος has supposedly

---

[81] See the opening of Chapter 1 for translation of the full passage.

[82] *Odyssey* 2.48: ἅπαντα; 2.49 πάγχυ, πάμπαν, and the assonant verbs διαρραίσει and ὀλέσσει.
See also Heubeck, West, and Hainsworth 1988:133 *ad loc.* From *Odyssey* 19.580 it is plain that
Telemachos overdraws his impending 'bankruptcy'.

[83] The ancient scholia rationalize the prince's statement as follows: 'οὐχ ὡς προκρίνων τοῦ
πατρὸς τὴν οὐσίαν, ἀλλὰ τὴν κατηγορίαν αὔξων τῶν νέων· ἄλλως τε τοῦτο μὲν ἀμφίβολον,
ἐκεῖνο δὲ πρόδηλον.' Cf. Heubeck, West, and Hainsworth 1988:133 *ad Odyssey* 2.46–49 and esp.
Dawe 1993:95 *ad loc.* ("crassly materialistic").

[84] Telemachos thinks in openly economic terms also in the same speech (*Odyssey* 1.74ff.: 'ἐμοὶ δέ
κε κέρδιον εἴη . . . ') and in his reply to Antinoos (*Odyssey* 1.133ff.).

[85] See Ferrari 2002:195 for the Classical evidence.

[86] Ferrari 2002:195, 198.

been destroyed. Moreover, given that patriarchy's "ground rule number one"[87] required the son to biologically perpetuate his father and his *genos*, how can Telemachos do so while his οἶκος is shrinking dangerously fast?

Patriarchy and *Kleos* in a Minor Key

Before treating the remainder of the δημηγορία 'public speech' it may be useful to roughly outline the structure of inner conflict in which the poet depicts Telemachos' character development, particularly in response to his dilemma at home. The quasi-legal question—insoluble in my view—of the ἐρημία, or 'heirless state',[88] threatening Odysseus' οἶκος and the related matter of Penelope's remarriage cannot concern the present discussion.[89] What is relevant is Homer's contrastive treatment of the *Telemachy*'s vacillating protagonist. In one view, as we will see in the next chapter, Homeric social convention has *already authorized* the youth to succeed his father as κύριος (in effect, 'lord of the manor'), provided that he first arranges for his mother's remarriage.[90] From a symmetrically opposite viewpoint, however, this son is *unqualified* to be declared κύριος: from this practical vantage-point, as Telemachos clearly demonstrates in his two main speeches in Book 2, he is unable to replace his father even temporarily (assuming he is alive), far less to succeed him in his own right (assuming he is dead). Under the patriarchal system of the epic as analyzed by Wöhrle, a son must at all costs prove successful—in respect of ἔπος 'word' and ἔγχος 'spearmanship, war', I might add (compare Nestor's two sons at *Odyssey* 4.211)—but he never is permitted to outshine his father so long as he lives.[91] Telemachos is therefore obliged indefinitely to remain a *Nebenfigur* overshadowed by Odysseus. 'Mentor' justifies the general state of paternal domination, a state of affairs that exists, notably, *at the expense of young men's kleos*. As 'Mentor' puts it in his exhortation in *Odyssey* 2.270–277:

Τηλέμαχ', οὐδ' ὄπιθεν κακὸς ἔσσεαι οὐδ' ἀνοήμων,
εἰ δή τοι σοῦ πατρὸς ἐνέστακται μένος ἠΰ,
οἷος κεῖνος ἔην τελέσαι ἔργον τε ἔπος τε.
οὔ τοι ἔπειθ' ἁλίη ὁδὸς ἔσσεται οὐδ' ἀτέλεστος.
εἰ δ' οὐ κείνου γ' ἐσσὶ γόνος καὶ Πηνελοπείης,
οὔ σέ γ' ἔπειτα ἔολπα τελευτήσειν ἃ μενοινᾷς.
παῦροι γάρ τοι παῖδες ὁμοῖοι πατρὶ πέλονται,
οἱ πλέονες κακίους, παῦροι δέ τε πατρὸς ἀρείους.'[92]

---

[87] Wöhrle 1999:35–36.
[88] MacDowell 1989, esp. 15 (cited by Ferrari 2002:195).
[89] De Jong 2001:29–31 (with bibliography) *ad Odyssey* 1.249–251.
[90] See de Jong 2001:33 *ad Odyssey* 1.296–297 for testimonia from the *Odyssey*.
[91] Wöhrle 1999:37–48.
[92] See Wöhrle 1999, esp. 41–44, and 124–125 for the proverbial (according to Stanford 1958:244 *ad Odyssey* 2.277) conviction that every generation is unavoidably worse than the preceding one. In

"Telemachos, in future you will not be fainthearted or unintelligent
if really your father's fine determination has been instilled in you—
considering what a man he was in carrying out both words and deeds—
then for you your journey will be neither in vain nor unfulfilled.
But if you are not his offspring and Penelope's,
then I do not expect that you will fulfill what you desire.
For few sons turn out to be like their father,
more are worse, and few [are] better than their father."

Prince Telemachos, cannot, as a *Nebenfigur*, be worthy of his father until he embarks on his mission abroad and gains *kleos*.

Telemachos' wavering behavior throughout the *Telemachy* and even beyond may be put down to the contradictions and tensions inherent in epic patriarchy: the son is a man, but not more so than his father; for, indeed, *there is no man equal to his father*, a fact Athena intimates at *Odyssey* 2.276 and which Telemachos bitterly underscores in the same book. On the other hand, as we just noted, the father exercises power over his son until he (the son) succeeds him—and in his turn exercises over *his* son the type of authority that holds in check this son's *kleos* and creates the same tensions between the two.[93] The contradictory nature of patriarchal ideology is reflected by certain of Telemachos' comments and is borne out by his parents' admission that their son now has the right κήδεσθαι τοῦ οἴκου 'to look after the house', see *Odyssey* 18.338–339, 19.85–88, 160–161. These conflicting positions may be summed up in this manner: a) 'I am a man equal to my father and lord of my manor (see *Odyssey* 1.358–359, 19.160–161) and therefore I may even kill the suitors when I return from my trip to Pylos and Sparta' (see *Odyssey* 2.314–318, compare 1.289–297); vs. b) 'There is no man <nor will there ever be a man> like Odysseus who might drive out the suitors' (see especially *Odyssey* 2.58ff., 16.71–72, 88–89).[94] These contradictions are not imposed by rhetorical

---

the light of Wöhrle's reading of *Odyssey* 2.270ff. the passage gains coherence, obviating the condemnation by Dawe 1993 of the essential verses 276–277. See also n93 immediately below. For a different reading of *Odyssey* 2.270ff., see Μανακίδου 2002:144–145.

[93] Wöhrle 1999:37–48. Symbolically speaking, there is perhaps no greater instance of this hegemonizing seniority system at work (for which cf. *Odyssey* 19.183–185) than *Odyssey* 21.128–129. Here Telemachos, literally equivalent in physical strength to Odysseus (see also *Odyssey* 14.175–177), is ready to string the bow when his father nods to him, checking him from doing this. See also n95.

[94] Haubold 2000:141–143 proposes a sociopolitical interpretation of ἀνήρ: particularly in Books 21 and 23 Odysseus is "the man" who will single out a group of "'non-people' which it [sc. the *Odyssey*] destroys in the interest of the larger whole." See also Chapter 6 for the liquidation of the "non-people" suitors.

requirements; see especially *Odyssey* 16.71–72, 88–89 above.[95] Rather, they delineate the structure of the prince's entrapment in the decaying state of Ithaka. This patriarchal system, as we have seen, on the one hand anoints him (at times objectively, at others opportunistically) *his father's successor*, and on the other hand, it disempowers him, denying him the external but also the deeper possibilities for acting as a *hero and a successor*. For the moment, he is incapable even of being a *Nebenfigur*. As for the *kleos* he is to gain through his voyage, Athena is most explicit: *it will be minor in comparison to his father's*.

∽

'ἐγὼ δὲ ἄλογος εἰμί.'

'ἐγὼ ἰσχνόφωνος εἰμί.'

Moses to Yahweh, *Exodus* 6:12, 30

Let us return to Telemachos' speech. In the "whining self-pity" of *Odyssey* 2.58ff.,[96] he makes a confession that is hardly flattering. It is in fact the reverse, indeed the subversion of heroic boasting:[97]

'οὐ γὰρ ἔπ' ἀνὴρ,
οἷος Ὀδυσσεὺς ἔσκεν, ἀρὴν ἀπὸ οἴκου ἀμῦναι.
ἡμεῖς δ' οὔ νύ τι τοῖοι ἀμυνέμεν· ἦ καὶ ἔπειτα
λευγαλέοι τ' ἐσόμεσθα καὶ οὐ δεδαηκότες ἀλκήν.
ἦ τ' ἂν ἀμυναίμην, εἴ μοι δύναμίς γε παρείη.
οὐ γὰρ ἔτ' ἀνσχετὰ ἔργα τετεύχαται, οὐδ' ἔτι καλῶς
οἶκος ἐμὸς διόλωλε. νεμεσσήθητε καὶ αὐτοί,
ἄλλους τ' αἰδέσθητε περικτίονας ἀνθρώπους,
οἳ περιναιετάουσι· θεῶν δ' ὑποδείσατε μῆνιν,
μή τι μεταστρέψωσιν ἀγασσάμενοι κακὰ ἔργα.
λίσσομαι ἠμὲν Ζηνὸς Ὀλυμπίου ἠδὲ Θέμιστος,
ἥ τ' ἀνδρῶν ἀγορὰς ἠμὲν λύει ἠδὲ καθίζει·
σχέσθε, φίλοι, καί μ' οἶον ἐάσατε πένθεϊ λυγρῷ
τείρεσθ', εἰ μή πού τι πατὴρ ἐμὸς ἐσθλὸς Ὀδυσσεὺς
δυσμενέων κάκ' ἔρεξεν ἐϋκνήμιδας Ἀχαιούς·
τῶν μ' ἀποτινύμενοι κακὰ ῥέζετε δυσμενέοντες,
τούτους ὀτρύνοντες. ἐμοὶ δέ κε κέρδιον εἴη
ὑμέας ἐσθέμεναι κειμήλιά τε πρόβασίν τε.

---

[95] In *Odyssey* 21.131–135 he pretends that he has regressed to the condition of feckless immaturity (*Odyssey* 21.132–133: 'νεώτερός εἰμι καὶ οὔ πω χερσὶ πέποιθα / ἄνδρ' ἀπαμύνασθαι . . . '); cf. *Odyssey* 2.62, where he is sincere.

[96] Dawe 1993:96 *ad Odyssey* 2.60–61 ("whining self-pity").

[97] For heroic boasts in Homeric and other epic, e.g. African, traditions see Chapter 1 n71.

εἴ χ' ὑμεῖς γε φάγοιτε, τάχ' ἄν ποτε καὶ τίσις εἴη.
τόφρα γὰρ ἂν κατὰ ἄστυ ποτιπτυσσοίμεθα μύθῳ
χρήματ' ἀπαιτίζοντες, ἕως κ' ἀπὸ πάντα δοθείη·
νῦν δέ μοι ἀπρήκτους ὀδύνας ἐμβάλλετε θυμῷ.'

Odyssey 2.58–79

"for there is no man at hand
such as Odysseus was to ward off disaster from this house.
Whereas we now are not such as to fight: indeed in this case [i.e. if we
    fight]
we shall be pathetic because untutored in combat.
Certainly, I would defend myself if [only] I had the strength.
For deeds that are tolerable no more have been brought about, and in a
    manner beyond decency [i.e. disgracefully]
 has my house been ruined. So feel indignant yourselves,
and feel shame before other neighboring men
because they dwell in this region; tremble in fear before the wrath of
    the gods,
lest they should change their attitude in their shock at these evil deeds.
I beseech you by Zeus Olympian and Themis
who dismisses and brings assemblies to their seats :
Hold off, friends! And leave me alone in [my] woeful pain
to be worn away—unless by any chance my noble father Odysseus
in his ill will harmed the well-grieved Achaians.
In return for which you are making me pay and harming me in your ill
    will,
by encouraging these [suitors]. For me it would be better
that you consumed my valuables and my flocks and herds.
If you at least were to consume these, there would be restitution at some
    time before long.
In this case we would sue throughout the city with words,
demanding [our] property until everything was given back.
As it turns out, you are causing me pointless pains in my heart."

He admits that a) as we have already noted, the security of his οἶκος 'house,
household' hinges on a single man but "such a man as Odysseus does not exist"
(*Odyssey* 2.58–59), and b) "*we do not have*"—the plural includes himself as well
as his mother, mentioned earlier, in verses 2.50ff.—"the physical strength"
(*Odyssey* 2.60; compare 2.62, where he refers to himself), "*nor have we learnt*

to fight" (2.61; compare again the plural)[98] "so as to drive out the suitors. Yet, if we attempted any such thing *we would seem* λευγαλέοι 'pathetic'" (2.61), an adjective that suggests contempt in the sight both of oneself and others.[99] Even so, the conclusion arising out of verses 58–61 is expressed in the singular by the verb ἀμύνειν 'defend, ward off', here repeated for a third time in four verses: in effect, "I want to resist the suitors but I cannot do this . . . " (*Odyssey* 2.62). The powerlessness to which the οἶκος (*oikos*) is reduced is collective, but in verse 62 it slips back into being individual: perhaps this 'inconsistency' realistically reflects Telemachos' confusion and anger (on which see below). In any case it is plain that the two qualities that Telemachos cites as indispensable to himself were considered in the Archaic period to be the typical attributes, alongside physical beauty, of an *ephebe*, particularly in the visual arts, namely, δύναμις 'physical strength' (*Odyssey* 2.62) and the capacity for violence (compare 2.61: ἀλκήν 'fighting, combat').[100]

'οἶκος ἐμὸς διόλωλε· νεμεσσήθητε καὶ αὐτοί' ("my house has been ruined; so feel indignant yourselves," *Odyssey* 2.64): he now continues, for about half a verse, to speak openly in the first person as the—admittedly *impuissant*—lord of the manor. Unable to muster the requisite external power and strength, he resorts to deploying evaluative language: αἰδώς 'shame', νέμεσις 'indignation' (usually leading to punishment), and the 'fear of the gods', three quintessentially social emotions that later oratory also mobilized.[101] Though he has arrogated a highly political matter, as we noticed, he contradicts this tack by rebuking the entirety of the δῆμος 'people, community', his very audience, for joint responsibility, if not culpability on account of their inaction (a topic that Mentor will handle more thoughtfully). The three consecutive imperatives, 'νεμεσσήθητε' (that is, "feel the indignation which the public outcry arouses and thus moves you to intervene", *Odyssey* 2.64), 'αἰδέσθητε' ("feel shame", *Odyssey* 2.65), 'ὑποδείσατε' ("tremble in fear", *Odyssey* 2.66) are encapsulated by two further imperatives in verse 2.70, 'σχέσθε' "hold off" and 'ἐάσατε' "leave, let", which spell out the desired consequence of νέμεσις, αἰδώς, and the fear of the gods: if the Ithakans feel these emotions they will carry out the somewhat diffuse central object of the speech, namely, 'stop [sc. encouraging the suitors]' and 'leave me alone in my extreme sadness!'

The culminating two commands are a *non sequitur*—and unfair. For one thing, the speaker, referring again to his πένθος 'suffering', addresses himself

---

98 See *Odyssey* 2.55: 'ἡμέτερον [sc. δῶμα]' and esp. 2.60: 'ἡμεῖς', which usually refers to the speaker's family (see Stanford 1958:237 *ad Odyssey* 2.60).

99 LfgrE, s.v. λευγαλέος.

100 Dover 1978:68–70 (iconography on Attic vases). See Telemachos' wish at *Odyssey* 3.205–206: 'αἲ γὰρ ἐμοὶ τοσσήνδε θεοὶ δύναμιν περιθεῖεν, / τίσασθαι μνηστῆρας . . .'

101 Dover 1994, esp. 169–170.

catachrestically to the δῆμος 'people', but this time he demands that they *desist from intervening* (thus contradicting the connotations of νεμεσσήθητε 'feel indignant', *Odyssey* 2.64); instead, the people must leave him alone. Second, there is a world of a difference, of which, however, Telemachos seems unaware, between inertia or apathy and active abetment (compare *Odyssey* 2.74: 'τούτους ὀτρύνοντες' "by encouraging these [sc. suitors]").[102] This blind spot is indicative of the speaker's immaturity. Heubeck, West, and Hainsworth 1988:135 ad *Odyssey* 2.70ff. put it well: "Instead of appealing for help against the suitors, Telemachos asks the Ithacans to stop encouraging them; his equation of apathy or acquiescence with positive complicity is surely to be seen as an emotional distortion betraying his youth and inexperience." φίλοι 'friends' (*Odyssey* 2.70) slightly softens the insulting blanket indictment. But there follows a compound conditional sentence of nearly four verses (2.71–74) that ironically and rather thoughtlessly plays on the concept of the ἐσθλός, or 'socially responsible', ruler.[103] These verses are a rhetorical *reductio ad absurdum* of the hypothetical counterargument that "your encouragement of the suitors is justified because Odysseus, my ἐσθλὸς πατήρ 'noble father' <and metaphorically your ἐσθλὸς πατήρ, instead of benefiting you > harmed you in the past." Here Telemachos confuses once more public with private, silence with criminal intent. Collectively the δῆμος 'community' harms him (*Odyssey* 2.73: 'κακὰ ῥέζετε' "you are harming"), apparently out of revenge for some injury Odysseus committed against them ('κακ' ἔρεξεν' "he harmed").[104] Yet how can ὁ ἐσθλὸς πατήρ have harmed his collective children? Although by definition this is quite out of the question, Telemachos has left the stinging accusation, summed up in the phrase 'τούτους ὀτρύνοντες' ("by encouraging these [sc. suitors]," *Odyssey* 2.74), dangling in the air.

The next verses, 2.74–75, express a simple thought, tactless and offensive in its turn. The indignant youth is forced to rectify it but he does this gauchely by rationalizing it into a supposition that is still more tactless. He uses, again, a compound conditional sentence: "If the Ithakans consumed our possessions, at least we would seek compensation through the customary procedure [sc. of *flagitatio*]" (*Odyssey* 2.76–78).[105] 'εἴ χ' ὑμεῖς γε φάγοιτε' ("if *you* at least were to consume these") is a pure condition that imputes, however obliquely, a crime to the audience in the second-person plural. As a whole, verses 2.74–78 are a pseudo-polite and hence ironical challenge, in effect, as Dawe phrases

---

[102] κακὰ ἔργα (*Odyssey* 2.67) is elucidated by verses 73–74: 'κακὰ ῥέζετε . . . / τούτους ὀτρύνοντες.'

[103] See Μανακίδου 2002:131n5 for the social meaning of ἐσθλός.

[104] Cf. also the symmetry between the *dêmos*' ill-will towards Odysseus and his putative ill-will towards the *dêmos*: see *Odyssey* 2.72: δυσμενέων, 2.73: δυσμενέοντες.

[105] *Flagitatio*: Jones 1991:139–140; Dawe 1993:97 ad *Odyssey* 2.70–79 considers the passage a *prolepsis* of the beggar Odysseus.

it, "pitch in and yourselves consume the property of Odysseus!"[106] It is obvious that Telemachos halts his speech because he is overcome with uncontrollable emotion. His final words are a direct ψόγος 'rebuke' of the people: 'νῦν δέ μοι ἀπρήκτους ὀδύνας ἐμβάλλετε θυμῷ' ("As it turns out, you are causing me pointless pains in my heart," *Odyssey* 2.79).

As in verses 2.44ff. and in the melodramatic appeal 'καὶ μ' οἷον ἐάσατε πένθεϊ λυγρῷ / τείρεσθ' ("And leave me alone in woeful pain / to be worn away," *Odyssey* 2.70–71), so also here, in the closing of his δημηγορία 'public speech' (*Odyssey* 2.79), the prince regresses to subjective πένθος 'suffering', having launched an attack on an unspecified culprit (*Odyssey* 2.44–45), then on specific culprits (i.e. the suitors) and finally co-culprits (i.e. the δῆμος 'people', *Odyssey* 2.73–74, and especially 79).

The Scepter as a Tennis Racket

Dropping the scepter, or staff, the symbol of the right of ἀγορεύειν 'speaking in public', on the ground, Telemachos is beside himself with anger (see *Odyssey* 2.80: ὣς φάτο χωόμενος 'so he spoke in anger'). He acts like a "less desirable kind of tennis player in moments of frustration."[107] The gesture stands in sharp counterpoint to his father's steady control of the scepter in *Iliad* 3.217–218: 'στάσκεν . . . / σκῆπτρον δ' οὔτ' ὀπίσω οὔτε προπρηνὲς ἐνώμα' ("He stood . . . / and he moved the scepter neither backwards nor forwards"). The prince's outburst of emotion locks him, as it were, in self-pity and juvenile ineffectiveness. The only thing he manages to accomplish is to move his audience to pity (*Odyssey* 2.81) and embarrassed silence (*Odyssey* 2.82), the very opposite of action.[108] Nevertheless, in spite of his naive outburst, he manages to unite the people emotionally, as Haubold also remarks.[109]

His μένος 'vehemence' is unstoppable, as Antinoos comments with condescension:

'Τηλέμαχ' ὑψαγόρη, μένος ἄσχετε . . .'

Odyssey 2.85

'Telemachos, lofty speaker, unrestrainable in your vehemence . . .'

---

[106] Dawe 1993:97 *ad Odyssey* 2.70–79. See also *Odyssey* 2.143 (not cited by Dawe).

[107] Dawe 1993:97 *ad Odyssey* 2.80: "The gesture of throwing down the sceptre is like that made by the less desirable kind of tennis player in moments of frustration." See also n108 immediately below.

[108] As a teacher of rhetoric Isokrates would have awarded low marks to Telemachos' performance. See Isokrates *Antidosis* 190: a gifted rhetor exhibits τόλμα 'daring'—but never ἀναισχυντία 'shamelessness'—as well as σωφροσύνη 'self-control'.

[109] Haubold 2000:111.

Besides Antinoos, the suitor Eurymachos will mention in passing the prince's anger when he berates Mentor (*Odyssey* 2.185: 'οὐδέ κε Τηλέμαχον κεχολωμένον ὧδ' ἀνιείης' ["and you would not be unleashing angry Telemachos in this way"]). Indeed, Telemachos' speech itself is a mixture of pain (see *Odyssey* 2.41, 70, 79) and anger. The latter emotion pervades the conditional sentence in verse 62: 'ἦ τ' ἂν ἀμυναίμην, εἴ μοι δύναμίς γε παρείη' ("Certainly, I would defend myself if I had the strength"). Achilles uses closely similar syntax to express his anger at his utter inability to ward off Apollo: 'ἦ σ' ἂν τεισαίμην, εἴ μοι δύναμίς γε παρείη' ("Certainly, I would avenge myself on you if I had the strength," *Iliad* 22.20; compare *Iliad* 22.10: 'μενεαίνεις' "you rage"). Telemachos' μένος 'determination, courage' proves to be as unstoppable as it is ineffectual. We have seen that Athena announces in the beginning of Book 1 that she intends to inspire the prince with μένος in order to move him to denounce the suitors before the ἀγορή 'assembly' (1.88–91); in the event, the young would-be ruler fails to put this fundamental emotion to political use.[110] Mentor, in contrast, draws a subtle distinction between inaction and complicity and avoids formulating head-on accusations and appeals. Odysseus' contemporary exploits the silence of the majority of Ithakans, turning this fact into an indirect call to action against the suitors, outnumbered by the δῆμος; see especially verses 1.239–241 (and de Jong 2001:57 *ad loc.*).

The poet will continue in the *Telemachy* to remind us of the youth's incompetence, or rather his relative immaturity, not merely in respect of ἔπεα 'words' and εὐβουλία 'good counsel' but also with regard to ἔργα 'deeds'. The deed Telemachos will be called upon to carry out—but which he confesses he cannot perform (see verses 2.60–62)—is τίσις 'requital, revenge'; in verse 2.144 the princeling in fact wishes 'αἴ κέ ποθι Ζεὺς δῷσι παλίντιτα ἔργα γενέσθαι' ("in case Zeus may perhaps grant that deeds of requital take place"). We have seen that revenge was the ἔργον 'deed, act' that marked the coming of age of 'far-famed' Orestes (*Odyssey* 1.30: 'τόν ῥ' Ἀγαμεμνονίδης τηλεκλυτὸς ἔκταν' Ὀρέστης' ["whom (sc. Aigisthos) the far-famed son of Agamemnon Orestes killed"]; 1.40–41: 'ἐκ γὰρ Ὀρέσταο τίσις ἔσσεται Ἀτρεΐδαο, / ὁππότ' ἂν ἡβήσῃ . . .' ["For from Orestes requital for the son of Atreus will come / when he comes of age . . . "]), the prodigious post-adolescent invoked as an example in the exhortations of Athena, Nestor, and Menelaos to Telemachos. Τίσις 'requital' represents an extreme form of heroic efficiency, which may more generally be conveyed by the verb τελεῖν 'to accomplish, fulfill' and

---

[110] *Odyssey* 1.320–321: τῷ δ' ἐνὶ θυμῷ / θῆκε μένος καὶ θάρσος (the 'descent' of Athena's spirit on Telemachos); cf. 13.387–388: 'στῆθι, μένος πολυθαρσές ἐνεῖσα, / οἷον ὅτε Τροίης λύομεν λιπαρὰ κρήδεμνα' (Odysseus to Athena).

the related τελευτᾶν 'to perform, conclude'. Consider the poet's pointed use of these verbs in two passages in Book 2. First, here is the suitor Leiokritos' prediction, spiked with malicious humor:

'ἀλλ', ὀΐω, καὶ δηθὰ καθήμενος ἀγγελιάων
πεύσεται εἰν Ἰθάκῃ, τελέει δ' ὁδὸν οὔ ποτε ταύτην.'

Odyssey 2.255–256

"But even so, I suppose, sitting long [at home] he will hear news (*angeliai*) in Ithaka, and never complete this journey."

Second, after the disbanding of the assembly, Mentor exhorts the prince using both verbs. His words reverberate like a riposte to the suitor's sarcasm:[111] see verses 2.272, 273, 275, 280.

In Book 4 Penelope characterizes Telemachos as νήπιος, an adjective connoting immaturity at its extreme:

'νήπιος, οὔτε πόνων εὖ εἰδὼς οὔτ' ἀγοράων'

Odyssey 4.818[112]

"childish, well-versed neither in difficulties [hardship] nor in assemblies
    [public deliberation]"

In her 'gloss' of the epithet the Queen divides it into two notional strands, giving it the nuance of 'incompetent in respect of deeds and words alike'. By clear implication, νηπιότης 'childishness' disqualifies the prince of *kleos* as distilled into its traditional ingredients. Indeed, in Book 2 Telemachos has proven νήπιος 'childish' in this twin sense. He lacks, for one thing, the skill of εὐβουλία 'dispensing counsel based on rational discussion', as we have seen. For another, as he admits in public himself, he lacks the ἀλκή 'fighting skills or spirit' to oust the suitors (compare πόνων 'difficulties, hardship' in Penelope's quote above). Disarmed of the possibility of action, he is far from carrying out τίσις 'revenge' like Orestes, who, on coming of age (ἡβήσσαντος), used βίη 'physical strength' so effectively. Having failed in public speech, combining and confusing emotion and tactics, the young man rather resembles savage (ἄγριος) Kyklops (compare *Odyssey* 1.70–71, 198–199, 2.19–20). When praying alone by the sea (*Odyssey* 2.262–266, compare 260: ἐπάνευθε κιὼν ἐπὶ θῖνα θαλάσσης 'after going aside to the seashore')—shortly after the dissolution of the assembly—he uses a

---

[111] De Jong 2001:60 *ad Odyssey* 2.270–280.

[112] In Phoinix's statement in *Iliad* 9.440–441 (cited by Heubeck, West, and Hainsworth 1988:244 *ad loc.*), the νήπιος individual has no knowledge of either war or ἀγοραί. For νήπιος, see Chapter 4 n10.

highly unusual formulation, which omits the prayer's petition. Thus he strays from standard adult conduct even in private prayer.[113] One might say that Telemachos occupies an intermediate position between civilized/prudent Orestes and uncivilized Kyklops.

~~

"in the Odyssey . . . he [sc. Telemachos] talks more than any other person except Odysseus."

Jones 1991:113 *ad Odyssey* 1.114–117

Certain scholars have remarked that even beyond the *Telemachy* the hero remains excitable in his conversations, but with the difference that he no longer loses control. In general Telemachos expresses ever-increasing self-confidence and adult authority, especially after reuniting with his father. Jones, who treats with much sensitivity the matter of the prince's gradual maturation, traces the process of the hero's development in his use of speech, and chiefly in his exchanges with Penelope and the suitors from Book 18 (verses 227–232) on.[114] In Book 20 (verses 309–310) his comment to the suitor Ktesippos forthrightly attests his graduation from the ranks of νήπιοι 'the childish' (ἤδη γὰρ νοέω καὶ οἶδα ἕκαστα, / ἐσθλά τε καὶ τὰ χέρεια· πάρος δ' ἔτι νήπιος ἦα' ["because now I perceive and know each and every thing, / good and bad alike; whereas before I was still childish"]).[115] He states that he is willing to die fighting the intruders (see especially *Odyssey* 20.315–319), a willingness reminiscent of a Hektor figure, ready ἀμύνεσθαι περὶ πάτρης 'to defend his country' if not on the battlefield, then at least in his own home. In this speech, in which he also denounces the suitors, he betrays again his 'psycho-linguistic' development. Stanford 1958:355 *ad Odyssey* 20.311 notes that the youth's emotional state results in a distortion of syntax in his speech: instead of a phrase standing in apposition to the pronoun τάδε 'these things' (*Odyssey* 20.311), Telemachos employs a genitive absolute (*Odyssey* 20:312–313):

---

[113] See Muellner 1976:22–23, who attributes this "substandard prayer" (similar to Achilles' in *Iliad* 1) to Telemachos' depression and immaturity: "Telemachus, who has just failed in his first attempt to play an adult role before the suitors and townspeople of Ithaca, is depressed and helpless."

[114] Jones 2002, esp. 192 *ad Odyssey* 20.309–310, 320–337, 338–344; see also de Jong 2001:497 *ad Odyssey* 20.257ff. (de Jong 201:371–372 *ad Odyssey* 15.222–283 cites Telemachos' reception of Theoklymenos as evidence of freshly acquired maturity, though her criterion here is not speaking style but the youth's overall conduct—he treats the fugitive as a friend rather than as a suppliant.)

[115] For νοέω as largely a mental operation, see Frame 2009, esp. 51. In the passage just quoted, Telemachos insinuates that he has now reached the stage of moral intelligence and agency signaled by epic μέτρον ἥβης, on which, see Ferrari 2002:133–135 (adducing classical evidence as well). See Frydenberg 1997:10: "*Moral reasoning* advances during adolescence to involve concerns about the *social order*" (my italics).

ἀλλ' ἔμπης τάδε μὲν καὶ τέτλαμεν εἰσορόωντες,
μήλων σφαζομένων οἴνοιό τε πινομένοιο
καὶ σίτου'

Odyssey 20.311–313

"Yet we have put up with seeing these things
our cattle and sheep being slaughtered and our wine being drunk
and food consumed."

Though his speech is temporarily deformed, the young man does not collapse emotionally, as when he criticized the suitors in his first δημηγορία 'public speech' in Book 2. His reaction now impresses Agelaos, who, reflecting the view of the other usurpers, at once complies with the prince's threat (*Odyssey* 20.320–337). Albeit briefly, the aura of *auctoritas* intimidates the supercilious suitors.[116]

Also indicative of the Telemachos' verbal and other maturation is the manner in which, across the distance of seventeen books, he responds anew to the suitors' suggestion that he arrange for Penelope's remarriage as soon as possible. Jones 2002:192 *ad Odyssey* 20.338–344 (see also 191 *ad Odyssey* 20.304–319) remarks that, whereas his response in *Odyssey* 2.129–145 is a veritable torrent of diffuse, πολύμυθα 'wordy' arguments, in *Odyssey* 20.338–344 his reaction is brief, well-targeted and suffused with "a self-confident authority." This maturity, reflected in Telemachos' more 'economical' (as the scholia would say) mode of self-expression, has been brought about by an educational event which Eurymachos registers with a sinking feeling as early as *Odyssey* 16.346–347:[117]

'ὢ φίλοι, ἦ μέγα ἔργον ὑπερφιάλως τετέλεσται
Τηλεμάχῳ ὁδὸς ἥδε· φάμεν δέ οἱ οὐ τελέεσθαι.'

"Friends, truly a great deed has been completed arrogantly
by Telemachos, this journey of his—and yet we said it would not be
achieved by him."

The ὁδός 'journey, voyage', as we have seen, is by itself a μέγα ἔργον 'great deed'; as a paideutic process it teaches Telemachos about the constituents—ἔπος 'word' and ἔργον 'deed'—of social identity, or *kleos*.[118] When Odysseus asks Athena why

---

[116] But cf. *Odyssey* 20.345–346 (the suitors laugh at him). Even as late as Book 21 these intruders do not take him seriously: Jones 2002:200–201 *ad Odyssey* 21.376.

[117] Though Antinoos utters the selfsame words in *Odyssey* 4.463–464, this statement, as Dawe 1993:203 remarks *ad loc.*, is less appropriate here, inasmuch as Telemachos has not yet completed his voyage.

[118] For διδάσκειν in the *Odyssey*, see Chapter 1.

87

she ever imposed the voyage on his son rather than informing him from the outset of his situation, she spells out her motive in *Odyssey* 13.422–423:[119]

‘αὐτή μιν πόμπευον, ἵνα κλέος ἐσθλὸν ἄροιτο
κεῖσ’ ἐλθών . . .’

“I myself was his guide, so that he might win a noble reputation (*kleos*) by going there . . .”

What does the goddess mean? Thanks to the ὁδός, the prince is meant to develop, to some degree at least, the compound identity known schematically in epic tradition as *kleos*. The rich gifts Telemachos receives from Menelaos and Helen are external tokens of this *kleos*.[120] Like Odysseus in Book 13, Penelope in Book 17 construes her son's ὁδός as an intelligence-gathering operation; hence she questions him about the ἀκουή 'news, hearsay' and ὀπωπή 'sight[ings]' of his father (*Odyssey* 17.41–44,104–106). Athena has unique insight into the educational dimension of Telemachos' trip, as will be argued in detail in Chapter 5.

In the books that follow on the *Telemachy* proper we noticed that Telemachos becomes better versed in words and deeds. If in Books 18 and 20 his manner of speech sounds more mature, by Book 21 his words to his mother have an even more impressive ring:

‘ἀλλ’ εἰς οἶκον ἰοῦσα τὰ σ’ αὐτῆς ἔργα κόμιζε,
ἱστόν τ’ ἠλακάτην τε, καὶ ἀμφιπόλοισι κέλευε
ἔργον ἐποίχεσθαι· τόξον δ’ ἄνδρεσσι μελήσει
πᾶσι, μάλιστα δ’ ἐμοί . . .’

Odyssey 21.350–353

“Return to your quarters and attend to your own tasks
with the loom and the shuttle and instruct the maidservants
to go about their work [sc. at the shuttle]; as for the bow [representing
        military matters], it will concern men,
all [sc. men], and especially me . . .”

---

[119] Dawe 1993:525–526 *ad Odyssey* 13.417–419, citing others, considers Athena's response “unsatisfactory,” a virtual pirouette by our poet! I hope in what follows to furnish a counter-argument to this interpretation.

[120] For these tokens of *kleos*, see Jones 2002:127 *ad Odyssey* 13.422. What is more, the luxurious hospitality offered to the prince (*Odyssey* 13.423–424) is commensurate with and emblematic of his *kleos*. Telemachos' gifts correspond to the bow given by Iphitos to the young Odysseus as a μνῆμα ξείνοιο φίλοιο during his mission abroad.

This is perhaps the pinnacle of the prince's self-expression as an adult.[121] (The speech is, to be precise, a signal specimen of εὐβουλία 'cogent advice'.) Homer is here deliberately echoing the much-discussed passage in *Odyssey* 1.356–359:[122]

'ἀλλ' οἶκον ἰοῦσα τὰ σ' αὐτῆς ἔργα κόμιζε
ἱστόν τ' ἠλακάτην τε, καὶ ἀμφιπόλοισι κέλευε
ἔργον ἐποίχεσθαι· μῦθος δ' ἄνδρεσσι μελήσει
πᾶσι, μάλιστ' ἐμοί ...'

Odyssey 1.356–359

"Return to your quarters and attend to your own tasks
with the loom and the shuttle and instruct the maidservants
to go about their work [sc. at the shuttle]; as for speech, it will concern
       men,
all [sc. men], and especially me ... "

Whereas at *Odyssey* 1.358 Telemachos arrogates μῦθος 'speech', in the later passage he invests himself with the aura of godlike omnipotence when he lays claim to the bow, an eloquent heroic emblem.[123] He designedly states that his 'education' has progressed from μῦθος to ἔργον. It is worthwhile to remark that after the *Telemachy*—on account of the journey he has embarked on in Book 2— the young man has undergone a 'change of gender'. Perhaps this is the juncture at which to examine the ὁδός as an 'initiatory', educational process.

---

[121] Telemachos' outburst of anger at his mother and the womenfolk may recall the standardized aggressive conduct exhibited by newly circumcised youths on returning home: they enter noisily, break small objects, and remaining silent for days they mock-beat their mother, sisters, and uncircumcised brothers. See Woronoff 1978:242–243 for the African field data.

[122] See also Jones 2002:200 *ad Odyssey* 21.350–358, who however does not remark the repetition ἔργα/ἔργον.

[123] Cf. *Odyssey* 21.344–345: 'μῆτερ ἐμή, τόξον μὲν Ἀχαιῶν οὔ τις ἐμεῖο / κρείσσων, ᾧ κ' ἐθέλω, δόμεναί τε καὶ ἀρνήσασθαι'; as magic spells also suggest, divine omnipotence consists in the ease with which a divinity can carry out A or, *if he/she wishes,* –A, its opposite. See Petropoulos 1993:43, 49–51.

4

The Little Prince's Voyage
on a Borrowed Ship

'ἄτοπος δοκεῖ εἶναι Τηλεμάχου ἡ ἀποδημία.'

Scholiast *ad Odyssey* 1.93 (Dindorf)

"Telemachos' going abroad seems absurd."

Telemachos and Eugene Onegin

LET US IMAGINE the world Telemachos has been living in before he sets off with his small crew on a borrowed ship.[1] When we first meet him, the post-adolescent hero is suffering from what we may call the 'Eugene Onegin syndrome'. B. Copley, in her psychoanalytical study of the portrayal of adolescence in literature, points out Onegin's "deficit" of experience in Pushkin's verse novel.[2] This protagonist lacks a father as well as meaningful contact with reality outside of the endless rounds of entertainment among Russian aristocracy. "Oppressed by emptiness of soul," Onegin lives his life largely through books, reading insatiably, striving "to achieve the appropriation of others' thought" (Pushkin 1979:1.44) in his own writings. He thus avoids drawing ideas from lived reality, slipping past the pains of growing up. Through his pseudo-experiences this young man develops into a pseudo-adult.

The Little Prince shows evidence of similar deficits of experience in Book 1. Trapped between two extremes, his own immaturity on the one hand and

---

[1] *Odyssey* 2.318–320,386–387. Why does Telemachos emphasize ἔμπορος 'passenger' in *Odyssey* 2.319? Dawe 1993:116 *ad loc.* suspects a *non sequitur* and therefore condemns verses 319–320. Yet Telemachos himself implies at least one reason why he has no ship of his own: the usurpers' dissipation even of Odysseus' fleet. The lack of a fleet is emblematic of the absence of great Captain (σημάντωρ) Odysseus; see *Odyssey* 19.313–315. For Telemachos' literal ἀπορία 'resource-lessness', see also Olson 1995:79–80 and below. Further on the ship and its tellingly small crew, see Chapter 5 n54 and n57.

[2] Copley 1993:61–64.

the geriatric decadence of his grandfather Laertes on the other,[3] he has difficulty conceiving his own father in plausible detail; at first he even boggles
at speaking his father's name, as we have seen. Life in the palace has turned
into a perverse, nonstop party in the company of the suitors (*Odyssey* 2.304ff.,
16.27ff., 18.164ff.) and his only exposure to male (Iliadic) *kleos*, it seems, are
the songs of Phemios (who performs under duress)[4] and other oral sources.[5]

At Ithaka—even before taking 'history lessons' in Pylos and Sparta—the
young prince grows up listening to tales about his father's *kleos*. As he later
avows to Odysseus:

'ὦ πάτερ, ἦ τοι σεῖο μέγα κλέος αἰὲν ἄκουον,
χεῖράς τ' αἰχμητὴν ἔμεναι καὶ ἐπίφρονα βουλήν'

Odyssey 16.241–242

"Father, truly I used to hear of your great reputation (*kleos*),
that you were warlike with your hands and wise in counsel"

Conventionally enough, Telemachos dissects the 'social identity' of *kleos* into
the standard Iliadic dyad, namely, βίη 'the exercise of physical strength' and
βουλή 'deliberation, discussion'.[6] Compare also *Odyssey* 23.124–125, where he
again talks to his father:

'σὴν γὰρ ἀρίστην
μῆτιν ἐπ' ἀνθρώπους φάσ' ἔμμεναι . . .'

"for they spread the word among men that your
cunning intelligence is the best . . ."

The verb φάσ' 'they say' conveys the rumors and hearsay presupposed by
kleos, as we saw in Chapter 2, while the phrase ἐπ' ἀνθρώπους 'throughout,
among men' likewise connotes the process of hearing.[7]

Just like Onegin, Telemachos lives in virtual reality, experiencing the
kleos of heroes second- or thirdhand, as if reading (like Onegin) a "book worn
through use" (Pushkin 1979:7.24). This parallel is tempting particularly if we

---

[3] For the portrait of the depressed, decrepit Laertes: *Odyssey* 24.226ff., esp. 231, 233 (πένθος);
also *Odyssey* 1.189–193, 11.187–196, 16.139–140.

[4] Yet another sign of the irregular state of affairs in the kingdom: *Odyssey* 1.154: ἤειδε . . .
ἀνάγκη.

[5] See Chapter 2.

[6] Jones 2002:152 *ad Odyssey* 16.242; further, see Chapter 3. Cf. e.g. *Odyssey* 1.258, 7.228, etc.

[7] Dawe 1993: ἐπ' ἀνθρώπους is properly used of "fame spreading" (814); see also Nagy 1974.
Here, however, Dawe suggests that the phrase pertains to ἀρίστη. Either way, Odysseus' reputation for his cunning will have spread globally, so to speak.

recall the quasi-textual character of *kleos* as argued in Chapter 1 (above). We have noted that Telemachos acquires *kleos* in stages, and particularly through his voyage to the Peloponnese, which, even without the envious suitors' ambush, proves perilous enough.

Telemachos and the Navajo

Unlike the majority of epic heroes,[8] the Little Prince has no father to 'teach' him *kleos*. G. Devereux, on the basis of his psychiatric fieldwork mainly among Hopi and Navajo Indians, highlights the patent 'educational' role a father plays in the establishment of his son's masculine identity:

> . . . a boy can become socio-culturally "masculine" *only if he models his behaviour on that of his father* or of some other male member of his own group. *If he models it on that of an alien male, his group may not consider him a "real" man.*[9]

Cross-culturally, it is this sense of connection with a paternal model and generally with the model of male ancestors that makes a boy into a man. In Homer, if a son feels himself unconnected to his father he is by definition νήπιος, as S. Edmunds has shown.[10] Other than the absent Odysseus, the prince has few plausible behavioral prototypes among men,[11] as we will note in chapter 5.[12] The only prototype he has, and the sole *kleos* he personally experiences in his single-parent family, is the sedentary, female *kleos* of his mother Penelope.[13]

Penelope's Antagonistic *Kleos*

> ἐπεί νύ τοι ἄρμενον ἦεν
> Ἡρακλῆα λιπεῖν· σέο δ' ἔκτοθι μῆτις ὄρωρεν,
> ὄφρα τὸ κείνου κῦδος ἀν' Ἑλλάδα μή σε καλύψῃ·
>
> Apollonios of Rhodes *Argonautika* 1.1290–1292

The most famous weaver in antiquity,[14] Penelope devises a notorious ruse that wins her a peculiar type of *kleos*. Antinoos decries this fact publicly in the ἀγορή

---

[8] But cf. Diomedes, who lost his father at a very tender age: *Iliad* 6.222–223 and Chapter 1 n94 and n98.

[9] Devereux 1985:19–20 (my italics). Similarly, according to Wöhrle 1999:32–48, the Homeric father is the cognitive model that shapes all of his son's social relations with other males.

[10] Edmunds 1990 and Chapter 3 above.

[11] See Olson 1995:67.

[12] Cf. the kourotrophic role of Iphidamas' grandfather (*Iliad* 11.221–224) and Chapter 5.

[13] See n20 below.

[14] Chapter 1 of Ferrari 2002. The ταφεῖον φᾶρος that the Queen weaves and then unravels is not a death shroud, but rather an ἐπίβλημα, that is, a cloth cover for Laertes' lying in state (πρόθεσις). Stretching beyond his corpse, it would cover the 'coffin' and would likely have been decorated

'assembly' (*Odyssey* 2.93–110). If broken down into pure narrative, this denunciation is part of the larger fabric of accounts that contribute to the queen's *kleos*. This particular narrative is the *historiola* about the ruse involving Laertes' ταφεῖον φᾶρος 'coffin cloth', a report that reveals and at the same time glorifies a woman, accomplished if devious (at least in the eyes of the suitors), who remains steadfast in her loyalty to her spouse and his οἶκος. Antinoos obliquely castigates Penelope; quite sensibly he places responsibility squarely on her shoulders for the ruin of this οἶκος 'house'. It is the Queen's resistance that has forced the suitors to wage a war of attrition on the royal estate: by deliberately consuming Odysseus' οἶκος—and the future household of his son—they have been applying pressure on Penelope to remarry before the estate evaporates. This tactic is recent, having been adopted by the usurpers when they discovered the ruse of the φᾶρος '[funeral] fabric', as *Odyssey* 13.377 makes abundantly clear.[15] In his criticism Antinoos unknowingly raises a matter that implicitly concerns Telemachos.

This woman's *kleos*, according to Antinoos, should be put down to her high intelligence and dexterity:

> ἔργα τ' ἐπίστασθαι περικαλλέα καὶ φρένας ἐσθλὰς
> κέρδεά θ', οἷ' οὔ πώ τιν' ἀκούομεν οὐδὲ παλαιῶν·

Odyssey 2.117–118

> "the knowledge of tasks [or handiwork, i.e. spinning and weaving] most
>   beautiful and fine intelligence
> and such ruses as we have never yet heard that even any of the women
>   of the past [knew]"

When it comes to the rumors (see *Odyssey* 2.118: ἀκούομεν 'we have heard' [literally, 'we hear']) circulating about her ingenuity, Penelope, as this suitor says, surpasses even the renowned women of more distant, mythical times.[16] These legendary women are Tyro, Nestor's grandmother, Alkmene, Herakles' mother, and Mykene, the daughter of the river god Inachos:

---

with parti-colored friezes representing his patron deity and narrating his feats and those of his ancestors. It is 'a eulogy on cloth'. As a number of diverse ancient sources suggest, the entire process of the fabrication and decoration of a φᾶρος of comparable proportions would indeed have required two or almost three years. See Barber 1991:350–383, esp. 378, 380, 382.

15 Heitman 2005:22–23, 26.

16 For these hyperbolic comparisons: Jones 2002:22 *ad Odyssey* 2.120. These heroines evoke an unusually distant and hence more definite past for the *Odyssey*'s protagonists. See Jones 1992:82 (who however argues that the past is conceived as recent in the poem).

'τάων αἳ πάρος ἦσαν ἐϋπλοκαμῖδες Ἀχαιαί,
Τυρώ τ' Ἀλκμήνη τε ἐϋστέφανός τε Μυκήνη·
τάων οὔ τις ὁμοῖα νοήματα Πηνελοπείη
ᾔδη . . .'

Odyssey 2.119–122

"of these [women] who were formerly Achaian ladies of beautiful curls,
Tyro and Alkmene and Mykene of the beautiful crown—
not any of these knew strategies similar to Penelope [i.e. to those of
Penelope] . . .'

Antinoos' extravagant compliment is mordant yet not unusual, echoing as it does a conventional politeness.[17] What is of particular relevance is his observation that through her obdurate faithfulness and her general evasiveness Penelope gains *kleos day by day*, even as he speaks. Her *kleos*, in other words, is still in a state of becoming; indeed, it veritably grows into her 'symbolic capital' at the expense of the literal estate of her son:[18]

'μέγα μὲν κλέος αὐτῇ
ποιεῖτ', αὐτὰρ σοί γε ποθὴν πολέος βιότοιο.'[19]

Odyssey 2.125–126

"a great reputation (*kleos*) for herself
she is creating, but for you a distressing lack of many possessions."

Shortly afterwards, Eurymachos' bilious comments (*Odyssey* 2.203–205; see below) in the assembly suggest that the queen's dilatoriness has all but destroyed her son's fleet.

The mother's *kleos*, moreover, develops at the cost of her son's *identity*. Idiosyncratic and so different from Odysseus' *kleos*—for it presupposes an introverted, sedentary, almost static lifestyle—the queen's 'fame' is nonetheless equal or at least equivalent to that of her husband.[20] Penelope's *kleos* overshadows her inexperienced son from the outset. This fact may explain why he invests so heavily in Phemios' song: confronted with the competition between maternal and

---

[17] Petropoulos 2003:20–21, 39–40.

[18] Bourdieu and Passeron 1964 and Robbins 1991. Ferrari 2002:11–12, following E. Keuls, regards Penelope's weaving as an act of political resistance.

[19] But cf. Jones 1991:141 *ad loc.*

[20] The beggar Odysseus' words to Penelope (*Odyssey* 19, esp. 108–109) are not a "deluge of insipid compliments" (*pace* Dawe 1993:693 *ad loc.* and similarly Jones 2002:176). The identical phraseology at *Odyssey* 9.20 (= 19.108–109), where the hero describes his *kleos* in the first person (see Chapter 1), implies on the contrary that in Book 19 he identifies with the *laudanda* or at least applies the terms of masculine *kleos* analogously to his wife.

paternal *kleos*, the youth turns to the thesaurus of song for some inkling not only of *kleos* (i.e. 'news') about his father, but also of his *kleos* in the sense of 'glory'.[21] Yet how can Telemachos learn about his father's *kleos* even indirectly, when Penelope's renown towers above him like a stifling tapestry?

Here it may be beneficial to attempt a brief psychoanalytical excursus, which may be of interest to students of literature: if we accept that the passage just cited (*Odyssey* 2.125–126) indirectly pertains to the competition or antagonism between two instances of *kleos*, we must at the same time suppose that the passage in its turn adumbrates an Oedipal conflict between father and son, or rather, an Oedipal attraction of the son to his mother.[22] This attraction is detectable in *Odyssey* 21.102ff., where Telemachos becomes a master of ceremonies, as it were, and advertises his mother as a bartered bride by using traditional hymeneal language:[23]

'ἀλλ' ἄγετε, μνηστῆρες, ἐπεὶ τόδε φαίνετ' ἄεθλον,
οἵη νῦν οὐκ ἔστι γυνὴ κατ' Ἀχαιΐδα γαῖαν,
οὔτε Πύλου ἱερῆς οὔτ' Ἄργεος οὔτε Μυκήνης·
οὔτ' αὐτῆς Ἰθάκης οὔτ' ἠπείροιο μελαίνης.'

Odyssey 21.106–109

"Well, come on, Suitors, since this [*pointing*] here prize is on display
the like of whom now there is no woman throughout the Peloponnesian
    land
nor in holy Pylos nor in Argos nor Mykenai,
nor in Ithaka itself nor on the dark mainland!"

After touting his priceless 'merchandise' as an ἄεθλον 'prize' (*Odyssey* 21.106–107), he rights himself, fully aware of the epithalamian undertones—namely, the αἶνος 'praise, encomium'—he has just evoked. His self-correction is at first sight explicable: praise (αἶνος) of this prospective bride (*Odyssey* 21.110: 'καὶ δ' αὐτοὶ τόδε ἴστε· τί με χρὴ μητέρος αἴνου;' ["and you yourselves know this; what need have I to praise my mother?"]) is superfluous. Immediately after this *praeteritio*, he hopes aloud that that he will succeed in "stringing

---

21 See Chapter 1.
22 For Penelope as an "analysand," see Devereux 1957:378–386 and Devereux and Κουρέτας 1958:250–255.
23 Parody is in tune with the young man's ironical, mocking mood, as can be seen in *Odyssey* 21.102–105 (esp. 105: 'αὐτὰρ ἐγὼ γελόω καὶ τέρπομαι ἄφρονι θυμῷ'). Nuptial discourse is echoed consciously in *Odyssey* 21.106–109; cf. the technical terms in verses 316 ('οἴκαδέ μ' ἄξεσθαι') and 322 ('οὔ τί σε τόνδ' ἄξεσθαι ὀϊόμεθ'); cf. also Odysseus' words to Nausikaa in *Odyssey* 6.149–169, 180–185 as well as the latter's reply in verses 243–245. *Odyssey* 6.227–235 may be based on the songs of praise accompanying the customary bath and preparation of the bridegroom, on which see Petropoulos 2003, chapter 2. Further on the 'intertextual' relationship between the above passages from Book 6 and ancient bridal songs, see Petropoulos 2003.

the bow and shooting an arrow through the iron" (*Odyssey* 21.114). Yet if he did this—according to the rules of the contest that Penelope has officially set (*Odyssey* 19.572–581)—he would win the 'prize', namely, his own mother! Such is the logical conclusion of *Odyssey* 21.106–114; but in verses 115–117 he corrects himself again, designedly avoiding the embarrassing associations that ensue and shifting to another related but safer topic (such avoidance also occurs in modern Greek folk song):[24]

'οὔ κέ μοι ἀχνυμένῳ τάδε δώματα πότνια μήτηρ
λείποι ἅμ' ἄλλῳ ἰοῦσ', ὅτ' ἐγὼ κατόπισθε λιποίμην
οἷός τ' ἤδη πατρὸς ἀέθλια κάλ' ἀνελέσθαι.'

Odyssey 21.115–117

"I would not be sorry if my lady mother were to leave this house,
going away with another [man], because I would be left behind
capable now of carrying off my father's beautiful prizes [i.e. the axes]."

Here the Oedipal allusions are drowned out through the use of the plural πατρός ἀέθλια 'my father's prizes' (*Odyssey* 21.117)[25] instead of the singular and highly emphatic τόδε ἄεθλον 'this prize' (21.106).[26]

Dawe 1993:757, commenting on Telemachos' *parapraxis*, or 'Freudian slip', himself commits a *parapraxis* that may help in the analysis of *Odyssey* 21.115–117. Like others, he does not take into account the significant detail that the suitors are young, some of them in fact being Telemachos' contemporaries. Consideration of this detail enhances the implications of his otherwise valid comments:[27] "If Telemachos is successful we tacitly assume that his success for the moment rules out the suitors as possible husbands, and so Penelope will not be departing anywhere . . . The only prize at stake is Penelope herself, and it is Oedipus's province, not Telemachos's, to go marrying mothers." Not surprisingly, Dawe athetizes verse 117.

Yet it is precisely these seeming incongruities that add psychological depth to the prince's chain of associations in verses 115–117. Nuptial language frames his spontaneous announcement that he too intends to take part in the shooting

---

[24] Petropoulos 2003:8–9 ("teasing technique").

[25] According to Jones 2002:198 *ad Odyssey* 21.117, these are Odysseus' old prizes, i.e. the axes, connoted in verses 61–62 by the phrase 'iron and bronze' (a *hendiadys*).

[26] The demonstrative pronoun τόδε suggests that Telemachos points with his finger or makes some other gesture in the direction of his mother.

[27] For the suitors' ages, see *Odyssey* 21.94, 179, 401, and Stanford 1958:363 *ad Odyssey* 21.179; cf. *Odyssey* 20.361, 24.107ff., and Dawe 1993:839 *ad Odyssey* 24.102. The suitors' youth is seldom mentioned by philologists but is highlighted by psychoanalysts, e.g. Devereux and Κουρέτας 1958:253. See also Chapter 6 for the social and cultural age of the suitors.

contest. He and the suitors alike are vying for his mother, the touted ἄεθλον 'prize'. The younger suitors, who are his contemporaries, have a filial rapport with Odysseus and, by extension, with the powerful 'mother of the people' Penelope.[28] A conspicuous case in point is the suitor Eurymachos, Odysseus' figurative son (see *Odyssey* 16.442–444), whose very name recalls 'Telemachos': this suitor has the greatest chances of marrying the Queen (*Odyssey* 15.16–18).[29] On the other hand, the more senior among the suitors are rather more like the Little Prince's antagonistic 'fathers', as witness, the notorious Antinoos and Telemachos' characterization of him at *Odyssey* 17.397.[30] It is therefore an inaccurate inference on the part of some scholars that the usurpers are Oedipal sons, one and all, of Odysseus and especially Penelope.[31] More valid is their assumption however that Odysseus' victory in the archery contest plays out the symbolic resolution (or better yet, the successful suppression) of the Oedipal complex.

Let us return to the competing 'fame' of Odysseus and Penelope, respectively. It is interesting that from the perspective of *Geistesgeschichte* the Oedipal conflict between son and mother is described by Antinoos in the language of *kleos*: Penelope's *kleos* grows every day, while Telemachos searches after Odysseus' 'fame' and 'news' every day. As noted, the former kind of *kleos* checks Telemachos' identification with his father's *kleos*. Penelope, in the simile she unapologetically applies to herself in *Odyssey* 19.518–524, is the suffocating infanticide Aedon; day by day she kills the prince's masculine identification with the king. This psychologizing interpretation of the repercussions of Penelope's *kleos* may seem untenable; even so, it is at least significant that the youth reacts aggressively to his mother's instructions to Phemios in Book 1 because he is intent on gaining access to his father's *kleos* (in both senses of the term).

---

[28] The Queen tenderly raises from her infancy Melantho, the maidservant (*Odyssey* 18.322–323): might this imply that Penelope is a collective mother? See Chapter 3 n70.

[29] See de Jong 2001:39 *ad Odyssey* 1.367–424 for these chances.

[30] A mordant comment that also acknowledges the suitor's seniority. The irony is especially pronounced because Telemachos' real father is present. For the suitors as substitute brothers and fathers, see below. Though in a sense a 'father' to Telemachos, Antinoos, if we judge by the way in which the Queen scolds him in *Odyssey* 16.418–421 ('καὶ δέ σέ φασιν / . . .μεθ' ὁμήλικας ἔμμεν ἄριστον / βουλῇ καὶ μύθοισι· σὺ δ' οὐκ ἄρα τοῖος ἔησθα') also poses smugly as Penelope's 'son' (cf. the manner in which she upbraids Telemachos in *Odyssey* 18.215–220). Antinoos' filial relationship stems, on the one hand, from his youth in relation to her and, on the other, from the paternalistic hierarchy that reduces social inferiors to the status of children: see *Odyssey* 4.31–36, Menelaos' stern words to his remiss servant Eteoneus. See also n33 below.

[31] Cf. Friedman and Gassel 1952:215–23.

Malvolio

"Not yet old enough for a man, nor young
enough for a boy . . . 'tis with him in standing water,
between boy and man."

Shakespeare, *Twelfth Night*

The suitors, many of whom are named, make up a cohesive group that stands apart from the anonymous λαός 'people'. All of the suitors are destined for decimation.[32] More or less contemporary with Telemachos—though some, as we saw, are older—they are also his *Ersatzbrüder* under the patriarchal system, aspiring to marry his mother, to whom they are sexually drawn (see *Odyssey* 1.366, 18.212–213).[33] These Oedipal rivals are the 'evil step-brothers' of fairy tales, venomous foes among whom the good prince has grown up. Only by killing his brothers/candidate fathers can Telemachos in his turn become a father and the husband of his mother.[34] Moreover, the usurpers constitute a gang of youths comparable, for instance, to the partisans who collectively oppose Romeo in Shakespeare's tragedy *Romeo and Juliet*.[35] The distinguished (κεκριμένοι)[36] *jeunesse dorée* of the kingdom are, from a psychosocial point of view, the crucial peer group that, theoretically at least, should have facilitated the development of his social identity.[37] The suitors' 'end' (in the Aristotelian sense) is marriage to Penelope, as Haubold points out.[38] By the same token, Telemachos' τέλος 'end, purpose' is κλέος ἔχειν, κλέος ἄρνυσθαι 'to win *kleos*', as Athena repeatedly asserts. Yet 'circumspect' Penelope thwarts both purposes. Through resistance and clever evasion for over three years, she effectively delays the maturation of these young men in particular. Given that marriage signals the decisive, quasi-initiatory step

---

[32] See Chapter 6.

[33] Cf. Felson-Rubin 1994: the suitors at times behave paternally towards Telemachos, and at times they are his "brothers": in the first case they are a foil to Odysseus, in the second they oppose Telemachos (177n14); also Wöhrle 1999: every suitor is an *Ersatzbruder* who however aspires to become the Prince's father or, better, his stepfather. As potential stepfathers, the suitors contend with Telemachos in a "battle of generations" (141). These 'half-brothers'/'step-fathers' have a father in common with Telemachos—Odysseus, the collective father, on whom see Appendix II.

[34] Cf. Wöhrle 1999:141. See the preceding section on epithalamian echoes in *Odyssey* 21.115–117.

[35] For this youth gang, see Copley 1993:101, 135–136, and Chapter 6. The suitors resemble a gang of youths in Copley's definition of the term: a gang provides its members with a) a *sense of identity* articulated through b) *violent behavior* (see ἀγήνορες) that also serves as the 'glue' for the gang; and c) a gang is "largely antisocial in its operations."

[36] For the suitors, see, *inter alios*, Hölscher 1990:264–267.

[37] Copley 1993:93; Wöhrle 1999: ordinarily the peer group would have facilitated the Prince's social integration by involving him, e.g., in pranks and jokes (119).

[38] See e.g. *Odyssey* 21.157–158 and Haubold 2000:138.

towards full maturity for both sexes,[39] Eurymachos' comment to Halistherses makes eminent sense. He charges Penelope with not only delaying but moreover altogether denying the suitors their chance to mature:

'ἡμεῖς δ' αὖ ποτιδέγμενοι ἤματα πάντα
εἵνεκα τῆς ἀρετῆς ἐριδαίνομεν, οὐδὲ μετ' ἄλλας
ἐρχόμεθ', ἃς ἐπιεικὲς ὀπυιέμεν ἐστὶν ἑκάστῳ.'

Odyssey 2.205–207

"we for our part, waiting on and on every day,
vie with one another on account of her general excellence (aretê), and
   we do not go
after other women, whom it would be [literally, is] fitting for each [of us]
   to marry."

The implication of the adverbial phrase ἤματα πάντα 'every day, day by day' (Odyssey 2.205) is noteworthy: time flows steadily and unstoppably at the cost of the suitors' designs of marriage to Penelope,[40] but this is to the benefit of her kleos, as Antinoos has earlier observed (Odyssey 2.125–128).

Just as she fails in the end to postpone the maturation of her 108 surrogate sons when she decides to hold the shooting contest, so also she proves incapable of putting off her real son's journey towards maturity. Her tearful

[39] In Iliad 11.225–228 marriage marks accession to the ἥβης μέτρον 'measure of maturity' in the case of the Trojan hero Iphidamas, who though newly married heads for battle from Thrace: see Ferrari 2002:133–134. In general, transvestism in myths and actual rituals (e.g. the Oschophoria) involving boys may be construed as symbolic preparation for the assumption of a heterosexual role in marriage. This view is argued by Waldner 2000 and cited by Ferrari 2002:123 and 283–284n65. That male initiation also aims at grooming a youth for a heterosexual role in society finds further support in the Telemachy: a) The two simultaneous weddings at Sparta (Odyssey 4.3–19) are neither merely an image of social normality with which Telemachos is unfamiliar (thus Jones 2002:35 ad loc.) nor an inessential and hence suspect scene (thus Dawe 1993:159–160 ad loc.) but rather part of the Prince's 'premarital' education, the doubling of a wedding feast being an emphatic educational device. b) Helen's innate sexuality, which is also made perceptible through her drug (Wöhrle 1999:128, 131n35), affords Telemachos a leisurely opportunity to become 'initiated' into female sexuality. c) The wedding gift that Helen, now the champion of matrimony, offers to the Prince (Odyssey 15.125–129), looks ahead to his maturity (possibly in the epic cycle outside the Odyssey): cf. Odyssey 15.125–127: 'τοῦτο δίδωμι, / . . .πολυηράτου ἐς γάμου ὥρην, / . . .τῆος δὲ φίλη παρὰ μητρὶ / κεῖσθαι ἐνὶ μεγάρῳ'. d) Athena herself predicts Telemachos' wedding (Odyssey 15.26). e) In general, military training, equipping a youth as it does with 'excellence' (ἀρετή), makes him attractive for a prospective bride, as suggested by Odysseus in one of his Cretan tales (Odyssey 15.211–213). See also Iliad 13.363ff. and the sexual 'initiation', which follows on their initiation proper, of Jason and other Argonauts at Lemnos in Apollonios of Rhodes and the African parallels: Woronoff 1978:246–249, 251, 257.

[40] See Odyssey 16.383, 390–392. Yet their general chances of marriage are not any fewer: Odyssey 2.206–207, 21.160–162. (Dawe and others consider Odyssey 21.157–162 an interpolation.)

reaction to the news that the prince has set out speaks volumes. Beneath the melodrama of her expostulation it is possible to discern the resolutely tight control she has exercised over him up to this point:

'εἰ γὰρ ἐγὼ πυθόμην ταύτην ὁδὸν ὁρμαίνοντα,
τῷ κε μάλ' ἤ κεν μεῖνε, καὶ ἐσσύμενός περ ὁδοῖο,
ἤ κέ με τεθνηκυῖαν ἐνὶ μεγάροισιν ἔλειπεν.'

Odyssey 4.732–734

"For if I had learned that he was contemplating this journey,
either right here he would have stayed, even though intent on his journey,
or he would have left me dead in the palace."

This possessive net had shown signs of slackening when in *Odyssey* 1.346ff. the prince delivered his tirade to his startled mother (*Odyssey* 1.360). Now Telemachos' departure brings this control to an unexpected end.

What form did such control conceivably take? In the *Vatersystem* so plausibly depicted by Homer, the only recourse open to a mother was to infantalize her son.[41] A mother had to persuade herself—and her son—that he was still νήπιος 'childish', in effect fixated at the stage of Hesiod's Silver Generation (*Works and Days*, especially 130–131). Penelope's ultimate aim is to keep her son at home. Wöhrle argues along these lines,[42] citing the following passage (where Penelope is talking in a dream to the disguised Athena):

'νῦν αὖ παῖς ἀγαπητὸς ἔβη κοίλης ἐπὶ νηός,
νήπιος, οὔτε πόνων εὖ εἰδὼς οὔτ' ἀγοράων.'

Odyssey 4.817–818

"And now my darling son has boarded a hollow ship,
childish, well-versed neither in difficulties [hardship] nor in assemblies
[public deliberation]."

Telemachos has been under her control until now—a pet she has manipulated to nearly the same degree that she has manipulated the suitors. Narcissistically exercising her charm over them, the Queen treats these youths like pet geese.[43]

---

[41] Wöhrle 1999:131.

[42] Wöhrle 1999:131.

[43] Cf. Penelope's dream of 20 geese (κατὰ οἶκον, *Odyssey* 19.536ff.), Felson-Rubin 1994:177n9 *ad loc.*, and esp. Devereux and Κουρέτας 1958:252–253, who note that χήν 'goose' is male in gender in ancient Greek. Cf. also Penelope as a child-slaying nightingale (above).

If the Little Prince is a hybrid ἀνδρόπαις[44]—that is, a *man* (ἀνήρ) whose biological maturation does not overlap with his psychosocial growth—we might say that the clinging queen focuses on the centripetal strand of παῖς 'child, boy'. At the same time Athena, especially when impersonating Mentes, counterbalances this by foregrounding the centrifugal strand of ἄνδρ in Telemachos' make-up. It is the latter component that the youth will bring to fruition once he returns from his mission. Parenthetically, Athena in her successive guises fulfills the educational role of Phoinix, who later in antiquity was considered the prototypical teacher. An *Ersatzvater*, Phoinix takes the infant Achilles as his charge (*Iliad* 9.485–91) and, significantly, accompanies the youth to Troy:

'νήπιον, οὔπω εἰδόθ' ὁμοιΐου πολέμοιο,
οὐδ' ἀγορέων, ἵνα τ' ἄνδρες ἀριπρεπέες τελέθουσι.'

Iliad 9.440–441

"childish, not yet knowledgeable about war that is impartial [?] to all
nor even about assemblies [public deliberation] where [sc. generally]
men become outstanding."

There he *teaches* Achilles the arts of rhetoric and good counsel as well as war, all of which, as we have seen, define mature heroic conduct.[45] The Iliadic passage that spells this out is well known and has already been cited:

'τοὔνεκά με προέηκε διδασκέμεναι τάδε πάντα,
μύθων τε ῥητῆρ' ἔμεναι πρηκτῆρά τε ἔργων.'

Iliad 9.442–443

"For this reason he [sc. Peleus] sent me to teach you all these things,
namely to be to be a speaker of words and a doer of deeds."

In her own words Penelope denies that her son possesses the two necessary ingredients of adult heroic identity. If she had her way, the prince would remain νήπιος 'childish', though she silently knows that he has indeed reached physical (chronological) maturity.[46] We noted in earlier chapters

---

[44] The term occurs in Aischylos *Septem* 533 (Hutchinson); Ferrari 2002, esp. 137, shows that this term refers to a hybrid, liminal stage embracing both "man and child."

[45] See Chapter 5 for the likely stages of Achilles' 'education' by Phoinix. Note τελέθουσι 'become' in *Iliad* 9.441 above, which connotes the 'hands-on' training of participation in the assembly. See also Chapter 3 and esp. n36 on Diomedes' schooling in speech.

[46] Cf. her explicit admission that 'νῦν δ'ὅτε δὴ μέγας ἐσσὶ καὶ ἥβης μέτρον ἱκάνεις' (*Odyssey* 18.217); also cf. *Odyssey* 18.269 and 19.160–161, where she calls her son *man* of the household, echoing Odysseus' observation at *Odyssey* 19.86ff.; see discussion below.

that her wish corresponds in large measure to her son's actual state since he has not yet been 'initiated' into heroic status. Antinoos' spontaneous curse (uttered before Penelope's oneiric conversation with her 'sister') is consistent with Penelope's statement in the dream:

> ἀλλά οἱ αὐτῷ
> Ζεὺς ὀλέσειε βίην, πρὶν ἥβης μέτρον ἱκέσθαι.'

Odyssey 4.668–669

> "but to his own detriment
> may Zeus destroy his strength before he reaches the measure of youth."

Scholars have been intrigued by the suitor's comment.[47] In effect Antinoos, like the Queen, rejects the reality that Telemachos has grown up, at least on the outside. Indeed, the completion of the "measure of youth" is a dire prospect for both and with good reason: in Archaic (and Classical) ideology ἥβη 'youth, coming of age' signals teleologically personal and civic agency, on the one hand, and, on the other, competence in warfare,[48] and, given the poem's particular ideology, the capacity for revenge.[49] The eventuality of personal agency threatens a mother; the second kind of agency, which Orestes embodies in exemplary fashion, threatens the suitors to their core. Yet before setting off on his ὁδός 'journey' Telemachos shows himself to be an ἀνδρόπαις 'man-child' in respect of both kinds of agency. It would be nice—according to his mother and the suitors—if he were to remain so.

---

[47] Heubeck, West, and Hainsworth 1988:235 *ad Odyssey* 4.668; Dawe 1993:203 *ad loc.*
[48] For ἥβη and agency, see Ferrari 2002:134–135, 163.
[49] Heitman 2005: Telemachos' beard forebodes his revenge (51). See Chapter 5 below.

5

Of Beards and Boar Hunts,
or, Coming of Age in the *Odyssey*

IN HOMER IT IS the connection with a paternal model and in general with the model of his male forebears that eventually makes a boy into a *man*. If the child is unconnected to his father, he is by definition νήπιος 'childish', as Susan Edmunds has shown.[1] Who then are the paradigms available to the young prince? Laertes, an obvious choice, lives in self-imposed exile and is not readily available. Autolykos, his maternal grandfather, who, as we will note, would institutionally have been the best substitute, is absent or dead. Eumaios, fatherly though he is, remains nonetheless an 'alien male', as Devereux would say, and hence is less suitable in the eyes of a patriarchal society. So too is Medon, the herald, for the selfsame reasons. *A fortiori*, the senior among the suitors who presumably entertained Telemachos regularly at their homes (*Odyssey* 11.184–187) would not be likely to fit the bill.

Faute de mieux the only person who can educate the prince in the ways of κλέος is Athena in her successive capacities as 'Mentes' and 'Mentor'. She serves the educational role of Phoinix, the surrogate father of the infant Achilles (*Iliad* 9.485–491), who later accompanies him to Troy. Even at Troy the young Achilles is still a 'child'—not biologically but developmentally, as Phoinix notes in *Iliad* 9.439ff., in respect of war (πόλεμος) and deliberation (ἀγοραί). Are we to assume that Achilles arrived on the foreign battlefield a virtual *tabula rasa*? What sort of 'education' had he most likely received previously in Thessaly? And what further training did he receive at Troy under the guidance of his 'mentor', Phoinix?

Education, glancingly alluded to in the *Iliad*, looms large in the *Odyssey*.[2] The so-called *Telemachy*—the nineteenth-century appellation for the first four

---

[1]   Edmunds 1990.

[2]   See *Iliad* 6.444–446: 'μάθον ἔμμεναι ἐσθλός . . .' (Hektor of himself); 9.440–443 (*locus classicus* of Phoinix's educational mission); 9.493–495 (Achilles as Phoinix's surrogate son, the son he would never have); 16.811: διδασκόμενος πολέμοιο (of the Trojan Euphorbos). For

books of the *Odyssey* as well as a large part of Book 15, and sections of 16 and 17—is rightly regarded by many scholars as a precursor to the *Bildungsroman*.[3] The educational strand of the poem was remarked upon, we have seen, as early as the fourth century AD by the Neo-Platonist Porphyry, who classified the tales of Telemachos as a παίδευσις 'education'.[4] In this chapter I will go one step further than ancient and modern scholars by arguing that the *Telemachy* was modeled on a recognizable standard component of aristocratic education.

Matters of education and of growing up, however, also surface outside of the *Telemachy* proper: this is scarcely surprising for a poem in which father and son move in parallel, the son imitating and re-experiencing on a micro-scale the travails, travels, and especially the seductive delays of his father. M. J. Apthorp, among others, has brought out the impressive formal and symbolic parallels between the ten-year wanderings of Odysseus and Telemachos' month-long voyage and sojourn in the Peloponnese.[5] (Needless to say, father and son never achieve parity, despite their common patterns: in accordance with Athena's master plan, Telemachos gains *kleos* as a direct result of his experiences—but this is *kleos* in a minor key, the kind of social recognition and status that more typically attaches to someone who has successfully gone through a 'life-crisis ritual', whether actual or metaphorical.) Apthorp, incidentally, leaves out one telling parallel between Odysseus and Telemachos that pertains to the *Odyssey*'s more general educational interests. It is this common feature that I would like to explore.

Education is, broadly speaking, initiatory, though not usually in van Gennep's sense of constituting a *rite de passage*. Conversely, as anthropologists note, initiation belongs to the genus 'education'.[6] Where then does the boundary between the two lie? Sir Kenneth Dover has argued that the difference between education and initiation resides in two criteria. As he puts it, "The most important criterion of initiation is in fact secrecy, which is absent from our kind of education; we do not forbid one sex to divulge the second law of thermodynamics . . . to the other sex. The intensity of symbolism is a secondary criterion." He adds: "The elements of secrecy and of symbolism

---

war figuratively as a βίαιος διδάσκαλος, cf. Thucydides 3.82.2 and Gomme 1956:373–374; Hornblower 1991:482 *ad loc.*
[3]   The term *Telemacheia* was most probably coined by the German scholar P. D. C. Hennings in 1858: see Heubeck, West, and Hainsworth 1988:52n5. On the work as a *Bildungs* (or *Entwicklungs*) *roman*, see e.g. Clarke 1963:140–141 with n16; Wöhrle 1999:140. Like others Clarke 1963:135ff. and Apthorp 1980:1ff. discuss the spilling over of the *Telemachy* beyond Book 4.
[4]   *Apud* scholia *ad Odyssey* 1.284.
[5]   Apthorp 1980:1–22.
[6]   E.g. *Encyclopedia of Social and Cultural Anthropopology*, s.v. 'education' (Barnard and Spencer 1996:178); Dover 1988:119.

in initiation procedures are, of course, variable between cultures."[7] Thus it is one thing to send pupils to school or, in the instance of the ancient Greeks, to immerse boys or young men in a set of cultural practices and mentalities in non-institutional contexts. It is quite another matter to follow the Bantu custom of secluding boys for three months in a lodge in the wilderness, submitting them to a series of hardships, instructing them in secret magico-religious formulas and finally reintegrating them into mainstream society. The custom I have just described resembles initiation rituals the world over: the individual experiences a symbolic death after withdrawal and at length is 'reborn', being rejoined (or 'incorporated') to his group with a new, often adult status.

Odysseus' boar hunt—the subject of the famed digression on the hero's wound in Book 19— represents, I believe, a culminating episode in Homeric education. Here I mean 'education' in the sense of "the unconscious inculcation of dispositions," according to Pierre Bourdieu's theory of *habitus*.[8] In this theory the learning process is not a matter of explicit tuition but rather is embedded in a variety of everyday contexts in which a person from childhood onward observes, imitates, and thereby internalizes cultural practices and social structures. As I will argue, despite its seeming casualness and certain inconcinnities, the hunting expedition is a formalized *Jünglingsprobe*—a traditional test which determines the candidate's status as that of a warrior-prince. In certain aspects this hunt resembles, at least superficially, a Cretan custom, reported by the historian Ephoros (fourth century BC), which Dover regards as a homoeroticized version of age-graded initiation.[9] Here, then, in Robert Fitzgerald's gripping

---

7   Dover 1988:119.
8   See Robbins 1991 for an explication of this and other theories in Bourdieu (1964). Morgan 1998 and Μπόκολας 2006 also make rich use of the concept of *habitus* in their studies of education.
9   Dover 1988:118; cf. Muellner 1998, esp. 18ff. The passage in question is Ephoros FGrHist 70 F 149.21 (*apud* Strabo 10.4.21 [Radt]): Ἴδιον δ' αὐτοῖς τὸ περὶ τοὺς ἔρωτας νόμιμον· οὐ γὰρ πειθοῖ κατεργάζονται τοὺς ἐρωμένους, ἀλλ' ἁρπαγῇ. προλέγει τοῖς φίλοις πρὸ τριῶν ἢ πλειόνων ἡμερῶν ὁ ἐραστὴς ὅτι μέλλει τὴν ἁρπαγὴν ποιεῖσθαι. τοῖς δ' ἀποκρύπτειν μὲν τὸν παῖδα ἢ μὴ ἐᾶν πορεύεσθαι τὴν τεταγμένην ὁδὸν τῶν αἰσχίστων ἐστὶν ὡς ἐξομολογουμένοις ὅτι ἀνάξιος ὁ παῖς εἴη τοιούτου ἐραστοῦ τυγχάνειν· συνιόντες δ', ἂν μὲν τῶν ἴσων ἢ τῶν ὑπερεχόντων τις ᾖ τοῦ παιδὸς τιμῇ καὶ τοῖς ἄλλοις ὁ ἁρπάζων, ἐπιδιώκοντες ἀνθήψαντο μόνον μετρίως τὸ νόμιμον ἐκπληροῦντες, τἄλλα δ' ἐπιτρέπουσιν ἄγειν χαίροντες, ἂν δ' ἀνάξιος, ἀφαιροῦνται· πέρας δὲ τῆς ἐπιδιώξεώς ἐστιν ἕως ἂν ἀχθῇ ὁ παῖς εἰς τὸ τοῦ ἁρπάσαντος ἀνδρεῖον (ἐράσμιον δὲ νομίζουσιν οὐ τὸν κάλλει διαφέροντα, ἀλλὰ τὸν ἀνδρείᾳ καὶ κοσμιότητι). καὶ ὁ ἐραστὴς ἀσπασάμενος δὴ καὶ ἐπιδωρησάμενος ἀπάγει τὸν παῖδα τῆς χώρας εἰς ὃν βούλεται τόπον· ἐπακολουθοῦσι δὲ καὶ τῇ ἁρπαγῇ οἱ παραγενόμενοι, ἑνεστιαθέντες δὲ καὶ συνθηρεύσαντες δίμηνον—οὐ γὰρ ἔξεστι πλείω χρόνον κατέχειν τὸν παῖδα—εἰς τὴν πόλιν καταβαίνουσιν. ἀφίεται δ' ὁ παῖς δῶρα λαβὼν στολὴν πολεμικὴν καὶ βοῦν καὶ ποτήριον (ταῦτα μὲν τὰ κατὰ τὸν νόμον δῶρα) καὶ ἄλλα πλείω καὶ πολυτελῆ, ὥστε καὶ συνερανίζειν τοὺς φίλους διὰ τὸ πλῆθος τῶν ἀναλωμάτων. τὸν μὲν οὖν βοῦν θύει τῷ Διὶ καὶ ἑστιᾷ τοὺς συγκαταβαίνοντας. εἶτ' ἀποφαίνεται περὶ τῆς πρὸς τὸν ἐραστὴν ὁμιλίας εἴτ' ἀσμενίζων τετύχηκεν εἴτε μή, τοῦ νόμου τοῦτ' ἐπιτρέψαντος, ἵν', εἴ τις αὐτῷ βία προσενήνεκται κατὰ τὴν ἁρπαγήν, ἐνταῦθα παρῇ τιμωρεῖν ἑαυτῷ καὶ ἀπαλλάττεσθαι. τοῖς δὲ καλοῖς τὴν ἰδέαν καὶ προγόνων ἐπιφανῶν μέγιστον αἶσχος ἐραστῶν μὴ τυχεῖν ὡς διὰ τὸν τρόπον

translation, is Homer's account of Odysseus' boar hunt (*Odyssey* 19.392–466 = Fitzgerald 1963:366–368):

αὐτίκα δ' ἔγνω
οὐλὴν, τήν ποτέ μιν σῦς ἤλασε λευκῷ ὀδόντι
Παρνησόνδ' ἐλθόντα μετ' Αὐτόλυκόν τε καὶ υἷας,
μητρὸς ἑῆς πατέρ' ἐσθλόν, ὃς ἀνθρώπους ἐκέκαστο   395
κλεπτοσύνῃ θ' ὅρκῳ τε· θεὸς δέ οἱ αὐτὸς ἔδωκεν
Ἑρμείας· τῷ γὰρ κεχαρισμένα μηρία καῖεν
ἀρνῶν ἠδ' ἐρίφων· ὁ δέ οἱ πρόφρων ἅμ' ὀπήδει.
Αὐτόλυκος δ' ἐλθὼν Ἰθάκης ἐς πίονα δῆμον
παῖδα νέον γεγαῶτα κιχήσατο θυγατέρος ἧς·   400
τόν ῥά οἱ Εὐρύκλεια φίλοις ἐπὶ γούνασι θῆκε
παυομένῳ δόρποιο, ἔπος τ' ἔφατ' ἔκ τ' ὀνόμαζεν·

τοῦτο παθοῦσιν. ἔχουσι δὲ τιμὰς οἱ παρασταθέντες (οὕτω γὰρ καλοῦσι τοὺς ἁρπαγέντας)· ἔν τε γὰρ τοῖς χοροῖς καὶ τοῖς δρόμοις ἔχουσι τὰς ἐντιμοτάτας χώρας τῇ τε στολῇ κοσμεῖσθαι διαφερόντως τῶν ἄλλων ἐφίεται τῇ δοθείσῃ παρὰ τῶν ἐραστῶν· καὶ οὐ τότε μόνον, ἀλλὰ καὶ τέλειοι γεγενημένοι διάσημον ἐσθῆτα φοροῦσιν, ἀφ' ἧς γνωσθήσεται ἕκαστος ʽκλεινόςʼ γενόμενος (τὸν μὲν γὰρ ἐρώμενον ʽκλεινόνʼ καλοῦσι, τὸν δ' ἐραστὴν ʽφιλήτοραʼ). ταῦτα μὲν τὰ περὶ τοὺς ἔρωτας νόμιμα. ("They have a peculiar custom in regard to love affairs, for they win the objects of their love, not by persuasion, but by abduction; the lover tells the friends of the boy three or four days beforehand that he is going to make the abduction; but for the friends to conceal the boy, or not to let him go forth by the appointed road, is indeed a most disgraceful thing, a confession, as it were, that the boy is unworthy to obtain such a lover; and when they meet, if the abductor is the boy's equal or superior in rank or other respects, the friends pursue him and lay hold of him, though only in a very gentle way, thus satisfying the custom; and after that they cheerfully turn the boy over to him to lead away; if, however, the abductor is unworthy, they take the boy away from him. And the pursuit does not end until the boy is taken to the 'Andreium' of his abductor. They regard as a worthy object of love, not the boy who is exceptionally handsome, but the boy who is exceptionally manly and decorous. After giving the boy presents, the abductor takes him away to any place in the country he wishes; and those of them who were present at the abduction follow after them, and after feasting and hunting with them for two months, (for it is not permitted to detain the boy for a longer time), they return to the city. The boy is released after receiving as presents a military habit, an ox, and a drinking-cup (these are the gifts required by law), and other things so numerous and costly that the friends, on account of the number of the expenses, make contributions thereto. Now the boy sacrifices an ox to Zeus and feasts those who returned with him; and then he makes known the facts about his intimacy with his lover, whether, perchance, it has pleased him or not, the law allowing him this privilege in order that, if any force was applied to him at the time of the abduction, he might be able at this feast to avenge himself and be rid of the lover. It is disgraceful for those who are handsome in appearance or descendants of illustrious ancestors to fail to obtain lovers, the presumption being that their character is responsible for such a fate. But the parastathentes (for thus they call those who have been abducted) receive honours; for in both the dances and the races they have the positions of highest honour, and are allowed to dress in better clothes than the rest, that is, in the habit given them by their lovers; and not then only, but even after they have grown to manhood, they wear a distinctive dress, which is intended to make known the fact that each wearer has become 'kleinos,' for they call the loved one 'kleinos' and the lover 'philetor.' So much for their customs in regard to love affairs.")

"Αὐτόλυκ', αὐτὸς νῦν ὄνομ' εὕρεο ὅττι κε θῆαι
παιδὸς παιδὶ φίλῳ· πολυάρητος δέ τοί ἐστι."
    Τὴν δ' αὖτ' Αὐτόλυκος ἀπαμείβετο φώνησέν τε·   405
"γαμβρὸς ἐμὸς θυγάτηρ τε, τίθεσθ' ὄνομ' ὅττι κεν εἴπω·
πολλοῖσιν γὰρ ἐγώ γε ὀδυσσάμενος τόδ' ἱκάνω,
ἀνδράσιν ἠδὲ γυναιξὶν ἀνὰ χθόνα πουλυβότειραν·
τῷ δ' Ὀδυσεὺς ὄνομ' ἔστω ἐπώνυμον. αὐτὰρ ἐγώ γε,
ὁππότ' ἂν ἡβήσας μητρώϊον ἐς μέγα δῶμα   410
ἔλθῃ Παρνησόνδ', ὅθι πού μοι κτήματ' ἔασι,
τῶν οἱ ἐγὼ δώσω καί μιν χαίροντ' ἀποπέμψω."
Τῶν ἕνεκ' ἦλθ' Ὀδυσεύς, ἵνα οἱ πόροι ἀγλαὰ δῶρα.
τὸν μὲν ἄρ' Αὐτόλυκός τε καὶ υἱέες Αὐτολύκοιο
χερσίν τ' ἠσπάζοντο ἔπεσσί τε μειλιχίοισι·   415
μήτηρ δ' Ἀμφιθέη μητρὸς περιφῦσ' Ὀδυσῆϊ
κύσσ' ἄρα μιν κεφαλήν τε καὶ ἄμφω φάεα καλά.
Αὐτόλυκος δ' υἱοῖσιν ἐκέκλετο κυδαλίμοισι
δεῖπνον ἐφοπλίσσαι· τοὶ δ' ὀτρύνοντος ἄκουσαν,
αὐτίκα δ' εἰσάγαγον βοῦν ἄρσενα πενταέτηρον·   420
τὸν δέρον ἀμφί θ' ἕπον, καί μιν διέχευαν ἅπαντα,
μίστυλλόν τ' ἄρ' ἐπισταμένως πεῖράν τ' ὀβελοῖσιν,
ὤπτησάν τε περιφραδέως δάσσαντό τε μοίρας.
ὣς τότε μὲν πρόπαν ἦμαρ ἐς ἠέλιον καταδύντα
δαίνυντ', οὐδέ τι θυμὸς ἐδεύετο δαιτὸς ἐΐσης·   425
ἦμος δ' ἠέλιος κατέδυ καὶ ἐπὶ κνέφας ἦλθε,
δὴ τότε κοιμήσαντο καὶ ὕπνου δῶρον ἕλοντο.
    Ἦμος δ' ἠριγένεια φάνη ῥοδοδάκτυλος Ἠώς,
βάν ῥ' ἴμεν ἐς θήρην, ἠμὲν κύνες ἠδὲ καὶ αὐτοὶ
υἱέες Αὐτολύκου· μετὰ τοῖσι δὲ δῖος Ὀδυσσεὺς   430
ἤϊεν· αἰπὺ δ' ὄρος προσέβαν καταειμένον ὕλῃ
Παρνησοῦ, τάχα δ' ἵκανον πτύχας ἠνεμοέσσας.
Ἠέλιος μὲν ἔπειτα νέον προσέβαλλεν ἀρούρας
ἐξ ἀκαλαρρείταο βαθυρρόου Ὠκεανοῖο,
οἱ δ' ἐς βῆσσαν ἵκανον ἐπακτῆρες· πρὸ δ' ἄρ' αὐτῶν   435
ἴχνι' ἐρευνῶντες κύνες ἤϊσαν, αὐτὰρ ὄπισθεν
υἱέες Αὐτολύκου· μετὰ τοῖσι δὲ δῖος Ὀδυσσεὺς
ἤϊεν ἄγχι κυνῶν, κραδάων δολιχόσκιον ἔγχος.
ἔνθα δ' ἄρ' ἐν λόχμῃ πυκινῇ κατέκειτο μέγας σῦς·
τὴν μὲν ἄρ' οὔτ' ἀνέμων διάη μένος ὑγρὸν ἀέντων,   440
οὔτε μιν Ἠέλιος φαέθων ἀκτῖσιν ἔβαλλεν,
οὔτ' ὄμβρος περάασκε διαμπερές· ὣς ἄρα πυκνὴ
ἦεν, ἀτὰρ φύλλων ἐνέην χύσις ἤλιθα πολλή.

τὸν δ' ἀνδρῶν τε κυνῶν τε περὶ κτύπος ἦλθε ποδοῖιν,
ὡς ἐπάγοντες ἐπῆσαν· ὁ δ' ἀντίος ἐκ ξυλόχοιο,   445
φρίξας εὖ λοφιήν, πῦρ δ' ὀφθαλμοῖσι δεδορκώς,
στῆ ῥ' αὐτῶν σχεδόθεν· ὁ δ' ἄρα πρώτιστος Ὀδυσσεὺς
ἔσσυτ' ἀνασχόμενος δολιχὸν δόρυ χειρὶ παχείῃ,
οὐτάμεναι μεμαώς· ὁ δέ μιν φθάμενος ἔλασεν σῦς
γουνὸς ὕπερ, πολλὸν δὲ διήφυσε σαρκὸς ὀδόντι   450
λικριφὶς ἀΐξας, οὐδ' ὀστέον ἵκετο φωτός.
τὸν δ' Ὀδυσεὺς οὔτησε τυχὼν κατὰ δεξιὸν ὦμον,
ἀντικρὺ δὲ διῆλθε φαεινοῦ δουρὸς ἀκωκή·
κὰδ δ' ἔπεσ' ἐν κονίῃσι μακών, ἀπὸ δ' ἔπτατο θυμός.
τὸν μὲν ἄρ' Αὐτολύκου παῖδες φίλοι ἀμφιπένοντο,   455
ὠτειλὴν δ' Ὀδυσῆος ἀμύμονος ἀντιθέοιο
δῆσαν ἐπισταμένως, ἐπαοιδῇ δ' αἷμα κελαινὸν
ἔσχεθον, αἶψα δ' ἵκοντο φίλου πρὸς δώματα πατρός.
τὸν μὲν ἄρ' Αὐτόλυκός τε καὶ υἱέες Αὐτολύκοιο
εὖ ἰησάμενοι ἠδ' ἀγλαὰ δῶρα πορόντες   460
καρπαλίμως χαίροντα φίλην ἐς πατρίδ' ἔπεμπον
εἰς Ἰθάκην. τῷ μέν ῥα πατὴρ καὶ πότνια μήτηρ
χαῖρον νοστήσαντι καὶ ἐξερέεινον ἅπαντα,
οὐλὴν ὅττι πάθοι· ὁ δ' ἄρα σφίσιν εὖ κατέλεξεν
ὥς μιν θηρεύοντ' ἔλασεν σῦς λευκῷ ὀδόντι,   465
Παρνησόνδ' ἐλθόντα σὺν υἱάσιν Αὐτολύκοιο.

Odyssey 19.392–466

                                    An old wound
a boar's white tusk inflicted, on Parnassos
years ago. He had gone hunting there
in company with his uncles and Autólykos,
his mother's father—a great thief and swindler
by Hermês' favor, for Autólykos pleased him
with burnt offerings of sheep and kids. The god
acted as his accomplice. Well, Autólykos
on a trip to Ithaka
arrived just after his daughter's boy was born.
In fact, he had no sooner finished supper
than Nurse Eurýkleia put the baby down
in his own lap and said:
                    "It is for you, now,
to choose a name for him, your child's dear baby;
the answer to her prayers."

Autólykos replied:
"My son-in-law, my daughter, call the boy
by the name I tell you. Well you know, my hand
has been against the world of men and women;
odium and distrust I've won. Odysseus
should be his given name. When he grows up,
when he comes visiting his mother's home
under Parnassos, where my treasures are,
I'll make him gifts and send him back rejoicing."
Odysseus in due course went for the gifts,
and old Autólykos and his sons embraced him
with welcoming sweet words; and Amphithéa,
his mother's mother, held him tight and kissed him,
kissed his head and his fine eyes.

       The father
called on his noble sons to make a feast,
and going about it briskly they led in
an ox of five years, whom they killed and flayed
and cut in bits for roasting on the skewers
with skilled hands, with care; then shared it out.
So all the day until the sun went down
they feasted to their hearts' content. At evening,
after the sun was down and dusk had come,
they turned to bed and took the gift of sleep.
When the young Dawn spread in the eastern sky
her finger tips of rose, the men and dogs
went hunting, taking Odysseus. They climbed
Parnassos' rugged flank mantled in forest,
entering amid high windy folds at noon
when Hêlios beat upon the valley floor
and on the winding Ocean whence he came.
With hounds questing ahead, in open order,
the sons of Autólykos went down a glen,
Odysseus in the lead, behind the dogs,
pointing his long-shadowing spear.

        Before them
a great boar lay hid in undergrowth,
in a green thicket proof against the wind
or sun's blaze, fine soever the needling sunlight,
impervious too to any rain, so dense
that cover was, heaped up with fallen leaves.

Patter of hounds' feet, men's feet, woke the boar
as they came up—and from his woody ambush
with razor back bristling and raging eyes
he trotted and stood at bay. Odysseus,
being on top of him, had the first shot,
lunging to stick him; but the boar
had already charged under the long spear.
He hooked aslant with one white tusk and ripped out
flesh above the knee, but missed the bone.
Odysseus' second thrust went home by luck,
his bright spear passing through the shoulder joint;
and the beast fell, moaning as life pulsed away.
Autólykos' tall sons took up the wounded,
working skillfully over the Prince Odysseus
to bind his gash, and with a rune they stanched
the dark flow of blood. Then downhill swiftly
they all repaired to the father's house, and there
tended him well—so well they soon could send him,
with Grandfather Autólykos' magnificent gifts,
rejoicing, over sea to Ithaka.
His father and the Lady Antikleía
welcomed him, and wanted all the news
of how he got his wound; so he spun out
his tale, recalling how the boar's white tusk
caught him when he was hunting on Parnassos.

Odyssey (tr. Fitzgerald) 19.392–466

For the benefit of my discussion I note the key passages in my own translation:

Αὐτόλυκος δ' ἐλθὼν Ἰθάκης ἐς πίονα δῆμον
παῖδα νέον γεγαῶτα κιχήσατο θυγατέρος ἧς·   400
τόν ῥά οἱ Εὐρύκλεια φίλοις ἐπὶ γούνασι θῆκε
παυομένῳ δόρποιο, ἔπος τ' ἔφατ' ἔκ τ' ὀνόμαζεν·
'Αὐτόλυκ', αὐτὸς νῦν ὄνομ' εὕρεο ὅττι κε θῆαι
παιδὸς παιδὶ φίλῳ· πολυάρητος δέ τοί ἐστι.'
    Τὴν δ' αὖτ' Αὐτόλυκος ἀπαμείβετο φώνησέν τε·   405
'γαμβρὸς ἐμὸς θυγάτηρ τε, τίθεσθ' ὄνομ' ὅττι κεν εἴπω·
πολλοῖσιν γὰρ ἐγώ γε ὀδυσσάμενος τόδ' ἱκάνω,
ἀνδράσιν ἠδὲ γυναιξὶν ἀνὰ χθόνα πουλυβότειραν·
τῷ δ' Ὀδυσεὺς ὄνομ' ἔστω ἐπώνυμον.   αὐτὰρ ἐγώ γε,

ὁππότ᾽ ἂν ἡβήσας μητρώϊον ἐς μέγα δῶμα   410
ἔλθῃ Παρνησόνδ᾽, ὅθι πού μοι κτήματ᾽ ἔασι,
τῶν οἱ ἐγὼ δώσω καί μιν χαίροντ᾽ ἀποπέμψω.᾽
Τῶν ἕνεκ᾽ ἦλθ᾽ Ὀδυσεύς, ἵνα οἱ πόροι ἀγλαὰ δῶρα.
τὸν μὲν ἄρ᾽ Αὐτόλυκός τε καὶ υἱέες Αὐτολύκοιο
χερσίν τ᾽ ἠσπάζοντο ἔπεσσί τε μειλιχίοισι·   415
μήτηρ δ᾽ Ἀμφιθέη μητρὸς περιφῦσ᾽ Ὀδυσῆϊ
κύσσ᾽ ἄρα μιν κεφαλήν τε καὶ ἄμφω φάεα καλά.
Αὐτόλυκος δ᾽ υἱοῖσιν ἐκέκλετο κυδαλίμοισι
δεῖπνον ἐφοπλίσσαι· τοὶ δ᾽ ὀτρύνοντος ἄκουσαν,
αὐτίκα δ᾽ εἰσάγαγον βοῦν ἄρσενα πενταέτηρον·   420

Odyssey 19.399–420

Now Autolykos, having come to the fertile land of Ithaka,
came upon the newborn son of his daughter.
Him Eurykleia placed upon his knees
as he was finishing his evening meal, and she spoke and addressed him by
       name:
"Autolykos, yourself [*autos*] now find whatever name you may have an
       interest in ascribing
to the beloved son of your son; surely he has been much prayed for."
Her in turn Autolykos answered and spoke to:
"My son-in-law and my daughter, ascribe [to him] whatever name I may
       utter:
since I have come this way having felt anger [*odussamenos*] at many,
men and women throughout the earth that feeds many flocks—
 therefore let him have the name 'Odysseus' as his meaningful name. And I,
when he, having come of age, to his mother's great [ancestral] home
comes on Mt. Parnassos where my possessions are,
some of these I shall give him as a gift and shall send him away rejoicing."
On account of those [objects] Odysseus had come: so that he [i.e.
       Autolykos] might present him splendid gifts.
So him Autolykos and the sons of Autolykos
welcomed with their hands [i.e. clasping his hand] and with words gentle
       as honey.
The mother of his mother Amphithee, hugging Odysseus,
kissed him on the head and both beautiful eyes.
Autolykos, meanwhile, ordered his glorious sons
to prepare the meal, and they heeded his urging,
and immediately they led in a five-year-old bull.

τὸν μὲν ἄρ' Αὐτολύκου παῖδες φίλοι ἀμφιπένοντο,　　　455
ὠτειλὴν δ' Ὀδυσῆος ἀμύμονος ἀντιθέοιο
δῆσαν ἐπισταμένως, ἐπαοιδῇ δ' αἷμα κελαινὸν
ἔσχεθον, αἶψα δ' ἵκοντο φίλου πρὸς δώματα πατρός.
τὸν μὲν ἄρ' Αὐτόλυκός τε καὶ υἱέες Αὐτολύκοιο
εὖ ἰησάμενοι ἠδ' ἀγλαὰ δῶρα πορόντες　　　460
καρπαλίμως χαίροντα φίλην ἐς πατρίδ' ἔπεμπον
εἰς Ἰθάκην. τῷ μέν ῥα πατὴρ καὶ πότνια μήτηρ
χαῖρον νοστήσαντι καὶ ἐξερέεινον ἅπαντα,
οὐλὴν ὅττι πάθοι· ὁ δ' ἄρα σφίσιν εὖ κατέλεξεν
ὥς μιν θηρεύοντ' ἔλασεν σῦς λευκῷ ὀδόντι,　　　465
Παρνησόνδ' ἐλθόντα σὺν υἱάσιν Αὐτολύκοιο.

Odyssey 19.455–466

The dear sons of Autolykos busied themselves with it [sc. the carcass]
and the wound of Odysseus the pre-eminent, the godlike
they bound up expertly, and with an incantation the dark blood
they staunched, and at once they went to the house of his dear father.
Now, him Autolykos and the sons of Autolykos,
after tending [him] well and after presenting splendid gifts [to him],
they speedily sent rejoicing to his dear native land,
to Ithaka. His father and lady mother
rejoiced at his homecoming [*nostêsanti*, literally, his having made his
　　　nostos] and they closely asked about every detail,
about the scar, how did he get it [literally, what happened to him]; and
　　　to them he narrated well [from the beginning to the end]
how a boar charged at him with its white tusk while he was hunting,
after going to Mt. Parnassos with the sons of Autolykos.

This test of manhood—if it is that—is deliberately announced elliptically at Odysseus' naming ceremony, during the very speech act that declares that his identity is to be a pun on the verb ὀδύσσεσθαι 'to feel anger' (*Odyssey* 19.406–409). His maternal grandfather Autolykos 'Lone Wolf'[10] has come from Parnassos to visit Laertes and Antikleia shortly after Odysseus' birth. Holding the baby symbolically on his knees, Autolykos names him, then ordains that as soon as the child becomes a young adult (ἡβήσας 'having come of age', *Odyssey* 19.411), he is to call on him at Parnassos; Autolykos will then award the young man a portion of his (ancestral) moveable possessions (κτήματα, *Odyssey* 19.411; cf. ἀγλαὰ δῶρα 'splendid gifts', 19.413) and afterwards send him

---

[10]　G. Nagy, personal communication.

back to Ithaka rejoicing (*Odyssey* 19.411–412).[11] What is Odysseus' grandfather alluding to? Jan Bremmer has come up with a cogent answer: Autolykos implies a ceremony by which Odysseus will be welcomed or (as Bremmer believes) "initiated" into his maternal family. According to this scholar's comparative analysis of myths and historical sources, a boy's maternal kin, and particularly his mother's brothers, would have had an "active hand" in his education, and they could even serve as his foster-father(s) until the boy's puberty.[12]

Surely enough, 18 or so years later, the hero journeys to Parnassos, ostensibly to claim the κτήματα 'possessions' pledged to him. There the youth joins Autolykos and his uncles. The men hold a bull sacrifice and a lavish feast that ends at nightfall. At the crack of dawn the party—grandfather, uncles, and Odysseus—set out to hunt with their dogs.

The men and dogs corner a boar, forcing it to emerge in anger from its lair; Odysseus, the first to attack, is wounded above the knee. Peter Jones, in his commentary, taxes the hero with impulsiveness, noting that Odysseus charges the animal, not vice versa.[13] Impulsive or just wet behind the ears? The best strategy would be for the entire hunting party to surround their prey and then *simultaneously* cast their spears, the tactic employed in the tragic boar hunt in Herodotos 1.43. Odysseus, moreover, ought to know that boars only counterattack and, even then, only when wounded. Once injured, a boar turns into a frenzied killer, capable of remarkable feats of strength and stamina. Imagine the charge of a well-muscled creature shielded with a virtually impervious hide and weighing between 140 and 300 kilos.[14] True to zoology, boars in Homer are always aggressive defenders, never attackers (unlike lions, which attack first).[15] Richard Rutherford, for his part, argues that the boar hunt in *Odyssey* 19 is only incidental to Odysseus' visit to Parnassos on the grounds that "in the text as it stands the initial purpose of Odysseus' journey to Parnassos is not to hunt (nor does Autolycus mention this aspect of the proposed visit), but to obtain gifts from his maternal relatives. *It is possible that gift-exchange rather*

---

[11] Perhaps one of these gifts is a boar's tusk helmet (κυνέη) such as the one Odysseus wears in his scouting mission in the *Doloneia*. In *Iliad* 10.261–271 the hero's κυνέη had once been stolen by his grandfather Autolykos, who gave it to Amphidamas, who gave it as a ξεινήϊον to Molos, who gave it to his son, Odysseus' squire Meriones, who put it on Odysseus in arming him for the mission. But why should Autolykos' possession have devolved upon Odysseus' squire and not Odysseus himself? Conceivably *Odyssey* 19.411 and 413 presuppose a more plausible version according to which Autolykos gives Odysseus his emblematic κυνέη after the lad has 'graduated' from the boar-hunting test.

[12] Bremmer 1983:173–186. As Bremmer remarks (178n30), the avunculate is also implicit in the tale of the Kalydonian boar hunt in *Iliad* 9.529ff., on which, see further n29 below. Another case, also noted by Bremmer (174), is the Thracian Iphidamas, raised by his maternal grandfather.

[13] Jones 2002:181 *ad Odyssey* 19.448.

[14] In 2006–2007 I 'interviewed' boar hunters in Serbia and Greece (w. Thrace).

[15] Muellner 1990:64.

than hunting is the underlying institution" [italics mine].[16] This is to ignore an obvious point, namely, the traditional educational value of the boar hunt as attested in Macedonian inscriptions and other sources from the fourth century BC onward.[17] M. B. Hatzopoulos, who has studied the Macedonian practice, shows it to be outright an educational institution that may be traced back to age-graded initiation of long standing.[18] (I will return to the highly ancient Macedonian custom shortly. For the moment I note that the hunt of the κάπρος 'wild boar' is but one of numerous similar educational practices evidenced Panhellenically, as Hatzopoulos demonstrates.)

Even Rutherford, despite his initial doubts, owns that Odysseus' expedition does have "something of the nature of a *rite of passage*, a transitional ritual between youth and manhood, literally a 'blooding'."[19] As students of anthropology well know, moreover, initiation activities often end with the bestowal of gifts upon 'graduating' initiates. Anthropologically speaking, it is rather the gift-giving that is an incidental (if symbolic) component of what transpires in the excursus in *Odyssey* 19. Autolykos, in keeping with the ideology of initiation, cryptically invites his grandson, once he becomes a young man, to come to Parnassos to receive gifts. The real reason for the pre-announced visit, however, is to undergo a test of manhood. If successful, Odysseus will win gifts, like the successful young hunter in Ephoros' account of pederastic abduction in Crete. After two months in the bush with his ἐραστής 'lover', the ἐρώμενος 'beloved' hunter receives from him an ox, a drinking-cup, and a combat outfit—all expensive gifts. And like the young Cretan hunter, Odysseus is to gain a new public status, as I will remark shortly.

Rutherford is still more helpful to my purposes, because he shows the extent to which the retrospective narrative about the killing of the boar incorporates telltale details from Iliadic battle descriptions: a total of six lines (433–434, 449, 451, 452, and 453) echo combat scenes word for word, while

---

[16] Rutherford 1992:186 *ad Odyssey* 19.410.

[17] Another point overlooked here is the condensed manner in which Homer may narrate the background, well known or culturally assumed by the audience, of an event. Thus the narrator's remark that young Odysseus went to Parnassos 'τῶν [sc. δώρων] ἔνεκ' (*Odyssey* 19.412) may be comparable with Tlepolemos' allusive remark that his father Herakles sacked Troy "for the sake of Laomedon's (half-divine) mares" (ἐλθὼν ἕνεχ' ἵππων Λαομέδοντος', *Iliad* 5.640). Sarpedon, his interlocutor, well knows the background, hence he implies in his riposte that the mares, 'ὧν εἵνεκα [sc. Ἡρακλῆς] τηλόθεν ἦλθε' (*Iliad* 5.651), had been pledged to but finally denied Herakles as compensation for an unspecified ἔργον, viz. the rescue of Hesione from a sea-monster. Each speaker assumes that the other knows why Herakles ultimately sacked Troy. ἔνεχ' ἵππων (*Iliad* 5.640) and ὧν εἵνεκα (*Iliad* 5.651) are shorthand for those in the know, including Homer's audience. Kirk 1993:123–124 *ad Iliad* 5.640–642 notes that the tale of Hesione's rescue by Herakles is alluded to three times in the *Iliad*.

[18] Hatzopoulos 1994:87–111, esp. 88–94.

[19] Rutherford 1992:186.

verse 454 replicates *Iliad* 16.469, which describes the death in battle of Patroklos' horse Pedasos.[20] As Rutherford remarks, such echoes remind the audience of martial epic.[21] They also suggest, as this scholar implies, that young Odysseus is consciously imitating the conduct of a typical warrior flushing out a camouflaged enemy who waits in ambush.[22] Odysseus, παιδνὸς ἐών 'being a child' (cf. *Odyssey* 21.21), undergoes, it appears, a standard exploit, which in its symbolism and danger prefigures his full-scale adult ἀριστεῖαι 'special periods of prowess', such as that in *Iliad* 11. 411–445.[23] There the action is introduced by a simile that likens the stranded hero Odysseus to a fearsome boar harried on all sides by hounds and brave *young* hunters;[24] the mature fighter Odysseus, in other words, is the analogue of the animal he killed as a young adult at Parnassos.[25] In three other Iliadic similes, warriors, Achaians, and Trojans alike share certain telling features with boars; so a boar, one might say, functions as a good *Ersatz*-enemy with whom to rehearse hand-to-hand combat.[26] Also suggestive, right after the boar simile in *Iliad* 11, Odysseus mortally wounds with his spear a Trojan in the shoulder (*Iliad* 11.420–421), another between the shoulders (11.447–448), and then is himself wounded. At Parnassos the hero, it will be recalled, pierces the boar through the shoulder with his ἔγχος 'spear', presumably striking its lung in much the same way that a matador lethally stabs a bull below the shoulder blade.[27]

---

[20] Rutherford 1992:187–188 *ad loc.*; de Jong 2001:478 *ad Odyssey* 19.428–456 ("a heroic patina"; but she omits a few epic reminiscences).

[21] Rutherford 2002:186 *ad Odyssey* 19.410.

[22] Rutherford 2002:186 *ad Odyssey* 19.410. I notice that the λόχμη 'thicket' (19.439–443) provides foolproof camouflage for Homer's boar, which like boars nowadays hides among leaves and bushes. Homer's boar in the λόχμη 'thicket' is the archetypal leader of an ambush (cf. λόχος).

[23] The Kalydonian boar hunt was the mythic *exemplum* for real-life 'initiatory' boar hunts; see below. A boar is the equivalent of a lion and other creatures at *Odyssey* 4.456–457, where Proteus changes into a lion, a serpent (δράκων), a leopard, and finally a *huge boar.* (Muellner 1990:63–64 remarks the interchangeability of the boar and lion in a number of Homeric similes.) On a late sixth-century B.C. Samian krater (in the Archaeological Museum at Vathy, Samos) a boar appears to be out-staring and out-growling a smaller lion.

[24] Hunting is a young man's activity: *Iliad* 11.414–415.

[25] Cf. Schnapp-Gourbeillon 1981 passim on the analogue of lion and aristocratic hero. Odysseus, as just noted, 'is' the wild animal he hunts. This equivalence explains the parallel descriptions, which Rutherford 1992:187–188 puzzles over, of Odysseus as a land-and-sea beast at *Odyssey* 5.478–483 and of the boar at 19.439ff., both disguised by thick vegetation (see n22 above).

[26] Other boar similes in the *Iliad*: 12.146–152 (of the Trojans); 13.471–477 (of Idomeneus' steadfastness); 17.281–287 (of Ajax's might in battle). See also Muellner 1990:63–64 on such similes. Cf. Atys' telling query (that seals this tale) in Herodotos I.39, 'ὑὸς δὲ κοῖαι μέν εἰσί χεῖρες …;' ('Has a boar got hands?'). Lastly, see Ma 2008:9–10 on the "parallelism between the 'fight' scene and the hunting scene" in the Achaemenid Çan sarcophagus (early fourth century B.C.); the two themes are linked in imperial ideology. (I thank Adrienne Mayor for the reference to this article.)

[27] Boars are extremely thick-skinned on the upper body; their neck may be up to 10cm thick, whereas the skin around the chest is thin, hence today hunters prefer to shoot at the animal's chest or head.

The hunting expedition in *Odyssey* 19 is far from incidental, as I have urged, and most likely reflects the social reality of the Archaic and earlier periods. Such a hunt was the key component of a traditional 'blooding' that followed a set procedure and was modeled on a military exercise.[28] The Iliadic overtones in the *Odyssey's* excursus bear out the latter aspect. If Macedonian practice is at all a reliable comparandum, this test, which myth retrojected ultimately to the Kalydonian boar hunt and to Herakles' similar exploit,[29] was essential to establishing a young man's masculine as well as his collective identity. Athenaios 1.18 reports that at Macedon men who had not killed a boar with a spear were debarred from reclining at dinner and that Kassandros for this very reason had to sit (like a woman) next to his father at meals until the age of 35, when he finally killed a boar.[30] 'Blooding' ideology clearly underlies the tomb fresco at Vergina, which includes two nude hunters with spears— but significantly without belts—pursuing a boar.[31] Hatzopoulos, who convincingly reads the fresco as a whole in terms of age-grades and royal hierarchy, classifies the hunters as not fully adult and not yet inducted into the army. Success in a boar hunt thus made one a man and a soldier in the archaizing kingdom of Macedon.[32]

Wounds sustained from the definitional hunt would have been marks of identity. As Dover notes,[33] injury itself serves as a test of endurance and also

---

[28] Actual boar hunts recalled, it appears, a type scene. As Nagy 1996:48–49n28 notices, at Bacchylides 5.125 the adverb ἐνδυκέως (cf. Latin *ducere*) refers to the fighting of warriors over the hide of the Kalydonian boar; at Pindar *Pythian* 5.85 the adverb refers to the set procedure or protocol of carrying out θυσίαι when receiving a guest.

[29] The mythical expeditions involved the use of spears, not nets: see Hatzopoulos 1994:94, following Vidal-Naquet 1991:170. Neither scholar cites Odysseus' boar exploit. According to Lonis 1979:202–203 and others, the Kalydonian boar hunt was arguably "le mythe étiologique d' un rite de sortie d' une classe d' âge." It involved some 16 ephebes (Meleager, Theseus, Jason, Kastor and Pollux, et al.), the maiden Atalante, and two adults (Meleager's uncles), the latter being the "parrains initiatiques" of the group, which was in effect an *agela*. Artemis' and her doublet Atalante's role in the myth points to her Kourotrophic aspect as "l' initiatrice par excellence," a role the goddess fulfilled in the fifth and fourth centuries B.C. in ephebic cults at Athens (Artemis *Agrotera*), the Piraeus, and Cos. There is one detail that has, as far as I know, escaped scholars' notice: the very name Κουρῆτες. In *Iliad* 9.529 the Κουρῆτες turn against Meleager and his fellow Aitolians; but this name, as Hainsworth 1993:132–133 notes *ad loc.*, "occurs by *coincidence* [italics mine] also in various Cretan rituals . . . and at a later date in association with cults in Asia Minor." Is this really coincidence? Further, as Hainsworth notes, the proparoxytone form of the name—Κούρητες—"means simply 'young warriors.'" Cumulatively this scholar's remarks suggest that Homer's κουρῆτες are a proper cultic name for a (rival?) *agela* of young warriors undergoing initiation.

[30] Cited by Hatzopoulos 1994:93–94, following Vidal-Naquet.

[31] See Hatzopoulos 1994:92ff. (and his Plate XXIV), not in Ferrari 2002.

[32] Further on 'educational' boar hunts in Macedonia, Sparta, and Crete, see Hatzopoulos 1994:132ff. and Bokolas 2006:228–230. On the edifying value of the hunt for young aristocrats: Plato *Laws* 823b; Xenophon *Hunting* 12.1–2: τὰ δὲ πρὸς τὸν πόλεμον μάλιστα παιδεύει.

[33] Dover 1988:119.

furnishes lasting proof of "transition to a new status, e.g. cutting off the fore-skin or knocking out one of the front teeth." Odysseus' φίλοι 'intimates' from childhood—people like Laertes, Eumaios, Philoitios the cowherd, and his former nurse—are proudly aware of the οὐλή 'scar'.[34] As an unmistakable signifier (liter-ally a σῆμα 'sign or token'), the scar is for Homer as potent a symbol of a change of gender as the sprouting of a beard. In a culture with a uniquely calibrated terminology for male facial hair, γενειάδες 'a beard' betokened the onset of ἥβη, or early adulthood.[35] Once arrived at the attractive 'full measure of ἥβη', a male possessed personal and civic agency and in particular, in Homeric ideology, the self-evident capacity to carry out acts of revenge.[36] At *Odyssey* 1.41 Zeus declares that Orestes behaves typically when he exacts τίσις 'retaliation, revenge' on Aigisthos as soon as he reaches ἥβη. And, as we learn at *Odyssey* 11.317–320, the gigantic twins Otos and Ephialtes would have toppled the Olympians had Apollo not killed them before they grew full, blossoming beards.[37]

Such an ideology requires that Odysseus should go boar-hunting only after growing a beard at ἥβη 'early adulthood, coming of age'. The sequence—beard, then boar hunt—was arguably standard in the pre-Archaic and Archaic periods. Not only is the hero's wound a metonym for ἥβη, but, located as it is above the knee (*Odyssey* 19.449–450), the notional seat of manhood,[38] the injury is compa-rable to the removal of foreskin in circumcision.

The young hero's coming of age culminates, it seems, in λεγόμενα 'things said' followed by δρώμενα 'things done'. First comes the twin cry of congratula-tion, 'ἀμύμων ἀντίθεος' ("the preeminent, the godlike"), as suggested by the phraseology in verse 456: ὠτειλὴν δ' Ὀδυσῆος ἀμύμονος ἀντιθέοιο ('and the wound of Odysseus the preeminent, the godlike').[39] Having earned two epithets typical of heroes, the wounded hunter enjoys permanently a new standing and high repute among his community. In like fashion, after his two-month stint, the Cretan hunter mentioned in Ephoros is entitled to wear at festivals the clothing awarded to him by his lover, and henceforth is reckoned κλεινός 'of high repute'. He has gained *kleos* in a minor key— the first glimmer of a grown-up's

---

[34] *Odyssey* 21.217–219 (Eumaios and Philoitios); 24.329, 331 (Laertes).
[35] Ferrari 2002:135–136 (the vocabulary of male pubescent hair); 116, 136–137 (fledgling beards in art).
[36] Ferrari 2002:163, 175 is fundamental.
[37] Ferrari 2002:135; cf. Heitman 2005:12, 58.
[38] Petropoulos 1994:42–43 (esp. n35); 85, on male reapers' weak knees in Hesiod *Works and Days* 586–587; also Bremmer 1983:178n29 on the initiatory significance of a thigh wound.
[39] I am here expanding on Rutherford 1992:198 *ad loc*. Odysseus' guardians treat his wounds by means of an incantation (*Odyssey* 19.457: ἐπαοιδῇ). Thus to their ululation ("Well done, ἀμύμων!") they merge the melody of magical song; anthropologically speaking, this is a fitting combination given that initiation often entails exposure of the initiand to magico-religious formulas, as noted earlier.

kleos. Then comes the award of ἀγλαὰ δῶρα 'splendid gifts' (*Odyssey* 19.460).[40] The hero, rejoicing, is seen off by his rejoicing grandfather and uncles. If we adopt, with Rutherford and Dawe,[41] the vulgate alternative φίλως χαίροντες instead of φίλην ἐς πατρίδ', the assonance in verse 461 (καρπαλίμως χαίροντα φίλως χαίροντες ἔπεμπον ['rejoicing in a spirit of intimacy, they speedily sent him rejoicing']) brings out the mutual pleasure of kin and grandson. The line also reproduces the bondedness of this all-male group.[42] On his return the young man gives an eloquent account of the exploit to his rejoicing parents (*Odyssey* 19.462–467). But this is no mere foretaste of Odysseus the raconteur and ἀοιδός 'singer of tales'.[43] A censored narrative by the initiate of his trials would have been a conventional sequel: the 'graduate' did not simply satisfy the curiosity of his family; he gave what was probably the first performance of his 'personal experience narrative' (or 'personal legend'). Telemachos' narrative, suitably censored for his inquiring mother in *Odyssey* 17.108–149,[44] may be an example of this standard *récit*; also compare his *récit* (not quoted however) to Mentor and other elders in *Odyssey* 17.68–70. Out of the wound emanates the young man's first 'personal legend or story'.

Having proved his mettle and stamina in the relatively controlled environment of the hunt—the other hunters would have stepped in if anything untoward had happened—the hero is now ready for a more advanced stage of preparation. This time the trial is more clearly a quest and is carried out in less of a controlled environment. This entails what Homer calls an ἐξεσίη, a 'mission abroad', across sea or land or both. Two heroes, Nestor (*Iliad* 11) and Odysseus (*Odyssey* 21), and *possibly* a third, Laertes (*Odyssey* 24.376–379), specifically undertake such a quest for the sake of gaining hands-on 'epic' experience. (In the third part of this chapter I will argue that Telemachos' ἐξεσίη, which is also called an ὁδός 'journey', represents such a grade-two test.) I turn first to Nestor's two junior exploits, which, if read back to back, shed light on the fundamentally educational nature of the ἐξεσίη 'mission abroad'.

---

[40] *Odyssey* 19.460 = 19.413; cf. 19.411: κτήματα; 24.335: δῶρα. (All three verses refer to the prize awarded after Odysseus' hunting venture.)

[41] See Rutherford 1992:189 and Dawe 1993:712 *ad loc.*, who renders the line thus: "they exchanged friendly farewells and sent him speedily to Ithaca."

[42] Cf. the feeling of *communitas, à la* Victor Turner 1974, which the ὁδός has engendered between the ὁμήλικες Telemachos and Peisistratus (*Odyssey* 15.197–198): 'ὁμήλικές εἰμεν / ἠδε δ' ὁδὸς καὶ μᾶλλον ὁμοφροσύνῃσιν ἐνήσει' (which plays on ὁμήλικες and ὁμοφροσύνῃσιν).

[43] Cf. Rutherford 1992:189 *ad Odyssey* 19.464; de Jong 2001:477 *ad loc.*

[44] See *Folklore, An Encyclopedia*, s.v. 'personal experience narrative' (Green 1997[II]:635–637).

At the height of a losing battle in *Iliad* 11, the veteran hero reminisces to Patroklos about bygone days (11.670–763).[45] He describes himself as a young man (*Iliad* 11.670, 684)—in the stage of ἥβη 'early adulthood'—when he leads a retaliatory raid on Elis (in the west Peloponnese) in order to recover a debt from the perfidious Eleans. He duly rustles large herds of cattle, swine, goats, and horses as repayment of the debt.[46] Armed lightly, with only a spear (*Iliad* 11.675), he also kills a prominent local, Ityoneus, and returns victorious to his proud father Neleus.[47] From Nestor's account and its sequel it is plain that this was a minor exploit more suitable for a young adult; dangerous enough to test him, yet not too dangerous. P. Vidal-Naquet regards this raid, which only involves the use of spears, as the first (and more elementary) of Nestor's two 'initiations' into war.[48] D. Frame (2009:110n7) puts it well: "the cattle raid still does not establish Nestor as a warrior; to become a warrior he must become a horseman and fight in a battle with other horsemen." In contrast, the exploit that immediately follows is not a raid and is more perilous according to Nestor. It involves heavy arms (cf. *Iliad* 11.718, 725) and fighting from a chariot.[49] Engagement with heavy arms was, as Vidal-Naquet argues, proper to adult warriors. So it is this adventure, which is a foil to the previous one, that fully 'initiates' Nestor into the adult world of horsemen. A few words about this exploit are in order.

Even as the Pylians are distributing the booty among themselves, as Nestor recalls, the Epeians (probably the same people as the Eleans) counter-attack with their allies. The invaders include the terrible Molione twins who, Nestor notes, are however παῖδες 'boys, children' still untutored in war: 'Μολίονε θωρήσσοντο, / παῖδ' ἔτ' ἐόντ', οὔ πω μάλα εἰδότε θούριδος ἀλκῆς' ("the Molione twins armed themselves, / 'boys' still, not yet knowing much about furious warfare," *Iliad* 11.709–710).[50] Nestor, at any rate, is eager to fight, but Neleus will not allow him to arm himself and hides away Nestor's horses, for in Nestor's words, "he said

---

[45] On this two-part story, the second longest para-narrative in the *Iliad*, see also Alden 2000:88–101 (a more literary interpretation) and now Frame 2009:105–130 on its connection to the Vedic *Aśvínā*, the cattleman and horseman twins, and its overlooked relevance to Patroklos.

[46] Iles Johnston 2003, esp. 159 (with n14): " . . . ancient Greek cattle-raid myths derive from Indoeuropean models and reflect the same ideologies. Under these ideologies the raid wins honour for the young hero and admission into the 'adult community.'" Nestor's tale follows the Indoeuropean paradigm closely according to Iles Johnston 2003:161.

[47] Vidal-Naquet 1986:118–119 singles out three elements in the "initiation" of a Greek warrior as characteristic of anti-hoplite/pre-hoplite and hence non-adult activity: a) the young warrior uses light arms (as here); b) he fights/hunts at night (see n48 immediately below); c) he employs deception.

[48] Vidal-Naquet 1986:119 means 'initiation' literally here. He is wrong to say that the fighting occurs at night (which would fit his 'Black hunter' thesis). Nestor fought by day, while the booty was driven to Pylos at night (*Iliad* 11.683).

[49] Otherwise unattested in Homer; see n52 below.

[50] The brothers foolishly enlisted and had to be saved from Nestor by Poseidon, their father (*Iliad* 11.750–752). In Archaic art they feature as Siamese twins: Snodgrass 1998:27–32.

that as yet I knew nothing of deeds of war" (*Iliad* 11.717–719, esp. 719: 'οὐ γὰρ πώ τί μ' ἔφη ἴδμεν πολεμήϊα ἔργα').[51] Yet the young man belies his father's fears, proving preeminent among charioteers (*Iliad* 11.720ff.).[52] Nestor is, in fact, the first to kill an Epeian, a spearman (*Iliad* 11.738ff.), then another hundred men, all charioteers, narrowly missing the Molione brothers. After the victory, the Achaian army—to quote Nestor's curious third-person formulation—"gave praise/thanks to Zeus among gods, and to Nestor among men" (*Iliad* 11.761: 'πάντες δ' εὐχετόωντο θεῶν Διὶ Νέστορί τ' ἀνδρῶν').[53]

Thus young Nestor's second exploit, considerably more dangerous and spectacular than his debt-collecting mission, pits him against the semi-divine Molione (who are themselves a bit wet behind the ears and need Poseidon's intervention). Neleus fears for the safety of Nestor, his only surviving son, as it turns out, considering him not fully mature as a warrior. But the lad (νέος, *Iliad* 11.684) triumphantly passes this unauthorized leap into adult warfare. As I have suggested, young Nestor's first proper test would have been the controlled experiment of a boar hunt. His second, intermediate test is the cattle-rustling ἐξεσίη 'foreign mission' in Elis.

In his youth Odysseus too conducts a vindictive debt-collecting raid on the Messenians, because, to quote Homer (*Odyssey* 21.15ff.), "Messenian men had lifted from Ithaka sheep / and three hundred herdsmen in ships with many benches for oarsmen . . ." The mission, which the poet terms an ἐξεσίη (*Odyssey* 21.20), is *arranged by his father and other elders*. The hero, a mere youth (παιδνὸς ἐών, literally, 'a boy, a child'), travels a long distance (πολλὴν ὁδὸν, *Odyssey* 21.20) southward to Messene. Compared with the distances and dangers of his later journeys, the assignment is truly minor, yet it affords him a relatively low-risk exposure to warfare and aristocratic courtesies; for during its course Odysseus also meets Iphitos, and the two exchange gifts.

---

[51] For the paradigmatic/rhetorical appositeness of this opposition to Nestor's entering the fray, see Alden 2000:94n46.

[52] Jones 2003:181–182 *ad Iliad* 11.747: "this is the only episode in the *Iliad* where the fighting is carried out from chariots, by (apparently) chariot squadrons."

[53] Cf. *Odyssey* 8.467: 'τῷ κέν τοι καὶ κεῖθι θεῷ ὡς εὐχετοώμην' (Odysseus' parting words to his savior Nausikaa): Garvie 1994:328 *ad loc.* interprets the verb as 'give thanks to'; see Muellner (immediately below). Why does Nestor speak of himself in the third person? There are to my mind two reasons: a) He deliberately delivers his entire "triumphalist narrative" in epic/Iliadic manner (Hainsworth 1993:298 *ad Iliad* 11.669) so as to foreground himself not as a self-conscious speaker but as a depersonalized epic *exemplum* worthy of imitation; cf. Martin 1989:82. b) Muellner 1976:59n82 notices the "close association of Zeus and Nestor in this line" and adduces further evidence for Nestor's immortality. See now Frame 2009, esp. 105, on Nestor as a reflex of the Vedic immortal cattleman twin. The exceptional employment of the derivative εὐχετάομαι + man (as opposed to deity) in the dative in *Iliad* 11.761 is, I suggest, practically a *catachresis*. As such it may be based on the fulsome words of Nestor's compatriots, whom in his objective mode he is quoting or paraphrasing. See also Sophokles *Ajax* 78, Plato *Symposium* 221b5 and Dover 1980:174–175.

Lastly, Laertes has also undertaken some such mission as a young man; *Odyssey* 24.376–379 may elliptically allude to this.[54]

Travel and a raid (a low-key military adventure) make up the preliminary quest or ἐξεσίη 'mission abroad' that three Homeric heroes embark on soon after reaching ἤβη 'early adulthood', recognizably the time of life when an aristocratic boy and girl were sent off from home.[55] *The quest makes good educational sense, particularly if the hero had already been introduced to quasi-combat in a boar hunt.*[56] A good parallel for the ἐξεσίη is the aristocratic custom, attested in numerous Greek inscriptions from the Hellenistic and Roman periods, of detailing young nobles to command small-scale military or paramilitary expeditions.[57] In some cases security forces were led by princes as young as 16.[58] The evidence for this educational practice, surveyed by M. Kleijwegt, may, I believe, help us in reconstructing Homeric educational ideology.

According to this scholar, the ancient Greeks, like other pre-industrial societies, conflated the stages of late childhood and adolescence with adulthood. Those who fell within the age-range of 14–20 years (men) and 12–18 (women) belonged to the wider if ambiguous category of 'youth'.[59] This was a period not of individual crisis or school-based subculture but of *apprenticeship*—Kleijwegt's most illuminating term—for adulthood. Youth was a form of proto-adulthood, and young people were judged according to adult standards, of which they constantly fell short. Apart from the inscriptions, the ideal of the τέλειος νέος 'perfect young man' was reflected, I might add, as early as the late fifth century BC by, *inter alia*, the numerous votive reliefs in Athenian gymnasia dedicated to Herakles.[60] In these the hero features as a role model for adolescent boys or those approaching adolescence. Perhaps this hero more than any other embodied the ideal youth, for Herakles was a precocious warrior already from the cradle, a 'wonder child' who, as one scholar notes, "grew abnormally fast,

---

[54] Ἀκεφαλλήνεσσιν ἀνάσσων' (*Odyssey* 24.378) in Laertes' 'nostalgic wish' (on the genre, see de Jong 2001:32 *ad Odyssey* 1.253–269) does not militate against my interpretation, especially if we assume that Laertes is already a prince detailed to mount a 'police' operation, on which see below. Tradition, at any rate, recorded that Laertes joined the Argonauts' expedition in his youth; see Apollodoros *Bibliotheca* 1.9.16. Conceivably this, then, was an alternative ἐξεσίη, particularly if his role was secondary or peripheral.

[55] Ferrari 2002:134.

[56] In general, bravery in combat (consequent upon participation in a boar hunt) raises one's ante as a prospective husband; cf. *Iliad* 13.363ff. The normative sequence argued for is deliberately (and fatally) inverted in Herodotos 1.34ff. Here Atys' wedding is premature, for ordinarily the lad should have married only after proving himself first in a boar hunt and then in a military ἐξεσίη.

[57] Chaniotis 2005, esp. 51, adduces evidence from Crete, Akarnania, Epiros, Asia Minor, and Athens; also Kleijwegt 1991, esp. 93–101.

[58] Kleijwegt 1991:95–96.

[59] Kleijwegt 1991, esp. 1–50.

[60] Shapiro 2003:96–97 (with fig. 13).

quickly bypassing the indignities of childhood"[61] and the continuing inept-
ness of adolescence.[62]

An inferior adult, the young man (or woman) was catapulted suddenly
into the adult world, a situation that Kleijwegt also compares to "practical
immersion in learning a foreign language."[63] Indeed, young men—Telemachos
is a plausible literary example—had to master this larger language by faithfully imitating their fathers and other male elders, especially (if Bremmer
is correct) their maternal grandfather and uncles.[64] Imitative behavior is
implied in Athena's revelation to Odysseus, in *Odyssey* 13.415, that his son
'ᾤχετο . . . μετὰ σὸν κλέος' (literally, "has gone off after your *kleos*"). Here, as
A. Hoekstra observes *ad loc.*, the prepositional phrase means both 'in quest of
news of you' and 'following the track of your *fame*'.[65] On the latter interpretation the young prince has consciously been following in his father's footsteps
in more than a geographical sense. If, with Redfield, we take κλέος as also
connoting something akin to 'social identity',[66] μετὰ σὸν κλὲος adumbrates
the educational purpose of Telemachos' voyage. By the prince's own admission (when recounting his adventures to his mother at *Odyssey* 17.108–149),
his travels intersect with his father's, albeit at multiple removes.

By the same token, as Kleijwegt demonstrates, young aristocrats in the
later inscriptions modeled their identity on that of their father.[67] Homer
and the inscriptions both reveal the same mentality concerning a youth's
prescribed relation to grown-ups. The twin ideals of imitation and confor-
mity give rise in the *Odyssey* to the paradox of the 'sensible youngster' (in
effect, a well-rounded miniature adult) as represented mainly by Nausikaa,
Peisistratos, and his brothers.[68] The young men in the inscriptions, also, are
too good to be true: brave in battle, public-minded, circumspect, intelligent,

---

[61] Beaumont 2003:71; cf. the funerary inscription for a six-year-old, I. Tomis 384, cited by
Kleijwegt 1991:124n304.

[62] Recall, e.g., the inept Molione brothers in *Iliad* 11. In general on the gerontocratic bias in favor
of precocious children and adolescents in post-Classical inscriptions, see Kleijwegt, 1991:123–
131, 221.

[63] Kleijwegt 1991:41ff.

[64] Plato confirms this adultocentric/gerontocratic model: *Laws* 2 provides for the early immersion of children in the music modes (and by extension, the ethical canons) established by the
best and *oldest* men.

[65] Heubeck and Hoekstra 1990:190 (italics mine).

[66] See Chapter 1 above.

[67] Kleijwegt 1991, esp. 49–50 (the pre-industrial paradigm), 69–71. Cf. p71: "Pride of descendance
and a tradition of behavioural similarity between father and son are banal features in Greek
and Roman honorary inscriptions."

[68] De Jong 2001:63 *ad Odyssey* 2.342 (with bib.); 76 *ad Odyssey* 3.124–125. She leaves out of account
a) Nestor's other sons, all of them married and 'πινυτούς τε καὶ ἔγχεσιν . . . ἀρίστους' (*Odyssey*
4.211); and b) Eumaios as a precocious (but innocent) child ('παῖδα . . . κερδαλέον', *Odyssey*
15.450–451).

well traveled, deeply educated. Though these texts have for obvious reasons censored the underside of the adultocentric ideal, the mundane average occasionally shows through in the *Odyssey*, κατ' ἐξοχήν in the treatment of Telemachos. As has been pointed out, Telemachos gradually grows into the formulaic epithet πεπνυμένος, which refers to him a total of 46 times, to the degree that he develops speech that becomes more and more characteristic of an adult in style and effect.[69] By the end of Book 16 the adjective suits the prince for the first time; up to this point there has been a variance between the young man's use of words and silences and his epithet. Reality also shows through when Penelope upbraids her son, rather unfairly I might add, for not protecting the beggar from the suitors' insults:

'Τηλέμαχ', οὐκέτι τοι φρένες ἔμπεδοι οὐδὲ νόημα·
παῖς ἔτ' ἐὼν καὶ μᾶλλον ἐνὶ φρεσὶ κέρδε' ἐνώμας·
νῦν δ' ὅτε δὴ μέγας ἐσσὶ καὶ ἥβης μέτρον ἱκάνεις . . .
οὐκέτι τοι φρένες εἰσὶν ἐναίσιμοι οὐδὲ νόημα.'

> *Odyssey* 18.215–220 (cf. n68 above
> *ad Odyssey* 15.450–451).

"Telemachos, no longer is your mind stable nor your thinking.
Even when still a child, you used all the more to exercise astuteness in
    your mind;
but now that you surely are grown and have reached the measure of matu-
    rity . . .
no longer is your mind just nor [is] your thinking."

Her words bear out that a young person was expected to behave as an adult and was regularly judged defective in this role.

Kleijwegt's study also has the great merit of invoking evidence of apprentice adults in other cultures, including Athens from the fourth century BC on and the modern-day Sarakatsani in northwest Greece.[70] At Athens the ephebate progressively became a low-key, quasi-intellectual apprenticeship; among the Sarakatsani today a youth becomes an apprentice shepherd at 13 and by 20 is reckoned a παλληκάρι 'all-round young man' and a shepherd in his own right. It is, I believe, because of such a traditional mentality that Athena motivates Telemachos' trip to the Peloponnese in Book 1. For the twenty-year-old prince *and* his crew of coevals the ὁδός 'journey' is, we have seen, full of real dangers, including the suitors' ambush off the coast of Ithaka.[71] Penelope, Odysseus,

---

[69] Heath 2005, esp. 100ff. and Chapter 3.
[70] Kleijwegt 1991:47–48.
[71] One detail that usually goes unnoticed by scholars (with the exception e.g. of Scheid-Tissinier 1993:16–17): the best among Ithakan κοῦροι are undergoing an 'initiation'/apprenticeship

Eumaios, and Laertes all realize these dangers and, in the light of the domestic situation, consider the voyage especially rash and pointless.[72] From the outside Telemachos' voyage may indeed seem poorly motivated, as even an ancient scholiast objected.[73] But we may compare an expedition described in a second-century BC ephebic inscription from Athens which A. Chaniotis calls "a harmless excursion."[74] To paraphrase the inscription: "Athenian youths under arms march to the borders of Attica, 'acquire knowledge of the territory and roads' ... visit Marathon, pay their respects there ... then march on to the sanctuary of Amphiaraos of Oropos. There they shout to pilgrims that Athens is the real owner of the sanctuary (which was not true at the time). This done, they march back to Athens." All of this has a rationale not obvious to an outsider, ancient or modern. Chaniotis detects here the substrate of some rite of passage; what is certainly clear is that the youths are reviewing and experiencing their city-state's history, geography, and territorial claims.

I return now to the *Odyssey*. Only Athena upholds the inner logic of Telemachos' voyage— its cultural rationale, as it were. When asked by Odysseus why she ever sent the lad on the voyage rather than simply tell him about his father, the goddess answers: "I ... guided him ... so that he might win *kleos* / by going there [sc. Sparta]" (*Odyssey* 13.422–423). Odysseus would have liked his son instantly and effortlessly to receive word (κλέος) about him. But that would have deprived Telemachos of the benefits of the incremental, nonlinear learning process encapsulated in his thirty-five-day apprenticeship.[75] We may also compare the eighteen–year-old Lykian aristocrat Marcus Aurelius Magas, who according to a funerary inscription led the police forces in his province. Kleijwegt stresses the "educational value of this phenomenon," which recalls Athenian ephebic patrols.[76] Incidentally, just as the content and tenor of the ephebate at Athens was 'intellectualized' gradually from the third century BC on, so also did the obligatory ἐξεσίη 'mission abroad' change, it would appear, from a bloody cattle-raid to an adventure abroad that, despite inherent dangers, was more clearly symbolic and intellectual. The preliminary boar hunt, however, conceivably continued to be *de*

---

alongside Telemachos, who is likewise a crew member under captain 'Mentor' until Book 15 (cf. *Odyssey* 4.652–544, etc.). In Book 15 the prince becomes captain: 44ff., 282, 503ff., 547ff.

[72] Penelope (*Odyssey* 4.817–823); Odysseus (*Odyssey* 13.417–419); Eumaios (*Odyssey* 14.178–179); Laertes (*Odyssey* 16.142–145).

[73] Scholia *ad Odyssey* 1.93 and 284 (noted in Chapter 4), whose views Heubeck, West, and Hainsworth 1988:53 seem to share.

[74] Chaniotis 2005:51–52.

[75] The phrase κλέος ἄροιτο (*Odyssey* 13.422, just cited) is suggestive. In his dictionary Snell notes (s.v. ἄρνυμαι) that the acquisition of κλέος (or κῦδος for that matter) is more of a casual, nonlinear process than, say, the concerted action of carrying off a physical object, e.g. the golden fleece.

[76] Kleijwegt 1991:95.

rigueur; the fact that Telemachos appears flanked prominently by two hunting dogs in *Odyssey* 2.11 and 17.62 may suggest that he has already passed this test.[77]

Within days of returning from his mission, a number of characters, including the suitors (*Odyssey* 16.374ff.), remark a change in the prince. At least three characters admit that he has grown.[78] As Eurykleia casually observes to Odysseus after the murder of the suitors: 'Τηλέμαχος δὲ νέον μὲν ἀέξατο' ("Whereas Telemachos has only recently started growing up," *Odyssey* 22.426), i.e. "until now Telemachos was too immature to exert control over the maidservants [but now he is mature enough to do so]."[79] And his mother, like the suitors a naysayer to the prospect of Telemachos growing up, twice registers his definitive adult status. The first time she does this is at 18.269–71, when she notes in public her son's beard:

"'αὐτὰρ ἐπὴν δὴ παῖδα γενειήσαντα ἴδηαι,
γήμασθ' ᾧ κ' ἐθέλησθαι, τεὸν κατὰ δῶμα λιποῦσα."
κεῖνος τὼς ἀγόρευε· τὰ δὴ νῦν πάντα τελεῖται.'

"'But the moment you see that our son has sprouted a beard,
give yourself in marriage to whomever you wish, after leaving behind your
        house.'
Thus he spoke. All this now is being fulfilled."

Presumably Telemachos had a beard even long before Book 1, despite Dawe's worries.[80] The prince certainly does not grow facial hair for the first time at the age of 20, far less in the 36 days between Books 1 and 19. What has changed is that his mother notices his beard and links it outright to her son's coming of age and right of succession. Τελεῖται 'is being fulfilled or brought to completion'

[77] Argos was also a hunting dog: *Odyssey* 17.315–317.
[78] Cf. also *Odyssey* 19.86–87 (Odysseus to Penelope); 19.160–161 (Penelope to Odysseus). Their testimony is particularly meaningful since they are φίλοι well acquainted, all save Odysseus, with the 'progress' of the prince. On the other hand, Homer's audience, who, like ourselves, were not φίλοι, probably noticed the V.I.P treatment, reflecting acknowledgement of his identity and status, as shown particularly by the gifts Telemachos receives at Sparta (see e.g. Jones 2002:137, section B). Scholars also bring out Telemachos' mature handling of the suppliant Theoklymenos (e.g, de Jong 2001:372), to which I add: the Little Prince has visibly graduated from apprentice crew member under 'Mentor' to captain commanding his ἑτάροι (like Odysseus at sea) to hoist the mast (*Odyssey* 15.287ff., n71 above).
[79] Cf. Heubeck's translation (Russo, Fernández-Galiano, and Heubeck 1992), 294 *ad loc.*: "Whereas Telemachus (I do not mention because he, δὲ) had only just started growing up." See *Odyssey* 18.338–342 (the maids seriously fear Telemachos).
[80] Dawe 1993:672 *ad Odyssey* 19.269–270. Compare Russo, Fernández-Galiano, and Heubeck 1992:66 *ad Odyssey* 19.269: Penelope is not lying to the suitors about Odysseus' parting instructions, the effect of which hinged on their son's growing a beard; her son assuredly had a beard years before the episode in Book 19, but the queen's stalling tactics prevented her from divulging the beard's pertinence to her remarriage.

(*Odyssey* 18.271) in Penelope's matter-of-fact statement connotes maturity and perfection, as if suggesting that the prince is at last τέλειος 'mature', literally, 'perfect'. Her statement is well timed in terms not only of her (controversial) ulterior motives but also her son's development. Until his voyage, Telemachos is not fully adult in status, like the thirty-five-year-old Kassandros. Had Telemachos not undertaken his apprenticeship, his beard would have meant very little to Penelope or to Homer's audience.

6

The End of the *Telemachy*
The Culmination of Extinction?

> " *. . . Time past and time future*
> *What might have been and what has been*
> *Point to one end, which is always present."*
>
> T. S. Eliot "Burnt Norton" (No. 1 of *Four Quartets*)

IF MUCH OF THE EMOTIONAL EFFECT of the first 21 books of the *Odyssey* turns on the relation or rather the heart-rending contrast between Odysseus' harmonious reign in the past and the dysfunctional, dejected present, the final two books derive their impact from the resolution of 'time past' into 'time future', to paraphrase T. S. Eliot. Italo Calvino[1] and others before him have well noticed that in keeping with its folk tale scheme Odysseus' final triumph, like Robin Hood's, for instance, also ushers in the restoration of a just society: so long as Odysseus will reign, Ithaka will be uniformly prosperous, peaceful, and oblivious to former conflicts, as Teiresias foretells in *Odyssey* 11.134–137.[2] Moreover, as Calvino crucially observes, in this restored society Odysseus' "true identity," like Robin Hood's, "will be recognised."[3] Before this happens father and son must strive along parallel courses and finally converge.[4] But, whereas Odysseus' identity is continuous and intact, if usually latent, needing to be revealed (for instance by his scar in *Odyssey* 19 or still more melodramatically when he heroically discards his beggar's disguise in Book 22), Telemachos' identity is discontinuous and disconnected from that of his father; the prince's 'personality' must evolve until it crystalizes, almost text-like, into the cumulative oral narrative about his ἐξεσίη 'mission abroad' that will make up his (admittedly subaltern)

---

[1]   Calvino 1999:14.
[2]   Cf. Zeus' concluding performative utterance at *Odyssey* 24.482, by which he ordains Ithaka's future; but it is a future that is limited to Odysseus' lifespan.
[3]   Calvino 1999:14.
[4]   See the preceding chapter.

kleos.[5] (This narrative, in other words, will be based typically on the 'reports', which even the suitors will come to hear, about his overseas adventures.)

The *Telemacheia* is taken up mainly with the prince's ὁδός 'journey', which, as I have argued, resembles an initiatory 'ordeal' characteristic of Homeric education. Having passed this conventional *Jünglingsprobe*, the initiated ephebe can fight confidently at his father's side in Books 22 and 24.[6] It is the merging of father and son in the latter half of the poem[7]—which I will touch upon shortly— that makes possible Telemachos' ἀριστεία 'special period of prowess', arguably the climax—the πείρατ' ἀέθλων 'end of trials'—of the *Telemacheia*.[8] As I see it, this secondary epic continues even beyond Book 17, which many scholars regard as the 'end' of the *Telemacheia*. The climax is duly registered in Book 24, as I will argue, by the 'group portrait' of grandfather, father, and son confirming their continuity as a *genos* (in the Homeric non-technical sense of 'family'). How far will this continuity extend? is a question that the poet seems to answer. Finally, another preliminary observation: if the dénouement (λύσις) of the *Odyssey* has rather the character of a contemplation on the future of the Arkeisiad *genos*, it is no less clear that in the latter part of the poem the poet is especially self-conscious about age categories and Ithaka's generational system. The Little Prince's coming of age, then, reflects closely the poem's vital thematic and dramaturgic stake in the social significance of age and personhood.

The Expendable Suitors and the Lonely Arkeisiads

The suitors, as a whole, constitute a group of young ὁμήλικες 'peers', most of them in their 20s, although a number of them are older (προγενέστεροι 'older', *Odyssey* 24.160; compare 434, 475).[9] Like Telemachos' crew, who are κοῦροι 'youths, young men' one and all (*Odyssey* 4.652ff.), the μνηστῆρες 'suitors' also bear this rather diffuse title (on which see Russo, Fernández-Galiano, and Heubeck 1992:224 *ad Odyssey* 22.30). Compare, for instance, Antinoos' 'epitaph' at *Odyssey* 22.29–30: 'φῶτα κατέκτανες ὃς μέγ' ἄριστος / κούρων εἰν Ἰθάκῃ ("you killed a man who was by far the best / of Ithaka's young men" [in the words of the other suitors]). As has been noted, despite occasional affinities with the λαοί 'people'—some of which are rhetorical pretensions, as at *Odyssey* 22.45–55—these

[5] See Chapters 1 and 3; cf. the discussion of Telemachos as νήπιος in Chapter 4.
[6] For his lack of self-confidence in lone combat (before meeting Odysseus), compare *Odyssey* 16.71–72.
[7] For his newly won confidence after being reunited with his father, compare *Odyssey* 20.313–319.
[8] Cf. *Odyssey* 23.248ff.: 'οὐ γάρ πω πάντων ἐπὶ πείρατ' ἀέθλων / ἤλθομεν' (Odysseus to Penelope).
[9] For the suitors' youth, see *Odyssey* 20.361, 24.106–107 with Dawe 1993:839 *ad loc.*; *Odyssey* 21.94–95 (Antinoos remembers Odysseus from his childhood, hence he must be at least 25); also *Odyssey* 21.179, 184, 361, 401 (they are νέοι); *Odyssey* 24.457 (they are παῖδες).

youths are in reality distinct from, and usually opposed to, the 'people'.[10] The suitors' sameness of age, moreover, is worth exploring briefly; for the terms ὁμηλικίη 'age group, generation' and ὁμῆλιξ 'of the same age, contemporary',[11] when used of young individuals, arguably connote the *education* of a specific age group (or class). Compare *Iliad* 3.175, where Helen regrets having left her ὁμηλικίην ἐρατεινήν, i.e. the group of graceful maidens who almost certainly trained with her in the same chorus. In *Odyssey* 15.197–198 Telemachos foresees explicitly that the common ὁδός 'journey'—a radically educational process, as argued in the previous chapter—undertaken by two ὁμήλικες 'peers', namely, himself and Peisistratos, will establish a 'feeling of bondedness' between them:

> 'ἀτὰρ καὶ ὁμήλικές εἰμεν·
> ἤδε δ' ὁδὸς καὶ μᾶλλον ὁμοφροσύνῃσιν ἐνήσει.'

"besides we are of the same age,
and this journey will involve us even further in mental togetherness."

The developmental undertones of these passages are strengthened by comparison with the collocation 'κεκριμένοι καὶ ὁμήλικες' in *Odyssey* 24.106–108, Agamemnon's generalization about the suitors' collective status. To quote his query to Amphimedon when they meet in Hades:

> 'Ἀμφίμεδον, τί παθόντες ἐρεμνὴν γαῖαν ἔδυτε
> πάντες κεκριμένοι καὶ ὁμήλικες; οὐδέ κεν ἄλλως
> κρινάμενος λέξαιτο κατὰ πτόλιν ἄνδρας ἀρίστους.'

"Amphimedon, what happened to you that you have gone down to the
Dark Land,
all select [men] and of the same age? Not any differently [i.e. better]
could one have selected and brought together the best men throughout a
city."

Agamemnon assumes that the select "'group' [sc. of contemporaries] must have met their end in some common venture" (Russo, Fernández-Galiano, and Heubeck 1992:372 *ad loc.*). Elsewhere Odysseus describes this elite collectivity as the ἕρμα πόληος 'the stone or prop, hence support of the *polis*', essentially a nautical metaphor, when he tells his son the following:

---

[10] Haubold 2000, esp. 110–125; Chapter 4 above.

[11] For the almost interchangeable terms ὁμηλικίη and ὁμῆλιξ in the *Iliad* and *Odyssey*, see Beekes 2010(I):515, s.v. ἧλιξ and especially Russo, Fernández-Galiano, and Heubeck 1992 (n16 below). For the moment I note that both terms may be taken either in an individual sense = 'contemporary', as in American English 'classmate', or in a collective sense = 'group of contemporaries', as in 'the Class of 1980'; cf. the Classical Athenian ἡλικία = '(military) call-up group' and n65 below.

‘ἡμεῖς δ’ ἕρμα πόληος ἀπέκταμεν, οἳ μέγ’ ἄριστοι
κούρων εἰν Ἰθάκῃ ...’

Odyssey 23.121–122

"whereas we have killed off the support of the [ship of] state, [those] who
        were the best by far
of Ithaka's young men ..."

What the two passages just cited may imply is that these ἄριστοι 'best' young men, all of them 'coevals', had been formally inducted into the status of junior adult at the same time. Anthropologists have established that many village and band societies, particularly in Africa, categorize males by virtue of their social (as opposed to their strictly chronological) age.[12] Each category is an 'age-set' which is given a special name. Thus, for instance, to quote one specialist, "those born between 1900 and 1909 would belong together throughout their lives in one set, and those born between 1910 and 1919 would belong to the next set. At intervals, *all the members of a set are initiated at one and the same ceremony* and then they move together through a series of roles or occupations."[13] These roles and occupations, which entail certain duties and responsibilities, signify a specific status or 'age-grade', for example, the 'warrior grade' or the 'grade of elders'.[14] Age-set members in, for example, Africa enjoy "a special feeling of solidarity *that cut[s] across domestic and lineage kin groups*."[15] On this analogy, the suitors must have belonged, by and large, to the same age-set of ephebes before achieving together the grade of 'warriors'.[16] In other words, if indeed the wide-ranging African evidence is a reliable guide, these young men were non-kin (a fact which Homer supports *e silentio*) and 'contemporaries' (ὁμήλικες, as Homer reports) in the cultural or ritual sense of having been initiated into manhood over the same span of, say, ten, twelve, or fourteen years.[17] Another defining trait was their feeling of *non-kin solidarity*, a sentiment that Telemachos (still an initiand in Book 17) cites as ὁμοφροσύναι 'togetherness of mind, mental harmony'.

It is this entire age-set alongside a group of προγενέστεροι 'older men' (presumably comprising one or more earlier sets) that Odysseus admits to

---

[12] Mair 1965:51; Orme 1981:150.

[13] Orme 1981:150; italics mine.

[14] Mair 1965:51.

[15] Harris 1987:190, citing the instance of East African pastoralists; italics mine.

[16] On ὁμήλικες as an 'age-group', see Stanford 1958 *ad Odyssey* 24.107ff., also Russo, Fernández-Galiano, and Heubeck 1992:258 *ad Odyssey* 22.209 (ὁμηλικίη) and n17 immediately below.

[17] Although it is not explicitly stated, the discussion in Russo, Fernández-Galiano, and Heubeck 1992 of the semantic shift of the noun ὁμηλικίη (from the abstract 'sameness of age' to the less abstract 'of the same age-group' to the concrete 'peer, contemporary') shows what a relative notion 'sameness of age' is, something which the African evidence bears out.

having liquidated. Haubold notes that suitors in Archaic hexameter poetry are by definition expendable; the *Odyssey* fatally pits them, the 'many', against the 'one' lucky ἀνήρ 'man'.[18] A suitor like Hippomenes in the Hesiodic *Catalogue of Women* must compete—to paraphrase Haubold—not only for a wife but also for his life.[19] In the *Odyssey*, by the same token, the μνηστῆρες 'suitors' cannot all succeed; only one—Odysseus, the arch and original suitor—will succeed, while the rest must die.[20] Penelope's suitors are all expendable, indeed.

Haubold calls the suitors an unsympathetic group, that is, within epic tradition, of 'non-people'.[21] By this he means that they are distinct from the undifferentiated mass of λαοί 'people' in epic, who are sympathetic to tradition. What is more, as this scholar points out, it is the suitors' loss and death at Odysseus' hands that assure the prosperity if not survival of the 'larger whole', which is the λαός/ λαοί.[22] The central νεῖκος or 'conflict' of the *Odyssey*, in my view, is not so much between characters as between *one* (emphasis mine) *genos* (which happens to be regnant, at least formally) and, on the other side, a *combinazione* of disparate aristocratic *genê* competing with the Arkeisiads and also with one another. In relation to one another but especially in relation to Telemachos, the suitors behave much like the feuding young gangs attached to the Montagues and Capulets, respectively, in Shakespeare's *Romeo and Juliet*. The *Odyssey*, at any rate, concludes with the 'continuation' of the Arkeisiads in power and the concomitant extinction of no less than two entire age-groups of young aristocrats from various *genê* 'families'.

The three Arkeisiads, encompassing as they do three living generations, are a quintessentially lone *genos* 'family line'.[23] This seeming eccentricity makes for the precarious situation in which Odysseus and his son find themselves, especially from Book 16 onward. Telemachos is a solitary resister from the beginning of the poem, one young man facing a host of other youths. The odds are intractably unfavorable. As he admits to Eumaios (Odysseus has not yet revealed himself to his son): 'πρῆξαι δ' ἀργαλέον τι μετὰ πλεόνεσσιν ἐόντα / ἄνδρα καὶ ἴφθιμον . . .' ("It is painfully hard to achieve anything, being one among greater numbers, / even if a man is brave . . . ," *Odyssey* 16.88–99). Then, in response to the beggar Odysseus' searching and ironical questions and pointed remark (a test,

---

18 Haubold 2000:140–141; also Chapter 4 above. Scheid-Tissinier 1993:17, 20–22 stresses, by contrast, that the deadly conflict in fact pits two different groups of budding warriors, namely Telemachos' 'contemporaries' and the suitors. The wholesale eviction or liquidation of an entire group of youths by another group within a city has, she notes, parallels in Archaic Sparta and Athens and subsequently in other Greek city-states.
19 Haubold 2000:139.
20 Cf. Haubold 2000:141.
21 Haubold 2000:141, 143.
22 Haubold 2000:143.
23 Also cf. Odysseus' maternal grandfather Autolykos, whose name may mean 'Lone Wolf' (see Chapter 5 above).

really, of his son's mettle) that if he were in the prince's place he would fight the suitors to the death even if single-handed (*Odyssey* 16.105–107), Telemachos self-consciously recites his genealogy, which is endangered, as he puts it exaggeratingly, by foes μυρίοι 'past counting':

'ὧδε γὰρ ἡμέτερην γενεὴν μούνωσε Κρονίων·
μοῦνον Λαέρτην Ἀρκείσιος υἱὸν ἔτικτε,
μοῦνον δ' αὖτ' Ὀδυσῆα πατὴρ τέκεν· αὐτὰρ Ὀδυσσεὺς
μοῦνον ἔμ' ἐν μεγάροισι τεκὼν λίπεν οὐδ' ἀπόνητο.
τῶ νῦν δυσμενέες μάλα μυρίοι εἴσ' ἐνὶ οἴκω.'

Odyssey 16. 117–121

"For in the following fashion the son of Kronos 'singled' our family:
to be a single son Arkeisios begat Laertes,
to be [a] single [son] in turn his father begat Odysseus; and Odysseus,
after begetting me in his palace to be [a] single [son], left me behind and
    did not even enjoy me.
Against this background, now evil-minded men past counting are in our
    house."

The Arkeisiads reach back to four generations, of which three survive in a sea of enemies. (At length, after his father has revealed his identity in the same episode, the prince renders a truthful account of the suitors, enumerating them finitely as his father requested [*Odyssey* 16.235, 245–253].)

To be sure, the survival of three generations of only sons does make the Arkeisiads seem a species possibly heading toward extinction. This is the more obvious implication of the quadruple anaphora of μούνωσε 'he singled' (i.e. 'made our family to have only one male in each generation')—μοῦνον 'single' in Telemachos' 'list of begats'.[24] Simon Goldhill has attractively suggested that Odysseus' family is both "at risk and perfect."[25] (I will extend this fruitful insight shortly.) Indeed, the generational structure of the Arkeisiads seems to me to be perfect in the sense that it is a culmination issuing in their extinction—and subsequent commemoration through Homeric poetry.

The uniqueness of the prince's *genos* 'family' may also reflect a trait typical of folk tale as analyzed by the Swiss folklorist Max Lüthi. This scholar has shown (1947) that, generally speaking, folk tale protagonists are isolated and lonely individuals, "helpless, forsaken and alone" (like Cinderella), often at the mercy of cruel/hostile outside forces.[26] All three Arkeisiads (not to mention

---

[24] This repetition takes up Odysseus' defiant μοῦνον ἐόντα in *Odyssey* 16.105. Note also the triple anaphora of τίκτω/τεκών, the 'begats' typical of actual genealogies.
[25] In a lecture delivered at the Triennial Conference at the University of Cambridge in July 2005.
[26] Lüthi 1976:61; Lüthi 1947, discussed in Χατζητάκη-Καψωμένου 2002:137.

Telemachos' maternal grandfather) fit the bill. It is perhaps no accident that Odysseus and Telemachos, in particular, are embarked on analogous adventures in which each is a lone protagonist confronting cruel characters and forces. Still more suggestive, in addition to their separate adventures, their very heredity also replicates—emphatically, as at *Odyssey* 16.117–121 (above)—the generic vulnerability and *Isolationstendenz* of Lüthi's popular heroes.

To return to the suitors, ironically Telemachos' coming of age has resulted in the annihilation of other young men (κοῦροι), most of them 'contemporary' initiates themselves. The Arkeisiads survive at the expense of at least two age-sets. What ensures this outcome is the symbolic merging of father and initiated son as well as their actual combination of forces.[27] A few words, then, about the decisive and deeply symbolic reunion of Odysseus and his son are necessary.

The Prodigal Son and Identity-switching

In Book 16 the kinship of Odysseus and Telemachos is asserted more frequently than in any other book of the poem. Their relationship is here celebrated, as it were, by repeated *antonomasia*: Odysseus is called 'father' four times, Telemachos 'son' no fewer than six.[28] Book 16 brings about not merely the desiderated eventuality of son meeting father but also the mutual transference—we might call it a *hypallage*—between the identities of father and son.[29] At *Odyssey* 16.17–21 the poet uses a 'role reversal simile' (to use de Jong's term)[30] in describing Telemachos' emotional reception by Eumaios. The prince, just returned from his fact-finding mission, has secretly gone to the swineherd's hut in the country:

ὡς δὲ πατὴρ ὃν παῖδα φίλα φρονέων ἀγαπάζῃ
ἐλθόντ' ἐξ ἀπίης γαίης δεκάτῳ ἐνιαυτῷ,
μοῦνον τηλύγετον, τῷ ἔπ' ἄλγεα πολλὰ μογήσῃ,
ὣς τότε Τηλέμαχον θεοειδέα δῖος ὑφορβός
πάντα κύσεν περιφύς, ὡς ἐκ θανάτοιο φυγόντα.

Odyssey 16.17–21

As a loving father emotionally welcomes his son
who has come back from a distant land in the tenth year,—
his only son, his special one, over whom he experiences [sc. experienced]
much distress,—

---

[27] Cf. *Odyssey* 16.300–301, 309–310: father tests son, son declares his determination. They then join forces.

[28] De Jong 2001:385.

[29] For this term, see Baldick 1990, s.v. 'hypallage': "a figure of speech by which an epithet is transferred from the more appropriate to the less appropriate of two nouns, [e.g.] . . . 'If Jonson's learnèd sock be on.'"

[30] De Jong 2001:389 *ad loc.*

so at that moment the excellent swineherd after embracing godlike
    Telemachos tightly
kissed him, as if he had escaped from death.

The simile, so affecting and at the same time so allusive, recalls the cross-cultural tale of the 'Prodigal son' (Luke 15:11–34).[31] De Jong (2001:389) registers the exchange, albeit temporary, of roles of father and son here: "the son in the simile is cast in the role of Odysseus . . . while the 'distresses' [sc. ἄλγεα] which the father in the simile has suffered on account of his son correspond to those of Telemachus during the absence of his father (cf. 4.164 and 16.188–9)." Further, she comments, "This role reversal underscores the similarity between the experiences of Odysseus and Telemachus."[32] But it may, I think, also be worthwhile to notice the 'educational' and encomiastic nuances of the cross-pattern that exalts the prince into a mature figure returned home after a ten-year absence abroad. The simile would indeed have been apter in a strict sense if Odysseus were the one being tearfully welcomed by his son, who has indeed suffered on account of his long absence (as is stated outright a bit later in the same book: *Odyssey* 16.188–189).[33] In the event, it is the father figure Eumaios—whom Telemachos affectionately calls ἄττα 'Papa' (*Odyssey* 16.31)[34]—who welcomes the 'prodigal son' back home; but as the simile unfolds, as I noted, the son shifts into a father and the paternal Eumaios into a hitherto helpless son. This unexpected rearrangement of terms can only make full sense in light of the fact that Telemachos has become an adult in the course of his ὁδός 'journey'. That said, the reversal of roles would have reverberated across nine books—from 16 to 24—during a live performance.[35] The audience would have been able to sense a reprise of Telemachos' teary welcome by the swineherd in the recognition scene of Odysseus and Laertes. In Book 24 Laertes has, like the surrogate father Eumaios, suffered because of his son's disappearance (esp. 233); furthermore, Laertes emotionally embraces Odysseus just as the swineherd embraces Telemachos (but goes one better than Eumaios by fainting). These congruities

---

[31] So Wöhrle 1999:114–115. I may add a crucial difference between Homer and Luke: in the *Odyssey* the long-lost son is an only son (*Odyssey* 16.19: μοῦνον τηλύγετον, on which see below), whereas Luke's returning son has a (virtuous) brother waiting for him.

[32] De Jong 2001:389. Also cf. the simile in *Odyssey* 5.394–399 in which Odysseus tellingly becomes a son overjoyed at his *father's* deliverance from illness; as de Jong 2001:144–145 remarks *ad loc.*, Odysseus is also implicitly the suffering father here.

[33] *Odyssey* 16.188–189: 'ἀλλὰ πατὴρ τεός εἰμι, τοῦ εἵνεκα σὺ στεναχίζων / πάσχεις ἄλγεα πολλά . . .'

[34] Eumaios calls the prince 'φίλον τέκος' (*Odyssey* 16.25).

[35] See Nagy 2003:16: "the resonances of Homeric cross-referencing must be appreciated within the larger context of a long history of repeated performances . . . the referent of a reference is not restricted to the immediate context but extends to *analogous contexts heard in previous performances*" (italics mine).

would confirm to the audience that in Book 16 the prince has briefly—and flatteringly—become an implicit Odysseus νοστήσας 'returned home'.[36]

This is a good juncture at which to return to Telemachos' rehearsal of his precarious lineage, quoted earlier (*Odyssey* 16.117–121). The prince's sparse family tree culminates in the fourth generation; its climax and conclusion—both notions are subsumed by the word τέλος—are Telemachos himself. Indeed, he fears that he may (barring some miracle) be the end of the Arkeisiad line. If the T scholia on *Iliad* 9.482 are correct in deriving the etymology of τηλύγετος 'special or favorite [sc. child]' from the word τέλος 'end', the prince is literally, as the above scholia note, ὁ τῆς γονῆς τέλος ἔχων, μεθ' ὃν ἕτερος οὐ γίγνεται 'he who finishes or completes the generation, after whom no other is born'.[37] As it happens, his *genos* 'family, lineage', incarnated as it is by three males, wins out in Book 24, as has been remarked. The triumph is facilitated, typically enough, by divine agency (Athena's and Zeus' intervention), but it actually is the direct result of the fortress-like compactness of this, the γένος βασιλήϊον 'royal family' (*Odyssey* 16.401, compare 17.291ff.).[38] The victorious trio—Odysseus, Telemachos, and Laertes—proclaim their family solidarity shortly before the attack on the suitors' allies:

αἶψα δὲ Τηλέμαχον προσεφώνεεν ὃν φίλον υἱόν·
'Τηλέμαχ', ἤδη μὲν τόδε γ' εἴσεαι αὐτὸς ἐπελθών,
ἀνδρῶν μαρναμένων ἵνα τε κρίνονται ἄριστοι,
μή τι καταισχύνειν πατέρων γένος, οἳ τὸ πάρος περ
ἀλκῇ τ' ἠνορέῃ τε κεκάσμεθα πᾶσαν ἐπ' αἶαν.'
Τὸν δ' αὖ Τηλέμαχος πεπνυμένος ἀντίον ηὔδα·
'ὄψεαι, αἴ κ' ἐθέλῃσθα, πάτερ φίλε, τῷδ' ἐπὶ θυμῷ
οὔ τι καταισχύνοντα τεὸν γένος, ὡς ἀγορεύεις.'
Ὣς φάτο, Λαέρτης δ' ἐχάρη καὶ μῦθον ἔειπε·
'τίς νύ μοι ἡμέρη ἥδε, θεοὶ φίλοι; ἦ μάλα χαίρω·
υἱός θ' υἱωνός τ' ἀρετῆς πέρι δῆριν ἔχουσι.'

Odyssey 24.505–515

At once he addressed his beloved son Telemachos:
"Telemachos, now you will learn this yourself—when you have come there,
     where
the best men as they fight measure themselves—

---

[36] These congruities are also cited by West 1997:436.

[37] So also Plutarch *Moralia* 94 A; see Vasilaros 2004:137–8 for bibliography and brief discussion and compare Beekes 2010 (II): 1479, s.v. τηλύγετος ('latecomer', sch. T on 9.482).

[38] Cf. also γένος βασιλεύτερον in *Odyssey* 15.533. See n41 below.

[namely] how not in any way to shame the family of our forefathers, us
    who since times past
have excelled in warfare and masculinity throughout the whole world."
To him prudent Telemachos responded:
"You will see, if you wish, dear father, me, in my present mood,
'not in any way to be shaming your family,' as you put it."
So he spoke and Laertes was overjoyed and spoke these words:
"What a day today is for me, dear gods! I really am overjoyed!
My son and grandson are competing over bravery!"

It is minutes before the curtain falls on the action of the poem. This is the last time we will see and hear the Arkeisiads. In its idealizing stylization the vignette conveyed in the verses quoted above is comparable to a 'graduation photograph', with the graduate flanked by his two elders. The three stages of life—old age, middle age, and youth—are summarized in this image.[39] Homer's group portrait condenses a moment of perfection, and it is the object of the final section of this chapter to elucidate this.

Closure: Joining the Γένος and Making the Grade

'ὡς ἀνδρῶν γενεὴ ἡ μὲν φύει ἡ δ' ἀπολήγει.'

Iliad 6.149

"So too one family of men grows and another dies out."

The brief exchange in *Odyssey* 24.505–515 concerns Telemachos, and it expresses not so much felicitation as recognition of his manly potential. Even more crucial, in this passage, as Graziosi and Haubold show,[40] the three speakers establish "continuity between three generations" by assessing the degree to which Telemachos has succeeded, as it were, to possession of ἠνορέη 'masculinity, manhood', a term I will deal with in a moment. Family continuity thus has the last word in the *Odyssey*. Before arguing this point I will discuss the social significance of the configuration of the three generations assembled on stage in the final scene of the *Odyssey*.

Archaeologists working at Athens, Lefkandi (Euboia), and elsewhere in Greece have noticed a three-generation limit to the reuse of family tombs, especially in the Geometric and Archaic periods. Carla Antonaccio has linked this

---

[39] Cf. the three-tiered Chigi vase (seventeenth century BC), featuring "the most successful portrayal of hoplite tactics that has survived" in the words of Murray 1993:130; in the lowest of the three bands on the *olpê* short-haired adolescent παῖδες are shown hunting rabbits, a junior activity; in the middle band we note slightly older males, with long hair, of whom five are hunting a lion, a conventional heroic adult activity; in the topmost band (still older?) *hoplites* march into battle.

[40] Graziosi and Haubold 2003:72–73.

phenomenon to "a three generation genealogical memory" which in her view points to, as she puts it, "a shallow time depth within lineage structures."[41] Such a restriction ruled out "long-term 'ancestor worship,'" she concludes.[42] Striking confirmation of this can be found, for instance, in the Athenian Agora and the Kerameikos. There, a number of stone enclosures, often triangular in plan, "stand near or mark earlier anonymous graves" that date from the sixth and fifth centuries BC.[43] These unroofed structures, enclosed by 'boundary walls', were called, fittingly enough, τριτοπατρεῖα.[44] They were essentially shrines used for tomb cult (not 'worship') of the family or civic τριτοπάτρεις, the illustrious male ancestors reaching back at least three generations. The famous shrine (*heroön*) of the early seventh century BC at Eretria actually contains offerings and evidence of sacrifices carried out over cremations of warriors from the period 720–680 BC. This structure, like two other possibly Archaic ἄβατα 'sacred areas' in the Lake Quarter in Delos, are almost perfect isosceles triangles in shape and are located at the intersection of three paths or τρίοδοι, described so handsomely by A. B. Cook as "that immemorial *rendez-vous* of family ghosts."[45] The Eretrian *heroön* is situated near the entrance of the civic cemetery; other comparable structures elsewhere are either near a cemetery or adjacent to a public assembly place.[46]

What is still more suggestive in light of the end of the *Odyssey*, the apex of the large isosceles triangle at Eretria faced north while the building as a whole was superimposed, to the east, on eight graves of incinerated adults and, to the west, on nine children's inhumations. The "collective σῆμα ['mound']," as Claude Bérard, the excavator of the site has termed it, was clustered around a 'prince'— if we judge by the unusually large number of weapons concentrated in one of the eight adult graves. The monument—to cite Bérard again—loudly proclaimed the glory of the dead ancestors and possibly served also as a *rallying point* for the

---

[41] Antonaccio 1993, esp. 63; to her bibliography (69n76) add: Lemos 2002, esp. 188 (at Protogeometric Lefkandi "members of the lineage or kin group were buried together"); Kitto 1951:18 (Homeric genealogies extend "up through three generations, then comes a god"); Thomas 1992:112 (the three to four generation limit to oral historical traditions in the Greek polis); hence, e.g., cf. *Iliad* 13.449–453 (Idomeneus' lineage); 14.113–118 (Diomedes' lineage); also cf. the Hesiodic Myth of the Five Generations, which are actually four if we exclude the intercalated *genos* of demigods. The phrase 'ἐς δεκάτην γενεήν' (see *Odyssey* 14.325, 19.294) is an exaggeration and does not upset the theory about a three to four generation upper limit. Nor does Theoklymenos' prophecy at *Odyssey* 15.533–535 ('ὑμετέρου δ' οὐκ ἔστι γένος βασιλεύτερον ἄλλο / ἐν δήμῳ Ἰθάκης, ἀλλ' ὑμεῖς καρτεροὶ αἰεί'), which dictated as it was by the soothsayer's need to flatter his host Telemachos, he subsequently replaces by a totally different prophecy (*Odyssey* 17.154–161).

[42] Antonaccio 1993:65.

[43] Antonaccio 1993:58.

[44] Antonaccio 1993:58.

[45] Cited by Bérard 1970:60.

[46] Bérard 1970:56–69 (full treatment with parallels); Ducrey et al. 2004:172–175 on the Eretria *heroön*.

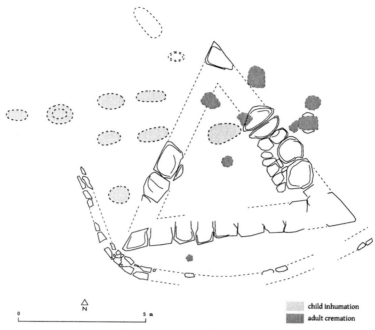

The Eretrian heroön: plan of the graves and triangular monument.
Courtesy of the Swiss School of Archaeology in Greece.

community and especially their leaders, who descended from the prince or his kin. The *heroön*'s proximity to the city's Archaic agora may well have been intentional, for here chiefs and other members of the *genê* 'families' assembled to honor their common ancestor in particular and to deliberate, under his protection, on public matters.[47]

From the archaeological findings emerge at least two facts that are relevant to my discussion of *Odyssey* 24. First, buried groups were based on close kinship that extended to only three generations, and, second, the cumulation of burial, iconography, and inscriptions functioned to reinforce the short-lived "ideal of family solidarity."[48] If, as Antonaccio observes, tomb cult thinned out after the third generation, it may be tempting to suppose that the group portrait in *Odyssey* 24 is meant analogously to memorialize family solidarity in its conventional form and duration. The end of the *Odyssey* features the Arkeisiads in triangular, as it were, configuration—Laertes at the northern apex, Odysseus and his son at the base—before they too taper off in Homeric tradition. (Of course Odysseus and his son were to 'survive' in the epic cycle, but that is another matter.) Is

[47] Bérard 1970:68–69.
[48] Antonaccio 1993, esp. 48.

it coincidence that the culminating exchange of father, son, and grandfather occurs in a book in which the first 204 verses are set in the 'underworld'? Now laid metaphorically to rest, this 'clan' is nonetheless capable of exercising its *"puissance des héros"*[49] via the monument of Homeric narrative.

Let us examine again this conversation (*Odyssey* 24.505ff.). Odysseus' words to his son are the standard paternal command not to shame one's forebears in battle, that is, to measure up to their prowess. In the prelude to his command (verses 506–507) Odysseus first spells out the experiential aspect of what lies immediately ahead for his son (*Odyssey* 24.506: 'ἤδη μὲν τόδε γ' εἴσεαι αὐτὸς ἐπελθών' ["now you will learn this yourself—when you have come there . . ."]). Then he generalizes that through such hands-on experience (compare again 24.506: αὐτὸς 'yourself' and ἐπελθών 'having come' [i.e. to the battlefield]) men 'κρίνονται ἄριστοι', literally, "separate themselves, hence measure themselves" (*Odyssey* 24.507).[50] The last phrase, 'κρίνονται ἄριστοι', recalls the description, already cited, of the suitors as κεκριμένοι καὶ ὁμήλικες 'select and of the same age' in *Odyssey* 24.107 and as ἄριστοι 'best' in *Odyssey* 23.121–122. Κεκριμένοι 'select, picked' implies Agamemnon's supposition that the suitors had already earned the title of *aristoi* in battle or battle-like experiences, all of them having advanced to the warrior-grade. Developmentally and also ritually most of them are, in fact, a grade ahead of Telemachos. The substance of Odysseus' προτροπή 'exhortation' can be found in verses 508–509. Compare the words Hippolochos spoke to his son Glaukos before sending him to war. As Glaukos recalls, indirectly quoting his father,

'πέμπε δέ μ' ἐς Τροίην, καί μοι μάλα πόλλ' ἐπέτελλεν,
αἰὲν ἀριστεύειν καὶ ὑπείροχον ἔμμεναι ἄλλων,
μηδὲ γένος πατέρων αἰσχυνέμεν . . .'

Iliad 6.207–209

"And he sent me to Troy, and sternly instructed me
always to be best and to be superior to others,
and not to shame the family of our forefathers . . ."

The conceit informing such statements is that genealogy,[51] in the first instance, naturally endows one with courage and imposes an obligation to excel in battle

---

[49] Bérard 1970:69 apropos of the talisman-like quality of a *heroön*.

[50] Cf. Russo, Fernández-Galiano, and Heubeck 1992:415 *ad loc.*: "'measure themselves' in battle." Leaf and Bayfield 1962:312 on the verb κρίνεσθαι at *Iliad* 2.385 note the "primary idea of *separation*" (their italics) that leads to contrasting and "measuring themselves" presumably in relation to the enemy.

[51] Cf. *Iliad* 5.253–254: 'οὐ γάρ μοι γενναῖον ἀλυσκάζοντι μάχεσθαι' (Diomedes to Sthenelos).

(ἀριστεύειν).[52] The typical warrior will assume, "I can and must fight according to the example of my forefathers," thus identifying with his γένος 'family, genealogy'. Odysseus does precisely this when he invokes his πατέρων γένος 'family of forefathers' in one breath (*Odyssey* 24.508) and then expressly appropriates his ancestors' ἀλκή 'valor' and ἠνορέη 'masculinity, manhood' in another (*Odyssey* 24.509). Now ἠνορέη, as Graziosi and Haubold have shown, is generally a positive quality.[53] In the *Iliad* the term is mentioned usually in conjunction with other virtues and connotes the state of being a man, a kind of masculinity that might prove socially beneficial if tempered by considerations of cooperation among equals on the battlefield. At *Odyssey* 24.509, its only attestation in that poem, ἠνορέη refers retrospectively to the Arkeisiads' renowned track record of bravery (compare 24.509: πᾶσαν ἐπ' αἶαν 'throughout the whole earth', for the extent of this renown). Haubold and Graziosi also remark that the degree to which Telemachos exemplifies this quality "is something still to be proven," for he "remains first and foremost a son, not a full-grown man" despite having participated in the πόλεμος 'war' (as Homer calls it) waged against the suitors.[54]

In his response Telemachos self-consciously echoes his father's injunction almost verbatim: 'οὔ τι καταισχύνοντα τεὸν γένος, ὡς ἀγορεύεις' (*Odyssey* 24.512) echoes 'μή τι καταισχύνειν πατέρων γένος' (*Odyssey* 24.508). Whether "with a touch of scorn" or not,[55] the prince signals to his father that he is quoting him.[56] But instead of repeating in his asseveration Odysseus' πατέρων γένος 'our fathers' *genos*',[57] Telemachos says τεὸν γένος ('your *genos*').[58] He admits by implication that he is not a full-fledged member of his father's *genos*. This variation in wording confirms, I believe, Graziosi and Haubold's diagnosis, which I cite again: "Telemachus remains first and foremost a son, *not a full-grown man fighting a war among other men on the battlefield*."[59] It remains for Telemachos, the last in line, to display ἠνορέη 'masculinity' in his own right, in a proper Iliadic battle (as opposed to the unusual indoor fighting of Book 22). This he promptly and spectacularly does (in verses 525–530) alongside his father and grandfather; the dynamic duo Odysseus and Telemachos would have decimated the enemy, the poet tells us, had Athena not intervened to stop the fighting (*Odyssey* 24.531–532).

---

[52] As I note in Chapter 3 where I follow others, genealogy raises the Homeric hero's statistical chances of excelling in battle and legitimates his efforts at ruling, but ultimately the touchstone of his overall excellence is his δύναμις, his 'bigman ability', to use the anthropological term.

[53] Graziosi and Haubold 2003, esp. 62–63, 71–73, to which this paragraph is indebted.

[54] E.g. *Odyssey* 24.475; see Graziosi and Haubold 2003:72–73.

[55] So Stanford 1958:429 *ad loc.*, who renders ὡς ἀγορεύεις as 'as you phrase it'.

[56] The echo is obvious even if we adopt Dawe's alternative (1993:867) 'in the way that you say' (= ὡς ἀγορεύεις), which would modify καταισχύνοντα.

[57] But cf. e.g. Dawe's translation (1993:867) 'your fathers, us who . . .'

[58] 'ἐμὸν γένος' would have been possible metrically, but Telemachos, as I will note, has not yet been fully incorporated in his father's γένος.

[59] Graziosi and Haubold 2003:73; italics mine.

So it is not until the very end of the poem that Telemachos proves himself truly worthy of his father's *genos* and is integrated *de facto* into it as a full-grown man.[60]

The Telemachos we see in the exchange of verses 505ff. is, I suggest, a Telemachos on the verge of coming fully into his own as a *man* possessed of ἠνορέη 'manhood'. In these verses the prince experiences some sort of symbolic induction into his *genos*, and the event is rendered most meaningful by the fact that it is overseen by his father and proud grandfather. It is pointless to speculate whether the poet is deliberately alluding to an actual practice or custom that an Archaic audience would have readily recognized.[61] In the Classical period, at any rate, an Athenian would have thought that Homer was conveying something of wider social importance in these verses. Telemachos' words, in particular, would have called to mind the beginning of the so-called 'ephebic oath', described by Dover as the "most comprehensive oath which an Athenian swore in his life" on being inducted into the status of ephebe at the age of 19 or 20.[62] The Athenian youth swore, "I will not *shame* the sacred arms . . ."[63] Of course the Athenian would have spoken in civic terms, while Telemachos speaks as a member of an aristocratic family.[64] What is beyond doubt is that the three-cornered conversation at the end of Book 24 espouses the ideal of family continuity across three generations, an ideal that can be corroborated by such evidence as the Archaic τριτοπατρεῖα or enclosures for burials of three generations. Showing ἠνορέη 'masculinity' in a spectacular outdoor battle, Telemachos becomes, by *Odyssey* 24.530, a man fully grown and 'graduates' to the grade of warrior.[65] He has upheld his genealogy by outgrowing his Homeric role of Little Prince. Like his genealogy, Telemachos has come to the end of the line.[66]

---

[60] Graziosi and Haubold 2003 do not envisage this development.

[61] Elsewhere in the *Odyssey* Homer seems clearly to echo marriage-song and custom (see Chapter 4) as well as educational practice (in the *anagnorisis* of Odysseus by Laertes in *Odyssey* 24, see Appendix III). As de Jong 2001:562 ad *Odyssey* 23.296 and others have argued, the poet plays up the reintegration of Odysseus in society through his 'remarriage' to Penelope. As for his reintegration into patriarchy in the *anagnorisis* in *Odyssey* 24, see Wöhrli 1999:111ff., to which I add Appendix III.

[62] For the text with discussion, see Tod 1985:303–306; Dover 1974:250; Siewert 1977:102–12. Note that Telemachos at 20 was still an ephebe by Athenian standards.

[63] Οὐκ αἰσχυνῶ τὰ ἱερὰ ὅπ/λα . . .

[64] But note the similar tripartite schema mirrored in the ephebic oath itself: the *ephebe* receives the 'fatherland' from his *forefathers* and swears to pass it on in his turn 'greater and better' to his *descendants*. For πατρίδα 'fatherland', cf. Odysseus' phrase 'πατρίδα γαῖαν' at *Odyssey* 24.322.

[65] In Classical Athenian terms he has passed scrutiny at the level of local *deme* and Athenian *Boulê* (cf. the formal terms ἀνὴρ γίγνεσθαι, δοκιμάζεσθαι εἰς ἄνδρας, etc.); but he has also become a hoplite and young adult (νέος) belonging to a given military ἡλικία (or call-up group): cf. Garland 1990:180–185 for the Athenian evidence.

[66] Now he is a man and no longer a *Nebenfigur*; he has as much a place in the *Odyssey* as a fully adult Harry Potter would have in the novels of J. Rowling. Cf. Martin 1993:222–240, esp. 240, for a metapoetic interpretation of the end of the *Odyssey*: Telemachos' failure to tell his own story symbolizes the end of a poetic tradition.

Appendix I

Ethnographically speaking, the relation of a rumor to an eyewitness account is not generally straightforward, as J. Vansina observes: "Very often, one can no longer ascertain whether the rumor derives from an eyewitness account or not. In most cases internal evidence itself will have to guide us . . . " (1985:6). Apart from this uncertainty we must also reckon with the element of exaggeration intrinsic to every rumor. Cf. Vansina's earlier remark: "Even if the bare facts are true enough, the spectacular parts are always overdone . . . " (6). On the other hand, Vansina very reasonably underrates the reliability of an eyewitness report as well: "Eyewitness accounts are only partly reliable" (5). As he argues, an eyewitness, when reconstructing an event in his/her telling, is apt to do so in a selective fashion, mentioning only certain elements and supplementing the gaps in his/her perception and memory with details he/she did not actually perceive but which he/she would expect to have seen or heard under the circumstances. In general, recollection forces the eyewitness to impose *coherence* on his/her narrative by adding the "missing pieces of observation" (5). The expected details and the coherence stem, moreover, from "popular paradigms of recollection" according to L. J. Kirmayer (1996:182). Homer perhaps implies the process of filling gaps with anticipated details when Odysseus extols above all else the *inner coherence and arrangement* (*Odyssey* 8.489: 'λίην γὰρ κατὰ κόσμον Ἀχαιῶν οἶτον ἀείδεις' ["for you sing of the fate of the Achaians in exceedingly proper order"]) exemplified by the 'construction' (cf. *Odyssey* 8.492–493: 'ἵππου κόσμον . . . / δουρατέου' ["the devising of the Wooden Horse"]) of Demodokos' song. It is obvious that according to Odysseus this coherence betrays the *truth-content* (or at least the reliability) of the bard's narrative: 'ὥς τέ που ἢ αὐτὸς παρεὼν ἢ ἄλλου ἀκούσας' ["as if somehow you were there yourself or had heard these things from someone else"] (*Odyssey* 8.491). The handling, κατὰ κόσμον 'in due or expected sequence', of the material, as de Jong 2001:214–215 argues *ad loc.*, suggests that Homer already acknowledges the principle of ἐνάργεια 'vivid evocation' of later rhetorical theory. Yet, *contra* de Jong, this passage does not imply that the *Odyssey*'s audience appreciated the vividness of a narrative at the expense of its truthfulness; on the contrary, it suggests that the mandatory vividness—stemming from the internal coherence and overall arrangement typical of eyewitness recollection—vouched for the narrative's truth.

Appendix II
"Gentle Father of the People"

For "gentle father of the people" in *Odysssey* 2.47 ('πατὴρ δ' ὣς ἤπιος ἦεν' ["and (who) was like a gentle father (sc. to you Ithakans)"]) compare Mentor's identical simile at *Odyssey* 2.234. Taking as my starting point Heubeck, West, and Hainsworth 1988:255 *ad Odyssey* 5.12 and de Jong 2001:57–58 *ad Odyssey* 2.234, I note that: i) the underlying image suggests the mutual yet asymmetrical emotional tie between Odysseus and the *laos*; ii) as social anthropology shows, this image presupposes a non-egalitarian social model; iii) in all three instances, *Odyssey* 2.47, 234, and 5.12, it is understood that within the setting of his social 'family' the 'father' exercises just rule. G. Wöhrle observes, in keeping with cross-cultural anthropological data, that intra-family patriarchy reproduces patriarchy outside the family, a condition that gives rise to rigidly hierarchical and occasionally violent power relationships (1999:11–22). Hence, in his view, the *basileus* is *a priori* a good father within and beyond his *oikos*. Indeed, as de Jong 2001:57–58 *ad Odyssey* 2.234 remarks, Odysseus' tender paternal relationship with his people will temper our sense of horror before his only act of cruelty, the murder of the suitors. This mass murder—to extrapolate from Wöhrle's analysis—represents the just punishment by a collective *paterfamilias* who is gentle in principle yet at the same time inexorable. And to extrapolate further, just as epic ideology accepts that there are just and unjust kings (e.g. Hesiod *Works and Days* 238–247), so also epic society understands that there are good and bad fathers. In *Odyssey* 2.46–47 (mentioned above) Telemachos has defensively 'split', as M. Klein would argue, the internal object of his 'father' and focuses wholly on the (idealized) 'good father'.

De Jong 2001:49 *ad Odyssey* 2.47 documents 'parent and children' comparisons in the *Odyssey* (including those involving animals); also see *Odyssey* 16.442ff. (which de Jong omits in the list of similes just noted). For Penelope as 'mother', in miniature, of the people, see *Odyssey* 18.323ff.; on her *kleos*, see Chapter 4.

Appendix III

G. Wöhrle is perfectly right in remarking that the scene in which Laertes recognizes his son in *Odyssey* 24 is "anthropologically acute."[1] In this scene Laertes and Odysseus reinstate together patriarchal succession, for an elderly king invariably needed the support of his son, and the son required acceptance and legitimation by his father in order for patriarchy to work.[2] If, as Wöhrle argues,[3] father-son competition is endemic in patriarchy, Odysseus' premeditated testing of his father (compare *Odyssey* 24.238–240) may be taken to betray this residual hostility, which also underlies Odysseus' and Telemachos' contest in ἀρετή 'bravery' (in effect) in the same book (compare *Odyssey* 24.515).[4] It is in the spirit of rivalry, then, that Odysseus puts not only his father's ἦθος 'moral character' to the test (as Aristotle would argue), but more pertinently the solidarity of his *genos*. It may repay attention to consider the anthropological and educational import of the two tokens—no less—of his identity, which Odysseus invokes in order to convince his father. As I shall argue, these σήματα 'indicia', namely, the well-known scar, on the one side, and the trees and vines in the orchard, on the other, cohere nicely, referring father and son back to two integral educational experiences, the second of which (unlike the scar) is known only to the two of them.[5]

First, Odysseus recounts and thereby relives his hunting expedition (*Odyssey* 24.331–335), a typical 'educational' ordeal.[6] The wound he suffered in that incident is token number one. Then, moving still farther back in his personal chronology, he recalls, in effect, the first lesson he received from his father in classification and the naming of objects, in this instance various

---

[1]   Wöhrle 1999:112–113.

[2]   Wöhrle 1999:116.

[3]   Wöhrle 1999, esp. 37–48 (paternal dominance, filial resentment, and father-son friction in the Homeric epics).

[4]   Cf. esp. 24.240. κερτομίοις (of his ἔπεα) = 'cutting to the quick' according to Jones 2002:222. For the "touch of scorn" in Telemachos' preceding words (*Odyssey* 24.511–512), see Stanford 1958:429 *ad loc.* and my discussion in Chapter 6 above.

[5]   Cf. Dawe 1993:854, de Jong 2001:581 and Heubeck 1992:389 *ad loc.*, who however do not correlate the σήματα to educational practice. On the scar as a necessarily 'public' badge, see Chapter 5.

[6]   See again Chapter 5.

trees and rows of vines (*Odyssey* 24.336–344). These were enclosed by a dry stone (?) wall (ἕρκος)[7] and lay within the large, luxuriant but 'well-ordered' orchard (ἀλωή,[8] ὄρχατος[9]) that formed a part of Laertes' 'well-cultivated' farm (ἀγρός) outside the city.[10] Now, 40 or more years on, Odysseus accosts Laertes here and enumerates the orchard's plants and trees (*Odyssey* 24.245–247).[11] Like the single scar, these collective tokens are prompts that generate a micro-narrative (to use N. Loraux's term) about a formative experience from Odysseus' early years, and his childhood in particular. An inquisitive boy, he had asked his dad about *each* tree and plant (*Odyssey* 24.337: 'ἐγὼ δ' ᾔτεόν σε ἕκαστα').[12] Laertes gladly obliged, "identifying" each tree "by species" (*Odyssey* 24.339: σὺ δ' ὠνόμασας καὶ ἔειπες ἕκαστα'); and in the course of naming each species Laertes also "told him about each."[13] The variety of identifiable vegetation, even of the vines, was considerable.[14] This elementary lesson in descriptive taxonomy encapsulates almost emblematically the process by which knowledge is passed on to the next generation in family life and play, among other social activities. The lad is here instructed by his father in "mundane categories," as Durkheim and Mauss would say.[15] Moreover, as anthropologists have recently argued, plant categories such as those Odysseus learned are, together with animal categories, among the most fundamental and enjoy a logical primacy in many societies.[16] The *analepsis* 'flashback' of Odysseus' boyhood experience of classification accords with the *Telemachy*'s general concern with growing up and cognition.

---

7 See Russo, Fernández-Galiano, and Heubeck 1992:387 *ad Odyssey* 24.224: ἕρκος.
8 *Odyssey* 24.336: 'ἐϋκτιμένην κατ' ἀλωήν'; cf. 24.226; 24.221: 'πολυκάρπου ἀλωῆς'.
9 *Odyssey* 24.222: μέγαν ὄρχατον; cf. 24.245. ἀλωή and ὄρχατος are here, it seems, synonymous; ὄρχατος denotes 'rows' (of trees, vines, etc.): Russo, Fernández-Galiano, and Heubeck 1992:385 *ad Odyssey* 24.222.
10 *Odyssey* 24.205–206: ἀγρὸν . . . / καλὸν Λαέρταο τετυγμένον; cf. 23.139, 359: πολυδένδρεον ἀγρόν.
11 *Odyssey* 24.338–339: 'διὰ δ' αὐτῶν [sc. δενδρέων] / ἱκνεύμεσθα'.
12 According to Dawe 1993:854 *ad Odyssey* 24.337 the intended sense must be "I asked *about* each of them" (his italics), echoed by "you named and told me about each" (*Odyssey* 24.339). I note that in the πεῖρα the mature Odysseus similarly decides to question Laertes *point by point*: ἢ πρῶτ' ἐξερέοιτο ἕκαστά τε πειρήσαιτο (*Odyssey* 24.238).
13 See Russo, Fernández-Galiano, and Heubeck 1992:399 *ad Odyssey* 24.339: ὠνόμασας; see also n12 above.
14 Hence *Odyssey* 23.139, 359: πολυδένδρεον ἀγρόν; 24.221: πολυκάρπου ἀλωῆς; 24.344: σταφυλαὶ παντοῖαι; 24.342: διατρύγιος 'ripening at different times' (so Russo, Fernández-Galiano, and Heubeck 1992:399 *ad Odyssey* 24.342), which is elaborated by παντοῖαι (*Odyssey* 24.344).
15 Durkheim and Mauss 1963.
16 Berlin 1992:342.

Because, as anthropologists also acknowledge, the distinction between the mundane and symbolic is often unclear, it may be worthwhile to consider whether the exercise in taxonomy (which typically involved matching objects and concepts to 'labels') bore symbolic allusions. The boy Odysseus was given, it appears, an incentive to learn the names of trees and plants. Each name corresponded to, say, a concrete apple tree that in turn became a gift—and a reward. Hence Odysseus recalls, 'ὄρχους δέ μοι ὧδ' ὀνόμηνας / δώσειν πεντήκοντα' ["the rows of vines, too, you specified in this way <and promised>/to give me fifty of them"] (*Odyssey* 24.341–342).[17] Gifts, as noted in the discussion of the boar hunt and other comparable 'ordeals', are often symbolic rewards for completion of a learning experience.[18]

In the case of Laertes' gifts, these symbolized, I propose, the signposts or ὅροι of the king's domains to which prince Odysseus would one day accede. The symbolism of the ὄρχατος 'orchard' may become clearer if we compare the "curious list of impersonal witnesses" to the ephebes' oath:[19] Ἵστορες [[ο]] θεοὶ Ἄγραυλος, etc., ὅροι τῆς πατρίδος, πυροί / κριθαί, ἄμπελοι ἐλάαι συκαῖ ["Witnesses (sc. are) the gods Agraulos, etc., the boundary markers of the fatherland, the wheat// the barley, the grapevines, the olive trees, the fig trees"]. Plutarch, in the *Life of Alcibiades* 15.7ff., far from distorting and misinterpreting the wording of the oath, indeed casts light on the 'patriotic' and educational symbolism of these landmarks.[20] I quote Plutarch: ὀμνύουσι γὰρ ὅροις χρήσασθαι τῆς Ἀττικῆς πυροῖς, κριθαῖς, ἀμπέλοις, συκαῖς, ἐλαίαις, οἰκείαν ποιεῖσθαι διδασκόμενοι τὴν ἥμερον καὶ καρποφόρον ("for they swear to use [regard] as boundary markers of Attika the wheat, barley, grapevines, fig trees, olive trees and [thus] they learn to treat as their own the cultivated, fruit-bearing land"). The ephebes, in other words, are made to learn that their πατρίς (a natural entity conceptualized in terms of descent from a common bloodline)[21] is coterminous with cultivated land (τὴν ἥμερον: by definition a 'cultural notion'), which includes, like Laertes' ὄρχατος, vines (ἄμπελοι) and olive trees (ἐλαῖαι). Homer, I suggest, is recounting something more momentous than a boy's promenade through an orchard with his fond papa.[22] Rather, he shows Odysseus acquiring with the help of 'names' a

---

[17] Russo, Fernández-Galiano, and Heubeck 1992:399 *ad Odyssey* 24.341: ὀνόμηνας and LfgrE, s.v. ὀνομῆναι (2b) and ὀνομάζω (b2): these verbs connote both *naming/listing* as well as *the promise of making a gift of the items listed/named*.

[18] Because Dawe 1993:855 *ad Odyssey* 24.341 overlooks this fact, he is led to puzzle over the use of ὀνόμηνας almost in the sense of 'to promise'.

[19] Tod 1952:204; see also Chapter 6 above.

[20] *Pace* Tod 1952:204.

[21] Cf. Hall 2002, esp. 9–10, 18 on ancient Greek ethnic identity.

[22] But cf. Dawe 1993:854 *ad Odyssey* 24.336.

taxonomy that is at once mundane and symbolic.[23] This excursion in symbolic territory takes place, appropriately enough, in a 'well-ordered orchard', itself a product of culture, in which the boy is being immersed.

---

[23] Nowadays anthropologists hold that language (i.e. 'names', 'labels') does not determine the parameters of categories: e.g. Berlin 1992. In the Archaic period, as Siewert 1977: 109 notes, Athenians tended to neglect or ignore the strategic and economic importance of Attica's mountainous districts and other remoter areas; perhaps this explains Laertes' focus on an orchard as emblematic of Ithaka's actual territory.

Bibliography

Alden, M. J. 2000. *Homer beside Himself: Para-Narratives in the Iliad*. Oxford.

Allione, L. 1963. *Telemaco e Penelope nell' 'Odissea'*. Turin.

Antonaccio, C. 1993. "The Archaeology of Ancestors." *Cultural Poetics in Archaic Greece: Cult, Performance, Politics* (eds. C. Dougherty and L. Kurke) 46–70. Cambridge.

Apthorp, M. J. 1980. "The Obstacles to Telemachus' Return." *Classical Quarterly* N.S. 30:1–22.

Austin, N. 1969. "Telemachos Polymechanos." *University of California Studies in Classical Antiquity* 2:45–63.

———. 1975. *Archery at the Dark of the Moon: Poetic Problems in Homer's Odyssey*. Berkeley and Los Angeles.

Autenrieth, G., A. Kaegi, and A. Willi. 1920. *Wörterbuch zu den Homerischen Gedichten*. Revised 14th ed. 1999. Stuttgart.

Bakker, E. J. 2002a. "Polyphemos." *Colby Quarterly* 38:135–150.

———. 2002b. "*Khrónos, Kléos* and Ideology from Herodotus to Homer." *Epea pteroenta: Beiträge sur Homerforschung. Festschrift für Wolfgang Kullman zum 75. Geburtstag* (eds. A. Reichel and A. Rengakos) 11–30. Stuttgart.

Baldick, C. 1990. *Oxford Concise Dictionary of Literary Terms*. Oxford Paperback Reference. Oxford.

Barber, E. J. W. 1991. *Prehistoric Textiles: The Development of Cloth in the Neolithic and Bronze Ages with Special Reference to the Aegean*. Princeton.

Barnard, A., and J. Spencer, eds. 1996. *Encyclopedia of Social and Cultural Anthropology*. London and New York.

Beaumont, L. A. 2003. "The Changing Face of Childhood." *Coming of Age in Ancient Greece: Images of Childhood from the Classical Past* (eds. J. Neils and J. H. Oakley) 59–83. New Haven, CT.

Beekes, R. 2010. *Etymological Dictionary of Greek* I, II. Leiden and Boston.

Benveniste, E. 1966. *Problèmes de linguistique générale*. Paris.

Bérard, C. 1970. *Eretria*. Vol. 3, *L' hérôon à la porte de l' ouest*. Bern.

Berlin, B. 1992. *Ethnobiological Classification: Principles of Categorization of Plants and Animals in Traditional Societies.* Princeton.

Bloch, E. 1959. *Das Prinzip Hoffnung.* Frankfurt am Main.

Blundell, S. 1995. *Women in Ancient Greece.* Cambridge, MA.

Bourdieu, P., and J.-C. Passeron. 1964. *Les héritier, les étudiants et la culture.* Paris.

Bremmer, J. 1983. "The Importance of the Maternal Uncle and Grandfather in Archaic and Classical Greece and Early Byzantium." *Zeitschrift für Papyrologie und Epigraphik* 50:173–186.

Butler, J. P. 1997. *Excitable Speech: A Politics of the Performative.* New York and London.

Bynum, D. E. 1968. "Themes of the Young Hero in Serbocroatian Oral Epic Tradition." *Publications of the Modern Language Association* 83:1296–1303.

Cairns, D. L., ed. 2001. *Oxford Readings in Homer's Iliad.* Oxford.

Calame, C. 1997. *Choruses of Young Women in Ancient Greece: Their Morphology, Religious Role, and Social Function.* Trans. D. Collins and J. Orion. Lahnam, MD. Originally published as *Chœurs de jeunes filles en Grèce archaïque. 1, Morphologie, fonction religieuse et sociale.* 1977. Rome.

———. 1999. "Indigenous and Modern Perspectives on Tribal Initiation Rites: Education According to Plato." In Padilla 1999:278–312.

Calvino, I. 1999. *Why Read the Classics?* Trans. M. McLaughlin. London. Originally published as *Perché leggere i classici.* 1991. Milan.

Carrithers, M. S., S. Cohen, and S. Lukes, eds. 1985. *The Category of the Person.* Oxford.

Chaniotis, A. 2005. *War in the Hellenistic World: A Social and Cultural History.* Oxford and Malden, MA.

Chantraine, P. 1968–1980. *Dictionnaire étymologique de la langue grecque.* Paris.

Chodorow, N. 1974. "Family Structure and Feminine Personality." In Rosaldo and Lamphere 1974:43–66.

Clairmont, C. W. 1970. *Gravestone and Epigram: Greek Memorials from the Archaic and Classical Period.* Mainz on Rhine.

Clarke, H. W. 1963. "Telemachus and the Telemacheia." *American Journal of Philology* 84:129–145.

Clarke, M. 2004. "Manhood and Heroism." In Fowler 2004:74–90.

Copley, B. 1993. *The World of Adolescence: Literature, Society, and Psychoanalytic Psychotherapy.* London.

Currie, B. 2005. *Pindar and the Cult of Heroes.* Oxford.

Danek, G. 1998. *Epos und Zitat: Studien zu den Quellen der Odyssee.* Wiener Studien Beiheft 22. Vienna.

Davies, M., ed. 1988. *Epicorum Graecorum fragmenta.* Göttingen.

Dawe, R. D. 1993. *The Odyssey: Translation and Analysis.* Lewes.

Devereux, G. 1957. "Penelope's Character." *The Psychoanalytic Quarterly* 26:378–386.

———. 1976. *Dreams in Greek Tragedy*. Oxford.

———. 1985. *The Character of the Euripidean Hippolytos: An Ethno-Psychoanalytical Study*. Chico, CA.

Dindorf, W., ed. 1855. *Scholia graeca in Homeri Odysseam ex codicibus aucta et emendata*. 2 vols. Oxford.

Dover, K. J. 1978. *Greek Homosexuality*. London.

———, ed. 1980. *Plato Symposium*. Cambridge.

———. 1988. "Greek Homosexuality and Initiation." *The Greeks and Their Legacy: Collected Papers*. Vol. 2, *Prose Literature, History, Society, Transmission, Influence* 115–134. Oxford.

———. 1994. *Greek Popular Morality in the Time of Plato and Aristotle*. Corrected reprint of the 1974 ed. Indianapolis.

Dowden, K. 2004. "The Epic Tradition in Greece." In Fowler 2004:188–205.

Ducrey, P. et al. 2004. *Eretria, A Guide to the Ancient City*. Trans. S. Rendall. Lausanne.

Durkheim, É., and M. Mauss. 1963. *Primitive Classification*. Trans. and ed. R. Needham. Chicago.

Easterling, P.E. 1991. "Men's κλέος and Women's γόος: Female Voices in the *Iliad*." *Journal of Modern Greek Studies* 9:145–151.

Edmunds, S. T. 1990. *Homeric Nēpios*. New York.

Felson-Rubin, N. 1994. *Regarding Penelope: From Character to Poetics*. Princeton.

Ferrari, G. 2002. *Figures of Speech: Men and Maidens in Ancient Greece*. Chicago and London.

Finnegan, R. 1977. *Oral Poetry: Its Nature, Significance, and Social Context*. Cambridge.

Fitzgerald, R. 1963. *Homer, The Odyssey*. Garden City, NY.

Foley, J. M. 2004. "Epic as Genre." In Fowler 2004:171–187.

Fowler, R., ed. 2004. *The Cambridge Companion to Homer*. Cambridge.

Fox, R. 1967. *Kinship and Marriage: An Anthropological Perspective*. Harmondsworth.

Frame, D. 2009. *Hippota Nestor*. Hellenic Studies 37. Washington, DC.

Friedman, J., and S. Gassel. 1952. "Odysseus: The Return of the Primal Father." *The Psychoanalytic Quarterly* 21:215–223.

Frydenberg, E. 1997. *Adolescent Coping: Research and Theoretical Perspectives*. London.

Garland, R. 1990. *The Greek Way of Life*. London.

Garvie, A. F., ed. 1994. *Homer, Odyssey: Books VI–VIII*. Cambridge.

Gennep, A. van. 1960. *The Rites of Passage*. Trans. M. Vizedom and G. Caffee. London.

Gerth, H. H., and C. W. Mills, eds. 1958. *From Max Weber: Essays in Sociology*. Oxford.

Gomme, A. W. 1956. *A Historical Commentary on Thucydides*. Vol. 2, *Books II–III*. Oxford.

———. 1970. *A Historical Commentary on Thucydides*. Vol. 4, *Books V, 25–VII*. Oxford.

Gray, J. 2003. *Straw Dogs: Thoughts on Humans and Other Animals*. London.

Graziosi, B., and J. Haubold. 2003. "Homeric Masculinity: HNOPEH and ΑΓΗΝΟΡΕΗ." *Journal of Hellenic Studies* 123:60–76.

———. 2005. *Homer: The Resonance of Epic*. London.

Green, T. A., ed. 1997. *Folklore: An Encyclopedia of Beliefs, Customs, Tales, Music, and Art*. Santa Barbara, CA.

Grethlein, J. 2006. "Individuelle Identität und Conditio Humana: Die Bedeutung und Funktion von ΓΕΝΕΗ im Blättergleichnis in *Il*. 6.146–149." *Philologus* 150:3–13.

Griffin, J., ed. 1995. *Iliad IX*. Oxford.

Hainsworth, J. B. 1993. *The Iliad: A Commentary*. Vol. 3, *Books 9–12*. Cambridge.

Halbwachs, M. 1980. *The Collective Memory*. Trans. F. Ditter, Jr., and V. Ditter. New York. Originally published as *La mémoire collective*. 1950. Paris.

Hall, J. M. 2002. *Hellenicity: Between Ethnicity and Culture*. Chicago and London.

———. 2007. *A History of the Archaic Greek World, ca. 1200–479 BCE*. Malden, MA.

Hammer, D. 2002. *The Iliad as Politics: The Performance of Political Thought*. Norman, OK.

Harris, M. 1987. *Cultural Anthropology*. 2nd ed. New York.

Hartog, F. 1996. *Mémoire d'Ulysse: récits sur la frontière en Grèce ancienne*. Paris.

Hatzopoulos, M. B. 1994. *Cultes et rites de passage en Macédoine*. Athens.

Haubold, J. 2000. *Homer's People: Epic Poetry and Social Formation*. Cambridge.

Heath, J. 2005. *The Talking Greeks: Speech, Animals, and the Other in Homer, Aeschylus, and Plato*. Cambridge.

Heitman, R. 2005. *Taking Her Seriously: Penelope and the Plot of Homer's Odyssey*. Ann Arbor.

Heubeck, A., and A. Hoekstra. 1990. *A Commentary on Homer's Odyssey*. Vol. 2, *Books IX–XVI*. Oxford.

Heubeck, A., S. West, and J. B. Hainsworth. 1988. *A Commentary on Homer's Odyssey*. Vol. 1, *Introduction and Books I–VIII*. Oxford.

Hölscher, U. 1990. *Die Odyssee: Epos zwischen Märchen und Roman*. Revised 3rd ed. Munich.

Hornblower, S. 1991. *A Commentary on Thucydides*. Vol. 1, *Books I–III*. Oxford.

Iles-Johnston, S. 2003. "'Initiation' in Myth, 'Initiation' in Practice: The Homeric *Hymn to Hermes* and its Performative Context." *Initiation in Ancient Greek Rituals and Narratives: New Critical Perspectives* (eds. D. B. Dodd and C. A. Faraone) 155–180. London and New York.

Jaeger, W. W. 1939. *Paideia: The Ideals of Greek Culture*. Vol. 1, *Archaic Greece: The Mind of Athens*. Trans. G. Highet. Oxford.

Jones, P. V. 1988. "The *Kleos* of Telemachus: *Odyssey* 1.95." *American Journal of Philology* 109:496–506.

———, ed. 1991. *The Odyssey 1 & 2*. Warminster.

———. 1992. "The Past in Homer's *Odyssey*." *Journal of Hellenic Studies* 112:74–90.

———. 2002. *Homer's Odyssey: A Commentary Based on the English Translation of Richmond Lattimore*. Revised reprint. London.

———. 2003. *Homer's Iliad: A Commentary on Three Translations*. London.

Jones, P. V., and G. M. Wright, eds. 1997. *Homer: German Scholarship in Translation*. Oxford.

Jong, I. F. de. 2001. *A Narratological Commentary on the Odyssey*. Cambridge.

Katz, M.A. 1991. *Penelope's Renown: Meaning and Indeterminacy in the Odyssey*. Princeton.

Kirk, G.S. 1993. *The Iliad: A commentary*. Vol. 2, *Books 5–8*. Reprint of 1990 ed. Cambridge.

Kirmayer, L. J. 1996. "Landscapes of Memory: Trauma, Narrative, and Dissociation." *Tense Past: Cultural Essays in Trauma and Memory* (eds. P. Antze and M. Lambek) 173–198. London and New York.

Kitto, H. D. F. 1991. *The Greeks*. Revised reprint of 1951 ed. London.

Kleijwegt, M. 1991. *Ancient Youth: The Ambiguity of Youth and the Absence of Adolescence in Greco-Roman Society*. Amsterdam.

Klein, M. 1932. *The Psycho-Analysis of Children*. London.

———. 1948. *Contributions to Psycho-Analysis*. London.

Klingner, F. 1944. *Über die vier ersten Bücher der Odysee*. Leipzig.

Kullmann, W. 1992. *Homerische Motive: Beiträge zur Entstehung, Eigenart und Wirkung von Ilias und Odyssee* (ed. R. J. Müller). Stuttgart.

Lacey, W. K. 1968. *The Family in Classical Greece*. London and Southampton.

Lateiner, D. 1993. "The Suitors' Take." *Colby Quarterly* 29:173–196.

Leaf, W., and M. A. Bayfield, eds. 1962. *The Iliad of Homer, Edited with General and Grammatical Introductions, Notes, and Appendices*. 2nd ed. 2 vols. London and New York.

Lemos, I. S. 2002. *The Protogeometric Aegean: The Archaeology of the Late Eleventh and Tenth Centuries BC*. Oxford.

Lewis, S. 1996. *News and Society in the Greek Polis*. London.

LfgrE = *Lexikon des frühgriechischen Epos*.

LIMC = *Lexicon Iconographicum Mythologiae Classicae*.

Lloyd-Jones, H. 1990. *Greek Epic, Lyric, and Tragedy: The Academic Papers of Sir Hugh Lloyd-Jones* II. Oxford.

Lonis, R. 1979. *Guerre et religion en Grèce à l'époque classique: Recherches sur les rites, les dieux, l'idéologie de la victoire*. Paris.

Lüthi, M. 1947. *Das europäische Volksmärchen: Form und Wesen*. Bern and Munich.

———. 1976. *Once upon a Time: On the Nature of Fairy Tales.* Trans. L. Chadeayne and P. Gottwald. Bloomington.

Ma, J. 2008. "Mysians on the Çan Sarcophagus? Ethnicity and Domination in Achaimenid Military Art." *Historia* 59:243–254.

MacDowell, D. M. 1989. "The Oikos in Athenian Law." *Classical Quarterly* 39:10–21.

Mair, L. 1965. *An Introduction to Social Anthropology.* Oxford.

March, J. R. 1987. *The Creative Poet: Studies on the Treatment of Myths in Greek Poetry.* Bulletin of the Institute of Classical Studies Supplement 49. London.

Marincola, J. 2007. "*Odyssey* and the Historians." *Syllecta Classica* 18:1–79.

Martin, R. M. 1989. *The Language of Heroes: Speech and Performance in the Iliad.* Ithaca, NY and London.

———. 1993. "Telemachus and the Last Hero Song." *Colby Quarterly* 29:222–240.

Marwick, A. 2001. *The New Nature of History: Knowledge, Evidence, Language.* Basingstoke.

Maslov, B. 2009. "The Semantics of ἀοιδός and Related Compounds: Towards a Historical Poetics of Solo Performance in Archaic Greece." *Classical Antiquity* 28:1–38.

Meyer, J. 2005. *L'éducation des princes en Europe du Xve au XIX siècles.* Paris.

Mintz, S. 2005. *Huck's Raft: A History of American Childhood.* Cambridge, MA.

Morgan, T. J. 1998. *Literate Education in the Hellenistic and Roman Worlds.* Cambridge.

Muellner, L. 1976. *The Meaning of Homeric EYXOMAI through its Formulas.* Innsbrucker Beiträge zur Sprachwissenschaft 13. Innsbruck.

———. 1998. "Glaucus redivivus." *Harvard Studies in Classical Philology* 98:1–30.

Murnaghan, S. 1989. *Disguise and Recognition in the Odyssey.* Princeton.

Murray, O. 1993. *Early Greece.* 2nd ed. London.

Nagy, G. 1974. *Comparative Studies in Greek and Indic Meter.* Harvard Studies in Comparative Literature 33. Cambridge, MA.

———. 1990. *Pindar's Homer: The Lyric Possession of an Epic Past.* Baltimore.

———. 1996. *Poetry as Performance: Homer and Beyond.* Cambridge.

———. 1999. *The Best of the Achaeans: Concepts of the Hero in Archaic Greek Poetry.* Revised ed. Baltimore.

———. 2003. *Homeric Responses.* Austin, TX.

Ober, J. 1989. *Mass and Elite in Democratic Athens: Rhetoric, Ideology, and the Power of the People.* Princeton.

Olson, S. D. 1995. *Blood and Iron: Stories and Storytelling in Homer's Odyssey.* Leiden.

Orme, B. 1981. *Anthropology for Archaeologists.* London.

Osborne, R. 1998. *Archaic and Classical Greek Art.* Oxford.

———. 2004. "Homer's Society." In Fowler 2004:206–219.

Otterlo, W. A. A. van. 1944. *Untersuchungen über Begriff, Anwendung und Enstehung der griechischen RingKomposition.* Mededeelingen der Nederlandsche Akademie van Wetenschappen, Afd. Letterkunde, nieuwe reeks 7.3. Amsterdam.

Padilla, M. W., ed. 1999. *Rites of Passage in Ancient Greece: Literature, Religion, Society.* Lewisburg, PA.

Patterson, C. B. 1998. *The Family in Greek History.* Cambridge, MA and London.

Petropoulos, J. C. B. 1993. "Sappho the Sorceress: Another Look at Fr. 1 (L.-P.)." *Zeitschrift für Papyrologie und Epigraphik* 97:43–56.

———. 2003. *Eroticism in Ancient and Medieval Greek Poetry.* London.

Pound, E. 1934. *ABC of Reading.* New Haven, CT.

Pushkin, A. S. 1979. *Eugene Onegin.* Trans. C. Johnston. Reprint of 1831 ed. Harmondsworth.

Radt, S., ed. and trans. 2004. *Strabonis Geographika.* Band 3, *Buch IX-XIII: Text und Übersetzung.* Göttingen.

Redfield, J. M. 1994. *Nature and Culture in the Iliad: The Tragedy of Hector.* 2nd ed. Durham, NC.

Reinhardt, K. 1960. *Tradition und Geist. Gesammelte Essays zur Dichtung* (ed. C. Becker). Göttingen.

Rengakos, A. 2002. "Zur narrativen Funktion der Telemachie." *La mythologie et l'Odyssée: Homage à Gabriel Germain* (eds. A. Hurst and F. Létoublon) 87–98. Geneva.

Robbins, D. 1991. *The Work of Pierre Bourdieu: Recognizing Society.* Milton Keynes.

Rosaldo, M. Z. 1974. "Women, Culture, and Society: A Theoretical Overview." In Rosaldo and Lamphere 1974:17–42.

Rosaldo, M. Z., and L. Lamphere, eds. 1974. *Women, Culture, and Society.* Stanford.

Russo, J., M. Fernández-Galiano, and A. Heubeck. 1992. *A Commentary on Homer's Odyssey.* Vol. 3, *Books XVII-XXIV.* Oxford.

Rutherford, R. B. 1986. "The Philosophy of the *Odyssey*." *Journal of Hellenic Studies* 102:145–160.

———, ed. 1992. *Odyssey, Books XIX and XX.* Cambridge.

Rycroft, C. 1995. *A Critical Dictionary of Psychoanalysis.* 2nd ed. London.

Scheid-Tissinier, E. 1993. "Telémaque et les prétendants. Les νέοι d'Ithaque." *L'antiquité classique* 62:1–22.

Schmitt, A. 1990. *Selbständigkeit und Abhängigkeit menschlichen Handelns bei Homer: Hermeneutische Untersuchungen zur Psychologie Homers.* Abhandlungen der Geistes- und Sozialwissenschaftlichen Klasse 5. Mainz.

Schnapp-Gourbeillon, A. 1981. *Lions, héros, masques: les représentations de l'animal chez Homère.* Paris.

Schofield, M. 1986. "*Euboulia* in the *Iliad*." *Classical Quarterly* 80:6–31. Revised reprint in Cairns 2001:220–259.

Scodel, R. 2002. *Listening to Homer: Tradition, Narrative, and Audience*. Ann Arbor.

Scott, J. A. 1917–1918. "Odysseus Disguised as an Aged Beggar." *Classical Journal* 13:214–215.

Segal, C. 1994. *Singers, Heroes, and Gods in the Odyssey*. Ithaca, NY.

Siewert, P. 1977. "The Ephebic Oath in Fifth-Century Athens." *Journal of Hellenic Studies* 97:102–111.

Silk, M. 2004. "The *Odyssey* and its Explorations." In Fowler 2004:31–44.

———. 2005. "Verbal Visions." *Times Literary Supplement*, January 14, 2005.

Snodgrass, A. 1998. *Homer and the Artists*. Cambridge.

Sokou, A. 2004. "Reconstructing the Past through Unreliable Voices: A Comparison between Oral and Literary Testimonies on the Asia Minor Disaster of 1922." Δελτίο Μικρασιατικών Σπουδών 14:279–310.

Sourvinou-Inwood, C. 1995. *'Reading' Greek Death: To the End of the Classical Period*. Oxford.

Stahl, S. K. D. 1989. *Literary Folkloristics and Personal Narrative*. Bloomington.

Stanford, W. B., ed. 1958. *The Odyssey of Homer* II. 2nd ed. Reprint 1978. London and New York.

Taplin, O. 1992. *Homeric Soundings: The Shaping of the Iliad*. Reprint 2001. Oxford.

Thalmann, W. G. 1984. *Conventions of Form and Thought in Early Greek Epic Poetry*. Baltimore.

Thomas, K. 1983. *The Perception of the Past in Early Modern England*. London.

Thomas, R. 1989. *Oral Tradition and Written Record in Classical Athens*. Cambridge.

———. 1992. *Literacy and Orality in Ancient Greece*. Cambridge.

Tod, M. N. 1951–. *A Selection of Greek Historical Inscriptions*. Vol. 2, *From 403 to 323 B.C.* Oxford.

———. 1985. *A Selection of Greek Historical Inscriptions from the Sixth Century B.C. to the Death of Alexander the Great*. Reprint of 1933–1948 Oxford ed. Chicago.

Tsagalis, C. 2004. *Epic Grief: Personal Laments in Homer's Iliad*. Untersuchungen zur antiken Literatur und Geschichte 70. Berlin and New York.

Turner, V. 1974. *Dramas, Fields, and Metaphors: Symbolic Action in Human Society*. Ithaca, NY and London.

———. 1986. *The Anthropology of Performance*. New York.

Vansina, J. 1985. *Oral Tradition as History*. Madison, WI.

Vermeule, E. 1979. *Aspects of Death in Early Greek Art and Poetry*. Berkeley and Los Angeles.

Vidal-Naquet, P. 1986. *The Black Hunter: Forms of Thought and Forms of Society in the Greek World*. Trans. A. Szegedy-Maszak. Baltimore.

———. 1991. *Le chasseur noir*. 3rd ed. Paris.

Waldner, K. 2000. *Geburt und Hochzeit des Kriegers: Geschlechterdifferenz und Initiation in Mythos und Ritual der griechischen Polis.* Berlin and New York.

Wees, H. van. 1992. *Status Warriors: War, Violence, and Society in Homer and History.* Amsterdam.

West, M. L., ed. 1966. *Hesiod, Theogony.* Oxford.

———, ed. 1978. *Hesiod, Works and Days.* Oxford.

———. 1997. *The East Face of Helicon: West Asiatic Elements in Greek Poetry and Myth.* Oxford.

Wöhrle, G. 1999. *Telemachs Reise: Väter und Söhne in Ilias und Odyssee order ein Beitrag zur Erforschung der Männlichkeitsideolgie in der homerischen Welt.* Hypomnemata 124. Göttingen.

Worman, N. 2002. *The Cast of Characters: Style in Greek Literature.* Austin, TX.

Woronoff, M. 1978. "Structures paralleles de l'initiation des jeunes en Afrique Noire et dans la tradition grecque." *Afrique noire et monde méditerranéen dans l'Antiquité: colloque de Dakar, 19-24 janvier 1976* (ed. Université de Dakar, Département d'histoire) 237–266. Dakar.

Bibliography in Greek

Βασίλαρος, Γ. 2004. *Απολλωνίου Ροδίου Αργοναυτικών Α΄*. Αθήνα.

Γκίκας, Γ. Π. 1983. *Ντελάληδες, Έρευνα και χρονικό*. Αθήνα.

Devereux, G., and Δ. Κουρέτας. 1958. "Ο χαρακτήρ της Πηνελόπης (Εφαρμογή της ψυχαναλύσεως εις το φιλολογικόν πρόβλημα των στίχων 218–224 της XXIII ραψωδίας της Οδύσσειας)." *Πλάτων* 19/20:250–255.

Edwards, M. W. 2001[2]. *Όμηρος, ὁ ποιητὴς τῆς Ἰλιάδος*. μτφ. Β. Λιαπής και Ν. Μπεζεντάκος. Αθήνα. Originally published as *Homer: Poet of the Iliad*. 1987. Baltimore.

Κοπιδάκης, Μ. Ζ. 2003. «*Ἐν λόγῳ ἑλληνικῷ*». Αθήνα.

Μανακίδου, Φ. Π. 2002. *Στρατηγικές της Οδύσσειας, Συμβολή στο ομηρικό ζήτημα*. Θεσσαλονίκη.

Μαρωνίτης, Δ. Ν. 1982[4]. *Αναζήτηση και νόστος του Οδυσσέα. Η διαλεκτική της Οδύσσειας*. Αθήνα.

———. 1999. *Ομηρικά Μεγαθέματα. Πόλεμος-ομιλία-νόστος*. Αθήνα.

———. 2006. *Ομήρου Οδύσσεια, Μετάφραση*. Ινστιτούτο Νεοελληνικών Σπουδών [Ίδρυμα Μανόλη Τριανταφυλλίδη]. Θεσσαλονίκη.

Μπόκολας, Β. 2006. *Παιδεία και πόλις: Η παιδεία στις ελληνικές πόλεις της ελληνιστικής και ρωμαϊκής περιόδου με βάση τις πηγές*. Διδακτορική διατριβή Πανεπιστήμιο Κρήτης, Π.Τ.Δ.Ε. Ρέθυμνο.

Πετρόπουλος, Ι. 2008. "Μαγεία και παραφροσύνη στον Όμηρο." *Η μαγεία στην αρχαία Ελλάδα* (επιμ. Α. Α. Αβαγιανού και Ε. Γραμματικοπούλου) 37–48. Αθήνα.

Σαρίσχουλη, Π. 2002. "Η λειτουργική εξέλιξη του ασυνδέτου σχήματος από την αρχαϊκή ποίηση ώς τους ρητορικούς λόγους." *Ελληνικά* 50:7–34.

Σημαντώνη-Μπουρνιά, Ε. 1988. *Αττικά κλασικά επιτύμβια ανάγλυφα*. Αθήνα.

Συνοδινού, Κ. 1995. "Ο Τηλέμαχος στην Οδύσσεια: πορεία προς την ενηλικίωση." *Φιλολογική* 51:4–10.

Χατζητάκη-Καψωμένου, Χ. 2002. *Το νεοελληνικό λαϊκό παραμύθι. Με φιλολογική επιμ. κειμένων Γ. Μ. Παράσογλου*. Θεσσαλονίκη.

Index Locorum

Aischylos
  Septem 533, 102n44
Apollonios of Rhodes
  Argonautika 1.1290–1292, 93
Aristotle
  Nikomachean Ethics: 1177b27–
    1178a8, 65n38; 1179b30–
    1180b28, 65n38; 1905b15, 60n14

Bible
  Exodus: 6:12, 79
  Luke: 15:11–34, 136

Cypria: fr. 1.1 Davies, 19n72

Diodorus Siculus: 5.31.2 (= Posidonius
  FGrHist 87 F), 48

EM *ad Odyssey*: 1.93 (Dindorf), 17–18,
  18n68
Ephoros
  FGrHist 70 F 149.21 (*apud* Strabo
    10.4.21), 107n9

Herodotus: 1.43, 115
Hesiod
  Catalogue of Women, 133
  Theogony, 48, 68n47
  Works and Days: 154, 26n99; 130–
    131, 101; 586–587, 119n38; 710,
    61n16

Homer
  Iliad
    2.260, 18
    6.149, 138; 6.206–211, 24;
      6.207–209, 141; 6.444–446, 25;
      6.490–493, 58
    8.192–193, 37
    9.440–441, 102; 9.442–443, 61,
      102
  Odyssey
    1.88–95, 1; 1.93–95, 76;
      1.114–118, 2; 1.158–170, 6;
      1.194–196, 14; 1.194–205, 11;
      1.206–210, 20; 1.214–220, 21;
      1.222–224, 23; 1.231–244, 26;
      1.265–270, 5; 1.301–302, 12;
      1.307–308, 12; 1.320–322, 13;
      1.346–348, 46; 1.356–359, 58,
      89; 1.384–385, 60;
    2.10–14, 70; 2.40–41, 72; 2.58–79,
      79; 2.85, 61, 83; 2.117–118, 94;
      2.119–122, 95; 2.125–126, 95;
      2.205–207, 100; 2.255–256, 85;
      2.270–277, 77; 2.303–304, 61
    3.83–85, 16; 3.93–95, 52; 3.98–
      101, 16; 3.184–187, 53; 3.254,
      54
    4.204–205, 63; 4.498, 56; 4.556ff.,
      56; 4.668–669, 103; 4.732–734,
      101; 4.817–818, 101; 4.818, 85

Subject Index

Achilles, 10, 35, 60, 84, 102, 105
aesthetic principles: verisimilitude, 55
Agamemnon, 41, 53–56, 64–65, 84, 131, 141
Amphimedon, 131
analepsis, 69
aner/ἀνήρ (man), 2n2, 22, 67, 72, 78n94, 79–80, 102; *agênôr*/ἀγήνωρ (of masculinity), 4n17, 6n24; *andropais*/ἀνδρόπαις (man-boy), 102, 103; *Mannwerdung*, 2n2, 7, 8n32, 78, 102, 137, 143; the 'one man', 56; anonymous man, 7–9
Antinoos, 61, 66, 76n84, 83–84, 87n117, 93–95, 98, 100, 103, 130
aoidos/ἀοιδός (singer of tales), 31, 43, 45–47, 58, 120. *See also* Demodokos; Muse(s); Phemios
Aristotle: *Nikomachean Ethics*, 65; *Poetics*, 63n25
Arkeisiads. See *genos*
Arkeisios, 134
Athena, 2, 5, 9, 14, 19, 20–21, 23, 26, 65–66, 68–69, 70, 72, 75, 78, 84, 87–88, 99, 101–102, 105–106, 124–126, 137, 142. *See also* Mentes/Mentor
Autolykos (Lone Wolf), 105, 112, 114–116

boar hunt: Atys' fatal accident, 117n26, 123n56; 'blooding', 116, 118; Çan sarcophagus, 117n26; Kalydonian, 118; Odysseus' boar hunt, 107–114, 115; 'personal legend' about, 120; scar from, 114, 119, 129; Telemachos' hounds as implying hunt, 70
boast, 19, 79

Demodokos, 35–36, 38
dêmos/δῆμος, 16, 27, 40, 60–63, 74–75, 81–84, 108, 112

education: as figurative initiation, 106; as inculcation of *habitus*, 107; 'awakening' of Telemachos, 8, 13; *Entwicklungsgang*, 8n32; 'history lessons' in Pylos and Sparta, 92, 126; hunt as educational ordeal, 107, 116, 123; Jaeger's model, 8n32; *paideusis*/παίδευσις, 106; processual aspect, 13, 65, 86–87, 89, 107, 126, 131; *Telemachy* as 'educational drama', 10, 17, 106; youth as an apprenticeship, 17, 123, 125. *See also* mission abroad; Mentes/Mentor; Orestes
epic cycle: as *oime*/οἴμη (song thread), 36; *Iliou Persis* (Sack of Troy), 36; *Little Iliad*, 37n14; *Nostoi* (Songs of homecoming), 45
Eretria, 139

inscriptions (Greek and Roman), 116, 123–124, 126, 140; funerary, 126. *See also under* oaths: ephebic

kleos (fame, reputation, glory): collective memory, 34, 37; diachronic aspect, 29, 31; *énoncé*, 30, 32; *histoire*, 30; history, 33–35; horizontal diffusion, 41n19; *klea gunaikon*/κλέα γυναικῶν (women's glories), 30, 93; 'life story', 28, 35–36; oral history, 1, 35, 37–38, 55, oral media, 35, 49; oral tradition, 28, 32, 35, 39, 48; 'personal (experience) story', 34, 120; (short-lived) 'personal tradition', 37; reliance on tomb, 26–29; social (including gender) identity, 17, 31, 32 and n124, 57–63, 92, 124; 'things heard', 30, 32; vertical diffusion, 33n130; virtual objects, 31. *See also under* Telemachos: minor key *kleos*; Telemachos: need to to achieve *kleos*
kleos (news, rumor, hearsay): accounts, 9, 29, 32, 35, 45, 52, 94; *aklees*/ἀκλεής (without report, unreported), 27, 29, 68; *akoue*/ἀκουή (hearing), 88; *angelie*/ἀγγελίη (news), 73, 85; autopsy/eyewitness, 49, 52–53, 56; Celtic bards as purveyors of, 48; gossip, 29, 40, 47, 49; hearsay, 21, 30, 35, 45, 48–52, 54, 88, 92; implications of, 49; information, 1, 15, 32, 39, 47, 55; Medon the 'messenger', 41–43, 44, 46, 105; modern Greek 'town crier', 41n22; *neôtatê aoidê*/νεωτάτη ἀοιδή (newest song), 46; *opope*/ὀπωπή (sight, seeing), 88; oral history, 32, 39, 48, 53; *Ossa*/Ὄσσα (Hearsay [deified]), 50; 'public opinion', 41; reminiscence(s), 5,

32–33, 39, 52, 55; scale of truth, 55; synchronic aspect of, 29, 33, 35, 37, 39; witness, 32–33, 52–55

Laertes: 'accurate' news about, 50; 'coffin cloth', 94; initiation, 120, 123; paternal model for Telemachos, 105; 'police' operation, 123n54
laos (λαός)/*laoi* (λαοί, people, community), 16, 70, 72, 99, 130, 133. See also *dêmos*

maturity: adult(hood), 1, 8, 13, 19–20, 23, 86, 89, 102, 107, 114, 117, 122–125, 127–128, 132, 136; civic agency, 86n115, 103, 119; 'graduation photograph' in *Odyssey* 24, 138; grown/grown up, 11, 20, 51, 99, 103, 125, 127, 143; *hebe*/ἥβη (youth), 102n46, 103, 119, 121, 123, 125; Herakles as perfect youth, 123; ideal of 'sensible youngster', 124; marriage as sign of, 99–100; *teleios*/τέλειος (perfect), 128; *teleitai*/τελεῖται (is brought to fruition), 127. See also *aner*; immaturity
Menelaos, 9, 28–39, 45, 48–50, 52, 54–56, 63–64, 84, 88. See also *kleos* (news)
Mentes/Mentor, 3, 5–6, 8, 10–15, 19–20, 22, 48, 50–51, 54, 57, 64, 77, 81, 84–85, 102, 105, 120
'mission abroad' (*exesie*/ἐξεσίη), 75, 78, 120, 123, 126, 129, as aristocratic custom, 120, 123. *See also under* Nestor: junior exploits; Laertes: 'police' operation; Odysseus: debt-collecting raid; Telemachos: *hodos*
modern Greek folk-song, 97. *See also* fairy tales
Muse(s), 48, 56

DICK WILSON

❖   ❖   ❖

Listening to Your Soul

❖   ❖   ❖

The Way to Harmony, Health & Happiness

Index compiled by Lyn Greenwood

SAFFRON WALDEN
THE C.W. DANIEL COMPANY LIMITED

First published in Great Britain in 1999
by The C.W. Daniel Company Limited
1 Church Path, Saffron Walden,
Essex, CB10 1JP, United Kingdom

© Dick Wilson 1999

ISBN 0 85207 328 3

The Random House Group Limited supports The Forest Stewardship
Council (FSC®), the leading international forest certification organisation.
Our books carrying the FSC label are printed on FSC® certified paper.
FSC is the only forest certification scheme endorsed by the leading
environmental organisations, including Greenpeace. Our
paper procurement policy can be found at
www.randomhouse.co.uk/environment

Printed and bound in Great Britain by Clays Ltd, St Ives PLC

Produced in association with Book Production Consultants, plc,
25–27 High Street, Chesterton, Cambridge, CB4 1ND
Typeset by Cambridge Photosetting Services, Cambridge

❖ ❖ ❖

Dedication

❖ ❖ ❖

To my Grandchildren, the new Generation,
with love and blessings.

Contents

Acknowledgements

I would like to express my deep-felt appreciation to Anthea Courtenay for all her assistance and encouragement during the writing of this book. I am truly grateful to Anthea for helping me to express and explain some very complicated and deep concepts so that, hopefully, those who are interested in this field can better understand the spiritual dimension involved in Health and Healing.

I would also like to acknowledge with gratitude the support I have received from Dennis Milner whose own two books contributed to my better understanding of this complex field.

Finally my thanks to everyone, particularly my family, who encouraged me to write this book.

❖ ❖ ❖

The Soul

❖ ❖ ❖

The Soul can be defined as our spiritual body: it has its roots in eternity. It carries the records of all our thoughts, activities and experiences acquired over many incarnations. These memories and records permeate every cell of the Physical Body, so that each of us is a reflection of the present state of our Soul on its long journey to spiritual perfection. The Soul is also aware of the experiences we need and choose to deal with in each lifetime and imbues our every cell with the mission to be accomplished in our current life. If we are not fulfilling our mission and have lost sight of our life plan, then we experience a persistent state of unease at a very deep level, caused by the conflict between our self and our Soul. Thus the lack of harmony between our spiritual purpose and the life we lead is one of the main causes of chronic illness today.

Introduction

❖ ❖ ❖

Over many years it has been my good fortune to be involved with both homoeopathic medicines and hands-on healing, and I have seen their positive effects over and over again. Yet I have never come across a satisfactory explanation of how they work, or of the real causes and cure of illness. This has puzzled and concerned me, particularly as it has become my vocation to promote both these safe and effective therapies, and I feel I should be able to explain what I am promoting.

In particular, I have been baffled by the many diverse and sometimes strange techniques employed by healers, on the whole successfully. In this field no-one, so far as I know, has yet provided an explanation that satisfactorily defines the principles which would apply to all these techniques.

I have always felt that there must be one principle underlying this whole field, but for a long time this eluded me. However, over the last few years, partly as a result of my close involvement with the manufacture and distribution of homoeopathic medicines and the Bach Flower Remedies, together with some profound and enlightening experiences in the field of healing, and partly from the many books I have read on this wide and complex subject, I have finally discerned a possible explanation. It is this explanation that I offer to readers, perhaps new to this field, not as the definitive answer but as one possibility, and as a basis for further exploration.

In all, there have been three strands to my thinking, which – together with my work with homoeopathy and the Bach Flower Remedies – have come together to provide this explanation. One is the work of Max Freedom Long, whose researches earlier this century in Hawaii – then the most geographically isolated part of Polynesia – resulted in books on the Huna philosophy of the ancient Polynesians. Discovering his book *The Secret Science Behind Miracles* was a defining moment for me. In it he describes the Huna beliefs and traditions, and in particular provides an understanding of some of the causes and successful treatment of illness.

I read Max Freedom Long's book with growing interest, for the ancient philosophy he describes seems to offer a convincing explanation not only of why people fall ill, but how they can be permanently cured of their illnesses, including the mental and emotional problems for which psychotherapy might be called on today. I went on to read all Long's books, as well as most of the others that have been written on the Huna tradition.

In this booklet I shall be describing, briefly and simply, the main tenets of the Huna tradition and how they can be applied to dealing with illness. I would urge readers who want more in-depth information on this fascinating subject to read the books by Max Freedom Long and others listed in the Bibliography.

The second strand of my thinking is my personal experience of etheric healing, to which I was introduced by my uncle, Andrew Wilson. In the 1960s he founded Thornhill Healing Centre, just outside Glasgow, which he ran successfully until the mid-1980s. He was not a healer himself, but had been interested in healing all his life, and had the motivation, commitment and resources to create a wonderful healing sanctuary.

I became involved with Thornhill during the 1970s and used to assist at healing sessions. These included the widespread method of laying on of hands, and also a more dramatic form of healing: the healer-medium, Albert Best, while under the direction of his spirit guides, would remove tumours, for example, from the patient's body.

Impressive as this type of healing can appear, what really interested me was the fact that although everyone experienced some or total relief of physical and emotional pain, not everybody was healed in the sense of being completely cured. It was amazing that some people could be reprieved even of terminal cancer, while others were not. This led me to wonder why – what was the missing factor? Many of the answers to this question were supplied by the Huna philosophy, and also communicated through the teachings of the spirit doctors who spoke through Albert Best.

The third strand of my thinking is based on beliefs that I have personally held for many years which in turn were derived from the teaching of the Austrian mystic, philosopher and educationalist Rudolf Steiner, and two important books by Dr Dennis Milner, a scientific researcher at Birmingham University.

In the 1970s Dr Milner produced two remarkable books, *The Loom of Creation*, co-written with Edward Smart, and *Explorations of Consciousness* (both unfortunately out of print). My uncle Andrew Wilson and his charitable foundation helped to finance the research for these books, which are serious studies by technological scientists into fields usually ignored by science – including para-psychology, mysticism and expanded awareness, mediumship, the human aura or energy field, and psychic surgery.

The Loom of Creation offers a model of the wider meaning of man's existence and true being, one which supplies the answers to many questions including the very purpose of our existence. *Explorations of Consciousness* describes the experiences of a group of research scientists and technologists who explored the expansion of their inner consciousness through trance techniques.

In the first two chapters of this booklet I have distilled, in a simplified form, much of the philosophy emerging from these two books and from Steiner's thinking, in order to provide a basic structure for the further theories outlined here.

Dick Wilson
October 1998

❖ ❖ ❖

1. What is a Human Being?

❖ ❖ ❖

It may be useful at the outset to explain some of the terminology used in this book, so that the reader can start with a clear picture. Different schools of thought may have different meanings and names for some of the terms. This does not make any of them 'wrong', and readers should not let this confuse them. The aim here is to express somewhat complex ideas as clearly as possible.

All esoteric and spiritual philosophies recognise that the human being consists of much more than the Physical Body. The world religions all acknowledge the existence of an eternal, undying Soul, depicted in different ways according to different cultures. At the same time, the ancient spiritual philosophies of the East describe systems of invisible energy surrounding and flowing through the body, which provide a link between our physical and spiritual selves. The role of these energies in our health is becoming widely accepted today in the field of complementary medicine and healing.

Chinese medicine, for example, is based on the existence of meridians, channels of energy running through the body; our physical health and emotional wellbeing depend on the harmonious flow of energy (*Qi*, pronounced 'chi') through these meridians. Indian yoga and medicine relate to a system of chakras, seven energy centres aligned down the body from the crown of the head to the base of the spine, which take in and give out energy (prana). Health and emotional harmony depend on the free, unblocked flow of energy within and between the chakras. Both these systems are becoming increasingly accepted in the western world, while in western spiritual thought we are hearing more and more about the existence of a Higher Self, the highest part of us, which is our link with our spiritual source.

How do all these elements fit together? The model I have found most helpful, and which is followed here, is based on the thinking of Steiner and Milner. According to this model, the human being consists of five main aspects: the Physical, Etheric and Astral Bodies, the Ego – which we know as our individual identity – and the Higher Self. The Soul [see p.12] encompasses three of these.

The Physical Body

The human body is the physical vehicle for the evolution of the Spirit. It is the result of aeons of evolution, which began when spiritual beings decided to incarnate on earth in order to experience the challenges of life within a material environment.

Human beings are therefore spiritual beings. Our ultimate purpose is to evolve sufficiently to return permanently to the spiritual realm from which we came, by developing our spirituality while in physical form. This process takes many lifetimes, in between which we return temporarily to our spiritual home to absorb and learn from our earthly experiences.

The body is surrounded by an energy field, invisible to most people but capable of being felt and sometimes seen by those whose sensitivities are developed. This energy field can be divided into two main parts, the Etheric Body and the Astral Body.

The Etheric Body

The Etheric Body is an energy body that closely surrounds the Physical Body and permeates every part of it. It is responsible for the body's form and functioning, maintaining its physical, nervous and chemical systems. It is a blueprint of every cell, tissue and fluid in the Physical Body.

The Etheric Body controls every action we perform, and all our involuntary bodily processes –

everything in fact but the voluntary muscles. It registers and stores as memory all our experiences, actions and thoughts throughout life.

The Etheric Body maintains our life processes at all times, including periods of sleep and unconsciousness. When it is separated from the body we are no longer alive. At death, its memory of our life experiences is absorbed and retained by the Soul.

The Astral Body*

The Astral Body is a key component of the spiritual make-up of the human being. It is the architect of the Etheric Body, which it surrounds like a multi-coloured, egg-shaped radiation of light. Steiner refers to it as our Soul-body, or the sentient part of the Soul. It is through the Astral Body that we experience sensations, thoughts, emotions, desires and reactions. It is the energy body responsible for our thinking, our voluntary actions and, importantly, through it we exercise our free will. When we wish to perform an action, we activate the Astral Body by thinking, and the thought process works through the Etheric Body in order for the Physical Body to act appropriately.

The Astral Body's natural environment is the spiritual world, and each night during sleep it returns to this realm. There it is balanced and restored to

*Some esoteric systems divide the Astral Body into a number of sub-divisions, but for the sake of simplicity these will not be expanded on here.

harmony, returning when we re-awaken to activity. During this time the bodily processes are kept going by the Etheric Body.

Without the active presence of the Astral Body within us, we remain unconscious, or in deep sleep.

The Ego

The Ego, our individual identity, is the active presence within the three bodies – the Physical, Etheric, and Astral. It is our eternal self. It is the original divine droplet, the God that dwells in all of us. Steiner compares the Ego to a drop of water taken from the ocean, which has the same composition as the ocean, but cannot claim to be the ocean. As the drop is to the ocean, so is our Ego to the Divine. Human beings can always find the Divine within themselves because it is from the Divine that their essential being springs.

Many human beings, however, are unaware of their own divine nature, and the Ego's task on earth is to develop the spiritual potential of its being, while temporarily cut off from its spiritual origins. This separation came about when human beings were first created: the Higher Selves of humanity could not incarnate fully into physical bodies without the risk of losing touch with their spiritual origins. It was therefore decided that only a part of the spiritual entity should be incarnated, in the form of the Ego: the part that remains in the spiritual realm is the Higher Self, the divine part of our Soul-being.

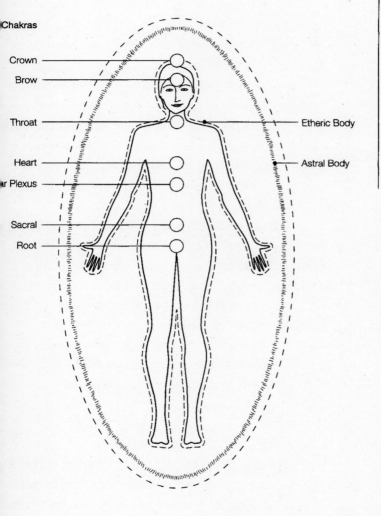

Chakras

Crown

Brow

Throat —————— Etheric Body

Heart

ar Plexus

Astral Body

Sacral

Root

The Human Energy System
The Seven Main Chakras,
the Etheric and Astral Bodies

The Higher Self

The Higher Self is our connection with divinity, it is the perfect part of the Soul which has never left the Godhead. Our main contact with it occurs during deep sleep and in meditation.

Connected with the Divine, it is constantly working to draw the rest of our Soul-being to an understanding of its own true essence and nature. When the rest of our Soul-being eventually comes to this perception, and has evolved to be of like kind and essence as the divine part of our Soul, our spiritual purpose will finally be fulfilled.

Thus there is the potential, through the guidance of the Higher Self, for the Ego to be in attunement with the whole. And no matter how far we go astray, there still remains within each one of us the pattern of and link to perfection through which we may regain full attunement with the whole.

The individual Higher Self is exclusive to human beings. Plants and animals possess group Higher Selves, and do not have individual Egos.

The Soul

The Soul can be defined as our spiritual body: it has its roots in eternity. It is said that God created man in His image: more accurately, the Soul was originally created in the image of God. It carries the records of all our thoughts, activities and experiences acquired over many incarnations. These memories and records permeate every cell of the

Physical Body, so that our Ego is a reflection of the current state of our Soul. The Soul is also aware of the experiences we need to deal with in each life-time, and imbues our every cell with the mission to be accomplished in our current life.

Although we refer to it as a unity, the Soul has three main components, the Ego, the Astral Body, and the Higher Self. While living in a physical incar-nation, the Ego is separated from the divine part of its Soul-being, the Higher Self. At death, however, the two are consciously re-united.

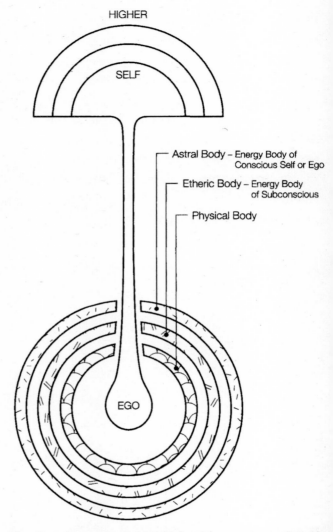

HIGHER

SELF

Astral Body – Energy Body of
Conscious Self or Ego

Etheric Body – Energy Body
of Subconscious

Physical Body

EGO

The Ego is our individual identity, our eternal Self.
It is the active presence within the three bodies –
the Physical, Etheric and Astral. It remains
connected to the Higher Self during our
physical incarnation.

❖ ❖ ❖

2. *The Purpose of Creation*

❖ ❖ ❖

Anyone who follows a spiritual path senses that life is more than a haphazard series of events: there is a meaning to existence, and an over-all purpose to the creation of the universe and humanity. For me, this has also been described most convincingly in the ideas of Steiner and Milner.

According to Steiner, human beings form only part of an evolutionary stream of spiritual beings, at the centre of which is the Godhead – not a personal God, and certainly not the judgmental God of the Old Testament, but a state of wholeness, the source of all consciousness from which everything in creation emanates. The Godhead is surrounded by a hierarchy of spiritual beings, all of whom are working towards the spiritual evolution of humanity, and of which our Souls are a part.

The evolution of humanity began when the Spiritual Hierarchy close to the Godhead decided to further the evolution of all Spirit beings by creating a world of matter. In the Spirit realm, they were unable fully to appreciate their own perfection, since they had nothing to contrast it with. *The only way they could experience their own spirituality, and appreciate the state of pure love in which they existed, would be to experience the opposite of this perfect state.* They could do this by undergoing life in a physical form in a material world, which would provide Spirit beings with experiences and challenges not available to them in the realm of pure spirit. To achieve this, it was necessary to create a material environment together with a physical vehicle, the human body, into which a Spirit being could incarnate.

In order to form the world of matter, the Spiritual Hierarchy contributed part of its Spirit body to make up the various forms of life. In the material world, therefore, all matter is ultimately formed of spiritual beings or entities at various levels of consciousness, fashioned by formative forces following the archetypal patterns of the Spiritual Hierarchy.

The Beginning of Creation: The Mineral Kingdom

From the beginning, creation has been controlled by two important life forces, one spiralling downwards and inwards, the other radiating upwards and outwards. On Earth, the one manifests as gravity, the other as the Sun. These two forces are in opposition to each other: the first condenses and solidifies matter to form the material world; the second raises the vibrational level of matter and provides the life force on which all living entities depend for their growth and development.

The Earth is in constant interplay with the two – the downwards and upwards, contracting and expanding, darkness and light (equivalent to the Chinese concepts of Yin and Yang). This interplay creates the ebb and flow of all our natural cycles: darkness and light, night and day, as well as the cycles of the seasons. It is the perfect balance of these forces that enables the material world to exist.

These forces also played their part in the long, slow process of creation which was to culminate in humanity. This began with the creation of the mineral kingdom which was fashioned from Spirit entities at a very low level of consciousness, virtually inert and unresponsive to stimuli. During this very early period the downward force was dominant. Eventually, through the action of the upwards life force, the Spiritual Hierarchy began to exert its influence on these beings. Those that were able to respond were activated to provide the building blocks of the next stage of creation, the plant kingdom. Those that could not remained as the mineral kingdom we know today.

The Second Stage: The Plant Kingdom

Plants range from very simple, near-mineral life forms to complex organisms with near-animal responses. Through their ability to respond to the forces in their environment, plants came to acquire invisible Etheric Bodies. This marked a crucially important development in evolution, since it enabled the interaction of the two opposing life forces to bring about the growth, fruition and decay of the plant.

Through the impulses from their Etheric Bodies, plants reached out into their environment to encompass the responsive beings of the mineral kingdom around them. These mineral beings were then raised to the same higher consciousness as the plant, and their activity helped to form the plant body by contributing the minerals essential to its growth. In this way the Earth, through the mineral kingdom, builds the body of the plant while the opposing force of the Sun encourages its growth.

Like all the kingdoms of nature, the plant kingdom exists between the spiritual and material worlds, reaching upwards towards the light and air, while rooted in the earth. It draws elements vital for growth from the mineral kingdom below, while taking in light and energy from the Sun and air above. Thus the interaction of the two opposing flows of energy produces the downward rooting and upward flowering of the plant.

The plant kingdom fulfilled one of the primary requirements of the second stage of creation:

sensitivity to the environment and the ability to respond to it. This was made possible by the acquisition of the Etheric Body – the energy body which surrounds and permeates all living things – which differentiated the plants from the purely physical mineral kingdom. It was the Etheric Body that enabled the Spirit beings from which plants were created to develop sensitivity and responsiveness to their environment.

This was an essential step towards the development of feelings and emotions, which would be vital for the creation of the human being. With their highly developed sensitivity, plants were the ideal vehicles in which to perfect all the positive emotional qualities, uninfluenced by the faculties of thinking and willing which colour the emotions in the human being.

Thus, over aeons of evolutionary development, the Spirit beings that animated certain plant species developed a resonance with particular human emotions; and within each of these species particular plants have evolved to the point where they can perfectly reflect a positive human emotion in a pure state.

With the establishment of the plant kingdom, half of creation was completed. This was a crucial stage in evolution: the entities then in existence had reached a stage of perfection which ensured the healthy, harmonious and perfectly balanced functioning of the whole natural world at that time. The Garden of Eden was established on Earth.

The Spirit beings of the Garden of Eden, or plant kingdom, have never left the Godhead and their divinity is still pure and perfect. Their role in nature is to hold the archetypal patterns of the plant kingdom and fashion the energy that holds these vibrating patterns into the physical structures we see all around us in the living world.

Because these beings have no individual Egos and are not hampered by material requirements, they are not exposed to the temptations of free will and materialism. They have thus been able to remain in a perfect state of harmony and balance. This makes it possible for humanity to turn to the plant kingdom for vibrational medicines (such as homoeopathic, herbal and flower remedies) to regain the balance and harmony appropriate to the needs of each individual.

The Third Stage: The Animal Kingdom

The plant has no independent control over its existence; life at the second stage therefore still lacked the opportunity for free will which would ultimately be necessary to the human being. For the next, third stage, the Spirit beings responsible for creation had to move beyond the plant-like state of consciousness, which simply reacts to the environment without thought or decision. This was achieved through the acquisition of a further energy body, the Astral Body, through which the faculties of thinking, feeling, and willing are experienced and controlled.

The Spirit beings responsible for the creation of the animal kingdom raised the level of physical life by building up a network of interrelating systems on which the human body would ultimately be based. These included a sophisticated nutritional system, and a nervous system that provided awareness not only of outward experiences but of internal events in terms of hunger, pain, sexual desire and so on. In this way, just as the plant kingdom perfected the human's emotional system, the animal kingdom perfected the physical.

Thus, through the development of the physical, chemical and nervous systems, together with the Astral Body, animals acquired awareness of both their internal and external worlds and of their responses to them, and also developed instinctive behaviour such as hunting and home-building. Finally, and very importantly, they developed the ability to relate to each other in social and family groups.

The Fourth Stage: Humanity

In the fourth stage the activities of the Spiritual Hierarchy finally reached their objective: the creation of the perfect vehicle for spiritual beings to live in the material world. Humans developed a higher level of consciousness than the animals, which gives them not only greater intelligence, but self-awareness in the form of the Ego, and the all-important faculties of independent thought and free will. And, as we saw in Chapter 1, we have five components: the Physical, Etheric and Astral Bodies, the Ego and the Higher Self, all of which have a part to play in our spiritual journey.

Humanity is therefore the end product of an unbroken chain of spiritual and physical evolution, without which we could never have come into being. *Thus we are linked, through our spiritual origins, with the rest of creation, and the quality of our material life depends on our recognising the part played by nature and working in co-operation with it.*

The Purpose of Human Existence

Human beings are ultimately spiritual beings, the outcome of a decision made at a high spiritual level. The whole purpose of creation is for individuals to learn and develop in a world of matter, until they are sufficiently spiritually evolved to return to their spiritual home. Our situation is like that of the biblical story of the Prodigal Son, who wanted to experience the materialism of the real world; after squandering his inheritance, he suffered all kinds of deprivations until – wiser and enlightened – he returned to his father's house, where he was made welcome.

The problem we face in life is the loss of contact with our spiritual origins resulting from physical incarnation. In order for spiritual beings to incarnate on Earth as humans, the Ego had to become split off from the rest of the Higher Self, the spiritual part of the Soul. It is possible – indeed, it is our task – to re-open and strengthen our spiritual connection through living in the material world. We can help ourselves by consciously working on our own development, with the help of the Higher Self.

Our Higher Selves, which live in the spiritual world, are aware of the purpose of creation. The Ego, however, may not be, and all too often the individual's lifestyle and behaviour conflict with this purpose. The disharmony this causes is experienced at a very deep level, often unknown to the individual but reflected by imbalances in the Astral Body. The more evolved the individual Ego the greater is the disharmony. This imbalance in turn distorts the Etheric Body, ultimately affecting our physical and emotional health. *Thus the conflict between our spiritual purpose and the life we lead is one of the main causes of chronic illness today.*

In order to restore some harmony, earthly life has been divided into two parts: at night, during the deepest periods of sleep, the Ego withdraws from the Physical Body, accompanied by the Astral Body. Together they visit the spiritual realm, the Astral Body's natural home, where they are rebalanced and restored to harmony by the Higher Self. The Ego is not generally aware of this support: on waking, it has no conscious recollection of the contact. The experience is, however, registered in the Astral Body, which is why we sometimes have flashes of awareness or understanding not gained from our everyday experiences.

Although our contact with our Higher Selves can initially be tenuous, and often remains so, the connection is never totally broken. This connection is like a cord; the stronger the cord the more in touch and evolved the person, the thinner and more thread-like the cord the less in touch, and the more unhappy or even hellish their existence. There are a number of ways of strengthening that link and becoming consciously aware of the role of our Higher Selves; we shall be looking at some of these in Chapter 7.

Thus we are equipped to work towards our ultimate purpose, which is to use our free will to develop our spirituality during our physical exist-ence, to the point at which we can return perman-ently to the spiritual realm. Human beings are at a fairly low level of the Spiritual Hierarchy, and every Ego has to work out its destiny slowly through many incarnations. At the end of each life, when we return to the spiritual realm, we have the oppor-tunity to reflect on the lessons of the previous life and on those we have yet to learn.

After death, the experiences of the Etheric Body are absorbed by the Soul. This process has been described by some people who have gone through near-death experiences as the experience of witnessing their whole previous life. During the time we spend in the spiritual realm between incarnations, we reflect on and learn from the experiences of our last life. When it is time to prepare for the next incarnation, the Soul creates a new Astral and Etheric Body, whose form will be based on the lessons needed for the Ego's spiritual development. This is why some people are born with special gifts or severe handicaps – not as a reward or punishment for past-life actions, but to provide the Ego with the challenges necessary to further its evolution.

Humanity and the Two Forces

The most important influence in our spiritual evolution is our constant exposure to the formative downward and upward forces that are constantly involved in creation. It is by means of the downwards force that the Spiritual Hierarchy has brought the Ego into physical existence on Earth. This also controls the first part of the individual's lifetime as it brings the Ego into full incarnation, through birth and childhood to adulthood. At this stage, the downward energy becomes progressively exhausted, and the upstream takes over, eventually taking the Ego back to the spiritual realm at death.

During every single lifetime, the individual is faced with finding a balance between these two forces. The downward force tends to direct people's attention entirely to the physical world and its materialism, to the detriment of their spirituality. The positive upward stream draws people to focus purely on the spiritual life, which can make them unrealistic and escapist, whereas in fact our destiny can only be fulfilled through acting in the material world.

However, the more the Ego tries to use its own resources to progress materially, the more cut off it becomes from its true, spiritual task. This is the stage we are at today: human beings have made huge technical advances, but the majority are unaware of their real role in the plan of evolution. As a result, both humanity and the environment are in a state of disharmony which is expressed in individuals as disease, unhappiness and chronic illness, and in society as crime, warfare, ecological problems, and the general suffering that pervades the planet. To reverse this state of affairs, we need to understand what we are really here for, and learn to work with and harmonise the two forces.

Finding the balance between the two is the key to continuous and perfect health. We have to grasp them both, and use them as the basis for developing our spirituality and for making our own contribution to carrying evolution further forward.

3. *Huna Beliefs and the Three Selves*

As we have seen, the human being consists of much more than is apparent to our everyday senses. The Physical Body is surrounded and interpenetrated by energy fields and systems, the importance of which are increasingly recognised by complementary therapists and healers. It is significant that the Kahunas, the doctor-priests of Polynesia, knew of similar systems thousands of years ago, including the existence of energy bodies and the Higher Self.

Through similarities in their language and symbols, it seems clear that the Huna philosophy and practices had their origins in Ancient Egypt. In Polynesia, the Kahunas were the custodians of this very ancient tradition; they were miracle-workers, revered by the local people who constantly sought their advice and help on life problems, and particularly on matters of health and healing. For centuries the Kahunas passed their teachings on to each generation so that their philosophy remained pure and uncorrupted.

The Huna tradition remained integral to the Hawaiian way of life until the end of the last century, when Western missionaries arrived and, as elsewhere in the world, progressively replaced the ancient native beliefs with Christian concepts. They outlawed the practice of Kahuna magic, and in time, the old Huna beliefs and practices succumbed to Christianity and died away, except in some small communities in remote islands. However, they have never been completely lost. Today, the increasing interest in such traditions has led to a revival of the Kahuna wisdom, and Western healers and therapists regularly visit Hawaii to train in Kahuna healing techniques which address the body, mind and spirit.

Long before the development of modern psychology the Kahunas knew that the human being was not a single unit. Only recently in the West have psychological pioneers like Sigmund Freud and Carl Jung recognised that the mind encompasses other, deeper levels than conscious, every-day thinking, while today transpersonal psychologists also recognise the existence of a Higher, or Spiritual Self. Very much longer ago, the Kahunas saw the individual as made up of three selves, separate but interdependent: this knowledge contributed radically to their ability to diagnose and heal physical and emotional illness.

The Make-up of the Human Being

According to Huna philosophy, the human being is made of several components:

> The Lower, or Subconscious Self – (Feeling Self)
>
> The Middle, or Conscious Self – (Rational Self)
>
> The Higher, or Superconscious Self
>
> The Etheric Body – the energy body of the Subconscious Self
>
> The Astral Body – the energy body of the Conscious Self
>
> The Physical Body
>
> Mana – The energy or vital force of the individual. (Referred to as *prana* in India, and in China and Japan as *Qi/Ki*)

In order to become fully developed human and spiritual beings, we need to acknowledge the existence of all these aspects of ourselves, and in particular to get to know the first three selves so that they can cooperate in our development.

These three selves have been given different names by various researchers in this field. To Max Freedom Long, the discoverer of Kahuna lore, they were the Lower, Middle and Higher Selves; Serge King, a contemporary writer on Kahuna wisdom, calls them 'Heart, Mind and Spirit'; they have also been called the Subconscious, Conscious and Superconscious Selves. The two selves constituting what we have earlier described as the Ego have also been referred to as the Child Self and the Adult Self, and the Feeling Self and the Thinking

Self. I have opted to call them the Feeling Self and the Rational Self, which seems to approach most clearly the Kahuna meaning.

The Feeling Self

Max Freedom Long calls this the Lower Self. It corresponds to a large degree with what psychologists call the Subconscious mind, and is also strongly connected to the Physical Body. Centred in the solar plexus chakra, it controls our involuntary bodily processes and everything but the voluntary muscles.

The energy body which envelops the Feeling Self is the Etheric Body, the blueprint of every cell, tissue and fluid in the Physical Body; it can slide into and out of the Physical Body, and it impregnates every part of the body and brain. All our thoughts, impressions and actions are stored as memory in that part of the Etheric Body which impregnates the brain, which thus becomes the repository of all our past experiences, and determines our individuality.

Very importantly, the Feeling Self is the seat of the emotions. Love, hate, greed and fear all arise from the Feeling Self in the form of strong emotions which can affect the will and the behaviour of the Rational Self, forcing it to share the feeling or to react to it. When these emotions are negative they may overwhelm us or lead us astray.

The Feeling Self receives sensory impressions

through the five senses, and presents them to the Rational Self for explanation and action, if required. It also records every impression and every thought we ever have. Thus memory is a key function of the Feeling Self. In addition, the Etheric Body is very sensitive to thought, so that if distorted thoughts are held in the mind for any length of time, the Etheric Body also becomes distorted, eventually leading to the impairment of the Physical Body.

The Feeling Self responds quickly to the Rational Self's demands to recall memories and experiences, and the Rational Self then uses this information to deal with day-to-day events and situations. This partnership can work successfully only when the memories and experiences have been properly understood and validated by the Rational Self before being stored away. For the Feeling Self lacks judgment. It acts rather like the memory of a computer, building up mental and physical habits, and automatic behaviour patterns and reactions. It often holds mistaken ideas which have not been rationalised by the Rational Self: the Rational Self may not even be aware that they exist. These in turn develop into fixations and complexes which can lead to major problems.

This process starts in childhood. The Rational Self only starts to reason in a limited way around the age of seven, and does not develop adequate understanding or full rational control of its thoughts and actions until the late teens – even later in some individuals. It is at this early stage of life that great damage can be inflicted which will surface later on.

Religious teachings, moral values, family customs and beliefs, social and racial conventions are instilled into children by well-meaning adults. In this way dubious moral values and social conventions (such as prejudice of various kinds, and unthought-out religious dogmas) are accepted as truths. The same applies to personal criticisms and judgments. If a small child is consistently told that it is stupid, naughty, deceitful, unacceptable, and so on, the Feeling Self will store these judgments as fact. The child's Rational Self is not yet developed enough to question this false information, which is then permanently stored and continually acted upon, unless something is done to change the programme. As a result, many people suffer in later life from faulty beliefs about themselves: these cause a great deal of illness and emotional suffering in the world today.

The Rational Self

The Rational Self (Long calls it the Middle Self) is the Conscious Self, the part of the mind we are aware of in ordinary daily life. It is the centre of the sensations, thoughts and feelings received through the Physical and Astral Bodies which enable us to act effectively in the material world; its energy body, the Astral Body, is located between the throat and brow chakras, and comprises the faculties of thinking, feeling and willing. It is the Astral Body that instigates our actions.

The Rational Self speaks, reasons, controls our voluntary actions, and also uses intuition to know and experience our material environment. Its primary role is to relate the body to the outside world through our five senses. While the data from our sensory systems is processed through the Feeling Self, only the Rational Self can put this information together to form a coherent picture.

The Rational Self has only a short-term memory; to make sense of the world it has to rely heavily on the Feeling Self for memories of past experiences. It has, however, the ability to reason, and to initiate decisions. One of its most important functions is to give clear directions to the Feeling Self.

The Higher Self

The Higher Self is the highest form of human consciousness. It is located outside the Physical Body above the crown chakra (at the top of the head), and is connected to the body by a golden cord rooted in the physical heart. Unlike the first two selves, the energy body which houses it does not interpenetrate the Physical Body.

The Higher Self accompanies the Feeling and Rational Selves throughout life, as guardian, guide and inspiration. It does not interfere unless specifically asked; it observes the principle of free will, so that the true purpose of our period in the material world can be experienced. It can be contacted through prayer and meditation.

The Kahunas recognised the existence of even higher spiritual beings, beyond human consciousness, but since they were unable to make direct contact with them, they made their prayers to the Higher Self which can call on these beings on our behalf.

To the Kahunas, the Higher Self was the 'utterly trustworthy parental Spirit', combining both mother and father. It watches kindly over us, and communicates with us during sleep and in meditation. Because we have free will it cannot intervene directly in our lives unless we ask it to: but when we give it the opportunity, it has the power to guide and advise us at all times.

The Physical Body

Together with the Etheric and Astral bodies, the Physical Body constitutes the vehicle through which we exist, have experiences, and act in the material world. It is also a physical manifestation of the acquired attitudes and habits of the Feeling and Rational Selves. This means that its appearance and state of health can be altered by changing our attitudes, habits and behaviour.

Energy

According to the Huna tradition there are three main forms of energy, which vibrate at different frequencies and which relate to the Feeling Self, the Rational Self and the Higher Self. (These three frequencies are known in other systems. In Chinese philosophy, they are known as *Qing* (ching), *Qi* (chi) and *Shen*. Similarly, healers recognise three levels of healing energy – usually termed magnetic, etheric, and spiritual.)

Mana – the Energy of the Individual

Mana is the primary energy, the energy of the Feeling or Subconscious Self, vibrating at the lowest level. It constitutes our vital energy or life force, and is created by the interaction of the food we eat and the oxygen we breathe. It is essential for the maintenance and day-to-day operation of the Physical Body: it keeps us alive and enables us to heal ourselves. It animates the circulation of our blood, our digestive processes and the electrical activity of the nervous system. All these essential life processes are made possible by the continuous movement of Mana, which flows through the body like an electric current, and around it like a magnetic field.

For good physical health the right amount and production of Mana is essential for one's bodily requirements, together with a strong circulation of Mana through the body. Factors that upset this vital function are poor nutrition and bad eating habits, poor breathing, inner stress and negative mental and emotional attitudes.

Mana-Mana

This is the energy of the Rational or Conscious Self, and is of a higher vibrational nature than Mana. It is important to us because it provides the energy for our willpower, which in turn activates our desires and intentional actions. As the tool of the Rational Self it allows us to have free will, but since it is related to our thinking it can have both positive and negative components and effects.

Mana-Loa

This is the energy of the Higher Self. Its vibrational level is much higher than that of the first two energies, and it acts in a very different way: this is the force involved in prayer and healing, which we shall be examining more closely in later chapters.

Thus there are three dimensions to all of us, and we live in all three dimensions simultaneously. Each of the three Selves exists in a specific realm of consciousness, the natural, the human, and the divine. Each is dependent on the other two for its own growth, so cooperation between them is essential.

4. *The Causes of Illness*

The challenge for all of us, and the way to perfect health, is to maintain a harmonious relationship between the triple aspects of ourselves: the Feeling, Rational and Higher Selves, and the Physical, Etheric and Astral Bodies. It is not only the Physical Body that needs to be nourished, exercised and rested. Our spiritual and emotional selves, which are linked to the Astral Body, also need to be attended to. Paying attention to the spiritual purpose of our lives, and resolving the emotional problems which often prevent us from fulfilling that true purpose, are vitally important if we are to evolve. Our lives need to include a balance between all these areas – something very few people manage. Most of us disrupt our potential harmony by the way we lead our lives, and one of the lessons to be learned in our current incarnation is the crucial importance of the need for balance.

The difficulty in achieving this was provided for in creation by the division of life into waking and sleeping; during deep sleep, when the Rational Self is withdrawn, our Higher Selves attempt to restore harmony without interference from our consciousness. But on awakening, the Rational Self reasserts control and the whole cycle begins again. If, after some time, a more regular state of balance is not established, the resulting disharmonies can manifest as illness. How long this takes, and how severe the disharmony experienced by any individual before serious illness arises, will vary according both to physical and genetic factors and to the individual's state of spiritual evolution.

Physical Factors in Illness

The body is formed and structured from energy; it is the distortion of this energy that creates illness. The discomfort experienced by the Soul whose Ego is going awry is reflected by imbalances in the Astral Body which in turn distort the Etheric Body, ultimately affecting the Physical. The body is then vulnerable to bacteria, viruses, pollution, and so on.

The causes of disharmony originating at the conscious and physical level include malnutrition, over-eating or drinking, an unbalanced diet, addictions, lack of exercise, and poor breathing. Accidents, of course, can also cause physical damage, and when this is serious the effects may be carried through to the Astral Body. And drugs and medi-cines intended to be therapeutic produce side effects which cause disharmony, particularly when taken over an extended period.

As for recreational drugs, their use temporarily displaces the Astral Body, leading to the so-called trip, in which hallucinatory experiences are in fact glimpses of the Astral Plane (the realm between the physical and the spiritual). The same phenom-enon occurs with the over-use of alcohol, which of course is also a drug. The danger is that once the effects of the drug have worn off, the Astral Body remains partially displaced and out of balance; it is then also vulnerable to negative influences which can affect the balance of the mind and give rise to uncharacteristic thoughts and behaviour. It is this displacement of the Astral Body that causes with-drawal symptoms, and the need for more of the drug to restore so-called normality to the user.

Disharmonies that are physical in origin can and need to be dealt with by eliminating the physical cause; if they are allowed to continue unchecked, their effects can penetrate to higher levels. But, except in extremely bad social conditions, it is rare for illness to be purely physical in cause. Most of us have choices in life. If we choose to adopt unhealthy habits, our choice is usually accom-panied by a negative attitude – conscious or uncon-scious – that contributes to our lack of self-care.

There is also a genetic factor in physical disease, of which modern medicine is aware. Heart disease, cancer, and other serious conditions are known to have an hereditary component. Medical research today is discovering new facts about our complicated body chemistry and how it works, and is even identifying the individual genes responsible for the more serious chronic illnesses. However, science has not yet addressed the reason why humanity has these potentially hostile genes in the first place, or what activates them to trigger serious illness in many sufferers.

What the medical profession does not teach us – and would probably laugh at – is the concept that our genetic system has a spiritual dimension. In fact, our genetic make-up represents an identikit picture of our selves, our strengths and our weaknesses, together with the attitudes acquired over many incarnations by our Feeling and Rational Selves.

For example, if a person dies of cancer without successfully identifying and dealing with the cause of the disharmony underlying that cancer, this will be retained in the Soul-body after death. The gene responsible for cancer will then appear in that person's make-up in their next incarnation. Likewise, if someone has an addictive gene, unless the addiction is faced and overcome, that genetic propensity will be carried through into the next life. In fact, all the genes responsible for potential negative conditions will continue to form part of our genetic package until we have addressed and eliminated each of those conditions.

The Emotional and Spiritual Causes of Illness

The causes of disharmony originating at the Sub-conscious and Etheric Level are negative thoughts, repressed emotions such as fear, sorrow, anger and rage, and negative attitudes and behaviours. These conditions cause the Etheric Body to become significantly unbalanced and blocked, and if they are not corrected serious chronic illness will eventually manifest in the Physical Body.

Practitioners of both natural and conventional medicine are increasingly aware of the role of stress and unhappiness in creating ill-health. The spiritual dimension of medicine goes even further: stress itself is often the consequence of an unrecognised but deep-rooted spiritual unease caused by the conflict between the Ego and the Soul. Unfortunately, Western medicine and religion have no all-inclusive system enabling us to integrate our physical, emotional and spiritual selves into both the material and the spiritual worlds around us.

A very common cause of inner conflict is the difference between the way the Ego wants life to be and the way it actually is. When life is as we want it, we experience pleasure and joy, which are health enhancing in themselves. Conversely, the disconnection between our spiritual nature and everyday living is often experienced as a dissatisfaction with life, a sense that something is missing – which is, of course, the case.

Unfortunately, people tend to seek this missing

part in material achievements and sources of satis-faction which are not ultimately satisfying. And when the Ego is not fulfilling the task for which it came into this life, when the individual's 'mission statement' – their life plan – has been lost sight of, there is a state of turmoil between the Ego and that part of our Soul which is connected with our Higher Self, which sooner or later affects the Physical Body.

The Meaning of Death

Losing sight of one's 'mission statement' is, I believe, one reason for premature death – either through serious illness or through accidents such as car crashes. Let us be clear: these are not visited on us as a punishment for failure. Rather, it seems that when people's lives are not working as they should, and may even have gone very wrong, they may have a subconscious desire to return to the starting post and begin again, rather than con-tinuing to erode their spirituality.

The decision to return to base takes place at a very deep level, guided by the Soul and the Higher Self. In most cases of terminal illness in which this is a factor, the individual Ego is not conscious of taking a decision to abort its present incarnation and return to the Spirit realm. This is different from suicide, when the individual consciously makes a decision which is often escapist and can have serious spiritual consequences.

At the same time, events that cut lives short – which may seem tragic in human terms – tend to have widespread effects beyond the individual life and death. One is to provide all those people linked to the person concerned with an opportunity for their own spiritual development or expansion of consciousness. A serious illness can give family, friends and carers an opening for expressing love and caring in a deeper way than before. Sometimes the ripples spread very wide: the death in 1997 of Diana, Princess of Wales affected a whole nation, giving people pause for thought about the values of our society.

Of course, another reason for apparently premature death is that one has successfully completed one's purpose for this particular incarnation. This can sometimes be seen with the deaths of children and young people. Often regarded as a meaningless waste, they may in fact be important contributions to the emotional development of the parents, or to an increased awareness of society's treatment of the young.

Most people, of course, live out their allotted span, particularly so long as they have a role to fulfil – in their work, as a husband or wife, or as a parent. But not everyone fulfils their spiritual role, and it is possible that much illness in middle and old age would be prevented if people were able to listen to what their symptoms of ill-health were telling them. For serious illness usually has an important purpose.

The Causes of Illness

The Message of Illness

Illnesses are actually a part of our self-healing process; many of them are caused by the efforts of the body and mind to resolve inner conflicts. The Feeling Self is quick to recognise any kind of imbalance in the body-mind system, and will try to communicate this imbalance to the Rational Self so that something can be done about it. Its customary method of communication is to produce signs and symptoms of illness; at an early stage these may manifest as stress symptoms, perhaps not very specific in nature, or as minor accidents. If, at this stage, the Rational Self takes note and acts sensibly, the process can be brought to a halt and health restored.

Stress is often at the root of health problems that we may not recognise as stress-related. Our physical responses to short-term stress are a natural way of preparing the body to take appropriate action (by producing adrenalin and raising the heart-beat, for instance). It is when stress becomes chronic that it is harmful, eventually leading to malfunction of the body's chemical and nervous systems, and eventually to the breakdown of the immune system which defends us against serious disease.

Stress is often caused by unresolved emotional problems like repressed anger, constant anxiety, unexpressed grief, and fear. Ignoring or suppressing these emotions can have profound effects. Negative feelings and behaviour patterns react on the Etheric Body so that it loses vitality; since the Etheric Body is the blueprint of the Physical, this loss of vitality is then reflected physically.

We all pay attention to the everyday communications of the body – hunger, thirst, sensitivity to heat and cold, the need to evacuate and to sleep, and so on. But we are not all aware of the signals sent by the Feeling Self to the Rational Self, to warn it that action must be taken before serious illness ensues.

All too often the Rational Self is unwilling to listen to the messages of the Feeling Self, or simply unaware that it is being given a serious warning. Busy with material preoccupations, the Rational Self will try to override these early-warning signals by taking a pill and trying to 'pull itself together' while it gets on with its daily business. However, if this continues for long enough, the Physical Body will eventually start to malfunction and real disease will take hold.

When a person begins to experience symptoms and fails to understand their message, they are more likely to see themselves as the victims of illness than that there is something fundamentally wrong with their lifestyle. If the Rational Self persists in believing in the illness, the Feeling Self will eventually believe in it too (since it is always influenced by the Rational Self), and will start to manifest something more serious.

Unless the cause is found and the relevant problems dealt with, the immune system will begin to fail and the process of illness will take its inevitable course until the individual becomes chronically sick. This can take time, and it may take a serious illness such as heart disease or cancer before the sufferer starts to re-think their real purpose in life.

The Rational Self, being only aware of the conscious world, will realise that the body is suffering, but will rarely understand why. Illness is still widely regarded as something visited on us from outside, rather than the result of our own internal processes. The medical profession and patients alike are only too willing to blame bacteria, viruses and the environment; some people, too, see illness as an imposition, or a test or even a punishment. Seriously ill patients often ask, 'Why me? What did I do to deserve this?' In fact, punishment is not a factor in illness – though responsibility often is.

To take responsibility for one's own illness involves recognising the role played by the Rational and Feeling Selves in causing or prolonging it; we need to understand that the illness is the body's way of letting us know that we have unresolved problems. Accidents, too, can be a way of drawing our attention to the fact that all is not well in our life; sometimes minor accidents precede serious ones, as if giving us warning that there is a problem to be dealt with. To restore our health, we need to resolve these conflicts. Even though we are already aware of many of them, there are often deep-seated underlying factors of which we are less aware.

What we can learn from the Kahunas is the vital importance of integrating the three selves, the Feeling, Rational, and Higher Selves. The purpose of illness is to draw our attention to the conflicts and imbalances between the three, and to the fears and guilts that prevent them form working together harmoniously. By eliminating these, we can enable the three selves to work in cooperation, bringing balance and wellbeing into our daily lives.

The Power of Thought

All our involuntary body systems – including our nervous, circulatory, muscular and digestive systems and, very importantly, our immune system – are under the direct control of the Feeling Self; in Kahuna terms, the Feeling Self is the manager of the Physical Body, and is also closely linked with the Etheric Body. In addition, the Feeling Self is responsible for our memories, thoughts and emotional reactions, and is strongly affected by them. When these are negative and painful, the conflict it experiences is inevitably reflected in the Physical Body.

The operation of our bodily systems is therefore influenced very directly by the way we think and feel. Negative thoughts cause blocks and distortions in the healthy flow of energy and reduce the ability of the immune system to ward off and fight disease. Positive thoughts, by contrast, produce positive energy and stimulate the immune system.

It is important to understand that thoughts are a form of energy, which becomes concentrated into what are called 'thought-forms'. According to the Kahunas, thought-forms have substance, and shape; they are active energy influences and, once born, can rule our lives. Even at a subconscious level, they still have power over us.

If you dwell on a thought continually, you not only become accustomed to it: you give it greater power and energy. It begins to take precedence over other thoughts, conditioning the rest of your thinking and your way of life. When more and more power is given to a negative thought over time, the thinker's own energy is depleted; this is a common cause of depression, as well as of chronic illness.

The Kahunas believed that the negative thought-forms which live within us impede our ability to function normally. Negative thoughts interpose themselves between the requests and commands of the Rational Self and the actions of the Feeling Self; they act as saboteurs, limiting our true abilities and potentials. They are often focused on fears and conflicts, remembrances of negative experiences and old hurts.

The Feeling Self and our Belief Systems

Why do we persist in thinking thoughts that may harm us? At the root of our thinking process there is always a set of beliefs, which are often both negative and erroneous. Negative belief systems are not only a cause of illness, but are at the root of a great deal of human misery; they underlie social problems such as failure, poor job performance, divorce, addictions, criminal behaviour and much more. Most faulty beliefs about ourselves and our environment are acquired in childhood; instilled into the Feeling Self by well-meaning adults, they become part of our accepted world view until we decide, or are forced to re-consider, their validity.

Our beliefs act as a filter, causing us to see the world differently from the way it really is. Negative beliefs can screen out positive information so that we only perceive what we believe to be true. A good example of this is prejudice; bigoted people who regularly express negative views on religion, race, skin colour, and so on, are generally unable to accept objective evidence that they may be wrong, and will focus on any events that seem to prove them right.

For example, if parents frequently tell a small child that he or she is stupid or naughty, the child – who cannot yet form an independent judgment – has no option but to believe them. Beliefs instilled at an early age by powerful authority figures become part of the child's make-up and personality, and the child will start to act accordingly. These beliefs are then likely to be reinforced, over and over again, both by past memories and present events. Poor exam results, criticism from teachers or employers, or put-downs from fellow students or colleagues, will be seen as proof that the individual really is stupid or unworthy and will discourage them from trying to see themselves in a different light.

Faulty beliefs like these interfere with the body's ability to function normally, and diminish its ability to maintain health. When we live by faulty beliefs we have considerable conflict in our lives. But since we dislike conflict and pain, we often either suppress our feelings or project them outside ourselves – blaming other people or conditions for our own unhappiness.

Guilt is another major cause of stress and illness, whether instilled by religious teachings or by over-critical parents, and whether or not it is deserved. Well-intentioned parents may have life-goals for their children which they are unsuited for, or unable to achieve. Many people experience conflict between the religious beliefs they were brought up with, or the expectations of their families, and the way they themselves want to live. Trying to follow one's parents' path rather than one's own destiny can create enormous inner conflict, while going against parental wishes can equally leave a lasting and painful sense of guilt.

Some religious and cultural groups still preach doom-laden dogmas against 'sins' which other cultures regard as normal activities. This can have lasting effects on psychological health. If you believe that sin is inevitably followed by retribution, your life will be shadowed by the fear of retribution – either in this life or the next. Few doctors recognise the destructive elements of some of these religious teachings, or realise the extent to which religious dogma causes chronic illness in the community. There is no medical formula for dealing with guilt, and it can take years of psychotherapy to overcome the emotional damage it causes. The Kahunas, however, in their healing rituals, laid great emphasis on freeing the sick from the damaging effects of guilt for real or imagined sins; we will be describing these further in Chapter 6 on page 77.

Guilt also contributes to a sense of personal unworthiness, an inability to love oneself. This is tragic, for love is the protector: it energises and maintains the immune system. Hence, when there is an absence of self-love and self-respect, the immune system, as well as the other bodily systems, tends to be below par. Other problems may well follow: alcoholism, excessive smoking and eating disorders all suggest that there is a significant breach in self-love and self-value.

If we have allowed guilt or other destructive thought complexes to take root in our Feeling Self, it is very likely that we will experience illness at some point. If, on the other hand, we can locate and eliminate these factors, we can improve our chances for a healthy, trouble-free life. For this, we need the cooperation of the Rational Self, which makes our decisions about how we live.

Throughout our development from infancy to adulthood, we are bathed by both positive and negative thought processes and belief systems. Ultimately, every individual must decide which to accept and which to reject. When someone accepts more negative than positive ideas, they end up with a negative mind-set. Conversely, accepting more positive than negative ideas will give them a positive outlook on life.

Thought-forms have energy, and energy cannot be destroyed. It can, however, be transformed. The Kahunas maintained that once a thought-form is created, it can be transformed or replaced with a new, healthier thought. Faulty beliefs can be thrown away and changed at any time, but in order to do this effectively *the Feeling Self needs to be reprogrammed to accept the new belief*. We will be discussing how to do this in Chapter 5.

❖ ❖ ❖

5. The Treatment of Illness

❖ ❖ ❖

The medical profession, and probably most patients, consider that once all the physical symptoms of an illness have been eliminated, the patient can be pronounced cured. In the main this is achieved by the chemical suppression of symptoms, together with the patient's natural powers of recovery. Visiting the doctor and being prescribed treatment can in themselves trigger the healing process. In fact, it could be said that the real healer is the patient, together with the power of his or her beliefs. Taking medication acts as a kind of ritual and reassurance, and is often understood by patients as a symbol of the doctor's power to get them better. In other words, what cures them is the Feeling Self. By seeking and accepting medical help, the person is giving a clear, decisive command to their Feeling Self to get them better.

This is fine when the illness is minor and temporary, as is often the case; many of us recover from transitory illnesses without further problems. It is when these recur or become chronic that we need to take serious note. In these cases, the type of recovery just described does not deal with the true cause of the problem, which usually lies beyond the physical. If there is a deep inner conflict, although health may apparently be restored, a permanent cure cannot be achieved until the underlying cause has been discovered and treated. Failing this, the condition may return in a more serious form, possibly after many years. So it is important to take note of the symptoms of illness at an early stage, and ask ourselves what message they are trying to convey.

The common cold is a very good example of the body's built-in early-warning system in action. We all tend to build up toxins in our bodies because of the nature of our lifestyles; for most people this unfortunately happens on a fairly regular basis. The classic symptoms of the common cold are a raised temperature, sweating, sneezing, coughing, and a runny nose: these are nature's way of getting rid of toxins. Rather than trying to suppress a cold by taking remedies, it is best to allow it to run its natural course, accompanied by rest and drinking plenty of fluids; this reduces the toxins to an acceptable level. Thus the cold serves as a cleansing process which prevents a build-up of toxins from bringing about a more serious illness.

It is obviously even more important to take note of the underlying message of more serious or debilitating symptoms, particularly if they recur regularly.

Natural Therapies

The natural or complementary therapies at least avoid the side-effects of medical drugs. They also take into account the deeper aspects of health and illness: most are based on the principle that human beings consist of more than their Physical Bodies.

As we have seen, disease comes about through disharmony resulting from hereditary, environmental, psychosomatic and spiritual factors. Good holistic therapists recognise all of these, and will treat individuals as individuals (unlike conventional medicine which tends to approach disease as though it existed independently of the patient). The majority acknowledge the role played by our thoughts, emotions and belief systems in health and sickness, while dealing with physical problems through diet, manipulation, the use of herbs, and so on. And nowadays a wide range of therapies address the patient's energy system.

Many complementary therapists recognise the existence of the chakras, the centres of energy which have long been integral to Indian and Tibetan medicine. These centres of whirling energy (chakra means 'wheel' in Sanskrit) are found in alignment between the crown of the head and the base of the spine; running through them and from them is an interpenetrating network of channels of etheric energy.

The chakras control the activity of the Etheric Body. They also govern the activity of particular physical organs, endocrine glands and internal systems, as well as our emotional and spiritual activity. When they are out of balance (under- or over-active, or blocked in some way), the person will be out of balance physically and emotionally. Certain of the natural therapies are particularly successful in restoring this balance.

A good natural therapist will be aware that an illness may be emotionally based, and may therefore respond best to a psychological approach or counselling. Other conditions may require a physical or other appropriate natural form of treatment to restore the harmonious functioning of the Physical and Etheric Bodies. Some will require more than one approach, and many natural therapies address body, mind and even spirit simultaneously.

A good example is acupuncture. This ancient Chinese therapy is based on the network of invisible channels, called meridians, which carry energy through the body. The meridians are connected with specific organs and body systems, and also with particular emotions. For example, the liver meridian is related both to the physical liver and to anger; the kidney meridian is associated with fear, and so on. The energy system connects the physical and the emotional: an imbalance in one will create an imbalance in the other. Likewise, correcting the one will help to correct the other.

If a person lives a harmonious and creative life, according to their level of spiritual development, their energies will circulate freely. However, in people who suffer from stress or frustrations which block the energy flow, the imbalance of energy can bring about a malfunctioning of the physical system. The skilled acupuncturist aims to restore a harmonious flow of energy throughout the body by applying fine needles or heat to specific points on the meridians. This has the effect of sedating over-active energy or encouraging stagnant energy to flow. Once the energy moves more harmoniously the patient experiences not only relief from physical symptoms but a greater sense of inner harmony and relaxation.

All complementary therapies focus on encouraging the patient's own self-healing powers, whereas conventional medicine tends to suppress symptoms with drugs. These in turn may suppress the immune or other systems, leading to debilitating side effects. I have been particularly involved with three forms of natural therapy, whose effects I have seen for myself over and over again: Homoeopathy, the Bach Flower Remedies, and Etheric Healing. Let us take a closer look at how and why they work.

Homoeopathy

The name 'homoeopathy' is derived from the Greek word '*homoios*', meaning 'like'. It is the practice of treating like with like: that is, treating an illness with a substance that is known to produce the same symptoms in a healthy person as those displayed by the sick person. Orthodox medical opinion believes that the symptoms are *caused* by the illness, and responds by prescribing medicine designed to eliminate them. Homoeopathy, by contrast, sees the symptoms as the body's reaction as its attempts to fight and overcome the illness; it therefore seeks to stimulate this reaction rather than suppress it. Homoeopathic remedies thus help the person to regain health by encouraging the body's natural forces of recovery.

Homoeopathic remedies are made from plant, mineral, animal and other natural products. They are made through a process of successive dilution and succussion of the starting material – succussion, or potentisation, as it is often called, is the vigorous shaking of the dilutant after each dilution. This diluting process is continued to a stage at which not even a molecule of the original substance is present in the remedy – one reason why the medical profession is sceptical about homoeopathy, despite the evidence of clinical research. In these extreme dilutions certain normally poisonous plants and mineral materials, known to produce the symptoms of particular illnesses, are often very efficacious remedies, based on the 'like cures like' concept.

There is also an energy factor in homoeopathic remedies. In Chapter 2 we saw how all matter and all plants comprise spiritual beings at various levels of consciousness and spiritual evolvement: this has an immensely important bearing on the quality and effectiveness of certain medicines.

Allopathic medicines – those used in conventional medicine – are usually made from chemical compounds, often originally derived from natural sources (aspirin, for example, comes from the willow). In its natural form, the active ingredient – the ingredient that does the healing work – constitutes only part of the total plant: plants which have a medical application have been endowed with a natural antidote to any potential side effects. This is one reason why herbal medicines are so effective, particularly when prescribed by a skilled medical herbalist: they make use of the whole plant. In allopathic medicine, by contrast, once the active ingredient has been identified by the pharmaceutical industry, it is usually isolated, analysed, and chemically reproduced. This is what gives rise to side effects which nature did not intend.

Once the active ingredient has been treated in this way, the spiritual beings associated with the original plant are no longer present in the compound, which is therefore inactive from the spiritual or energy point of view. The drug is directed to the physical plane only, and cannot affect the patient's Etheric and Astral Bodies, which is where the correction needs to take place. In the Physical Body it will have only a temporary effect, and as this wears off the condition often returns: sufferers from complaints like high blood pressure, arthritis, and so on are often on drugs for their whole lives. They may also have to take further pills to counteract the side effects.

Homoeopathy, by contrast, uses the whole plant or substance, incorporating the spiritual beings that went into its creation, together with the life-force energies that formed it. Through the diluting and potentising stages these spiritual beings, and the associated life-forces, are progressively and harmoniously released, freeing their spiritual qualities. Since the life-force energies are the same forces that bring about the harmonious activity of the living world, they can be very efficacious in treating malfunctioning systems in the human body.

When homoeopathic remedies are taken, they are absorbed by the patient and raised up through the successive levels of the Physical, Etheric and Astral Bodies. During this process the spiritual qualities pertaining to each plant or substance become conscious and active, contributing their vibrational energy to the patient. If the remedy corresponds to the type and level of disharmony in the patient's energy bodies, it will correct the imbalances at all levels.

In addition, homoeopathy concentrates on treating the individual person rather than the disease. Identifying the correct remedies for reasonably serious conditions requires the involvement of an experienced homoeopathic practitioner, who will take into account not just the person's symptoms but their personality, physical make-up, habits and lifestyle. Once the correct course of treatment has been completed, the patient's system will be rebalanced and restored to harmony: when the vibrational distortion in the Etheric Body is corrected, physical symptoms will automatically disappear.

The Bach Flower Remedies

Flower remedies have evolved in this century to heal and balance emotional and spiritual qualities. The pioneer in this field was Dr Edward Bach (1886–1936), a Welsh physician and homoeopath. He spent his life seeking ever more refined methods of healing, particularly of the emotions, which he considered the main cause of ill-health. Constantly experimenting on himself, he discovered thirty-eight remedies, most of them based on trees and flowers, which have the potential to heal thirty-eight negative states of mind, including fear, loneliness, anger, and so on. The majority are made simply by floating the flower heads in spring water in full sunlight. The water becomes imbued with the energy of the plant, and is then bottled and preserved with a little brandy, to be further diluted when taken.

The Bach Flower Remedies, which first appeared in the 1930s, have become popular worldwide, chiefly by word of mouth. How do these gentle remedies restore emotional harmony? As we saw in Chapter 2, when the plant kingdom was created, the spiritual beings that were embodied in their creation developed the perfect form of particular human emotions. The flower remedies are in fact tinctures of liquid healing energy, each one embodying part of the conscious life-force of the plant.

Absorbing the energy of a plant that possesses the qualities of a human emotion in its perfect, positive form counteracts the negative vibration from which the person is suffering. When someone is given a remedy which is appropriate for their condition, the plant's essence within that person helps them to regain perfect balance in the desired quality. Thus, fear is replaced by courage, anxiety by confidence, anger and resentment by love and forgiveness.

Over the past few years, a number of therapists and researchers have been discovering more and more remedies based on the energies of plants, and also on those of gems and minerals. There are now literally hundreds of remedies on the market, coming from all over the world, to deal with a huge range of emotional and spiritual imbalances.

Etheric Healing

Healing by the laying on of hands or prayer is an extremely ancient form of therapy. It comes under various names: spiritual healing, psychic healing, bioenergetic therapy, faith healing, and so on. Here it is referred to as etheric healing, since it works through and on the etheric energies of the human body. For a long time regarded with suspicion and scepticism, healing today is becoming increasingly widespread and accepted, even by some medical doctors. In the 1990s it seems that we are becoming more open to the potential of therapies that are not 'scientifically' explicable.

Healers work in a variety of ways and give a variety of explanations for how healing works. The most widespread is that the healer acts as a channel for a cosmic or spiritual energy that passes through them to the patient, stimulating the patient's own self-healing process. Some healers are aware of being helped by healing guides, some put their results down to religious faith, and some work purely with energy; nowadays many also use tools like sound, colour and crystals. This variety of beliefs and techniques does not generally affect the benefits of the healing received by patients. Successful healing seems to depend not on techniques but rather on the quality of the healer and their ability to channel the highest form of spiritual energy.

The effects of etheric healing vary from mild relaxation and pain relief to results that can only be described as miraculous. The Kahunas, according to Max Freedom Long, were able to perform extraordinary instant healings. And at Thornhill in the 1970s, I witnessed the healer Albert Best causing tumours and arthritic deposits to disappear. How do these apparently 'miraculous healings' come about?

Energy vibrates at various levels – the Kahunas referred to three levels (see Chapter 3). The most powerful healing draws on the highest and most powerful frequency – energy its highest form. The Kahunas called it Mana-Loa ('the strongest force'): healers today often refer to it as spiritual energy. It is the energy of the Higher Self.

Directed by the healer's Higher Self to the patient, it has the effect of raising the vibrational frequency of the affected part of the body until it is no longer solid. In this energy form it is healed before being rematerialised in the Physical Body. Since the Etheric Body forms a blueprint of every cell of the Physical Body, it provides a perfect template for every limb, organ and tissue. When the energy form of the dissolved area reverts to its normal solid frequency in the etheric mould, it is restored to a healthy condition.

Having witnessed the work of Albert Best at Thornhill, I can authenticate that this type of healing can and does take place. Albert was a highly gifted channel; in trance, he was taken over by two Spirit doctors in turn, who carried out operations through his hands, without opening up the Physical Body. Albert used to place his hands over the relevant area of the patient's body. The patient would feel a powerful, warm, tingling sensation, as the Spirit guide raised the vibrational frequency of the area being treated until it was no longer solid.

Albert would then withdraw from the body the energy form of the affected part, and immediately plunge his hands into a bowl of water. The water absorbed and dissipated the energy, preventing the diseased tissue from resolidifying when it returned to its normal vibrational state. He would then replace his hands on the patient, and heal the relevant area of the Etheric Body. This done, the patient could expect healing or relief from suffering. It was not uncommon for tumours to be removed in this way.

Healing of this magnitude can only be performed with the participation of the Higher Self. The Spirit guides often spoke to us through Albert during the healing. They told us that any one of us who were healers could perform similar feats, if only we had the confidence. In fact, they said that Albert did not really need their help; if he could only be convinced, he could perform this kind of healing on his own, with the help of his Higher Self.

Now, the Higher Self will never interfere in any human activity, including healing, without being asked. At Thornhill, those present often heard one or other of Albert's Spirit guides requesting the help of his Higher Self, whom he addressed as 'Father' (reminiscent of the Kahunas, who called the Higher Self 'the parental Spirit').

To contact the Higher Self the Kahunas themselves followed a specific procedure. They held that contact with the Higher Self should be initiated by the Lower or Feeling Self, who must request its participation in the healing. The reasons for this were firstly, that the Feeling Self produces the vital energy (Mana) needed by the Higher Self. Secondly, it controls all the healer's bodily functions including those involved in the healing. Thirdly, unless all three selves operate as one, complete healing cannot take place. The active participation of the Feeling Self – which constitutes 50% of our earthly being – is essential.

The Feeling Self always has to be instructed to play its full part in the healing activity, and the Kahunas achieved this through the use of ritual. The Mana, or vital energy, presented by the Feeling Self, could then be raised by the Higher Self to the highest frequency.

As we saw in Chapter 2, *The Purpose of Creation*, it was the action of consciousness upon energy that brought about the creation of the universe. Similarly, it is the consciousness of the Higher Self that causes energy to become sufficiently high in frequency to bring about changes in physical matter. And – as Long emphasises – this high-frequency energy then responds to the direction of the healer's conscious intention *almost as though it were itself conscious.*

The majority of healers ultimately derive their healing ability from their Higher Selves, whether or not they are aware of it; the exception is that when a channel like Albert Best is taken over in trance, the healing energy appears to come from the Higher Self of the Spirit doctor working through him. Most healers, however, work in a conscious state: when Spirit guides work with them, it seems that the guides draw on the energy of the healer's own Higher Self. Whether or not healers work with guides, I believe that they would all have the potential to heal as effectively as the Kahunas, if they included the Feeling Self in the process.

It is true that healers who are unaware of this concept still obtain good results. I believe this is because the majority adopt some kind of ritual before giving healing, in the form of a prayer, meditation, a breathing exercise, a request to their guides or, indeed, to their Higher Selves.

The Feeling Self is very responsive to ritual and these practices in themselves alert it to become involved with the Higher Self. However, unless the healer *consciously* invokes the participation of the Feeling Self, and instructs it to make contact with the Higher Self, the link is still tenuous and the energy less powerful than it could be. Conversely, the more aware healers are of the role of the Feeling Self, the more open they can become as channels for truly powerful healing.

At Thornhill, people came to Albert Best with a variety of complaints, including cancer: I witnessed many cases of cancer eliminated and arthritic joints restored to movement, as well as a wide range of other cures. Even so, not everyone was healed, in the sense of being cured. What was consistent was that they were relieved of physical pain and mental suffering, for truly spiritual healing affects all levels, including the emotions and the Soul-being, as well as the physical. But, as with the other forms of treatment discussed here, when an illness is serious the correction of symptoms through healing does not always lead to a permanent physical cure. We will be discussing how to achieve this in the next chapter.

6. *The Cure of Illness*

Of the three phases of illness – cause, correction of symptoms, and cure – the all-important third phase is often neglected. As far as the medical profession is concerned, once symptoms have been dealt with, the battle is over. But when a serious emotional and/or spiritual imbalance is involved, ill-health is sooner or later likely to return. For anyone suffering from a chronic illness, or who wants to prevent chronic illness from setting in, the first step is to understand that recurrent problems usually have an underlying cause of an emotional and possibly spiritual nature.

Once this cause has been identified and accepted, we can set about dealing with it by making the appropriate changes in lifestyle, attitudes and beliefs. This demands our active and willing participation: no matter what treatment we receive, or how effective it is in the short term, only we ourselves can bring about the state of permanent harmony that leads to real healing. This requires us to understand the role of the three selves, and – perhaps for the first time – to engage the support of the Feeling Self.

Together, the Feeling and Rational Selves form the two halves of the Ego, our total earthly self. It is the Feeling Self that not only controls the processes and wellbeing of the Physical Body; it also holds our memories and emotions, and the flawed beliefs that are so often the key to disharmony. Yet all too often the Feeling Self goes unheeded or unheard. In dealing with chronic ill-health, the Feeling Self must be convinced that the Rational Self has effectively dealt with the problem that started it in the first place: otherwise it will continue to respond as before. Therefore, for a permanent cure, there must be a joint involvement and commitment by both the Rational and the Feeling Selves.

This process of inner change does not have to be as difficult as we are sometimes led to believe. The Kahunas had some practical and extremely effective ways of embarking on this journey – and a fascinating phenomenon today is that much of the ancient wisdom known to the Kahunas is re-emerging in various ways. For example, self-help techniques like visualisation and affirmations which are encouraged by New Age therapists and self-development groups are actually methods of communicating with the Feeling Self and persuading it to change its negative beliefs.

In the field of psychology, new therapies are being developed which do not involve years of analysis, or wallowing in painful memories. In Cognitive Therapy, for instance, the psychologist helps the client to examine the truth of habitual ways of thinking and to replace negative, often irrational statements (such as, 'I am always a failure') with more positive ideas (such as recalling past successes). Neuro-Linguistic Programming (NLP) is another method of rapidly changing attitudes, which often engages the Feeling Self very directly through bodily sensations and actions. Other new, forward-looking therapies are emerging all the time, based on changing negative beliefs and attitudes.

While it can be helpful to seek the support of a counsellor or self-development group, this is not always essential. The key to good health – emotional as well as physical – lies in establishing a new relationship with the Feeling Self.

Identifying the Cause of Disharmony

People are often aware, or partly aware, of the emotional problems underlying their chronic ailments, but are unwilling or simply unsure how to deal with them. Others know that something is not working in their lives, but do not necessarily relate it to their state of health. Not everyone wants to: life would obviously be much easier if health could be restored simply by taking pills or undergoing surgery, without the need for self-examination. Unfortunately, this rarely happens.

The Kahunas spoke of the barriers to healing as 'something eating inside', which they often identified as guilt. These barriers also include factors like fear of failure (or of success), anxiety, unexpressed grief, suppressed anger, or feelings of general unworthiness and inadequacy.

Such emotions can affect people's health in various ways, *some of which* have a very clear connection with their physical symptoms. For example, fear of failure can lead to stomach upsets before exams or interviews. The sense of being overburdened can produce shoulder problems or backache. A sore throat may result from failing or fearing to express oneself. In fact, one clue to the cause of an illness is to ask yourself, 'What does this prevent me from doing?' Sometimes the links are less obvious, perhaps because the memory of a painful experience has been suppressed. Patients who visit natural therapists – particularly those who practise counselling, or who are strongly intuitive – may find the cause emerging through discussion during their therapy.

In fact, there is a part of you which knows very well why you are ill – the Feeling Self. And you may find that it is very willing to tell you, if you ask it. Simply go into a relaxed, meditative state; then tell your Feeling Self that you would like its help, and ask it what you need to know. The answer will come in the form of a mental message: it may come in words, images, or a feeling. If you do not get an immediate answer, it may well come a little later in the form of a dream.

It is also by working with the Feeling Self that you can eradicate the cause. Before describing how to do this, however, it may be useful to review the roles and qualities of the three Selves.

The Role of the Three Selves

The Subconscious, Rational and Higher Selves are three separate parts of us, each of which has an individual and necessary role: the more they can work together, the healthier and more effective we can become.

The Feeling Self is close to though not quite synonymous with, the subconscious mind. It controls our involuntary bodily systems, and holds our memories and emotions. These three are strongly linked (emotional memories are stored not only in the Etheric Body, but also in the cells and muscles of the Physical Body), and it is with these that we find the key to 'the thing eating inside'.

As we saw in Chapter 4, the cause of illness very often lies with the flawed beliefs and attitudes instilled into the Feeling Self in childhood. These may conflict with ideas which the Rational Self acquires later in life – particularly as the Feeling Self makes no distinction between past, present and future. When the conflict is strong enough, the

Feeling Self will react with physical symptoms, or highly charged emotional responses.

The Feeling Self occupies the centre of the body – the area corresponding to the solar plexus chakra, which governs self-esteem, and feelings of fear or courage.

A misunderstanding of psychology commonly leads people to believe that the Feeling Self is something to be feared. This is far from the case. It is much more like a child which has the capacity for all the positive emotions, as well as the less positive ones. It is, as Long puts it, 'dear and bright and loving... endlessly faithful and willing and eager.' It corresponds very closely to what New Age therapists call the 'Inner Child'. It has the capacity to be joyful, creative and intuitive and, with the help of the Rational Self, it can become our ally.

The Rational Self, or Conscious Self, is logical and unemotional. Its role is to act as parent, guide and teacher to the Feeling Self. Unfortunately, unless we are aware of this concept, it is only too easy either to suppress the Feeling Self or to let it run the show – in the form of over-emotional reactions, for instance, or by continuing to hold negative beliefs about oneself and life in general. It may stop us from doing something the Rational Self has agreed to do – such as giving up addictions and making other changes in lifestyle. When we start consciously communicating with the Feeling Self, however, the Rational Self can begin to take charge of the situation, and change it.

The Higher Self is our connection with the spiritual realm. It is in turn parent and guide to the two other selves, and like a good parent it will only intervene if we ask it to. It is reached through meditation and during our periods of deepest sleep, and the most powerful form of contact with it is made via the Feeling, or Lower Self (see Chapter 7). It is vitally important, therefore, that we begin to communicate with the Feeling Self.

Befriending the Feeling Self

To begin a dialogue with the Feeling Self, choose a time when you will not be disturbed, and sit down quietly. Allow yourself to enter a relaxed, meditative state, and invite your Feeling Self to make itself known. You can do this silently, but it will probably be more effective to speak out loud. It can help if you imagine the Feeling Self sitting in a chair opposite you.

The Feeling Self may reply in the form of words, mental pictures, or feelings. It may even want to write or draw its answers, so have a pen and some paper handy. You can experiment with your method of communication: regard it as a game, rather than a serious test – the Feeling Self enjoys games.

If you do not get a strong response on the first occasion, don't lose patience: if it has never been truly listened to before, the Feeling Self may be hesitant at first – particularly if it has come in for a lot of criticism in the past. You may need to repeat the process more than once before you can com-municate fully.

The Feeling Self may need reassuring that you are on its side and want its wellbeing. If, as a child, you did not receive all the love you wanted, the Feeling Self will still be carrying that sense of being unloved. Now is the time when your Rational Self can give it the love and approval it needs. We are often told that it is important to love ourselves, and this becomes much easier if you imagine that unloved self as a little child, eager to be appre-ciated and to cooperate in this new game.

It is easier to communicate with the Feeling Self if you give it a name – which need not be the same as yours. Ask it what it would like to be called, and listen to what comes into your mind. Then, in future, always address it by name. Max Freedom Long called his 'George'; he began his own communication with 'George' by asking it for pleasant childhood memories, and was flooded by warm memories to which he had given little thought over the years.

Through communicating with the Feeling Self, you can learn a great deal about it, and its beliefs – as well as the cause of any physical problems you are suffering from. This may stem from beliefs that the Rational Self is already aware of, but has not managed to change – or you may be surprised by something completely new. The next step is to find ways of persuading the Feeling Self to change the beliefs that are impairing the healing process.

Guilt and Forgiveness

For the Kahunas, the 'thing eating inside', which activated most problems and prevented a full cure, was a sense of sin or guilt; they held that if the Feeling Self believed a person had 'sinned' and deserved punishment, it would punish them through illness or accidents. Healing could only take effect if the Feeling Self believed it deserved to be healed. It was therefore important to clear any guilt feelings, however minor, for full healing to take place.

Many people harbour underlying guilt feelings. Few of us go through life without doing a few things of which we feel ashamed. This can be worsened by a strictly religious upbringing (which can leave rational adults with a sense of sin about enjoying all kinds of pleasures), by a childhood in which normal childish activities were labelled 'naughty' or 'wicked', or by parents who told us we caused them pain or disappointment when we did not follow their chosen path for us.

The Kahunas themselves taught that the only sin was to hurt another person – to which we might add 'or any living being'. They summed this up neatly in the phrase, 'No hurt, no sin.' While they recognised the existence of Higher Beings, they also saw that by their very nature, there was nothing a human being could do that would hurt such beings. This is very important: if you believe in a God of love and forgiveness who is a perfect spiritual being, that spiritual being *cannot* be hurt by our activities. Nor is a perfect Spirit likely to indulge in the very human emotion of anger. What can happen, if we behave badly enough, is that we become cut off from our Higher Selves. This may sadden the Higher Self, it will not hurt it. The loss of contact will, however, diminish our own lives.

Looking rationally at the cause of your guilt, your Rational Self may see that it is in fact quite undeserved. But it is the Feeling Self which needs to be convinced. The Kahunas dealt with this by performing specific rituals, which included fasting, purification (through washing or bathing), and giving away money or goods. These very physical activities helped to convince the Feeling Self that the sin was expiated and forgiven.

You may like to try carrying out such a ritual for yourself. Fasting could take the form of a complete fast, or of giving up something you like for a day or two. Take a bath specifically for the purpose of washing away past sins or guilts. If you have hurt someone in the past, you could write them a letter of apology – it is not necessary to send it unless this is appropriate. Finally, give some money to charity, over and above what you normally give, or perform some other generous action. You can then, as Rational Self, reassure the Feeling Self that it has been forgiven.

Re-examining Your Beliefs

A problem which is possibly even more common than guilt – though closely allied to it – is low self-esteem. In our communications with the Feeling Self, therefore, it will respond to praise and encouragement.

Even well-meaning parents may feel it right to focus more on criticism than praise, instilling into children the feeling that they are not quite good enough. As a result many people carry into adult life a view of themselves that does not tally with reality, and which affects their general potential as well as their health. (We should not forget, of course, that the converse may also be true: it is possible to grow up with an over-inflated idea of one's talents and self-importance. This can also lead to inner and outer conflict in adult life!)

In adulthood, the Rational Self may form new opinions about its self-worth, or may *want* to form them but is obstructed by the Feeling Self. It may not even be aware that the Feeling Self's beliefs are erroneous, formed as they were in childhood when the Rational Self was not yet able to judge their validity. Faulty childhood beliefs are sometimes held with absolute conviction by otherwise intelligent, rational people: over-judgmental parents, for instance, were probably themselves brought up to believe unquestioningly that children benefit from constant criticism.

Some beliefs appear rational because they are held by society at large. For example, many people unthinkingly accept society's view that the way to happiness is found through achieving material success, despite evidence to the contrary. Beliefs about racial or religious superiority or inferiority may be held without question – until a whole nation is forced to reconsider them, as with South Africa. Such beliefs may appear to be consciously formed, but are in fact strongly held by the Feeling Self, which is why it can require a major upheaval to change them. A classic case is that of Northern Ireland, where intelligent people have found it almost impossible to shift their stance, having been brought up from infancy to hold fixed attitudes about people whose beliefs differ from their own.

You can tell if a belief is also held by the Feeling Self if contradicting it evokes an emotional response; such beliefs may need some reconsideration. Changing flawed beliefs will benefit not only your health, but your future activities and relationships.

Changing your Beliefs

Having understood and accepted the cause of your health problems, the next stage in the healing process is to convince the Feeling Self that the beliefs that triggered them can be changed. As you communicate with the Feeling Self, you will make a good start simply by gaining new insights into the truth of its beliefs; the Feeling Self is often willing to change illogical beliefs once the Rational Self shows that they *are* illogical.

Remember that thought-forms are bundles of living energy; as you change your beliefs, you can replace unwanted, unrealistic thought-forms by positive, more realistic ones. Focusing on these, and acting on them, will give them the energy to grow in strength so that they can eventually materialise in reality.

You can back up this process in a number of ways. Bear in mind that the Feeling Self is very responsive to repetition and habit. It also responds to physical stimuli, which include speech, the written word, images, and physical actions. One method of helping it to absorb your new beliefs is the use of affirmations, positive statements about oneself, which should be written, or spoken, in the present tense: for example, 'Every day in every way I am getting better and better.' They should be repeated a number of times. The act of speaking or writing helps to get the message through to the Feeling Self by giving it a physical role in the process.

There is one caution here. You may find your Feeling Self having a strong negative reaction to some affirmations. Repeating, 'I am a confident person' will change nothing if your Feeling Self repeatedly responds, 'But I'm not!' So take note of any responses like this, together with your physical reactions, and talk with your Feeling Self about the source of its belief and how it could be changed. For instance, you could write a description of the way you want to be, or draw a picture of yourself in the situation you want, and put it up where your Feeling Self can see it. This will help your Feeling Self to understand that change is possible.

Visualisation is another tool which you can use to picture yourself in a perfect state of health. Presented with this positive image, the Feeling Self takes it as reality, which encourages it to make the necessary bodily changes to bring it about. While visualising, the more relaxed you are the more effective this will be. Don't worry if you can't 'see' very clearly at first, and make use of your senses of feeling and hearing as your visual imagination. You can also use visualisation to picture yourself acting in new ways, such as behaving confidently at a job interview, or remaining calm in a situation which would normally upset you.

Affirmations and visualisation are both ways of creating new thought-forms: they are all the more effective if you can consciously engage the Feeling Self in the activity. The more you practise them, the stronger the new, positive thought-forms will be.

Make it a point, too, to *act* on the beliefs that you want your Feeling Self to hold. If you want it to feel valued, behave in a way that shows you value it: this might involve making changes to your life-style, like adopting a more balanced diet, or taking regular exercise. If you want to deal with an addiction, explain to the Feeling Self why you need to give up smoking or chocolate. Then keep to your decision, so that the Feeling Self understands that you mean business. You can also, of course, reward it with praise or by doing something you and it enjoy.

A highly effective physical means of impressing the Feeling Self is to clear up your environment; getting rid of unwanted rubbish from cupboards or shelves demonstrates to it that you are also clearing out out-dated beliefs and ideas. If you have a garden, make use of the act of weeding by doing it with the consciousness that you are 'weeding out' unwanted negative thoughts.

To help the Feeling Self absorb the new ideas you want it to hold, make it a habit to read books that support your new way of thinking (some are listed at the back of this book). It can be very helpful to join a self-development class or group, where you will get the support of other people on a similar path. For example, if self-esteem is a basic problem, assertiveness training classes not only encourage you to examine your beliefs about yourself, but enable you to literally act out new ways of being and reacting.

You can also support the changes you want to make by taking flower remedies, taking up appropriate, energy-oriented exercise (like Yoga, T'ai Chi or Qi Gung), and listening to great music. Try to cultivate a positive outlook on life, not by denying what is wrong but by seeking the good in the people and events around you.

The Feeling Self and the Emotions

When you embark on this process of self-exploration, you are likely to come across negative feelings such as fear, or anger, or unexpressed grief. All emotions come from the Feeling Self, and they need to be paid attention to.

Whatever emotions are causing problems, remember that *the emotions are the province of the Feeling Self alone.* This can help the Rational Self to regard emotions dispassionately, without being overwhelmed by them or attempting to suppress them. Nor is it necessary to wallow in them: the Rational Self can help the Feeling Self to overcome bad memories by giving it new, constructive lines to work on, in the form of new beliefs and activities. But painful emotions do need to be acknowledged if they are to be healed.

If the Feeling Self is fearful, the Rational Self must patiently allow it to express its fears – which may well include the fear of change – and reassure it that there is no longer any need for fear. In the case of anger, speaking your anger aloud (not necessarily to the person who caused it) helps to move the energy that has been holding it in. If the Feeling Self is full of grief, it may be that as a child you were not allowed to shed the tears you needed to. The Rational Self, as a kind parent, must allow the Feeling Self to express that grief.

If you find yourself getting into painful emotions, don't stay with them for too long: give yourself a time limit, and always end such sessions with some positive statements and actions. Energetic physical activity like walking, running and dancing, also help to release the physical effects produced by deep emotions, while flower remedies can help to heal them. Some people may need the support of a counsellor or therapist: no-one should be afraid of seeking professional help at times of emotional crisis.

When Cure is Slow

The methods outlined above, if taken seriously and practised regularly, can not only affect the course of chronic illness but can improve life all round. Do not expect results to be instant, particularly when a condition has been present for some time; ideally these techniques could be used to prevent ill-health from setting in in the first place. If an illness has taken some time to build up, it can also take time to cure, and there may be some conditions which cannot be cured completely if a great deal of physical deterioration has already occurred.

There may be also cases, as we saw in Chapter 4, when there are spiritual reasons for a person unconsciously choosing to experience the discomforts of a disabling or terminal illness, or even a premature death. They may be part of the lifeplan chosen by the Soul in order to further one's spiritual development by undergoing particular experiences. They also often serve the evolution of those around, giving them the opportunity to grow through experiencing a caring role.

Even if you do not achieve a full recovery, establishing a new, creative collaboration with your

Feeling Self can only benefit your life and your relationships; it will help you not only to understand why you have become ill, but to come to terms with the problem. And, whether you are ill or not, your life will be greatly enhanced if you also use the Feeling Self to build stronger links with your Higher Self, and to align yourself more closely with your true purpose.

❖ ❖ ❖

7. Living in Harmony with the Higher Self

❖ ❖ ❖

When you begin a regular dialogue with the Feeling Self, you will probably find aspects of your life changing, or demanding to be changed. Try to pace these changes; when you are learning any kind of new skill, periods of focussed learning need to be followed by periods of assimilation.

As a result of your new relationship with yourself, you may be making new discoveries about your self-worth, your values, and your potential. You may discover that you and your Feeling Self need to express more creativity, or you may decide to develop other gifts that have been lying latent. You should also find that any self-imposed limitations begin to lift, as you give yourself permission to live more fully. All of these will feed into your working life and your relationships with others, and set you on the path for a fruitful future life, as well as a healthier one.

When we look at old people, it is possible to recognise those who have developed a good relationship with their Feeling Self, and those who have not. In old age, some people revert to childish patterns of behaviour and can become decidedly cantankerous, selfish and unreasonable, as the control exercised by the Rational Self weakens. It is true that some people often find themselves obliged to be dependent upon others, and they may resent this. If they have not understood the role of their Feeling Self, it is liable to express its resentment in a childish way, not understanding that there is a spiritual purpose behind this loss of independence.

There are two important learning periods in our lives, one in childhood, and one in old age. Losing one's independence in old age provides a final opportunity for self-development by experiencing a different relationship with those around – by learning to receive care instead, perhaps, of always being in the role of provider and controller. If we can learn, at any age, to live in greater harmony with ourselves, our relationships with others can only benefit both in the short-term and for the remainder of our lives. Life then becomes a continuing journey of growth towards greater wisdom, rather than an inevitable deterioration.

As we saw in Chapter 2, the purpose of human existence is for us, as spiritual beings, to experience life in a material environment, so that we can ultimately return to the spiritual realm to which our Souls belong. You can be greatly helped in this by making contact with the Higher Self, the spiritual part of you that is watching over your progress and longs to give help and guidance, if only you will let it.

Contacting the Higher Self

In New Age circles today, people are encouraged to make contact with their Higher Selves, and many in fact achieve this. However, there is a risk of seeking enlightenment through the Higher Self alone, while by-passing the Feeling Self. This not only makes the contact less powerful than it might be: it could be the reason why some apparently very spiritual people nonetheless have problems with their relationships and day-to-day living. As outlined in Chapter 2, we are subject to two forces: the upward, spiritual force, and the downward, material force. If only one predominates, we are thrown out of balance. It is important to remember that our object is to experience ourselves as spiritual beings *within a physical body and a material environment*. And the Feeling Self is, of course, the controller of the Physical Body.

The desire to go straight to the Higher Self is partly the result of the Western religious tradition, with its belief – still held in some quarters – that the body and its natural feelings are sinful, and must be denied or 'overcome'. In Eastern traditions the role of the body has been better understood, and many Eastern forms of meditation engage the Feeling Self through the body by means of physical exercises – Yoga in India and T'ai Chi in China, for instance. In their healing activities, the Kahunas made a point of building up vital force (Mana) before offering it to the Higher Self to be raised to its highest form. Yoga and T'ai Chi are both methods of building up energy, so are deep relaxation, breathing exercises, and some forms of dance. And since they all involve the body, they are all ways of encouraging the participation of the Feeling Self. So even if you do not practise a specific technique, it can be helpful to do some physical stretching and deep breathing before contacting the Higher Self.

Choose a quiet time and place for this. Remember that the Feeling Self likes symbols and physical acts: lighting a candle or placing a favourite crystal in front of you will alert it to the fact that you are engaging in something special. If you practise this regularly, remember that the Feeling Self is a creature of habit, and if possible choose a regular time, place, and symbolic act to alert it to your intentions.

Sit with your spine straight (but not rigid) and your feet flat on the floor, and close your eyes. Now, become aware of your breathing, and allow it to become slower and deeper (deep breathing should not be forced). This will help you to quieten the mind to achieve a meditational state.

Next, first make your need known to the Feeling Self: tell it that you would like guidance from your Higher Self. If you have a specific question or problem, now is the time to pose it. Then sit quietly with your eyes closed, and allow the Higher Self its space in your mind.

Do not expect anything dramatic to occur; you may only be conscious of your mind becoming calmer. Some people experience a feeling of love and security. Sometimes the answer to a problem simply drops into the mind in the form of words, a mental image, or just a sense of knowing. Quite often the answers you seek will come less directly, and not necessarily at the time of asking. You might find yourself being led to a particular book, or an unexpected meeting or conversation may provide you with new information or a new insight. With regular practice you will also find that as you go about the day your intuition will be sharper, and you will have a clearer sense of direction.

Sleep and Dreams

We are all in touch with our Higher Selves during our deepest periods of sleep. These are the times when the Ego and the Astral Body together leave the Physical Body to be renewed and re-balanced in the realm of Spirit. As a rule we have no conscious recollection of these journeys, though most people will have some inkling of them at times – it is quite common, for example, to wake up knowing the solution to a problem. This can be encouraged by asking your Astral Body before you go to sleep

Living in Harmony with the Higher Self

to seek the answer to any question that is bothering you. The first time I tried this myself, immediately on waking I found myself going to a particular book; it opened at a page which included the answer to that question. This is a natural human faculty which everyone could use to advantage.

It is also very common to receive guidance through dreams, so it is worth paying them some attention. Not all dreams have significance, of course; many are simply a way of clearing the brain of the mental business of the day. Dreams that have important meanings for us tend to be the ones that wake us up, or leave us with a deep and lasting impression. Recurring dreams are always important; they indicate that we need to pay attention to something we may be trying to ignore.

Keeping a dream diary encourages the process of communication; if you start writing your dreams down in a note-book they will become progressively easier to remember. Keep a pen and paper by your bed, so that you can note them down as soon as possible after waking, before the details fade away. Some people prefer to keep a tape-recorder at the bedside, which enables them to record any dreams during the night without having to put the light on. When you come to write the dream out next day, you may be surprised to realise its meaning.

Learning the language of your dreams can take a little practice. Though they come from the Higher Self, they are always mediated by the Feeling Self, which tends to pass the information on to us in symbolic form, or through puns or word-play. For instance, dreaming you have something in your eye may signify that there is something your 'I' is not seeing clearly. So pay attention to any elements in your dreams that do not have an immediately obvious meaning, and ask yourself what they might symbolise.

It is also worth explicitly asking for helpful dreams before you go to sleep. Remember that the Higher Self *wants* the opportunity to help and guide you.

Planning Your Life

It can be useful to take time now and again to think about what you really want to happen in your life. While the Feeling Self deals with past memories, it is the Higher Self that helps us to form the future, using the thought-forms created by the plans and desires of the two lower selves. The clearer and more decisive you are about what you want and where you want to go, the clearer the thought-forms which go to construct your future. The reason people so often do not get what they want is that the thought-forms of what they desire are mixed up with the fears and doubts of the Feeling Self.

Ultimately, what happens in our lives is a result of the thought-forms, and clusters of thought-forms, created by both the Rational and the Feeling Selves. Thought-forms have an energy and power of their own, which materialise in real events. Albert Best's

Spirit guides used to tell us, 'Thoughts are real and living things, so you should be extremely careful about what you think. They often cause a lot of problems.'

Everything that you think is potentially capable of being materialised. This is why some people suffer from 'self-fulfilling prophecies': the person who says, 'I never have any luck' is literally building for themselves a luckless future. On the other hand, re-programming the ideas of the Feeling Self, as described in Chapter 6, depletes the energy of negative thought-forms; focusing on new, positive beliefs will create new thought-forms, while repetition will energise them. Ultimately that energy will create the new reality you want to bring about.

Planning is best done by the Rational Self, but you can engage the help of the Feeling Self by letting it know that you are allowed to have what you want (providing it hurts no-one else). Make sure that you have its full participation. For example, the Rational Self may decide quite logically that you need a larger income. If the Feeling Self has at some stage been taught that the desire for money is greedy or even sinful, it will need to be convinced otherwise so that it does not sabotage your efforts.

You can also help the Feeling Self to cooperate by taking some active or symbolic step towards getting what you want. For example, if you want a new home, buy an object or a piece of furniture that you intend to put in it. Affirmations and visualisation are also useful: the Kahunas would pray aloud for what they needed, and repeat the prayer three times, to ensure that the Feeling Self carried the thought-form to the Higher Self.

Your Higher Self and Other People

You can use your contact with your Higher Self to improve your relationships with other people, and to help others if you wish, through prayer or meditation. Incidentally, if you already use prayer in your life, do not be concerned about the idea of praying to the Higher Self: as mentioned earlier, the Kahunas believed in the existence of higher beings, and regarded the Higher Self as the intermediary in contacting those higher beings. Similarly, all our prayers, whoever they are directed to, reach their destination through the mediation of the Higher Self.

If you are having difficulty with a particular person, it may help to remember that *everyone* has a Higher Self: that we are *all* spiritual beings and that at a much higher level, we are all part of the same whole. There is a level at which all Higher Selves are linked: this is one reason why group meditations and prayers can be so powerful.

You can help to resolve a problem with someone else by engaging both the Feeling Self and the Higher Self, either in meditation or before going to sleep. If, for instance, someone has upset you, remember that the emotional upset is the response of the Feeling Self, which may be reacting like a hurt child. You can help to get rid of the upset both by recognising this, and by explaining the situation to your Feeling Self. It is quite likely that the other person's Feeling Self is also behaving childishly! Then ask your Higher Self to contact the Higher Self of the other person, and to help to harmonise the relations between you. Then, stop thinking about the problem – brooding over it will only perpetuate it by continuing to energise negative thought-forms. Dealt with in this way, solutions to interpersonal problems often come about in unexpected ways: you may wake up seeing things quite differently, or receive a different reaction from the other person next time you meet, or they may simply move out of your orbit.

In Chapter 6 we described the importance of forgiving yourself, to free yourself of real or imaginary guilt. Forgiving others is another important way of clearing negativity from your system. It is not always easy to do, for if someone has treated you badly the Feeling Self may continue to feel hurt for a long time. Since it has no sense of past or future, it can go on holding that sense of hurt in the present unless the Rational Self takes action to change it.

Forgiving others does not mean that you con-done or approve of their behaviour: rather, it is a way of releasing the effects of their behaviour from your system. In fact, the person who benefits most will be yourself, since emotions like anger and resentment deplete energy, and are definitely harmful to long-term health. So, explain to your Feeling Self why you need to let go of that past experience. It can be helpful to visualise the other person sitting opposite you. Be aware that they, too, have a Higher Self; then, tell them how their behaviour made you feel, and imagine them telling you they are sorry for their actions. This may be what the Feeling Self needs to hear in order finally to forgive them and let go of the hurt.

You can also ask for the help of the Higher Self in healing or praying for others. When you pray for another person, or send them healing thoughts, your thoughts will automatically go to the other person's Higher Self as well, maximising the healing energy available to them.

Going Further

I have tried to share with you here what I have found to be a rational explanation as to the causes and cures of ill-health, and my own understanding of the importance of the spiritual dimension in health – one that tends to be overlooked or not properly understood. It is offered for readers to take as a possible model of healing, which they can explore further if they wish. Following the methods outlined here will help you to heal the conflict between the over-all needs of your Soul and the needs of the Ego – including the body, mind and emotions – in the material world. For those who want to explore them more deeply, a number of books are recommended for further reading on page 98.

❖ ❖ ❖

Further Reading

❖ ❖ ❖

Edward Bach, *The Twelve Healers and Other Remedies*, The C W Daniel Company Ltd, 1933

Edward Bach, *Heal Thyself, An Explanation of the Real Cause and Cure of Disease*, The C W Daniel Company, 1931

Gill Edwards, *Stepping Into the Magic, A New Approach to Everyday Life*, Piatkus, 1993

Homoeopathy, The Family Handbook, Thorsons, 1992

Serge Kahili King, PhD, *Mastering Your Hidden Self, A Guide to the Huna Way*, The Theosophical Publishing House, 1985

Serge Kahili King, PhD, *Urban Shaman, A Handbook for Personal and Planetary Transformation*, Simon & Schuster, 1990

Dr Andrew Lockie, *The Family Guide to Homoeopathy*, Elm Tree Books 1989; (paperback) Hamish Hamilton, 1990

Max Freedom Long, *The Secret Science Behind*

Miracles, DeVorss Publications, 1948, 1976

Max Freedom Long, *The Secret Science At Work*, DeVorss & Company, 1953, 1988

Dennis Milner and Edward Smart, *The Loom of Creation*, Neville Spearman, 1975

Dennis Milner (ed.), *Explorations of Consciousness*, Neville Spearman, 1978

Mechthild Scheffer, *Bach Flower Therapy, Theory and Practice*, Thorsons 1986

Mechthild Scheffer, *Keys to the Soul*, The C W Daniel Company, 1997

Steiner, Rudolf, *Theosophy*, Anthroposophic Press, 1922

Steiner, Rudolf, *The Occult Science – An Outline*, Rudolf Steiner Press, 1909

Nora Weeks, *The Medical Discoveries of Edward Bach, Physician*, The C W Daniel Company Ltd, 1973

Index